# SENSATION AND JUDGMENT
## Complementarity Theory of Psychophysics

# SCIENTIFIC PSYCHOLOGY SERIES

Stephen W. Link & James T. Townsend, Editors

## MONOGRAPHS

**John C. Baird** • Sensation and Judgment: Complementarity Theory of Psychophysics

**Gordon M. Redding and Benjamin Wallace** • Adaptive Spatial Alignment

**John A. Swets** • Signal Detection Theory and ROC Analysis in Psychology and Diagnostics: Collected Papers

**William R. Uttal et al.** • The Swimmer: An Integrated Computational Model of a Perceptual-Motor System

**Stephen W. Link** • The Wave Theory of Difference and Similarity

## EDITED VOLUMES

**F. Gregory Ashby** • Multidimensional Models of Perception and Cognition

**Hans-Georg Geissler, Stephen W. Link, and James T. Townsend** • Cognition, Information Processing, and Psychophysics: Basic Issues

# SENSATION AND JUDGMENT
## Complementarity Theory
## of Psychophysics

**John C. Baird**
*Dartmouth College*

**LEA**   LAWRENCE ERLBAUM ASSOCIATES, PUBLISHERS
1997   Mahwah, New Jersey

Lawrence Erlbaum Associates, Inc., Publishers
10 Industrial Avenue
Mahwah, New Jersey 07430

**Library of Congress Cataloging-in-Publication Data**

Baird, John C.
     Sensation and judgment : complementarity theory of psychophysics /
John C. Baird.
         p.   cm.
     Includes bibliographical references (p.      ) and indexes.
     ISBN 0-8058-1830-8 (cloth : alk. paper)
     1. Psychophysics.   2. Senses and sensation.   3. Judgment.
     I. Title.
     BF237.B35   1996
     152.1—dc20                                            96-26481
                                                              CIP

Books published by Lawrence Erlbaum Associates are printed on acid-free paper,
and their bindings are chosen for strength and durability

Printed in the United States of America
10  9  8  7  6  5  4  3  2  1

*FOR COLLEAGUES*

# Contents

# Preface

An empirical science invites characterization in one of two distinct ways. Either the field appears as a singular whole with all the parts fitting together in just the right places, or the field appears strewn with the disconnected results of experimental tests. Confronted with the first situation, the theorist can "admire" the packaging or take steps to "unwrap" it. Confronted with the second situation, the theorist can refuse the challenge or attempt to combine the pieces into a new whole. In this way, theoretical efforts undergo cyclical shifts in emphasis. Once a neat package is assembled, the chief option is to unwrap the packaging, and once this is done, the chief option is to reassemble the facts into a new arrangement. The field waxes and wanes, with each succeeding cycle leading to a deeper understanding of the empirical phenomena.

In this book I offer a theory to unify the apparently disconnected findings of psychophysics. I argue that some experimental outcomes are best attributed to sensory processes, whereas others are best attributed to judgment processes. Other results can be viewed equally well from either perspective. The two alternatives each have special advantages, and together they provide a dual characterization of the field that is complementary and "mutually completing."

The first chapter outlines the overall theme of the book, followed by six chapters discussing the implications of a sensory orientation to psychophysics. This section considers the major psychophysical laws (Weber, Stevens, and Piéron) and suggests how these laws interrelate at the neural level. Chapter 7 ends the first part of the book by extending the reach of sensory modeling to memory psychophysics.

The next two chapters (8 and 9) introduce the judgment orientation to psychophysics, and succeeding chapters (10 through 15) detail the implications of this orientation for topics such as the effects of stimulus range, sequential dependencies, and the comparison of results gathered by different methods. This section is followed by a chapter on multidimensional psychophysics. The volume closes by discussing the broad implications of the principle of complementarity for sensory physiology and behavioral perception.

The book was written while I was associated with three educational institutions. I completed most of the work in my capacity as professor of psychology and mathematical social sciences at Dartmouth College. I would like to thank all my colleagues there for helping me see which of my ideas deserve public attention and which deserve pruning or abandonment. In particular, the modeling sections profited from my ongoing conversations with Robert Z. Norman. One of my co-workers, Kathleen Harder, provided constructive comments on the initial drafts of the entire manuscript, and John Jalowick and Kate Buhrmaster made helpful comments on various aspects of the manuscript and figures. Susan Miller offered her usual expert advice on editorial matters.

Much of the conceptual thinking behind the theory took shape during my sabbatical leave at the University of Stockholm. I would like to thank my longtime collaborator, Birgitta Berglund, and all the graduate students in her laboratory for their intellectual interest in the project, and for sharing with me their knowledge of psychophysics.

Parts of the final draft were written while I was a visiting research scholar at Colby College. I appreciate the hospitality shown me by the members of the psychology department there, and in particular, I am grateful to Diane Winn for her comments on drafts of several chapters.

Many other friends and colleagues offered pertinent suggestions on some of the chapters. In particular, I wish to acknowledge the valuable comments of Anna Garriga-Trillo, Lawrence E. Marks, A. A. J. Marley, Elliot Noma, Martha Teghtsoonian, Robert Teghtsoonian, and Mark Wagner. I am also grateful to all the researchers who sent me the raw data on which much of the present theory is grounded. A special word of thanks goes to R. Duncan Luce who has a rare knack for clarifying ideas with which he does not always agree. On more than one occasion he helped me disperse clouds of misunderstanding that potentially could have paralyzed the entire enterprise.

Finally, I want to extend my warmest appreciation to my series editors, Stephen W. Link and James T. Townsend, who never flagged in their encouragement and professional advice.

*—John C. Baird*

# 1 Complementarity Principle

Events transpiring in the physical environment are registered by the senses and subsequently represented in human awareness. The environmental events of interest are physical stimuli whose quantifiable characteristics vary along dimensions, such as chemical concentration, visual luminance, and tonal amplitude. Ever since Fechner (1860/1966), the focal aim of psychophysics has been to determine the relation between the physical world of stimulus objects and the psychological domain of conscious awareness. In modern research laboratories, this enterprise involves an experimenter presenting a subject with a stimulus that is measured by a physical instrument, with the subject indicating the perceived magnitude of the stimulus in some observable way, and the experimenter then relating the perceived magnitude to the stimulus intensity. Psychophysical laws codify the quantitative relation so established between dimensional variations of objects and corresponding changes in conscious experience, as reflected in the subject's responses (Baird & Noma, 1978; S. S. Stevens, 1975). These laws, their variations and violations, constitute the empirical picture that must be elucidated by a theory of psychophysics.

Before embarking on this venture, certain philosophical questions require some attention. Three such questions are especially salient. The first concerns whether a theory of psychophysics should be modality specific, or instead, deal with phenomena that transcend sense modality. The theory presented here concerns phenomena that occur in most sense modalities.

The second question asks whether all forms of psychophysical judgments depend on the same sensorineural code, or, conversely, whether they depend on different neural structures. The position herein is that different psychophysical methods induce the subject to rely on the same neurophysiological code. Specifi-

1

cally, the code associated with stimulus discrimination at the local level of the Just-Noticeable-Difference is the same code associated with the more global scaling of stimulus magnitude. In this respect, this approach is more closely allied with that of Fechner (1860/1966) than it is with S. S. Stevens (1975). This is not to say that exactly the same aspects of the neural code are relevant for all experimental methods. Under some conditions, the subject's response may reflect the activity of a single neuron, different from trial to trial; while under other conditions, the mean output of an ensemble of neurons may be the determining factor.

The third question asks whether a single model can explain the full spectrum of laboratory results, from those most probably associated with peripheral, sensory events to those most probably associated with central, brain events. In shorthand notation, this issue is often presented as a distinction between the influence of "sensory" and "cognitive" variables. A single model cannot accommodate both types of data, and it is time to frankly admit that attempts to explain all the facts from only one of these standpoints has failed.

In this work, psychophysics is looked at through two complementary lenses: One model considers the effects of sensory factors, and the other the effects of cognitive factors. The theory proposed, therefore, consists of two distinct explanatory schemes, joined by a superstructure that directs empirical phenomena to the model most likely to succeed. These two approaches are proposed as situationally applicable alternatives, rather than as intellectual competitors.

## DUAL MODELS

In recent years, psychophysical theory has undergone a bifurcation. On one side, theorists treat phenomena and empirical laws as chiefly due to sensory processes (S. S. Stevens, 1975). Contextual effects arising through the use of particular methods, such as numerical response preferences in Magnitude Estimation, are seen as an unwanted nuisance whose influence must be reduced to a minimum in order to isolate the "true" sensory scale. Such models assign no additional role to central, cognitive processes.

On the other side, theorists consider psychophysics purely in terms of the influence of cognitive variables, such as the strategies induced by instructions, and the response biases associated with different scaling methods (Parducci, 1982; Poulton, 1989). Sensory factors play a minor role in such approaches. The physiological concomitants of psychophysics are said to be centrally located in the brain, not in the peripheral sense organs themselves.

Experiments conducted within either tradition are often designed to minimize the chance of unearthing new facts that might lend support to the opposition. Expressing the situation in the starkest terms, one school ardently embraces sensory interpretations of psychophysical phenomena and ignores cognition; the other school ardently embraces cognitive interpretations and ignores sensation. Attempts have been made to reconcile these two extreme positions (Baird, 1970a, 1970b), but until recently, not many such arguments have received a full hearing (Algom, 1992b). This book carries this reconciliation one step further by arguing that the same psychophysical phenomena should be conceptualized in two alternative ways. The implications of this analysis are similar to, but not identical with, those earlier theories that gather sensory and cognitive variables under the same umbrella.

## INTERPRETING THE POWER LAW

The sharp divergence of perspectives is aptly illustrated in the interpretation of Stevens's Power Law relating magnitude estimates to physical intensity, and more particularly, in the meaning attached to the exponent of that functional relation (Equation 1.1).

$$R = \lambda S^\gamma \tag{1.1}$$

The original interpretation, strongly advocated by S. S. Stevens (1971a, 1971b, 1975), is that the exponent ($\gamma$) reflects the influence of sensory transducers, single neurons or groups, whose operating characteristics differ, as indicated by variations in the size of the exponent. The multiplicative constant ($\lambda$) in this scheme is a scalar term devoid of psychological meaning. For example, nonlinear response compression (exponent less than 1) occurs for sound intensity, nonlinear expansion (exponent greater than 1) occurs for the force of handgrip, whereas the function is linear (exponent equal to 1) for the perceived length of lines.

The Power Law and its exponent are, therefore, the result of biological processes in the periphery and not in the brain. The brain issues commands to the motor system so that a faithful rendition of the sensory percept is reflected in an overt response. This mapping task presumably is accomplished without error. The variance observed in subjects' overt responses to repeated presentations of the same stimulus is said to be caused by variability of functioning in the different components of the sense organ.

The obvious fault with this simple conception is that it is contradicted by a wealth of empirical data. If the Power Law arises from transformations taking place at the periphery, then this law should be unaffected by factors having nothing to do with sensory processing. Contrary to this, however, the exponent's value is influenced by numerous factors whose impact on the senses must be either nonexistent or extremely weak. Such factors include the position of a standard (with a preassigned value) in the stimulus series (Engen & Ross, 1966) and the range of intensities presented for judgment (Poulton, 1989).

These empirical facts continue to subvert a theory that refers only to unadulterated sensory events. However, if experimental conditions are held constant, and the stimulus quality (such as light, sound, odors) is varied, then relative changes in the exponent of the power function can be attributed with some degree of confidence to variations in the ability of different sensory systems to process incoming stimulus information.

The opposing view is that the Power Law of Equation 1.1 and its exponent are due solely to the operation of cognitive variables. For instance, a person's everyday experience with the physical units by which a stimulus is commonly measured might determine how well the person estimates it in the laboratory setting (Poulton, 1989; R. M. Warren, 1981). According to a "physical-correlate theory," either people have been reinforced in the past for estimating relative intensities accurately, as might be true with visually presented distances that can be estimated by using familiar units (inches, centimeters, etc.), or judgments of one dimension are based on a learned association with another.

In the way of example, people may judge the brightness of a light based on how distant a physical source would have to be in order to appear equal to its apparent value at some standard distance. Because the light flux reaching the eye decreases inversely with the square of the source's distance, rather than linearly, this would lead to compression of the response range when compared against the range of light intensity actually present. Because a person is not perceptually attuned to the inverse square law, changes in brightness are drastically underestimated. One troublesome spinoff of this idea is that it predicts the wrong value for the exponent. According to the inverse square law, the exponent for brightness should be 0.5. It typically is found to be closer to 0.3 (S. S. Stevens, 1975).

The deeper problem encountered by this notion of the exponent's underlying source, however, parallels that encountered by an exclusively sensory interpretation. There exist substantial empirical facts contradicting the main assumptions (Baird, 1981). The physical-correlate theory of brightness and loudness perception rests on the incorrect notion that subjects accurately perceive visual distance. But decades of experimental evidence show that distance estimates are as malleable as other physical continua. They too depend on stimulus context and on the many other factors that affect psychophysical judgments (Baird, 1970c). Recent data serve to buttress these early conclusions (Baird & Wagner, 1991; Wagner, 1985).

For example, the exponent relating judged and actual distance is slightly greater than 1 when based on changes in the visual angle of a frontal stimulus, and much less than 1 when based on extent along the ground stretching away from the observer (reviewed by Loomis, Da Silva, & Fujita, 1992). The physical-correlate theory should predict brightness and loudness exponents greater than 0.5 when distance is estimated on the basis of frontal size, but less then 0.5 when the critical dimension is distance along the ground. Yet, how do we know when the subject is relying on the stimulus array comprising the frontal or horizontal plane? It remains hard to see how this theory can be brought into line with a host of well-established psychophysical facts. A similar note of caution must be sounded about other purely cognitive approaches to psychophysics (e.g., Poulton, 1989).

The Power Law and its exponent depend on numerous factors, including the sensory attribute, the stimulus context, and the exact wording of the instructions for making judgments. As a compromise between extreme positions, several hybrid theories have appeared. They classify influences as either sensory or cognitive variables (e.g., Baird, 1970a,1970b; Curtis, Attneave, & Harrington, 1968; Rule, Curtis, & Markley, 1970). The goal is to separate and identify independent components of the exponent, much in the way that the Theory of Signal Detectability (TSD) distinguishes between sensory and cognitive elements in the study of stimulus thresholds (Green & Swets, 1966/1974; Macmillan & Creelman, 1991). The related theories applied to the Power Law have had marginal success, primarily because statistical measures, comparable to $d'$ and $\beta$ of TSD, have not been developed for the exponent.

## DUALITY ACCEPTED

Experimentalists tend to favor one or the other branch (sensory and cognitive) of psychophysical theory, and are eager to find ways to neutralize the influence of variables that fall outside the sphere of their preferred theoretical orientation. So there is plenty of data for and against both sides. As the facts accumulate, however, unification becomes more and more problematic. With the passage of time, the two camps drift farther and farther apart, with less and less fruitful collaboration. Against this movement toward bipolarity, equal validity is assigned here to all the reliable data collected by either camp. At some point in the ongoing debate, we simply must admit that there is a real necessity for accepting two alternative, seemingly contradictory, views of psychophysics. This acceptance of opposites is called for because some empirical phenomena are best explained in terms of sensory processes, whereas others are best ascribed to central causes.

For instance, it seems unlikely that a cognitive theory would ever be able to explain the phenomenon of dark adaptation in vision or the change in the shape of the psychophysical function obtained from people who have suffered damage to the auditory nerve. On the other hand, it is not obvious how sensory factors can account for number biases in Magnitude Estimation or for the disagreements between the results obtained by the methods of Magnitude and Category Estimation. It may be possible to squeeze out explanations for all psychophysical phenomena by firmly adhering to one-sided principles, but it is doubtful if such a stance will achieve universal acceptance, because a large fraction of the available data will still remain untouched.

Responsibility for explaining phenomena that do not lend themselves to one interpretation is best left to the alternative. The underlying assumptions of a sensory model are inherently of a different sort from those of a cognitive model, and both may be right inasmuch as they make accurate predictions within their own region of applicability, yet fail to varying degrees when extended to phenomena outside these limits.

In sum, different experimental procedures and paradigms lead to different experimental results, which are difficult or impossible to reconcile with each other. Therefore, it is time to explore new directions, neither driven by the desire to establish sensory scales nor by the desire to establish cognition as the sole explanatory force in psychophysics.

## COMPLEMENTARITY PRINCIPLE

It appears that the field is at a crossroads not unlike that faced by physics at the beginning of this century (a comparison alluded to by Ward, 1990). Because of the intractability of the empirical facts to be explained, physicists were led to accept the validity of two seemingly contradictory views of the nature of light (Bohr, 1961; Feynman, Leighton, & Sands, 1963, chaps. 37 & 38). Concepts of light as consisting of packets of energy were appropriate for certain phenomena but not for others. On the other hand, treating light as waves rather than as packets of energy explained phenomena that were not dealt with by the opposing view. The Complementarity Principle of Niels Bohr, stated originally in his lecture at the International Congress of Physics at Como (published in *Nature*, 1928), accepted both concepts into the circle of legitimate theory and recognized that each was needed for solving some problems arising in the physics laboratory but not others. The application of one or the other model of light depends on the nature of the phenomenon to be understood. In this sense, the two models are "mutually completing" (Murdoch, 1987).

The Complementarity Theory of Psychophysics proposed here also stresses the "mutually completing" nature of apparently contradictory models, though neither has anything to do with the physical concepts of light. In this situation, the two opposing extremes are sensory and cognitive interpretations of psychophysical results. The initial part of this book gives detailed predictions of a neural model whose components are presumed to involve peripheral mechanisms. This model addresses a wide array of well-established sensory facts and laws, but has almost nothing to say about the genesis of context effects, which are endemic to all scaling methods. The latter part of the book pays scant attention to the possible existence of sensory effects, and explains context effects in terms of a judgment model, and its variations, whose physiological manifestation is most certainly in the brain and not in the periphery. In neither model is any attempt made to specify the actual, detailed structures in the nervous system that represent these hypothetical concepts.

At the heart of the separation between the sensory and cognitive (judgment) interpretations are the alternative processes thought to underlie the distribution of responses obtained when a single stimulus is presented on multiple occasions. The Sensory Aggregate Model posits that the variability of responses occurs because a subpopulation of neurons are excited whenever a single stimulus is presented, and that its members do not all fire at the same rate. Therefore, response variability is a consequence of the brain taking samples of the firing rates of different subsets of neurons on different trials. A critical point here is that the entire distribution of neuronal firing is available each time a stimulus is presented. It is never the case that the firing of a single neuron is the only option open to the subject when required to give a psychophysical judgment (for an alternative view, see Norwich, 1993).

The Judgment Option Model posits that response variability occurs because the subject is uncertain about exactly which response should be given on any trial. The uncertainty is in the judgment domain rather than in the sensory domain. According to this view, the sensory representation is identical each time the same stimulus occurs, but the subject is uncertain about the judgment most appropriate to characterize this stimulus. Thus, different judgments are given for the same stimulus because the same response option is not always selected from the available pool. Once again, however, the judgment uncertainty occurs on each and every stimulus occasion. An entire distribution of options is available to the subject on each trial, but only one of these is eventually transformed into an overt response.

At this specific level, therefore, the Complementarity Principle refers to the mutually completing nature of two quite different conceptions of the processes presumed to underlie the response distribution associated with a single stimulus intensity. Nonetheless, it would be unwise to draw a sharp line between the realms of application covered by these two alternatives. Although distinct explanations are needed to do justice to the field as a whole, one approach is only favored over the other when used to address certain well-known problems, the most important of which are examined in the ensuing chapters.

It should be mentioned as well that the choices made between the two approaches is based not just on quantitative Goodness-of-Fit arguments, but sometimes on personal hunch and common sense. Later developments may lead to more rational procedures for deciding which model is best suited for which phenomena. Some concrete suggestions in this regard are offered in the final chapter.

## PHILOSOPHICAL IMPLICATIONS

Philosophy is implicated as much as psychology in formulating a complementarity principle. Yet the argument favoring dual models arose from the empirical demands of psychophysics and not from the abstract demands of philosophy. If a decision is made to fasten onto a single position—sensory or cognitive (judgment)—it becomes impossible to predict certain key experimental outcomes. It is the failure of prediction that is critical, not the preexistence of a philosophy purporting to tell us how psychological science should be conducted. This caveat is as critical in psychophysics as it is in physics. In considering the philosophical implications of quantum mechanics, Feynman et al. (1963) made the point succinctly:

> "As always, there are two aspects of the problem: one is the philosophical implication for physics and the other is the extrapolation of philosophical matters to other fields. When philosophical ideas associated with science are dragged into another field, they are usually completely distorted. Therefore we shall confine our remarks as much as possible to physics itself. (p. 38-8).

This warning is to be taken seriously, and it should be made clear at the outset that a complementarity principle is not being entertained for psychophysics as a copycat reaction to its proven success in physics. Rather, the introduction of complementarity is a reaction to the gradual, but inexorable, changes taking place within the field of psychophysics. The dual conceptions are motivated by a desire to predict the outcome of experiments, past and future. The philosophical implications of this duality should be confined to this realm. Extrapolation of arguments to other areas of psychology, or to other scientific fields, will probably be less successful, though perhaps worth the effort.

## OVERVIEW OF THE BOOK

The succeeding theoretical analysis reviews the major findings of psychophysics that have withstood scientific scrutiny since Fechner's day and the laws and principles that accurately codify these findings. The journey, however, will not begin by traversing old and venerated ground. The new theoretical ideas will be presented upfront before introducing the empirical data. Only after the conceptual foundation is laid will predictions be compared against the empirical data of the past and against knowledge that might be gained in the future. This organization of the material provides a framework for discussion that would have quite another twist if the factual material were presented first, and the models advertised as inductive steps from a solid empirical base. By initially spelling out the assumptions of the models, this volume provides reasoned guidelines for reaching a satisfactory understanding of the empirical base behind the general theory.

The goal throughout is to discuss previous works in as faithful and fair a light as possible. The models are created to accommodate empirical results. In no way does this volume imply that theory blossomed forth from abstract mathematical or philosophical sources outside of psychophysics. The data were there and the models evolved to explain them. In presenting the theoretical arguments initially, it is possible to see these empirical facts as integral components of a coherent pattern, rather than as isolated findings devoid of theoretical meaning.

In summary, the Complementarity Theory finds expression in two distinct models. The first assigns importance to populations of sensory neurons acting in the aggregate and is formulated to deal with sensory effects. The second assigns importance to judgment uncertainty and to the strategies induced in subjects by experimental procedures. The latter model is formulated to explain context effects. In both instances, the mode of exposition is not a formal argument couched in mathematical terms, but is a mix of mathematics, graphs, and computer simulations, interlaced to reveal the complementary nature of psychophysical explanations.

# 2 Sensory Aggregate Model

Theoretical statements concerning sensory psychophysics are usually couched in physiological terms unique to each sensory modality or to the stimulus attributes processed by that modality.[1] Models emerging from such theorizing look very different for different modalities because transformations of physical energy into a neural state are not the same for all the senses (Barlow & Mollon, 1989; Geldard, 1972). The anatomy and physiology of the visual system clearly do not take the same form as those of the auditory system. Nor for that matter do the gustatory, cutaneous, and olfactory systems suggest close anatomical kinship.

Modality-specific theory is prevalent because the majority of psychophysicists are experts in one sensory system, and in some instances, one subspecialty such as color vision, taste quality, or loudness perception. These researchers are knowledgeable about the intricacies of their discipline at all scales, stretching from the broadest strokes of behavioral perception down to the cellular details of sensory physiology. Their interest in psychophysics is driven by a desire to thoroughly explore one aspect of sensation in all its guises. Psychophysical methods are seen as interchangeable tools for reaching this goal.

Because their aim is to plumb the depths of one sense modality, the existence of similarities across modalities is of secondary interest (for exceptions to this research attitude, see Geldard, 1972, and Marks, 1974b). The explanatory models are themselves expressed in modality-specific language, and it is especially difficult for anyone to extract principles from these models that transcend the modality to which the empirical phenomena are so intimately connected.

An alternative approach to the study of sensory psychophysics, also deeply

---

[1] I cover issues concerned with multisensory integration (Stein & Meredith, 1993) in Chapter 16.

imbued in tradition, focuses on method. The same experimental paradigm is used with different sense modalities or stimulus attributes, and theory is confined to the results obtained by this one method or class of methods. Examples of such paradigms are the classical discrimination methods systematized by Fechner (1860/1966), the direct scaling approach of S. S. Stevens (1975), and the reaction time methods popularized by Piéron (1952).

One advantage accruing from this method-bound tradition is that the same methods, as well as their associated statistical and theoretical underpinnings, are readily generalized to psychological problems outside the boundaries of psychophysics—prime examples are preference and decision making, memory and pattern recognition. Method-oriented research has the disadvantage that it tends to divide opinion into separate camps that have little interaction with each other. Each camp strongly believes their chosen method is superior to all others at revealing the empirical facts of psychophysics, and there is no point in trying to incorporate their findings into a larger scheme that includes data collected by their competitors. Such an attitude does not encourage general theory aimed at finding a home for all the reliable facts, regardless of the means by which they are determined.

## THE FUNCTIONAL THESIS

In contrast to an approach that favors particular sense modalities or methods, the thesis of the present work is that general principles emerge when considering the results from all the senses and from all psychophysical methods taken as an indivisible whole. Once the findings are summarized in the language of mathematics and modeled by computer simulation, the physiological and psychological explanations are stripped of all but their most salient features, and these are the features of interest to the general theorist.

By this way of reckoning, each sense modality performs the same function: to transform physical energy into a neural format that the brain uses to learn about environmental events. Each psychophysical method is one of many avenues for discovering this connection between external stimulation and perceptual experience. In addition, the functional rules relating stimulus to judgment must be examined, not the exact way in which these rules are instantiated in neural mechanisms. Such broad themes are emphasized in this work, because the intent here is to explain as many empirical relations as possible that transcend psychophysical method and stimulus attribute.

## LOCAL AND GLOBAL PSYCHOPHYSICS

A handful of equations describe the relations between perceptual and physical magnitudes, and because of their ubiquitousness, they are often referred to as *psychophysical laws.* There is no disputing their faithful description of data obtained under well-defined experimental conditions. These equations, along with theories tracing their roots back to sensory mechanisms, fall within the jurisdiction of psychophysics. But there are two major subdivisions to this discipline, designated here as *local* and *global* (Luce & Green, 1974; Luce & Krumhansl, 1986). Global psychophysics refers to the conglomerate of methods and models that treat functional relations over a substantial range of stimulus intensities, the dynamic range spanning a person's ability to perceive values along a stimulus dimension, such as that characterized by light, sound, and odor intensity. Local psychophysics involves those methods and models pertaining to the perception of small stimulus differences measured along these same physical dimensions.

Local psychophysics employs the classical techniques for studying discrimination, as introduced by Fechner and his contemporaries in the last century (e.g., methods of Constant Stimuli, Limits, and Adjustment), as well as the more recent techniques supporting the Theory of Signal Detection (Green & Swets, 1966/1974; Macmillan & Creelman, 1991). Global psychophysics uses the scaling methods made famous by S. S. Stevens and his students in the latter half of the present century, including such techniques as Magnitude Estimation, Magnitude Production, and Cross Modality Matching (Marks, 1974b; S. S. Stevens, 1975). Included also among the global methods is "Absolute Identification," which parts company with the others by permitting feedback after each judgment (Baird & Noma, 1978, chap. 14, this volume).

The supposed link between planes of analysis is a recurrent source of disagreement in psychophysics, and theoretical work often turns on questions about whether or not the sensory processes underlying the laws of local and global psychophysics are the same. This chapter provides a framework for a sensorineural model that predicts the laws on both planes, as well as their linkages. The next five chapters show how such a model elucidates the major findings of sensory psychophysics. In placing this theme within the realm of physiology, almost no emphasis is given to psychological factors, such as procedural context effects and the cognitive strategies engaged in by subjects. These topics are given their due later on.

## NEURAL PSYCHOPHYSICS

Most would agree there is a sensorineural basis to psychophysics. This volume claims further that all the sensory systems solve the major problems of perception in a similar manner, though the anatomical means by which this is accomplished are remarkably diverse. A related position taken by Norwich (1993) explains the laws of psychophysics by a single unifying equation based on the uncertainty inherent in the activity of single neurons. In contrast, the present analysis is grounded in the premise that variability observed in psychophysical judgments is due to the involvement of neuronal aggregates, rather than to the noise resulting from the activity of single neurons.

Like Norwich's thesis, the proposed model is an abstraction, derived from anatomical and physiological facts known about specific sense modalities, but expressed in functional terms intended to capture the essence of such facts, rather than their physiological manifestations. Of course, unique sensorineural analogues of psychophysical phenomena do exist in each sense modality, and variability within a single neuron certainly commands interest. These are not the chief concerns of this work.

The targets for analysis are those aspects of the neural code potentially responsible for psychophysical results. In the past, there have been two broad answers to the question of the appropriate neural code. Fechner (1860/1966) believed that the same neural substructure underlay both the micro and the macroanalysis of psychophysics. He proposed that the Just-Noticeable-Differences (JNDs) on the microlevel were the building blocks determining the overall shape of the psychophysical function observed over the full range of a stimulus dimension. He believed further that moving between levels of scale was symmetrical in the sense that if one understands the macropicture, one can simply shift attention to the microlevel without loss of understanding. According to Fechner, the law relating subjective sensation to the material world of physics was an invariant that did not undergo change according to the scale at which it was observed.

As is well known, Fechner's (1860/1966) creative hunch on the morning of October 22, 1850 was that the global law of psychophysics is in fact logarithmic and can be derived by concatenating JNDs based on stimulus discrimination (Baird & Noma, 1978, chap. 2; Boring, 1950). In the spirit of Fechnerian lore, Thurstone (1927) took response variability as a unit of measure marking off distances along psychological scales. Extensions of these early formulations continue to appear in the literature on judgment and choice (Baird & Noma, 1978; Green & Swets, 1966/1974; Link, 1992; Luce, 1977; Restle, 1961). Restricting attention only to psychophysics, the classical Fechnerian tradition implicitly assumes that all empirical laws are supported by variations of the same sensory code.

Contrary to this opinion, S. S. Stevens (1975) advocated that a separation be maintained between the neural underpinnings of local and global psychophysics. In his view, discrimination between stimuli that are near each other along a stimulus dimension must be explained in quite another way than how one explains the subject matter of global psychophysics. According to Stevens, coupling the two levels, either by integrating constituents to reveal the whole, or by differentiating the whole to examine the constituents, was not legitimate. In particular, the Power Law effective in relating subjective magnitude to stimulus intensity should not be considered as a logical implication from perceptual discrimination data at the local level. Stevens thought the subject's discrimination of small stimulus changes was the result of neural processing that was fundamentally different from that invoked in the scaling of large stimulus changes.

The evidence from neurophysiology provides no definitive resolution to the conflicting views of Fechner and Stevens. Neurophysiological measures, just like their psychophysical counterparts, come in a variety of forms. Even when the model is based on the activity of single neurons, there are several prime candidates for the correlate of physical intensity. Neuronal firing rate is a strong possibility, but so is the onset time of neural discharge, or even the variability of firing rate (Norwich, 1993). If aggregates of neurons are considered, the number of candidates proliferates to include the specific neurons excited, the total number involved, or their average firing rate. In like fashion, the neural code underlying Weber's Law relating the stimulus JND to stimulus intensity (Baird & Noma, 1978, chap. 3) may reside in the operating characteristics of the single neuron or in the concerted action of groups.

One thing is apparent: The neural infrastructure is sufficiently rich to provide reasonable explanations for many of the outcomes observed psychophysically. There is no need to interleave sensory and cognitive factors into one model in order to handle a substantial proportion of the available psychophysical data.

For purposes of creating a sensory model, therefore, the strong claim is made that much, but not all, of psychophysics can be understood in terms of sensory physiology, without having to enlist the services of central/cognitive mechanisms. In order to explain the rest of the results obtained in the psychophysics laboratory, it is necessary to start with entirely different assumptions concerning the underlying source of response variability. This alternate route claims that response variability is due to the subject's decision uncertainty and is unrelated to the intrinsic variability of the senses. The implications of this perspective are examined after we address sensory phenomena.

## THE SENSORY AGGREGATE MODEL

The model proposed is founded on assumptions in four areas: the transfer function between neural discharge rate and stimulus intensity, the dynamic range of an individual neuron, the stimulus-contingent neuronal thresholds, and the distribution of thresholds over the range of stimulus intensity to which the sense organ can respond without damage.

### Neural Transfer Function

The firing rate of a sensory neuron typically increases sharply following stimulus onset and then tapers off to a sustained rate. The onset time of a neuron, at least when measured on the scale of milliseconds, is proportional to this sustained rate

(Getchell, 1986; Smith, 1988). It is sometimes said that onset time is a function of stimulus intensity, but this is not strictly accurate, because not all neurons are selectively tuned in the same way to qualitatively distinct stimuli (e.g., sound frequency, wavelength of light). In any event, the stabilized firing rate of a neuron is usually a decelerating function of stimulus intensity over its effective range.

The function's exact shape, however, varies widely. For example, in the cat, the neuronal response to noxious skin heating is linear over much of its range, though it does eventually asymptote (Carstens, Fraunhoffer, & Suberg, 1983). Certain neurons, acting alone or in groups, reach a peak rate and then decline with further increases in intensity (Gulick, Gescheider, & Frisina, 1989, chap. 9; S. S. Stevens, 1975, chap. 7), and so forth.

Early physiological studies indicate that the transfer function for individual neurons is logarithmic, in accord with Fechner's Law (Hartline & Graham, 1932; S. S. Stevens, 1975), but a power function also does a respectable job fitting data that are in fact logarithmic. Thus, S. S. Stevens argued that the power function, found so often with psychophysical methods, operates in the neural arena as well. He also reviewed a considerable body of evidence upholding the notion that the discharge rate of the peripheral nerve bundle follows a power function more often than a log function (1970, 1971a, 1971b). In point of fact, it would be difficult to decide between these two representations on mathematical grounds, and therefore, even harder to decide categorically on a single, all-inclusive equation for the neural transfer function.

A possible resolution of the conflict between these competing laws is to claim that different transfer functions exist for different dependent measures. Wasserman, Felsten, and Easland (1979) demonstrated this by recording intracellularly from the photoreceptor cells of the horseshoe crab (*Limulus*). They observed both a logarithmic and a power function for the magnitude of the receptor potential in response to a light flash, where the best-fitting function depends on the response measure. They recorded the electrical response of the cell over a 15-sec period after stimulus onset. Using the peak neural response over this period as the dependent measure, the transfer function is logarithmic, though it clearly saturates at the upper end of the stimulus range. When the integral (area) under the same response curve is the dependent measure, no saturation is observed and the output of the cell is a power function of physical intensity. It would seem that either a power or a logarithmic function can characterize the receptor potential in the *Limulus* eye for individual neurons, depending on the choice of response measure.

An ancillary problem with assuming the power function characterizes all the relevant data on neural transfer functions is that psychophysical results at the behavioral level show that some attributes, such as lifted weight and warmth on the skin, yield exponents greater than 1. A search of the literature did not find any reports of individual sensory neurons that respond in a positively accelerating fashion to increases in stimulus intensity over their full dynamic range. This hole in the physiological record causes embarrassment for any theory that proposes a one-to-one correspondence between psychophysical and sensory power functions for individual neurons.

It has also been noted that the relation between firing rates of neurons and stimulus intensity is often S-shaped for both vision and hearing (Gulick et al., 1989; Naka & Rushton, 1966; Sachs & Abbas, 1974; Viemeister, 1988). For descriptive purposes, a number of distinct mathematical functions can be fit to such a relation: a higher order polynomial, the logistic, or the hyperbolic tangent function (Naka & Rushton, 1966; Sachs & Abbas, 1974). Figure 2.1 shows sample hypothetical data from five auditory neurons illustrating an S-shaped function (Gulick et al., 1989). The lower section of each curve is positively accelerated, but with further increases in intensity, the curvature reverses in sign, and eventually the function asymptotes. This graph also illustrates that the thresholds of the neurons are staggered (distributed) along the intensity dimension by which the location of the absolute threshold is defined. This aspect of the data is central to the present argument, and is discussed more fully in a moment.

Each of the functions in Figure 2.1 asymptotes as the intensity of the stimulus reaches the highest levels. Saturation of this sort is a common finding in studies of neural transfer functions, another example is presented in Figure 2.2. Here, the firing rate (on a linear scale) of an auditory neuron is shown as a function of sound pressure level in dB (logarithmic scale) of a 2900-Hz tone (based on an unpublished experiment by Brachman, 1980, and Smith, 1988 on the Mongolian gerbil). The crosses indicate maximum firing rates during a 1-msec time interval following stimulus onset. The squares indicate firing rates during a 20-msec interval following onset. Both functions are negatively accelerated over their early course, but the rate for the 20-msec interval eventually saturates at the higher stimulus intensities.

In sum, the neural transfer function shows us many faces, and hence, a single

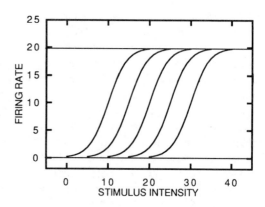

FIG. 2.1. Idealized rate-intensity functions for neurons with staggered thresholds. After Gulick et al. (1989).

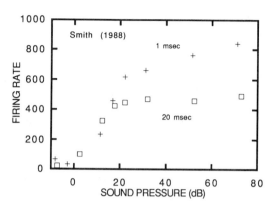

FIG. 2.2.  Firing rate of an auditory neuron from the Mongolian gerbil as a function of sound pressure level in dB (logarithmic scale). After Smith (1988). The crosses indicate firing rates during a 1-msec time interval following stimulus onset. The squares indicate firing rates during a 20-msec interval following onset.

equation is unlikely to hold true for all attributes under all conditions of stimulation. Moreover, the activity of a neuron is potentiated or inhibited by its neural neighbors (Shepherd, 1983, chap 8, 1990). Despite this influence of adjacent neurons on the activity level of a single fiber, the key property of most neural transfer functions is that they are negatively accelerated over the middle range of intensities. It is possible that this is the only critical section of the function in terms of signaling the brain that a neuron has been activated, but, of course, there is no way to tell if this is correct.

In terms of computer simulation, it makes little difference to the final outcome if one employs any of a number of the neural transfer functions identified in the literature. Admittedly, most such functions look a bit like an S-shaped curve (normal ogive) or some other function that saturates at high intensities.[2] It is not clear, however, whether the lower and upper tails of the function convey any critical information to higher centers in the brain. For example, the slowest firing rates may be indistinguishable from background noise in the system. And a neuron that fires at a sustained and constant rate despite changes within the region of strong physical intensities may not be especially informative. The middle part of the function, where the first derivative is greater than zero, may provide the most useful indication of response magnitude. Because the neural transfer function gradually bends over in this section, its shape is approximately logarithmic.

In order to move on and begin making predictions of specific empirical outcomes, it is assumed that the firing rate for individual sensory neurons is a logarithmic function of stimulus intensity, but only up to a saturation point

---

[2]A logistic function does this. Its formulation is $\dfrac{L}{1 + e^{a-bx}}$, where L is the upper limit, $a$ is a constant, and $b$ is the rate of increase (Larsen & Marx, 1981, p. 440). This equation has the advantage that it produces a saturation point.

(discusssed later). By endorsing this assumption, it is possible to build a model whose predictions are invariant under transformations of stimulus range. This does not occur with many of the alternative mathematical representations. This advantage will crop up again in our discussion of the role of stimulus range in determining the exponent of the Power Law (chap. 6).

## Dynamic Range of Individual Neurons

The saturation or slowing of firing rate evident in Figures 2.1 and 2.2 suggests that the effective range of a neuron is limited, and in fact, this limit is the source of a long-standing puzzle in sensory neurophysiology. The dynamic range of the senses, when measured at the behavioral (psychophysical) level, is enormous relative to the effective range of a single neuron. This is especially true for vision and hearing where populations of neurons, apparently working in concert, are able to differentially code stimulus intensities over a range that is at least two, and perhaps as much as five, times greater than the known range of single neurons (Barlow, 1989a, 1989b; Evans, 1981; Luce, 1993; Viemeister, 1988). This is the main reason for assuming that aggregates of neurons code intensity, rather than leaving the task to single fibers.[3]

Therefore, a second abstraction from the neurophysiological data is that the dynamic range of an individual sensory neuron is limited and more restricted than the stimulus range to which the sense modality is responsive.

The upper constraint on the firing rates of individual neurons suggests that intensity is coded by subpopulations of neurons acting together. This view has been entertained by physiologists and psychologists for some time (e.g., Barlow, 1989a; Viemeister, 1988). For example, Wever's (1949) well-known "volley principle" incorporates this notion in explaining the neural coding of sound frequency. Squads of neurons fire intermittently with other squads in order to increase the overall firing rate of the aggregate. On the other hand, a quantitative model has not been proposed until now concerning the means by which a population of fibers act together to produce an output corresponding to judgments obtained in the psychophysics laboratory. Before delving into the details of such a model, it is necessary to review the neurophysiological findings regarding the way in which populations of neurons might share the work load in this regard.

## Stimulus-Contingent Thresholds

Although in some way patently obvious, it still is worth emphasizing that stimuli delivered to the senses can vary in both quantity and quality. It is impossible to

---

[3]This statement is not intended to exclude neurons whose dynamic ranges can be reinstated at higher intensity levels by introducing background stimulation, such as holds true in the visual system (R. L. DeValois & K. K. DeValois, 1988).

present one without the other. A light has both a brightness and a tint or shade, a sound has both a loudness and a pitch or timbre. It has been evident for some time that application of an external stimulus does not produce the same excitation in all sensory neurons. For example, in vision, the absolute threshold for lights of different wavelength depends on the particular receptor type sampled. The basis of color vision in the three-cone system, together with the differential response of the rods over the same continuum, indicates that different intensity is needed to trigger a response in the same receptor, depending on the stimulus wavelength (see, e.g., Pugh, 1988). The source of these stimulus-contingent thresholds is definitely at the receptor level, because the electroretinogram representing the response of the entire eye, and the absorption curves of individual receptors, match the psychophysical data remarkably well (Armington, 1974).

Individual neurons in the cochlea are also tuned to respond preferentially to certain sound frequencies (Gulick et al., 1989; Kiang, 1965). An example of such a stimulus-contingent tuning curve is shown in Figure 2.3 for three fibers whose optimal frequencies are at 100, 1000, and 10,000 Hz. The y axis indicates the amount of energy needed to excite the cell for different sound frequencies. The least amount of energy is required when the frequency exactly fits the characteristic frequency of the cell. With sufficiently intense sounds, each fiber shows some degree of activation across a band of frequencies. The enclosed area of each "V" indicates all the combinations of intensity and frequency giving rise to a neural response by the fiber type indicated on the x axis. Different fibers have different sound frequencies to which they are maximally sensitive, and, in this way, it is supposed that the cell population handles the whole frequency spectrum to which the auditory system responds (Luce, 1993, pt. III, sec. 4; Pickles, 1988, p. 84).

Similar stimulus-contingent fibers are found in olfaction and taste. Sicard and Holley (1984) discovered that cells in the frog's olfactory epithelium do not respond with equal vigor to a variety of odor qualities and even cells in the same

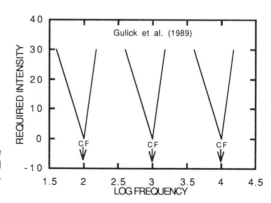

FIG. 2.3. Idealized response area of auditory neurons tuned to different frequencies (CF). After Gulick et al. (1989).

location have different response profiles over qualitative changes in odor. The absolute threshold of a fiber, though broadly responsive, is sensitive to a limited range of odor qualities in a manner reminiscent of tuning curves in audition and photoreceptor curves in vision (Cain, 1986; Getchell, 1986; Kauer, 1974).

Stimulus-contingent thresholds have been identified for taste as well. Frank (1973, 1975) classified taste fibers (in rats and hamsters) according to their selectivity to chemical stimuli. She reported that some fibers have minimum thresholds for salt, others for hydrochloric acid, and still others for sucrose or quinine. Figure 2.4 shows typical results for this selective tuning to stimulus quality for four fiber types, as designated by the different point symbols (for review of this literature, see Bartoshuk, 1986). The x axis indicates each of the four chemicals. The y axis is the mean response rate.

It has also been noted that taste qualities do not fall into a handful of subjective categories or "primaries," such as those envisioned by early investigators (Henning, 1916). Schiffman and Erickson (1971, 1980) argued that taste qualities and their neural counterparts should be treated as points in a continuous multidimensional space, rather than as representatives of distinct qualities, such as sweet, sour, salty, and bitter. They emphasized that a variety of neurons fire in response to a single tastant and the coding of intensity and quality is not so much the result of optimal firing by a "selectively tuned" neuron as it is the result of the firing pattern produced by an entire cadre of neurons.

In summary, the evidence for selective tuning in any modality is usually depicted by plotting the absolute threshold or firing rate on the y axis as a function of stimulus quality on the x axis. The differential tuning is indicated by a dip (minimum threshold) or a peak (maximum sensitivity) in the function at the particular quality for which a fiber is maximally sensitive. The relevance for intensity coding is that different types of neurons contribute to the impression of intensity, but the thresholds of these neurons are staggered over the range of intensities to which a sensory system is responsive. It may be that cells with the same response profiles over changes in stimulus quality also vary in terms of

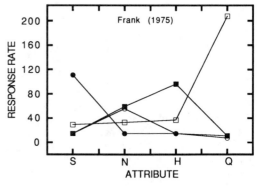

FIG. 2.4. Mean response rate of four taste fibers (different symbols) selectively tuned to four different chemicals (x axis). After Frank (1975).

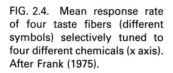

their absolute intensity thresholds, but this conclusion is more speculative (Gulick et al., 1989; Sachs & Abbas, 1974; Smith, 1988).

It is established that each sensory system contains fibers with diverse thresholds for the same stimulus quality, be it a particular wavelength (vision), frequency (audition), odor quality (olfaction), or chemical (taste). A general principle for the coding of stimulus intensity can therefore be proposed: The absolute thresholds of the neurons responsible for the coding of intensity for a particular stimulus attribute or quality are staggered over the range of intensities to which the sense modality is responsive.

## Distribution of Neuronal Thresholds

One final assumption is necessary before turning to a neural model of intensity coding that applies to all sense modalities. This assumption has no direct support in the electrophysiological data, but it is an integral component of the present model. It is assumed that the logarithm of neuronal thresholds over the intensity continuum is normally distributed.

When the senses are treated as physical measuring devices, there is circumstantial evidence suggesting that sensory thresholds are normally distributed on a log scale (Barlow, 1989a). Moreover, any system whose components are arranged hierarchically, as is often true for the neural components of the senses (as well as their representation in the cortex), can be modeled so they produce output roughly approximating a log function (one such example is given in Baird, 1975a).

The lognormal distribution has two parameters: the mean and the standard deviation. As is demonstrated later, the variation of parameter values describing matters in the neural domain supplies a rationale for variations in the parameter values of psychophysical laws. That is to say, differences in the processing of stimulus qualities (attributes) are simulated by using different values for the mean and standard deviation of the hypothetical lognormal.

To recap, the central assumptions underlying the Sensory Aggregate Model are that the transfer function for individual neurons is logarithmic and limited in dynamic range, and the thresholds of stimulus-contingent neurons are distributed in a lognormal fashion over the range of intensities to which a sensory system responds. Implications of the model are examined in succeeding chapters, and predictions made for a number of empirical phenomena. In practice, one can alter the details of these assumptions and still have a quantitative simulation that arrives at the same end point. These related models are not considered here. I turn next to a quantitative description of the model under discussion.

## FORMALIZATION

The goal of formalization is to derive equations that yield statistical measures of the firing-rate distributions associated with each of the stimulus intensities presented in a psychophysical experiment.[4] The analytic approach is complicated by the fact that there are two types of logarithmic variables involved, and they do not pertain to the same thing. First, there is the lognormal distribution of thresholds, and second, there is the firing rate of a single neuron that is a function of the logarithm of stimulus intensity in respect to a threshold. It is helpful to keep in mind that these two variables are not the same.

First, find the mean firing rate for a single stimulus intensity. This illustrates the procedure to calculate other statistical measures such as the variance and skewness. Laboratory scientists are used to calculating the mean of a set of observations by adding up all the values and dividing by the number of cases. This is done in Equation 2.1:

$$\overline{M} = \frac{\sum_{i=1}^{N} x_i}{N} \ .$$

(2.1)

Another way to write Equation 2.1 is

$$\overline{M} = \sum_{i=1}^{N} \frac{1}{N} x_i \ .$$

(2.2)

This emphasizes the weighting $(1/N)$ that occurs for each of the $x$'s in the sum. More generally, the weight is a probability, represented as the relative frequency of occurrence:

$$\overline{M} = \sum_{i=1}^{N} p(x_i) x_i$$

(2.3)

The continuous version of Equation 2.3 gives the expected value of $X$:

$$E\ [X] = \int_{A}^{B} xp(x)dx$$

(2.4)

Next, the various terms of Equation 2.4 are defined by relying on the assumptions of the Sensory Aggregate Model. After doing this, we return to the discrete case in order to find tractable expressions for purposes of calculation.

## Neural Transfer Function

The variable $x$ in Equation 2.4 is the neural firing rate $(F)$, which is defined for a single stimulus $(S)$ in terms of its magnitude relative to a fiber's threshold $(S^*)$.

---

[4]I am grateful to R. Duncan Luce for his valuable assistance in developing the argument in this section.

Because the stimulus intensity is constant, the random variable of interest is the threshold. Consider a fiber that has threshold $S*$ and maximum effective stimulus $S_m$. Its firing rate in this range is assumed to be

$$F = log\ (S/S*),\ (0 < S* \leq S \leq S_m). \tag{2.5}$$

In the computer simulations described later, a parameter was included as a multiplier to produce reasonable firing rates. A further limitation at the upper end of the stimulus continuum is also introduced to make it clear that the fiber has a finite region of effectiveness. It is assumed there is some maximum firing rate $F_m$, such that

$$F_m = log\ (S_m/S*),$$

and $F_m$ is independent of $S*$, that is,

$$S_m = S*e^{F_m}.$$

The value of $F_m$ represents the dynamic range of the neuron, which is a free parameter, but one that is not manipulated in the present applications. In the simulations that follow, the range of a neuron's effectiveness is the same (1.5 log units) for all neurons in the ensemble, though of course individual thresholds vary.

## Threshold Limits

The problem is to calculate, as a function of $S$, the expected firing rate when the fibers have an assumed distribution of thresholds. In particular, assume $log\ S*$ is a truncated normal where the truncation is given by the requirement

$$0 \leq log(S/S*) \leq F_m.$$

So, by rearranging,

$$log\ S \geq log\ S* \geq log\ S - F_m. \tag{2.6}$$

## Distribution of Thresholds

The probability density depends on the distribution of fiber thresholds $(S*)$, which are staggered along the intensity dimension. This is schematized in Figure 2.5.

The firing rate is plotted as a function of stimulus intensity in arbitrary units for nine idealized neurons, whose thresholds vary along the intensity dimension. Each of the nine log functions has the same dynamic range from a minimum at 1 to a maximum of approximately 20, but the full extent of all but the neuron with the lowest threshold is not visible on the graph, because of the arbitrary upper cutoff on the intensity scale. In the computer simulations of the model, the distribution consists of 1000 neurons.

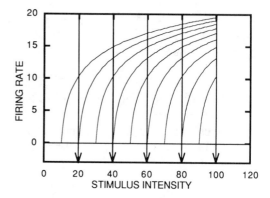

FIG. 2.5. Firing rate as a function of stimulus intensity for nine hypothetical neurons with staggered thresholds. The intersections of the vertical lines with the firing-rate curves indicate the varied rates across the ensemble of neurons responding to each stimulus.

The vertical lines in Figure 2.5 mark the location of the stimuli. The aggregate output for each stimulus arises from the joint contribution of all the activated fibers. That is, the intersections of each vertical line with the individual transfer functions designates the set of firing rates within the aggregate for that one stimulus intensity. The statistical properties of the distributions of firing rates are the basis for explaining psychophysical laws and their parameter values for different attributes (qualities), psychophysical methods, and stimulus conditions. These details gradually unfold as the implications of the model are spelled out.[5]

One of the critical aspects of the Sensory Aggregate Model, not shown in Figure 2.5, is the distribution of the neural thresholds over the intensity dimension. In the figure, the thresholds are equally spaced. In the model they are not. The neural aggregate that signals intensity is comprised of all the neurons activated by that stimulus. In other words, the only neurons at issue are those whose thresholds are exceeded and whose dynamic ranges include the stimulus intensity. For the example, then, the lognormal has to be restricted in order to only evaluate those thresholds lying equal to or below the stimulus intensity. The probability density of relevance, therefore, is the truncated lognormal whose truncation points are given by Equation 2.6. Thus, the expected value is

$$E[F(S)] = \int_{log\ S\ -\ F_m}^{log\ S} log(S/S^*)p(log\ S^*)d(log\ S^*) \ , \qquad (2.7)$$

where

$$p(log\ S^*) = \frac{\varphi(log\ S^*)}{\Phi(log\ S) - \Phi(log\ S - F_m)} \ . \qquad (2.8)$$

---

[5]The next section relies on the presentations by Bury (1975, chaps. 5 & 8) and by Johnson and Kotz (1970, chaps. 13 & 14).

In this notation, $\varphi$ is the normal density function and $\Phi$ is the corresponding distribution function.

In the present theoretical context Equation 2.7 is somewhat unrealistic because neurons and their firing rates are discrete, not continuous. Evaluating Equation 2.7 is also unwieldy without the use of a computer, though everyone in this field has one. It is easier to work with a discrete approximation. This essentially involves discretizing the truncated lognormal. Returning to the example for the mean expressed by Equation 2.3, we can write

$$\overline{M} = \sum_{i=1}^{N} p(F_i)F_i , \qquad (2.9)$$

where N is the number of fiber thresholds, and $p(F_i)$ is a fiber's probability density divided by the sum of such probabilities for all the relevant fibers (those with thresholds below the stimulus).

## DEPENDENT MEASURES

The argument to this juncture describes the neural activity corresponding to stimulus intensity. The dependent measures of interest arise from the activity of the full aggregate. For each stimulus, the aggregate consists of neurons whose dynamic range encompasses the stimulus intensity. The composition of each distribution consists of the firing rates of individual neurons, as indicated by the vertical cuts through the curves in Figure 2.5. The intersection of the vertical line with a particular log function indicates the firing rate associated with that stimulus on the x axis. Because of the different prevalence of threshold types, due to the lognormal distribution, all statistics summarizing the firing-rate distributions are weighted values.

Figure 2.6 depicts a three-dimensional view of the threshold distributions associated with each of six stimuli ($S_1$ to $S_6$), equally spaced along a log scale. Each distribution is a truncated version of the entire normal curve (with unit area) that extends over the intensity range to which the sense modality is responsive. Only thresholds falling below a stimulus intensity contribute to the neural aggregate responsible for signaling its presence. The upper truncation of each distribution marks the position of the stimulus intensity relative to the lowest fiber threshold—the weakest intensity is represented by the distribution in the foreground, the most intense stimulus by the distribution furthest back in the diagram. The Stevens exponent ($\gamma$) is explained in chapter 3.

This activated pool of neurons has the restriction that each component must have a dynamic range that envelops the stimulus. For example, suppose the dynamic range of each neuron is 1 log unit and a stimulus is located at a position of 2.5 log units. Then a neuron with a threshold located at 1.5 log units will

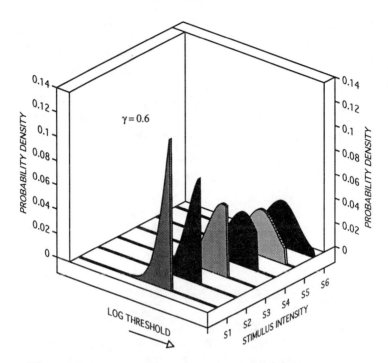

FIG. 2.6.    Probability density of thresholds associated with each of six stimuli (**S**₁ to **S**₆). Distributions are truncated lognormals. Stevens exponent of 0.6. Standardized probabilities sum to 1.0.

contribute to the aggregate because its dynamic range extends up to the stimulus $(1.5 + 1 = 2.5)$, whereas, neurons with thresholds falling below 1.5 do not enter the picture. The assumption of a sharp break in whether or not a neuron contributes to the aggregate is somewhat arbitrary, because a neuron's firing rate might be expected to either asymptote or decline with increases in stimulus intensity beyond its nominal dynamic range. Introducing this additional layer of complexity, however, seems unwarranted at this stage of model building.

The firing rates for individual neurons contributing to the aggregate depend on how far below the stimulus their respective thresholds lie. A neuron whose threshold falls just below the stimulus will be firing at a slow rate. A neuron with a threshold far below the stimulus will be firing at a fast rate. Figure 2.7 shows the predicted firing-rate distributions for each of the six hypothetical stimuli. These distributions represent the combined action of the sensory correlates for psychophysical judgments.

It is informative to compare Figures 2.6 and 2.7. Consider the peaked threshold distribution in Figure 2.6 associated with the weakest stimulus intensity. It is highly skewed to the left (negatively). This is to be compared with the corresponding firing-rate distribution, which is skewed in the opposite direction (Fig-

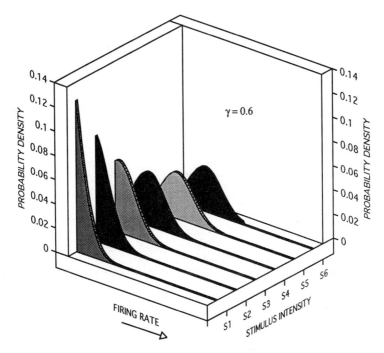

FIG. 2.7. Probability density of firing rates associated with each of six stimuli (**S₁** to **S₆**). Stevens exponent of 0.6. Standardized probabilities sum to 1.0.

ure 2.7). That is, it helps in tracking the workings of the model to keep in mind that the neurons with the lowest thresholds (Figure 2.6) are associated in the aggregate with the highest firing rates (Figure 2.7).

## STATISTICAL PROPERTIES

The statistical properties of the distributions in Figure 2.7 are the dependent measures used in making predictions of psychophysical results. Of special interest for applications of the model are the mean, the standard deviation, and the skewness. These measures are all expressed in linear units.

### Mean Firing Rate

For each stimulus intensity, the firing rate of the ensemble of active neurons is a weighted average of the firing rates of the components. If threshold is indexed by j, the mean is

$$\overline{M}(F) = \sum_{j=1}^{N} p[log\ (S/S_j^*)]F_j\ . \tag{2.10}$$

## Variance

The dispersion of a distribution is defined by the variance of firing rates in the aggregate:

$$\text{Var } (F) = \sum_{j=1}^{N} p[log \ (S/S_j^*)][F_j - \overline{M}(F)]^2 \ . \tag{2.11}$$

## Standard Deviation

The square root of the variance yields the standard deviation:

$$sd \ (F) = [Var \ (F)]^{1/2}. \tag{2.12}$$

## Skewness

The symmetry of the distribution is defined by its skewness (in a dimensionless form):

$$Sk \ (F) = \frac{\sum_{j=1}^{N} p[log \ (S/S_j^*)][F_j - \overline{M}(F)]^3}{[sd \ (F)]^3} \ . \tag{2.13}$$

## PSYCHOPHYSICAL IMPLICATIONS

Psychophysical laws capture the invariant relations between perceived magnitude and physical intensity. It is the functional relation between judgments and stimulus parameters that must be traced back to the neural level. The Sensory Aggregate Model offers a framework for describing and predicting these invariances. The main question is whether one can select the parameters of the model in a manner so as to generate an output that matches the judgments subjects give in psychophysical experiments. Such judgments are assumed to depend on neural processes associated with the common methods used in stimulus scaling and discrimination.

The model postulates a situation in the sensory domain that is in one-to-one correspondence with psychophysical judgments. That is, the sensation aroused by external stimulation is presumed to be faithfully represented by psychophysical judgments. The possible influence of procedural factors, such as the format in which the subject's response is expressed, is not part of the model. As becomes apparent, a rather impressive list of psychophysical phenomena are clarified without involving cognitive or response factors in any way.

Also note that the Sensory Aggregate Model is underdeveloped analytically, which means the laws of psychophysics are not derived mathematically from the equations. The model's performance is tested by computer simulation. The statistical measures are based on the data generated by this simulation, and plotting these measures against stimulus measures depicts the predicted psychophysical relations.

Two broad classes of phenomena are reviewed in the chapters that follow. The first involves global scaling of stimulus intensity, and, for this class, it is assumed that aggregate firing rate is responsible for the data observed. The major results considered are the Power Law relating response magnitude to stimulus intensity (Stevens functions) and the relation between reaction time and stimulus intensity (Piéron functions).

The second class of results involves discrimination between stimuli at a local level. Neuronal firing rate is the key factor in discrimination as well. If on each trial the brain samples a single value from the firing rates of the neural aggregate, then the variability within the aggregate determines the ability to discriminate between stimuli that are near each other in intensity: the greater the variance, the less the discrimination. In other words, the standard deviation of the neural aggregate is an index of the Just-Noticeable-Difference that enters into Weber's Law relating variability to stimulus intensity (Baird & Noma, 1978, chap. 3).

Before expanding on these themes, three caveats are in order: First, discussion of cognitive factors in psychophysics is being postponed, not ignored. Such factors are often crucial in determining the judgments given by subjects in psychophysical experiments. These contributions receive a full airing later in the book. This section on neural modeling means to convey that much of psychophysics can be explained by arguments based entirely on sensorineural mechanisms. Because of the inescapable influence of cognitive factors in the psychophysics laboratory, it is true that the operation of sensory processes can be superseded or hidden under a cloak of psychological variables. The Sensory Aggregate Model applies to phenomena that would be evident if this cloak were removed.

Second, the model is not exhibited on a pedestal as the one and only hope for establishing a neurophysiological basis for psychophysics. Reliable features of the empirical data at the neural level were emphasized in fashioning this model, but no doubt there are alternatives, based on the same set of physiological facts. The aim is to suggest a broad direction for neural modeling, not a narrow, straight path. In presenting the assumptions and subsequent implications of the model, however, it is necessary to become rather specific. Otherwise, a convincing case cannot be made for turning to sensory neurophysiology as one of the two pillars supporting the Complementarity Theory.

Third, the model are a hypothetical structure and, therefore, an abstraction. The raw empirical data are not simply lifted from the neural realm and, by induction, applied to behavior. This task would prove fruitless, unless a separate model were formulated for each of the sense modalities and for each of the stimulus attributes processed by that modality. Instead, an abstract structure transcending modalities and emphasizing their commonalities, rather than their idiosyncracies, is offered. Because of this abstraction, the model performs best when explaining the laws of psychophysics that appear for all sense modalities. The approach is less suited to handling data that are modality specific. Only in a secondary manner, or by way of illustration, are findings with implications for perception of but a single attribute considered.

# 3 Stevens Functions

There are two suppositions for experiments on psychophysical scaling at the global level. First, the human being is considered a measuring instrument whose properties remain the same for all manner of sensory inputs but whose sensitivity depends on the physical attribute being assessed. Second, quantitative judgments are the consequence of this measurement and, as such, can be ordered along psychological *scales*. Tradition holds that these scales come in four varieties: ratio, interval, ordinal, and nominal (S. S. Stevens, 1946, 1951). The mathematical rules governing the legitimate use of these scales have been well documented by S. S. Stevens (1975), Senders (1958), and others (Baird & Noma, 1978; Gescheider, 1985), and a major aim of the field, at least as an empirical enterprise, is to determine the scale type most appropriate for representing judgments.[1]

S. S. Stevens (1975) also proposed a distinction between *prothetic* and *metathetic* attributes, by which he meant to classify two types of sensations. One is indexed by continuous functions between stimulus intensity and perceived magnitude (prothetic), and the other is not (metathetic). In discussing this issue, Stevens drew a line, albeit fuzzy, between "quantity and quality, or magnitude and kind, or size and sort" (1975, p. 12). Prototypical examples of the two classes are loudness and pitch, which he contrasted by claiming that "loudness is

---

[1]An alternative to the scaling approach of empirical psychophysics is the axiomatic approach of measurement theory. This enterprise is concerned with the relations that must exist within a body of empirical data to allow measurement scales to be constructed (Luce & Krumhansl, 1988). It is claimed by measurement theorists that Stevens's original scale types do not exhaust all the possibilities (Luce, Krantz, Suppes, & Tversky, 1990, chap. 20).

an aspect of sound that has what can best be described as degrees of magnitude or quantity. Pitch does not. Pitch varies from high to low; it has a kind of position, and in a sense it is a qualitative continuum. Loudness may be called a *prothetic* continuum, and pitch a *metathetic* one" (1975, p. 13).

At a physiological level, the difference between prothetic and metathetic continua has to do with whether the process involves addition or substitution. In the prothetic case, an increase in the intensity of the physical attribute augments the set of neurons or their firing rates, whereas in the metathetic case the set of active neurons is shifted, some drop out of the ensemble and others take their place.

Although Stevens felt it reasonable to ask someone to give numerical estimates of the intensity (loudness) of a tone, he was less comfortable asking for an estimate of the tone's frequency (pitch), at least in the form of a perceived ratio between the target tone and some other frequency. Additional metathetic continua included visual position of a point and inclination of a line (S. S. Stevens, 1975).

One might quibble about which attribute belongs in which class, but for the present purpose, nothing is gained by challenging the particulars of Stevens's binary classification. More relevant is the fact that the bulk of empirical studies are reported for prothetic attributes. Based on this source, explanations of global psychophysics are formulated in terms of the sensory aggregate model whose structure was detailed in the preceding chapter.

## STEVENS FUNCTIONS

Research on prothetic attributes indicates that sensory systems yield data that can be represented along a ratio or interval scale. Despite this fact, sensory instruments are often nonlinear in their processing of intensity information. That is, whatever the scale type, a nonlinear relation is repeatably found between stimulus intensity and the expressed magnitude of the corresponding experience. This much is beyond dispute. The most robust of empirical laws dealing with such relations is the power function, associated closely with the pioneering work of S. S. Stevens (1975), and expressed as

$$R = \lambda S^{\gamma}, \tag{3.1}$$

where $R$ is perceived magnitude, $S$ is stimulus intensity (measured in units appropriate for each stimulus dimension), and Greek letters stand for free parameters fit to the data points. The logarithmic form of Equation 3.1, producing a straight line in double logarithmic coordinates, is commonly used in fitting data, that is,

$$log\ R = \gamma\ log\ S + log\ \lambda. \tag{3.2}$$

Differences in response sensitivity to values along different physical dimensions (attributes) are presumed to reflect the transduction properties of the sense modalities involved, where the index of relative sensitivity among the senses is the exponent of the Power Law. An exponent less than 1 implies that the sense modality compresses the range of perceptual magnitude relative to the range of physical intensity. An exponent greater than 1 implies that the modality has an expanded range, whereas an exponent of 1 implies that the modality accurately mirrors physical ratios.

Stevens functions are referred to as the mapping between observable stimuli and responses usually described by the Power Law. This mapping also covers other quantitative relations—such as the logarithmic function, which often provides a good description of data trends obtained by the Method of Category Estimation (Baird & Noma, 1978). Because the differences between the results from Magnitude and Category Estimation are unrelated to the precipitating sensory events (cf. Marks, 1974a), or to stimulus conditions (cf. Norwich, 1993), such differences are ignored throughout this chapter, but not throughout the book. The differences between the two methods are best considered from a judgment perspective, which is the side of the Complementarity Theory covered in later chapters.

## SCALING METHODS

Most experiments undertaken to test the Power Law employ methods instructing the subject to use numbers to convey the ratios perceived among a set of stimuli that usually contains 7 to 10 discrete members, spaced logarithmically and presented in a random sequence. In the most popular Method of Magnitude Estimation, one stimulus may be given first as a standard and assigned a numerical value (modulus) by the experimenter, or subjects may be allowed to choose their own numbers, without the constraint of a standard (Baird & Noma, 1978, chap. 5). Based on two decades of experimentation (1953–1975), S. S. Stevens (1975) compiled a representative list of exponents from data collected on groups of subjects tested with a variety of stimulus attributes. This list is reproduced in Table 3.1. Although by no means exhaustive, the values accurately summarize the full scope of laboratory findings.

In production methods, the response scale under the control of the subject is not the number continuum but a physical dimension such as luminance, sound amplitude, or the force of handgrip exerted by squeezing a dynamometer (S. S. Stevens, 1975). In Magnitude Production, a trial consists of the experimenter stating a number that the subject is asked to match by adjusting the intensity of a physical stimulus. In Cross Modality Matching, stimuli along a non numerical dimension (such as luminance) are matched to those along another (such as sound amplitude).

TABLE 3.1
Representative Exponents of the Power Law
(after Stevens, 1975, p. 15)

| Attribute | Exponent | Stimulus Condition |
|---|---|---|
| Loudness | 0.7 | Sound pressure of 3000-Hz tone |
| Vibration | 1.0 | Amplitude of 60 Hz on finger |
| Vibration | 0.6 | Amplitude of 250 Hz on finger |
| Brightness | 0.3 | 5° target in dark |
| Brightness | 0.5 | Point source |
| Brightness | 0.5 | Brief flash |
| Brightness | 1.0 | Point source briefly flashed |
| Lightness | 1.2 | Reflectance of gray papers |
| Visual length | 1.0 | Projected line |
| Visual area | 0.7 | Projected square |
| Redness (satur.) | 1.7 | Red-gray mixture |
| Taste | 1.3 | Sucrose |
| Taste | 1.4 | Salt |
| Taste | 0.8 | Saccharine |
| Smell | 0.6 | Heptane |
| Cold | 1.0 | Metal contact on arm |
| Warmth | 1.6 | Metal contact on arm |
| Warmth | 1.3 | Irradiation of skin, small area |
| Warmth | 0.7 | Irradiation of skin, large area |
| Discomfort, cold | 1.7 | Whole body irradiation |
| Discomfort, warm | 0.7 | Whole body irradiation |
| Thermal pain | 1.0 | Radiant heat on skin |
| Tactual roughness | 1.5 | Rubbing emery cloths |
| Tactual hardness | 0.8 | Squeezing rubber |
| Finger span | 1.3 | Thickness of blocks |
| Pressure on palm | 1.1 | Static force on skin |
| Muscle force | 1.7 | Static contractions |
| Heaviness | 1.4 | Lifted weights |
| Viscosity | 0.4 | Stirring silicone fluids |
| Electric shock | 3.5 | Current through fingers |
| Vocal effort | 1.1 | Vocal sound pressure |
| Angular accel. | 1.4 | 5-sec rotation |
| Duration | 1.1 | White noise stimuli |

In all these methods, the average estimates[2] or settings given by one or more subjects are the response values ($R$) in Equations 3.1 and 3.2. A variation on this practice occurs when experimenters are interested in direct comparisons between the exponents from estimation and production methods. When plotting the results of the production method it is convenient to designate the produced inten-

---

[2]The arithmetic mean is typically used for individuals, whereas the geometric mean or median is used for groups.

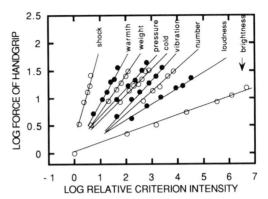

FIG. 3.1. Median force of handgrip exerted on a dynamometer to match criterion intensities for different attributes (log–log coordinates). The positions of the functions are shifted along the abscissa. After J. C. Stevens et al. (1960).

sity (dependent variable) as the $S$ value in the equations and the experimenter's stated number or other stimulus (independent variable) as the $R$ value. This is done so that the slopes (exponents) from the two types of methods can be compared directly, but it is not always obvious in the original papers that this reversal of roles has occurred. This can create some confusion in the mind of an unwary reader.

According to Equation 3.2, on a log–log plot, points should fall on a straight line with slope of $\gamma$ and y intercept of $log\ \lambda$. Data that are adequately fit by a linear function in logarithmic coordinates are given in Figure 3.1, which illustrates sample outcomes from Cross Modality Matching (J. C. Stevens, Mack, & S. S. Stevens, 1960). The points represent the median force of handgrip exerted on a dynamometer by a group of subjects attempting to match five to seven criterion intensities for the attributes noted. The positions of the functions have been shifted along the abscissa to aid in viewing. The slopes (exponents) extend from numbers much greater than 1 (electric shock) to those much less than 1 (brightness). The stimulus ranges differ in Figure 3.1 and lower exponents are generally associated with larger ranges. This outcome has fueled a long-standing controversy over the proper interpretation of the size of exponents for different attributes (an issue brought to prominence by Poulton, 1967, and R. Teghtsoonian, 1971). This matter is discussed in chapter 6.

## THE SENSORY AGGREGATE MODEL

### Neural Aggregates

S. S. Stevens viewed the Power Law as intrinsic to the senses themselves. The receptors in the eye, ear, tongue, and skin transduce the energy impinging on the sense organ according to a power function, and the exponent of that function faithfully reflects this transduction process. In discussing transducer physiology and its potential role in elucidating the mechanisms behind psychophysical judgments, he stated his challenge: "The development of transducer physiology remains a challenge for the future, but one of its concerns will be to explicate the mechanisms that generate the psychophysical power functions. The Power Law tells us *what* the transducer does. We have yet to learn *how* it does it" (1975, pp. 207–208).

This challenge is addressed here and a neurophysiological basis for the Power Law is proposed. The claim is that the form of the Power Law is due to the aggregation of outputs from pools of neurons with staggered absolute thresholds—a transducer process whose details are embodied in the Sensory Aggregate Model described in chapter 2.

## Computer Simulations

A computer program was written to calculate various statistical measures of firing rates predicted by neural aggregation of 1,000 neurons over a single log cycle of stimulus intensity. The position of the absolute threshold was defined in terms of the minimum stimulus intensity required to excite the neuron. All calculations were made with the absolute thresholds spanning a range from a minimum of 0 log units to a maximum of 3 log units. The effective window, within which hypothetical stimuli were located, was the log cycle between 2 and 3. Ten equally spaced log stimulus intensities were distributed over this range. These particular choices are somewhat arbitrary and should be treated as demonstrations of the model's effectiveness, rather than as binding strictures.

The parameters of the simulation were the dynamic range of individual neurons ($\delta = 1.5$ log units), the mean ($\mu$), and standard deviation ($\sigma$) of the lognormal distribution of threshold types. Because the firing rate of each neuron spanned a range of 1.5 log units, the cells determining the response magnitude for the weakest intensity of 2 log units must have thresholds greater than or equal to $2 - 1.5 = 0.5$ log units. Cells with lower thresholds contributed nothing to the outcome in this particular application. The dynamic range of the neurons was the same in all simulations.

The point was to find sets of values for the mean and standard deviation of the threshold distribution that yielded sets of exponents of the power function ranging from 0.2 to 2. The eventual solutions are not unique examples; that is to say, several sets of parameter values lead to the same exponent with about the same correlation. The data presented here are for simulations yielding the highest correlation between the obtained and target function.[3]

---

[3]This was accomplished in practice by starting with a target exponent and varying the two parameters of the threshold distribution until achieving the closest fit between the simulation data and a hypothetical function with the requisite exponent.

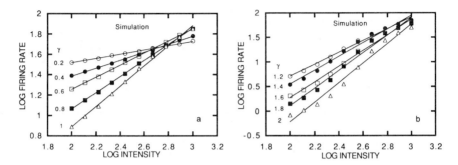

FIG. 3.2.    Mean firing rate as a function of stimulus intensity (log–log coordinates) generated by the Sensory Aggregate Model. The γ values indicate the slope (exponent) of each function. (a) 0.2 to 1 (b) 1.2 to 2.

The mean and standard deviation of firing rates (responses) produced by the neural aggregate for each intensity were determined by an evaluation of the relevant equations given in chapter 2 (Equations 2.10 and 2.12). These calculations yield the results shown in Figure 3.2.

This graph presents mean firing rate as a function of stimulus intensity in double-logarithmic coordinates for a variety of means and standard deviations of the hypothetical neural thresholds. Straight lines emphasize the linear trend in the means for each of the conditions. The functions in the left panel (Figure 3.2a) have exponents less than and equal to 1; the functions in the right panel (Figure 3.2b) have exponents greater than 1. The parameter values of the lognormal distribution of thresholds leading to each of these power functions are listed in Table 3.2, together with r, Pearson's Product Moment Coefficient.[4]

The linear fits (r ≥ .99) were excellent in all cases, but some curvilinearity is apparent for the highest exponents. It is especially difficult to obtain good fits for functions having exponents above 2, but the range of power functions in Figure 3.2 covers perhaps 95% of the empirical data ever reported with the Method of Magnitude Estimation. The only attribute left out by this analysis is "electric shock," which Stevens indexed by the remarkably high exponent of 3.5 (S. S. Stevens, Carton, & Shickman, 1958). Other investigators have since reported lower values for electric shock that may be closer to the truth (Cross, Tursky, & Lodge, 1975; Ekman, Frankenhaeuser, Levander, & Mellis, 1964; Ekman, Fröberg, & Frankenhaeuser, 1968; Sternbach & Tursky, 1964).

The major factor driving the simulation is the standard deviation of the lognor-

---

[4]Despite its drawbacks (Birnbaum, 1973), this measure is used throughout the book. Any deviations from linearity are obvious in the accompanying graphs and these deviations are discussed whenever the situation warrants it.

TABLE 3.2
Parameter Values of the Lognormal Distribution of Thresholds
Associated with Different Parameter Values of Steven's Law

| Simulated Power Law | | Threshold Distribution | | Correlation |
|---|---|---|---|---|
| $\gamma$ | $\log \gamma$ | $\mu$ | $\sigma$ | $r$ |
| 0.2 | 1.1 | 3.0 | 0.73 | 1.0 |
| 0.4 | 0.6 | 2.5 | 0.47 | 1.0 |
| 0.6 | 0.06 | 2.3 | 0.34 | 1.0 |
| 0.8 | −0.52 | 2.3 | 0.24 | 1.0 |
| 1 | −1.1 | 2.3 | 0.18 | 1.0 |
| 1.2 | −1.7 | 2.3 | 0.14 | 1.0 |
| 1.4 | −2.2 | 2.3 | 0.11 | 0.99 |
| 1.6 | −2.9 | 2.4 | 0.09 | 0.99 |
| 1.8 | −3.5 | 2.4 | 0.08 | 0.99 |
| 2.0 | −4.2 | 2.5 | 0.06 | 0.99 |

mal. Larger standard deviations are associated with smaller exponents. It is also possible to alter the exponent by changing the mean of the threshold distribution. When this manipulation is done, an increase in the mean leads to a decrease in the exponent. The exponent is inversely related to both the mean and the standard deviation of the lognormal distribution of neural thresholds. Inspecting the threshold distributions generated by the lognormal (chap. 2, Figure 2.6) may help the reader conceptualize this situation. Recall that the closer a threshold is to the stimulus intensity being evaluated, the slower is that neuron's firing rate.

Appropriate scalar transformations of the relevant stimulus and threshold parameters responsible for any one function in Figure 3.2 lead to a rich array of exponents over an arbitrary range of stimulus intensities. Therefore, even an exponent of 3.5 can be matched by the proper selection of model parameters. At this juncture in the theoretical development it is enough for the reader to realize that different exponents are produced with exactly the same stimulus range. This consequence of the model requires some care in its elaboration, so further consideration is reserved until chapter 6, where a unification of psychophysical laws is presented in terms of the model.

## VARIATIONS ON THE POWER LAW

Although the fits of the power function to empirical data are usually satisfactory, nonlinearities sometimes appear in the log–log plot at the low end of the stimulus dimension. The nature of this nonlinearity is a slight downward concavity (Baird & Noma, 1978, chap. 5; Mashhour & Hosman, 1968).

In order to secure a better fit to empirical data, it has been standard practice for some time (Ekman, 1956b) to modify Stevens's Law by subtracting a constant from each stimulus before raising it to a power. That is,

$$R = \lambda(S - S_0)^\gamma \tag{3.3}$$

In the initial tests of the Power Law, researchers tried to relate the size of this constant to absolute threshold, but such attempts were largely unsuccessful (Baird & Noma, 1978) and have remained so until now. Nonetheless, it is not unusual for researchers to modify the Power Law according to Equation 3.3, with the justification that they are "correcting for threshold." But, the real reason for including another constant is that the trend of the untransformed data points is not always given justice by a straight line in log–log coordinates. The additional constant transforms the curved line into a straight one, avoiding the need to reject Stevens's Law.

One consequence of modifying the Power Law in this way is that the exponent is smaller than it is when the constant is not included. In the case of electric shock, for example, Lawrence Marks (personal communication April, 1995) finds that the exponent is closer to 1.0 when Equation 3.3 is applied to some data collected by Bujas, Szabo, Kovacic, and Rohacek (1975). This value is far below the exponent of 3.5 so often referenced in the literature. Just as is true with empirical data, slight downward bowing in the psychophysical functions (in logarithmic coordinates) produced by the Sensory Aggregate Model can be straightened by application of Equation 3.3.

Another example of conditions leading to deviations from the Power Law is reported in a study by J. C. and S. S. Stevens (1963). They adapted the eye to different luminance levels and had subjects estimate brightness. For the dark-adapted eye, the exponent of the power function is approximately 0.3, but the exponent rises as the eye is adapted to brighter and brighter background lights and then tested with exactly the same intensities. A summary of their results is given in Figure 3.3. The lines summarize the overall trends. The straight lines extending from the smallest y values for each function were drawn as a reasonable guess about how the data might behave for these lower intensities (see also, S. S. Stevens, 1975). It is safe to assume that the lack of empirical data in this lowest part of the function is due to the lack of the subject's ability to resolve differences between the stimulus and the background (adapting stimulus). The important point here is that the brighter the adapting light, the more the entire function is shifted to higher starting positions along the luminance dimension.

Cain and Engen (1969) reported a similar effect near threshold for judgments under conditions of olfactory adaptation. The Stevens functions for n-amyl alcohol ($C_5$) and n-propyl alcohol ($C_3$) both bow downward near the concentration of the adapting stimulus (Figure 3.4). This is indicated in the figure by the differences between the circles, squares, and the crosses. The circles and squares represent results for low-intensity adaptation where the subject drew three and

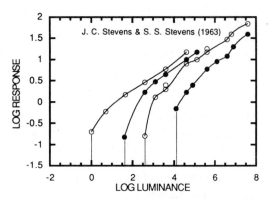

FIG. 3.3. Mean brightness estimate as a function of light intensity (log–log coordinates) with different levels of luminance adaptation (indicated by vertical lines intersecting the x axis). After J. C. Stevens and S. S. Stevens (1963).

eight breaths of air, respectively. The crosses are for high-intensity adaptation where the subject drew three breaths before rendering a judgment. The influence of concentration is obviously greater than stimulus duration (indexed by number of breaths) in shifting the threshold and altering the shape of the Stevens function (see also, Cain, 1986). Similar bowing occurs for other modalities as well, when either an adapting or masking stimulus is introduced (Gescheider, 1988; Marks, 1974a; S. S. Stevens, 1975; Zwicker & Fastl, 1990).

Much of this distortion of a pure power function is remedied by subtracting a constant from the stimulus before raising it to a power (Equation 3.3), but this is a temporary bandaid solution without any deep theoretical meaning. The Sensory Aggregate Model offers a more rational explanation for this effect—fibers sub-

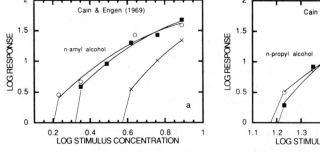

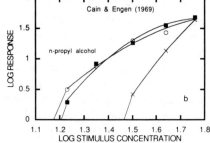

FIG. 3.4. Mean odor estimates of n-amyl alcohol (a) and n-propyl alcohol (b) as a function of intensity under different states of adaptation. Circles and squares represent low-intensity adaptation (with three and eight breaths of air). Crosses represent high-intensity adaptation (with three breaths). After Cain and Engen (1969).

suming the representation of intensities below the point of adapation are rendered inoperative. Before examining this explanation, consider a distortion of the psychophysical function that has a more apparent physical cause, but that can be explained along the same lines as masking and adaptation phenomena.

## AUDITORY RECRUITMENT

A dramatic bowing of the function on a log–log plot occurs for judgments of sound intensity by subjects with known cochlear impairment. Thalman (1965) had patients with hearing loss adjust the amplitude of a vibration applied to the finger to match the loudness of a 1000-Hz tone. For patients with cochlear damage, the matching function shifted to the right along the intensity dimension and became noticeably steeper in the log–log plot. S. S. Stevens (1975) offered an interpretion of this finding: "Loudness grows abnormally rapidly when the sound stimulus is increased. At the level of 100 decibels the hard-of-hearing ear has caught up with the normal ear. The steep loudness function constitutes a phenomenon known as recruitment" (p. 132).

Evidence for "recruitment" is seen in Figure 3.5, which shows data from a typical listener with hearing damage (Hellman & Meiselman, 1990).[5] Results for a normal listener would be linear throughout the stimulus range (as shown on the graph). These researchers conducted an extensive study of 100 people diagnosed as having sensorineural hearing impairment. Their loudness judgments are negatively accelerated on a log–log plot, indicating a bowing of the function from the point of damage.

For the hearing-impaired subject, the Stevens function is steepened for intensities falling just above the elevated threshold, as if the auditory system somehow is able to "recruit" the service of additional neural fibers in order to compensate for the injury. A physiological explanation of this phenomenon is offered by Evans (1989), who proposed that recruitment "is likely to be related to the abnormally rapid spread of activity across the neural array with increase in intensity, which would be expected to occur on account of the broader tuning of cochlear fibres in cochlear pathology" (p. 323).

That is to say, more neurons are involved in representing intensity in the damaged ear compared to the normal ear. The manner in which this model predicts the quantitative details, including the steepening of the psychophysical function, remains unclear. It is also difficult to see how such an argument explains the effects of sensory adaptation and masking, when the power function is concave downward in a log–log plot and shows an apparent enhancement in processing weak intensities.

---

[5]I am grateful to the authors for providing me with their original data.

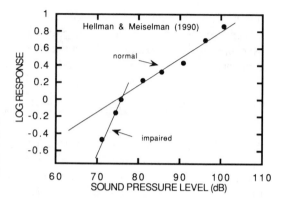

FIG. 3.5. Loudness judgments as a function of sound pressure level (log–log coordinates) for normal and hearing impaired subjects. After Hellman and Meiselman (1990).

All the foregoing situations have one empirical trait in common: Processing by the sensory system at or below the point of negative impact (measured in terms of the absolute threshold) is hampered or shut down entirely. This much is not surprising. The puzzle arises when we learn that the impaired ear's performance in the region just above the point of impact appears to be somehow better (in the sense that the slope of the function is steeper) than it is in the normal ear. That is to say, the data indicate that the impaired ear exhibits greater sensitivity to stimulus changes in this region of the continuum than does the normal ear.

These phenomena probably have a shared neurological basis, but it is probably not a recruitment of fibers that causes the apparent improvement. For stimulus masking and adaptation, the neurons responsible for signaling intensity are temporarily ineffective, and, in the case of hearing loss, the neurons near the absolute lower threshold (measured psychophysically) do not fire because they are damaged. None of the neurons with thresholds below a critical point are part of the aggregate, and immediately above the point of impact, the only neurons firing are doing so at a very slow rate. As intensity increases, however, the aggregate is composed of these same neurons firing at higher rates, thus causing the function to steepen. The main point here is that more and more neurons are not *added,* above and beyond the usual aggregate, as intensity increases. Rather, the situation is that fewer and fewer neurons are *missing* from the full complement of fibers that normally subsumes the processing of intensity.

A simulation of conditions leading to "recruitment" effects by the Sensory Aggregate Model produces results that are consistent with the "missing neurons" hypothesis concerning the shift in position and shape of the Stevens function. The simulation was conducted by omitting the contribution of neurons below some cutoff along the stimulus dimension. Therefore, these neurons do not contribute to the neural aggregate that signals stimulus intensity. The results are shown in Figure 3.6 where the logarithm of the mean firing rate is plotted as a function of the logarithm of stimulus intensity. Results there are based on the

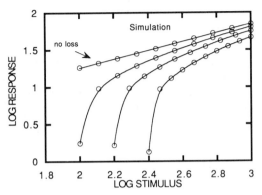

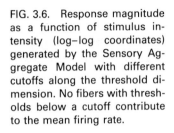

FIG. 3.6. Response magnitude as a function of stimulus intensity (log–log coordinates) generated by the Sensory Aggregate Model with different cutoffs along the threshold dimension. No fibers with thresholds below a cutoff contribute to the mean firing rate.

same parameter values of the model used in calculations leading to the data in Figure 3.2a, described by a power function with an exponent of 0.6. The modification here was to redo the calculations with several cutoffs along the stimulus dimension, below which a neuron contributed nothing to the aggregate. These cutoffs were situated at points that were 95% of the intensity of the first stimulus for each of the functions shown on the graph.

The familiar bowing of the psychophysical function is seen in the simulation, and the degree of curvature is greater as the cutoff advances up the intensity dimension. In addition, the mean responses for each function converge to a maximum at the upper end of the dimension. This pattern is the same observed in the empirical results obtained under conditions of masking in vision, hearing, and olfaction (see J. C. Stevens, 1974), as well as in the impaired ear (Hellman & Meiselman, 1990).

The present model explains these phenomena by claiming that different neurons are responsible for the coding of intensity at different intensity levels. The elimination of certain groups of neurons, those falling below a cutoff due to neural masking or damage, has less and less impact on the total aggregate as stimulus intensity increases. For weak intensities, the elimination of neurons with low thresholds has a marked effect on the pooled output. For strong intensities, however, the elimination of these same neurons has little or no influence on the aggregate, because these low-threshold neurons no longer contribute— their dynamic range does not extend far enough into the higher regions to influence the result by either their presence or absence.

For the particular case of auditory impairment, the neural output for strong stimuli remains intact, whether or not the auditory system is able to process weak sounds in a normal fashion. The distinctive feature of this explanation in comparison with the "recruitment" hypothesis is as follows: According to the Sensory Aggregate Model, the weakening of a subtractive force due to inhibition, adaptation, or damage produces the steepening of the psychophysical function, whereas according to the recruitment hypothesis, the weakening of an additive force (accrual of fibers to the normal complement) causes the steepening as intensity increases.

Changes in the shape and variability of the psychophysical response distributions are also anticipated for a person with cochlear damage. Discovery of such variation in response distributions might provide further insight into the cause of the shift and steepening of psychophysical functions. An insufficient number of responses are collected in such studies to permit an evaluation of this hypothesis.

## RANGE EFFECTS

It has been known for some time that stimulus range affects the exponent of the Power Law. An increase in range is accompanied by a decrease in exponent (Poulton, 1989; R. Teghtsoonian, 1973). The change of range, in this context, refers to within-attribute variation. Separate experiments are run for the same stimulus attribute with different ranges, and the relation observed between the exponent and the range (in log units).

Figure 3.7 shows several examples of range effects from data collected in the Stockholm psychophysics laboratory in the 1960s and assembled in this format by Poulton (1989, chap. 8). The original investigators used the Complete Ratio Method in which each stimulus is paired with every other stimulus, and subjects express their magnitude estimates in terms of the perceived relative intensity between members of the pair. Only visual attributes were tested: numerosity of dots (Strangert, 1961), distance (Künnapas, 1960), length of lines, and area of circles (Björkman & Strangert, 1960).

The exponent declines somewhat with increases in log range and probably would reach a lower asymptote with sufficiently large ranges (R. Teghtsoonian,

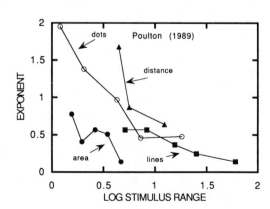

FIG. 3.7. Stevens exponent as a function of logarithm of stimulus range for different visual attributes. After Poulton (1989).

1973, 1978). The largest exponent is for numerousness of dots for the narrowest range. Similar effects on the exponent are observed for attributes yielding exponents less than 1, such as loudness and brightness (Poulton, 1989, chap. 8), but most of these studies only tested two ranges (small and large), and hence, the specific quantitative relation between exponent and range cannot be confidently determined.

Figure 3.8 shows data generated by the Sensory Aggregate Model, evaluated with the same parameter values behind the exponents in Figure 3.6. The variation in range is obtained by beginning with a single log cycle, and then, incremental reductions in the total range are achieved by simultaneously increasing the minimum and decreasing the maximum of the original range. The resulting functional relations are all linear. This follows directly from the fact that each psychophysical function is roughly linear in its entirety. For hypothetical attributes yielding exponents greater than 1 (3.8b), there is a sharp decline in the exponent as a function of range, but this effect is attenuated for hypothetical attributes yielding the shallowest exponents (3.8a). There are slight effects there as well, but the decline is not always noticeable on the graph.

Although the range is less than those in the studies summarized in Figure 3.7, the results of the Sensory Aggregate Model are invariant over linear transformations of all parameter values. Therefore, the results shown in Figure 3.8 are applicable to any range, not just those illustrated. No effort was made in describing the model's performance to fit laboratory data. The goal here is only to argue that the patterns produced by the model are similar to the patterns observed empirically.

The most prevalent interpretation of range effects is that they reflect response biases of some sort and are not due to sensory mechanisms (Poulton, 1989). The Sensory Aggregate Model, on the other hand, suggests that the cause of within-

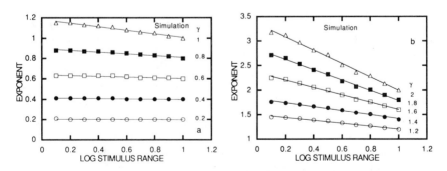

FIG. 3.8. Stevens exponent as a function of logarithm of stimulus range for functions yielding exponents ($\gamma$) of 0.2 to 1 (a) and exponents ($\gamma$) of 1.2 to 2 (b) for the largest range. Simulation data generated by the Sensory Aggregate Model.

attribute effects may reside in neurophysiology. The reason the model produces such effects at all is that the relation between mean firing rate and stimulus intensity is not exactly a power function. The Power Law is only an approximation, albeit a very convincing one under most circumstances. In this regard, the effect on the exponent depends critically on the exact way in which the range is altered. For example, if the overall Stevens function bows downward near the lower end of the stimulus dimension (Equation 3.3), then the exponent will obviously be higher if stimuli are distributed over that small region. Experimenters have not paid sufficient attention to exactly how physical range is varied. Different choices in this regard will lead to different relations between stimulus range and the exponent (Ahlström & Baird, 1989).

The aforementioned results apply only to within-attribute effects. Predictions concerning between-attribute effects depend on whether one believes that differences in the exponent occur because of differences in the stimulus range typically used to investigate the Stevens function (Poulton, 1989; R. Teghtsoonian, 1971). According to one such view (Poulton), variations among exponents are due to response biases and, consequently, have little to do with attribute variations in the transduction properties of sensory systems. This conclusion is consistent with one possible interpretation of the Sensory Aggregate Model, because stimulus conditions can be arranged in the computer simulations so that firing rates are constant for all stimulus ranges; hence, the exponent becomes inversely related to range. More is said about this topic in chapter 6.

## DETECTION THRESHOLDS AND THE POWER LAW

The least intensity necessary to trigger detection some specified percent of the time (e.g., 50%) is considered to be the absolute threshold. It is the focus of countless studies over the past 150 years and, in many ways, best exemplifies the Fechnerian legacy in psychophysics. In the older literature, this threshold is called the *stimulus threshold* because it was thought that in everyday commerce with the world values are not detected along continuous, abstract dimensions; rather, actual objects, such as a candle flame or a cow bell, are identified. Some investigators use the terms *absolute lower threshold,* or, more parsimoniously, the *absolute threshold.* The decision about terminology may be important because labels have surplus meanings that can subtly influence the type of explanation provided for the phenomenon being named. In this regard, the term *detection threshold* seems more neutral and is used in what follows.

The majority of experiments on detection thresholds involve tests of the eye and ear, whose sensitivities have been thoroughly investigated for a wide array of stimulus conditions (Barlow & Mollon, 1989; Marks, 1974b). There are several questions of interest, but an important one concerns whether the detection threshold for intensity is affected by other stimulus parameters, such as wavelength (light) or frequency (sound). Assuming such differences are found, is the pattern of relative threshold values maintained as the intensity of the stimulus is increased over the range of values to which the eye and ear respond? This is of interest because it allows for an internal check on the validity of the global scaling procedures. An assessment is made about the agreement between a matching technique (Adjustment) and Magnitude Estimation.

## Sample Data

Figure 3.9 gives a schematic rendition of typical data for brightness (Judd, 1951). The detection threshold in log energy units is plotted against the wavelength (linear units) at which measurements were made. The stimulus parameter producing the various functions is the adapting luminance of the background. The lowest curve on the graph indicates the relative detection sensitivity for wavelength in the dark-adapted eye. Maximum sensitivity is about 505 nm. As the wavelength shifts above or below this point, sensitivity drops rather precipitously, inasmuch as more energy is required to reach the same criterion level of detection.

The top curve illustrates data for an adapting intensity that is 5 log units above that used for the dark-adapted condition. Two observations should be made in this regard: First, the minimum point on the curve shifts to a higher wavelength, from 505 nm to about 550 nm. Second, the shape of the function at the highest level of adapting light is very similar to the shape at the lowest level. In other words, as one moves to higher and higher adapting lights (increased intensity), the shift of the peak sensitivity increases along the wavelength continuum in a systematic fashion. This is due to the shift from rod to cone vision, but there is little alteration in the overall shape of the curve. This implies that the same absolute intensity is required to be added to a blue light in order to match the brightness of a bluish-green light presented under the same state of adaptation.

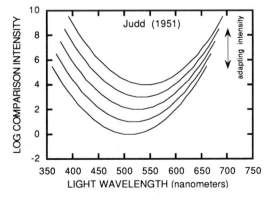

FIG. 3.9. Schematic rendition of the detection threshold of light (logarithmic units) as a function of wavelength (linear units). The adapting luminance of the background is the stimulus parameter associated with the different curves. After Judd (1951).

The picture is not the same for sound. The relevant data are well summarized by Gulick et al. (1989). Figure 3.10 presents a schematic rendition of the classic results of Fletcher and Munson (1933), who had listeners make matches between the loudness of a 1000-Hz standard tone, presented at a constant intensity, by adjusting the intensity of each of 10 comparison tones, ranging in frequency between 62 Hz and 16,000 Hz. In different conditions, the intensity of the standard was set at different levels above the detection threshold. Figure 3.10 indicates the relative matches (in schematic form), where the parameter responsible for shifting the height of the curves is the intensity level of the standard. As with vision, the minimum detection threshold falls at an intermediate frequency (1000 Hz to 3000 Hz). The intensities of sound frequencies above or below this region must be increased in order to match the loudness of the 1000-Hz standard.

In contrast to the situation for vision, however, the shape of the equal-loudness curves depends on the level of the standard to be matched. The depression of the curve is most pronounced when comparisons are matched to the softest standard, and as intensity of the standard is increased, the curve gradually becomes flatter over the frequency continuum. This lack of parallelism is the reason that good audio equipment permits some control (equalization or loudness) over it.

## Implications of Detection Curves

The fact that the equal-brightness contours maintain their separation over changes in wavelength implies that the exponent of the power function should be independent of wavelength. This can be understood by considering the vertical distance between the lowest and highest curves in Figure 3.9. The separation is the same for all wavelengths. Therefore, if a subject were asked to adjust the intensity of a blue light to match a series of green lights of different intensity, the adjustments (in terms of absolute luminance range) would be the same as when a

FIG. 3.10.  Schematic rendition of the detection threshold of sound (logarithmic units) as a function of frequency (logarithmic units). A comparison sound was matched to a standard whose intensity varied (different curves). After Fletcher and Munson (1933).

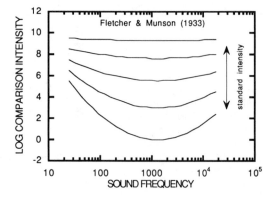

green light was adjusted to match a red light. Because the response range is identical for all such matching tasks, the visual system must process intensity in the same way for all wavelengths. Hence, the exponent from a magnitude estimation task (using numbers to match intensity) should not depend on wavelength. The empirical evidence is somewhat ambiguous on this point (Marks, 1974b, pp. 65–68), but most available data suggest that the exponent for brightness does not change substantially for lights of different wavelengths (e.g., Ekman, Eisler, & Künnapas, 1960a, 1960b; Wilson, 1964). This means the matching data corroborate the data from Magnitude Estimation.

On the other hand, the fact that the equal-loudness contours are separated by different amounts at different tonal frequencies implies that the exponent of the power function for loudness should depend on the tonal frequency at which it is assessed. And it does. The supporting evidence is thoroughly reviewed by Marks (1974b, pp. 70–74). For example, Hellman and Zwislocki (1968) reported that the loudness exponent is higher for low frequencies (100 Hz) than for high ones (1000 Hz), and this finding is also reported by Schneider, Wright, Edelheit, Hock, and Humphrey (1972). This is what one would expect based on the fact that the matching data in Figure 3.10 indicate that the absolute range of intensity "matches" separating the lowest and highest intensities is different for different frequencies. The required range is smaller for 100 Hz than it is for 1000 Hz, meaning that perceived intensity grows more rapidly for the lower frequency.

The relevance of data on detection thresholds and psychophysical functions from the standpoint of the Sensory Aggregate Model is the implied interaction of a prothetic and a metathetic continuum. The two prothetic continua are the brightness of the light and the loudness of the sound. The associated metathetic continua are the wavelength of the light and the frequency of the sound. These empirical facts lead to the conclusion that the fiber threshold types for light are distributed in exactly the same manner for each wavelength, whereas the distribution of threshold types for sound depend on frequency.

If the exponent of the power function depends on frequency, then the mean and/or standard deviation of the underlying lognormal distribution of thresholds also depend on frequency. This prediction could be tested if it were possible to tally the number of neurons subsuming intensity coding at different levels. Some day this may be possible.

## OVERVIEW

The power function is among the most celebrated "laws" in psychology. Only a dozen years after S. S. Stevens (1953) and his colleagues began intense work on this problem, Ekman and Sjöberg (1965) reflected on the success of the Power Law: "As an experimental fact, the power law is established beyond any reasonable doubt, possibly more firmly established than anything else in psychology"

(p. 467). Today, this law, as a mathematical description of psychophysical results, is even more firmly established; hence, it must be squarely faced by any theory of psychophysics.

This chapter has demonstrated that the power function and its exponent is predicted by a Sensory Aggregate Model that does not contain any parameters pertaining to the role of cognitive/central processes. The perceived intensity of a stimulus is the result of an aggregation of the firing rates of a population of neurons whose stimulus-contingent thresholds are lognormally distributed over the intensity dimension, and whose firing rate of individual neurons is logarithmically related to stimulus intensity. The next chapter considers the variability of the firing rates produced by the computer simulations, and compares the results with laboratory findings.

# 4 Weber Functions

Global psychophysics involves situations in which the stimulus intensities are clearly distinguishable from each other. The subject's task is to scale stimuli and, in so doing, reveal the mapping between physical intensity and perceived magnitude. This chapter focuses on local psychophysics (Luce, 1993; Luce & Krumhansl, 1986). Here the stimuli are highly similar, and the subject's task is to discriminate between them rather than to scale their magnitudes. The aspect of local psychophysics of special interest is the measurement of Just-Noticeable-Differences (JND) between stimuli and the functional relation between the JND and the stimulus intensity at which it is determined. This relation is typically linear over much of the dynamic range of a stimulus attribute (Weber's Law), but deviates from this pattern near the ends of the stimulus range, especially in the vicinity of the lower absolute threshold. The size of the JND across changes in physical intensity is thought by many theorists to indicate the sensitivity of the sense modality. The relative size of JNDs in respect to the intensity at which it is measured is an index of potential neurophysiological significance.

The previous claim must be qualified, however. Recent developments in measurement theory bring into question the notion that results of local psychophysics, and global psychophysics as well, are meaningful indices of the relative perceptual sensitivity of different sense modalities; at least there are problems in stating a general rule that applies to all physical dimensions (Narens & Mausfeld, 1992). These concerns are ignored here and the implications of the measurement results are discussed in chapter 6.

The classic model of JNDs (difference thresholds) claims that perceptual discrimination depends on the ability of the sensory/brain system to register and compare internal effects (perhaps neuronal firing rates) arising from presentation

51

of one or more suprathreshold stimuli. The origins of this model can be traced back to Fechner (1860/1966), whose position on this matter is still respected: Repeated presentations of the same stimulus produce a Gaussian distribution of effects of a sensory nature, because there is either variability in the stimulus or variability in its impact on the sensory system. When a subject compares the intensity of two or more stimuli, samples are taken from these sensory distributions, and a decision rendered about the relative magnitudes of the two physical stimuli based on the relative magnitudes of the two internal events. A variation on this proposal is that subjects sample from the Gaussian distribution of internal events on successive trials and the variability of the sensory impact of a stimulus is reflected in the variability of the responses.

Early in this century, Thurstone (1927) extended the Fechnerian model to handle more complex, nonsensory situations, such as preference for wrist watches and the perceived seriousness of crimes. His work in turn is a precursor to the modern Theory of Signal Detectability (TSD) (Green & Swets, 1966/1974; Macmillan & Creelman, 1991). A thorough review of the history and current status of the Fechnerian viewpoint concerning stimulus discrimination is given by Link (1992); a more concise summary is provided by Melara (1992).

The thread maintained throughout the evolution of the classic view purports that the basis for all judgments of stimulus intensity is "effective sensory magnitude." One stimulus is judged greater than another because it excites the greater internal effect sampled on that particular occasion. The basis of this comparison may occur in the peripheral sense organs, as when the subject performs sensory discrimination, or it may occur more centrally, as when the subject states preferences or opinions about complex stimuli, such as the importance of Swedish monarchs or the tastiness of different brands of chocolate. The general model is a mathematical abstraction whose assumptions have never explicitly identified the physical nature and locus of internal events responsible for such distributions, though mechanisms have been proposed that are specific to the sense modality under examination.

After reviewing the empirical evidence on local psychophysics, an explanation of stimulus discrimination consistent with the traditional Fechnerian view, but built on the assumptions of the Sensory Aggregate Model, is proposed. The source of internal variability is ascribed to the firing rates of neurons comprising the ensemble of excitation associated with each stimulus. The standard deviation of this firing rate distribution is the sensory correlate of the JND obtained psychophysically.

## WEBER'S LAW

The oldest way to determine perceptual sensitivity is to ask what minimum stimulus change is necessary for a subject to notice a difference. Using the approach introduced by Weber (1846) and Fechner (1860/1966), it was proposed in the last century that the JND is a linear function of the intensity at which it is determined. Weber's law describes this empirical relation, where $\Delta S$ is the JND, $S$ is the standard, and $k$ is the Weber fraction.

$$\Delta S = k\mathbf{S} \tag{4.1}$$

The value of $k$ reflects the discriminability of closely spaced stimuli: the higher $k$, the lower the sensitivity. Table 4.1 lists typical Weber fractions for a variety of stimulus attributes. The values range from 0.02 for electric shock to 0.24 for odor. (These values are taken from empirical studies cited in Baird, 1970a, and Baird & Noma, 1978).

Figure 4.1 presents Weber functions for line length. The data are from a study by Kiesow (1926), who used the Method of Limits to obtain a difference threshold on both ascending (filled circles) and descending (open circles) trials (see Engen, 1972, or Laming, 1986, for descriptions of this and related experimental procedures). The graph depicts the relation between the size of the JND and the size of the standard line length. Both relations are fairly linear for the smaller standards, in keeping with Weber's Law, but at the topmost end of the stimulus scale they each begin to level off (in addition, an order effect is evident in that the ascending threshold is usually greater than the descending threshold). Laming (1986) summarized data for other attributes that obey Weber's Law over a substantial stimulus range.

TABLE 4.1
Representative Weber Fractions (after Baird
& Noma, 1978)

| Attribute | Weber Fraction $\Delta S/\mathbf{S}$ |
|---|---|
| Finger span | 0.02 |
| Saturation (red) | 0.02 |
| Electrical (skin) | 0.03 |
| Position of point (visual) | 0.03 |
| Length of lines (visual) | 0.04 |
| Area (visual) | 0.06 |
| Heaviness | 0.07 |
| Brightness | 0.08 |
| Loudness (1000 Hz, energy units) | 0.10 |
| Taste (salt) | 0.14 |
| Taste (sweet) | 0.17 |
| Skin vibration (100 Hz–1100 Hz) | 0.20 |
| Smell | 0.24 |

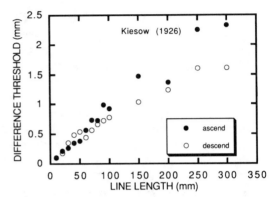

FIG. 4.1. Difference threshold for visual line length as a function of standard length, as determined by the Method of Limits (ascending and descending trials). From Kiesow (1926).

## DEVIATIONS NEAR ABSOLUTE THRESHOLD

Experimentalists agree that Weber's Law holds over the middle range of stimulus intensities, but sensitivity decreases near the lower—and sometimes near the upper—absolute threshold (Falmagne, 1986; Ward & Davidson, 1993; Woodworth & Schlosberg, 1954). The entire relation is best appreciated by rearranging Equation 4.1 and then examining a plot of the Weber fraction ($\Delta S/S$) as a function of stimulus intensity (S). These plots are presented either in linear or logarithmic coordinates, depending on the size of the ranges to be accommodated. Figure 4.2 gives examples of such a plot from two classic studies: one concerning the discrimination of luminance (König & Brodhun, 1889), the other concerning the discrimination of sound intensity (Riesz, 1928). If Weber's Law held exactly, the functions would be horizontal to the x axis throughout their course. It is evident, however, that the fraction increases precipitously as it

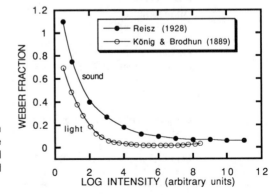

FIG. 4.2. Weber fraction as a function of logarithm of the standard intensity for sound and light. From Riesz (1928) and König and Brodhun (1889).

approaches the lower absolute threshold, and, in the case of luminance, shows a very slight upward turn near the upper absolute threshold.

## Affine Generalization

Because of the failure of Weber's Law at the extremes, other equations were introduced over the years to describe such nonlinearities (Baird & Noma, 1978; Falmagne, 1986). The entire class of models relating the JND to the intensity of the standard are referred to as *Weber functions*. Murray (1992) reviewed the historical development of such functions. For example, he noted that Helmholtz (1856–1866/1962) was aware of the shortcomings of Weber's Law and thought that for the brightness of lights at least, it should be modified to account for the fact that the sensation of brightness is added to a "natural light of the retina." This modification took the form of adding a constant to each stimulus intensity, such that

$$k = \Delta S/(S + c').$$

Rewriting in the linear form relating $\Delta S$ to $S$,

$$\Delta S = kS + kc'.$$

Letting $c = kc'$,

$$\Delta S = kS + c. \qquad (4.2)$$

This more general Weber function is also advocated by others since Helmholtz (e.g., Baird & Noma, 1978; Miller, 1947). The reason for preferring Equation 4.2 over Equation 4.1 is based on descriptive, rather than theoretical concerns. The Weber fraction ($\Delta S/S$) is often too large at small values of $S$; they are too large in the sense that, as is evident in Figure 4.2, it steadily drops as intensity increases, until leveling off at the intermediate intensities where the fraction is more stable. In some experiments, the fraction actually continues to decline over the entire stimulus range, though by far the most dramatic changes occur near threshold (Falmagne, 1986). Neither Equation 4.2, nor any others, actually used to fit data accommodates the fact that the Weber fraction sometimes increases at the upper limit of sensory functioning (though see Valter, 1970). Nonetheless, the interpretation of this increase has always seemed obvious: There are definite limits on the physiological ability of the sense organ to follow changes in intensity. Even the most skilled experimenter will be unable to coax a response from a burned-out sense organ.

It is not evident what the prediction should be when the stimulus exceeds the ability of the sense organ to process stimulus differences. From a physiological standpoint, the variance of a set of adjustments of a comparison intensity to match a very intense standard should approach zero, and therefore, if the JND is equated with the standard deviation of the adjustments, one would falsely conclude that the subject is exhibiting high sensitivity. In fact, the subject cannot distinguish among the intense standards. On the other hand, at extreme intensities, naive subjects may react negatively to the whole experimental procedure, seeing it as irrational and possibly dangerous to one's health. Under these circumstances, response behavior may be erratic and highly variable. The experimenter would then conclude that sensitivity is poor. This conclusion also does not seem quite right, because the result is due more to the subject's aggravation than it is to sensory processes. Very little is known about the behavior of the Weber fraction for very intense stimuli, and for obvious ethical reasons, it is unlikely that more can be learned through further experimentation with humans.

## The Near Miss

A second variation on Weber's Law is attributed to Guilford (1932), who proposed that the JND was equal to a constant multiplied by the stimulus intensity raised to a power:

$$\Delta S = k\mathbf{S}^\alpha \tag{4.3}$$

This formulation should not be confused with Stevens's Power Law, which relates global scaling responses to physical intensities. Guilford's lobbying effort for Equation 4.3 turned on his analysis of discrimination experiments conducted by E. S. Robinson and F. R. Robinson (1929) and Kiesow (1926) in which the Methods of Adjustment and Limits (respectively) were employed with standard lines of different lengths (Figure 4.1). After plotting his data in the usual way, Guilford rejected the possibility that Weber's Law was the appropriate model, because the y intercept (c in Equation 4.2) was not zero for either data set. This is not an especially telling criticism, because psychophysics is no different from other sciences in accepting the reality that empirical laws have limits of application. In any event, Guilford rejected Weber's Law, and in its place offered the power function (Equation 4.3) for which he found an exponent of 0.59 for the E. S. Robinson and F. R. Robinson data and 0.86 for the Kiesow data.

It is clear from inspection of the original data referred to by Guilford, however, that a linear equation (Equation 4.2) provides an equally good fit to these two data sets. In fact, in a later report, Hovland (1938) reanalyzed these results and found that for the E. S. Robinson and F. R. Robinson study, the linear equation

$$\Delta S = 0.035 \ \mathbf{S} + 5.99$$

yields a correlation of 0.99 between theoretical and observed values. This marginally exceeds the correlation of 0.97 Guilford finds when using Equation 4.3. Neither of these formulations are satisfactory for describing relations that asymptote at high intensities (e.g., Kiesow's data in Figure 4.1).

Sound intensity is another attribute for which a power function represents the

Weber function. Jesteadt, Wier, and Green (1977) published one of the most thorough studies of this topic. They also compared their data with that of several earlier investigators who had commented on this relation. The authors used the Two-Interval Forced Choice method to determine intensity discrimination of pulsed sinusoids for various frequencies and intensities. A single equation handles the data from all conditions:

$$\Delta S/S = 0.46 \, (S/S_0)^{-0.07}$$

Setting the scaling factor ($S_0$) to 1, this equation can be rewritten by multiplying both sides by S to obtain

$$\Delta S = 0.46 \, S^{0.93}. \tag{4.4}$$

McGill and Goldberg (1968) referred to such a result as the "near miss" to Weber's Law. Jesteadt et al. went on to show that data from a number of experiments on intensity discrimination of pure sounds are well fit by Guilford's equation (Dimmick & Olson, 1941; Harris, 1963; Penner, Leshowitz, Cudahy, & Richard, 1974; Schacknow & Raab, 1973). On the other hand, the affine form of Weber's Law (Eq. 4.2) seems to fit the discrimination data for white noise (Luce, 1993; Miller, 1947).

Although there is little doubt that the results on loudness discrimination are described well by a power function with an exponent somewhat less than 1, the same data are adequately fit by a linear function of the form given by Equation 4.2. In order to demonstrate this, the multiplicative constants and exponents reported by Jesteadt et al. for each of the aforementioned studies were used to generate hypothetical JNDs based on the evaluation of Guilford's equation for 100 stimulus intensities, equally spaced in logarithmic units, over the range of 1 to 10,000 (the number of stimuli is not critical). Then, linear functions (Equation 4.2) were fit to these data; acceptable fits were obtained in all cases, as evidenced by the fact that $r^2 = 1$. A linear equation can also be satisfactorily fit to the early Riesz (1928) data on JNDs for a 1000-Hz tone (Figure 4.2), though the additive constant (c in Equation 4.3) is much larger than that in the studies mentioned, and the linear fit is not as good. Upon visual inspection of all the available data, the results from some experiments are best fit by the linear generalization of Weber's Law, whereas others are best fit by Guilford's power function (Luce, 1993; Luce & Green, 1974).

Equation 4.5 is quite general and encompasses all the various Weber functions:

$$\Delta S = kS^\alpha + c \tag{4.5}$$

Weber's Law holds when $\alpha = 1$ and $c = 0$. The affine version of Weber's Law holds when $\alpha = 1$ and $c > 0$, and Guilford's power function results when $c = 0$ and $\alpha > 0$.

In most instances, the use of either a linear generalization of Weber's Law or a power function provides an adequate description of the relation between the stimulus JND and the standard at which it is measured. The key parameter is the Weber fraction, which indexes the differences in perceptual sensitivity exhibited by the different sense modalities (attributes). This fraction is never constant over the entire range of stimulus intensities, but it is reasonably so in the middle region of the intensity scale.

## NONMONOTONIC WEBER FUNCTIONS

Laming (1986) reviewed Weber functions and distinguished between experimental methods in which the standard and comparison are successively presented as discrete entities and methods in which an increment is added to an existing standard. He referred to the result of the first method as a *difference* threshold, and the result of the second as an *increment* threshold. His reading of the literature lead him to propose that Weber's Law, or its affine generalization, faithfully represents the difference threshold, whereas a square root (power) function is more appropriate for the increment threshold when it is measured in the vicinity of the detection threshold. Laming also claimed that the appearance of a breakdown in Weber's Law coincided historically with a switch in methodology from one of obtaining difference thresholds to one of obtaining increment thresholds. It should also be noted, however, that the affine generalization of Weber's Law produces a nonlinearity near threshold when $\Delta S/S$ is plotted against $S$ (Baird & Noma, 1978, p. 51), and this fact was under discussion by the end of the last century (Woodworth & Schlosberg, 1954).

Laming (1986) also referred to data showing a nonmonotonic Weber function when tests are conducted near detection threshold. That is, for very weak standards, the JND is approximately equal to the size of the absolute threshold. Then the JND drops to a minimum with further increases in the standard and climbs according to Weber's Law for more intense stimuli. Figure 4.3 shows loudness data collected by Raab, Osman, and Rich (1963). In this graph, the JND (increment required to detect a difference) is plotted against the sound pressure of a masking noise. Both scales are logarithmic (dB). These results have since been corroborated by Viemeister (reported by Green, 1988) and by Hanna, Von Gierke, and Green (1986).

The curious empirical finding is that the JND for a suprathreshold standard in the vicinity of the absolute threshold is smaller than the increment needed to detect stimulus presence (Laming, 1986, chap. 8). The nonmonotonic behavior of the JND near the auditory detection threshold is attributed to "negative masking." The notion is that a suprathreshold standard inhibits the perceived stimulus level when tests are done very close to absolute threshold. As the standard increases, this inhibition lessens, thus leading to an improvement in sensitivity as indicated by the smaller size of the JND. Laming (1986, chap. 8) reviewed

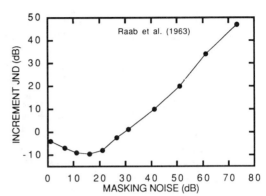

FIG. 4.3. Detection of an increment of wide-band noise as a function of background masking noise of the same spectral composition. After Raab et al. (1963).

studies showing that this pattern occurs in a variety of sense modalities, including vision and touch, and he proposed a model to explain it. Green (1988, chap. 3) also discussed the phenomenon and presented corroborative evidence for the case of loudness (intensity) discrimination. Despite these theoretical efforts, the physiological basis of the effect remains obscure. It is not predicted by the Sensory Aggregate Model, which does quite well in predicting other results of local psychophysics.

## SENSORY AGGREGATE AND THE JND

Knowledge of the relation between the mean magnitude estimate and stimulus intensity, as summarized by a Stevens function, does not imply knowledge of the relation between the variability of estimates around the mean and the associated stimulus intensity. In order to make predictions of this kind, it is necessary to have a theory about the physiological and/or psychological processes occurring when subjects estimate stimulus intensities using global methods such as Magnitude Estimation and Cross Modality Matching, or local methods such as Adjustment, Limits, and Constant Stimuli (Engen, 1972).

It is also important for theoretical reasons to distinguish between variability of responses obtained from the same individual and variability occurring among members of a group. Whereas it seems plausible to believe that between-subject variability arises because of differences in the ability of sensory systems to process environmental input, as indicated by differences in the parameter values of Stevens functions, this suggestion has little or no chance of explaining variability observed within the same subject. Whereas not denying that the firing rate of a single neuron may fluctuate over time due to random neurochemical processes (Norwich, 1993), the response variability in global psychophysics is too large to attribute solely to the vagaries of single neurons. A more plausible explanation is that different components of the same complex ensemble of neurons are sampled on different trials; and hence, the same stimulus does not always elicit the same response.

According to the Sensory Aggregate Model, this complex event is the firing rate distribution of neurons that selectively react to a stimulus possessing such properties as luminance (light), amplitude (sound), and concentration (odor). Thus, response variability arises over trials because the subject takes solo samples from a complex sensory representation. Psychological processes, too, may play a modulating role, but these processes enter the picture at a higher stage of neurophysiology and are not part of the model. They do, however, play a major role in the Complementarity Theory of Psychophysics.

## FIRING RATE DISTRIBUTIONS

If sensory mechanisms are the only determinants of global responses, an overview of the response variability is achieved by considering the hypothetical firing rate distributions. Figure 4.4 gives examples of firing-rate distributions for six

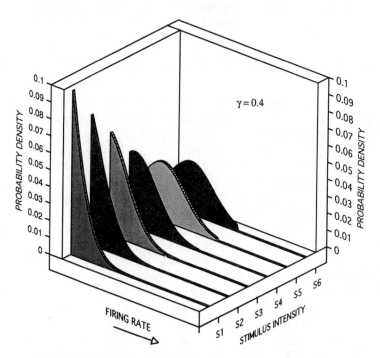

FIG. 4.4.   Probability density of firing rates associated with each of six stimuli ($S_1$ to $S_6$). Stevens exponent of 0.4. Standardized probabilities sum to 1.0.

intensities, spaced logarithmically over a single log cycle. The parameter values of the lognormal distribution of sensory thresholds responsible for producing these distributions are those associated with a Stevens exponent of 0.4.

Two features of the graph stand out. First, variability increases and skewness decreases with increases in stimulus intensity. Second, the distributions for the weakest stimuli are compact and positively skewed, whereas the distributions for the intense stimuli are broad and more symmetric about the mean. Laboratory data are not plotted in the manner shown in these figures, so it is necessary to compute statistical measures in order to make comparisons with empirical findings.

## VARIABILITY OF NEURAL FIRING RATE

### Weber Functions

Figure 4.5 shows the standard deviation as a function of the stimulus intensity for the 10 Stevens functions discussed in chapter 3, based on predictions of the Sensory Aggregate Model. It is important to realize that the standard deviation is an approximation of the JND and is not expressed in stimulus units.

A negatively accelerated curve is evident in all instances, but Guilford's power function (Equation 4.3) only provides an adequate fit for the data associated with Stevens exponents less than 1 (4.5a). Overall, the standard deviation is smaller for Stevens functions with higher exponents. The functions in Figure 4.5b asymptote at high intensities, suggesting that a logistic function would provide a better description of these results than Equation 4.3. No effort was made in the simulation to find parameter values of the underlying threshold distributions producing the best agreement with any of the Weber functions in the literature. The simulations were conducted with a different purpose in mind: that

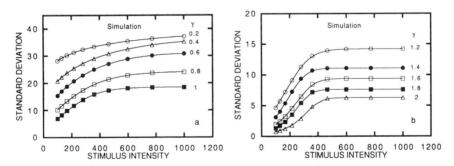

FIG. 4.5. Standard deviation of firing rate as a function of stimulus intensity. Data generated by the Sensory Aggregate Model yielding Stevens exponents listed to the right of the functions: (a) 0.2 to 1 (b) 1.2 to 2.

is, to minimize the fit between the obtained data and the Stevens functions. The JND data are from the same simulations.

## Weber Fractions

The Weber fraction for the simulation data is the standard deviation divided by the mean (relative error). This value is plotted as a function of stimulus intensity in Figure 4.6. The left panel (4.6a) shows the results for Stevens functions with exponents ranging from 0.2 to 1. The right panel (4.6b) shows comparable results for exponents greater than 1. The left panel shows a decline in the Weber fraction as the stimulus intensity increases. The functions all tend to level off at the higher intensities indicating a Weber fraction approaching a constant.

Figure 4.6b shows a similar decline near threshold, but some of the functions are nonmonotonic. It should be noted that the y axis here varies from 0 to 0.05, spanning values much smaller than those in Figure 4.6a for Stevens exponents less than or equal to 1. At the higher intensities, the Weber fractions continue their decline, but the overall change in the fraction over the entire stimulus course is not very substantial for the values associated with the highest Stevens exponents.

In none of the functions is there an increase in the Weber fraction for the most intense stimuli. The Weber fraction just continues to drop as intensity advances out to the limit evaluated by the simulation. Therefore, this aspect of the empirical data is not captured by the model. One modification that would create higher variability at the upper end of the stimulus range would be to assume that some of the neurons have lower firing rates at high intensities. In the present version of the model, a neuron simply stops firing when its dynamic range is exceeded.

The most striking aspect of the overall Weber function is how it depends

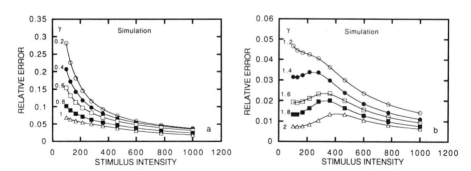

FIG. 4.6.  Relative error (standard deviation divided by the mean) of firing rate as a function of stimulus intensity. Data generated by the Sensory Aggregate Model yielding Stevens exponents listed to the left of the curves: (a) 0.2 to 1 (b) 1.2 to 2.

systematically on the Stevens exponent. The higher the exponent, the lower the Weber fraction. Because of the curvature exhibited in Figure 4.6, however, it is not possible to obtain a single index that represents relative sensitivity for each curve.

The opportunity to secure such an approximate index is afforded by plotting the data in Figure 4.6 in double logarithmic coordinates. This is done for all 10 functions in Figure 4.7. Most of the functions are reasonably linear, suggesting that the parameters of a straight line through the points are indices for summarizing the relative sensitivity exhibited by different sensory attributes in terms of their associated response variability. The equation describing each of these linear functions is expressed as

$$log\ (\Delta S/S) = v\ log\ \mathbf{S} + log\ \varphi, \qquad (4.7)$$

where the parameter of interest is the y intercept ($log\ \varphi$), though the slope = $v$ would serve equally well (see Ward & Davidson, 1993). The higher the value of $log\ \varphi$, the higher the Weber fraction and the lower the sensitivity. Table 4.2 gives a list of y intercepts, together with their associated Stevens exponents. The implications of this link between the Stevens exponent and the size of the Weber fraction are spelled out in chapter 6, which considers the relations among psychophysical indices for a variety of stimulus attributes.

## Counting JNDs

None of the Weber functions proposed in the literature captures the asymptotic behavior of the simulation data in Figure 4.5. A possible measure of sensitivity applicable for any Weber function is the number of JNDs stretching from the lower to the upper absolute threshold. In the present case, it is more convenient to determine the stimulus range required to accommodate a fixed number of JNDs for different Stevens exponents.

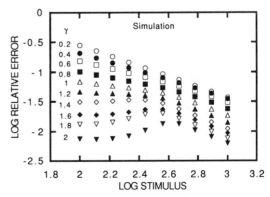

FIG. 4.7. Relative error (standard deviation divided by the mean) of firing rate as a function of stimulus intensity (log–log coordinates). Data generated by the Sensory Aggregate Model yielding Stevens exponents from 0.2 to 2.

TABLE 4.2
Results of Computer Simulation

| Exponent | log φ | Log Range |
|----------|-------|-----------|
| 0.2 | 1.2 | 1.43 |
| 0.4 | 0.84 | 0.81 |
| 0.6 | 0.57 | 0.53 |
| 0.8 | 0.25 | 0.42 |
| 1 | −0.006 | 0.34 |
| 1.2 | −0.25 | 0.30 |
| 1.4 | −0.50 | 0.26 |
| 1.6 | −1.41 | 0.23 |
| 1.8 | −1.4 | 0.21 |
| 2 | −2.2 | 0.18 |

Because the variability is so great for the lowest exponents, a single JND "step" is arbitrarily defined as 10% of the standard deviation of the firing rate. Beginning at the lowest stimulus value ($log$ $\mathbf{S}$ = 2), the first step is defined as the mean firing rate for that stimulus plus 10% of the standard deviation. The next stimulus intensity (in log units) is then determined as follows: Let $Y$ be the response to stimulus $\mathbf{S}$ and $Y + \Delta Y$ is the response to stimulus $\mathbf{S} + \Delta \mathbf{S}$. Then, assume

$$log \left( \frac{Y + \Delta Y}{Y} \right) = \gamma \, log \left( \frac{\mathbf{S} + \Delta \mathbf{S}}{\mathbf{S}} \right),$$

where $\gamma$ is the Stevens exponent. Rearranging,

$$log \, (\mathbf{S} + \Delta \mathbf{S}) = \left[ \frac{(log \, (Y + \Delta Y) - log \, Y)}{\gamma} \right] + log \, \mathbf{S} . \tag{4.8}$$

The standard deviation (10% of which is $\Delta Y$) for stimulus $\mathbf{S} + \Delta \mathbf{S}$ is then found by the simulation. Ten percent of this is the second step, and so forth, until a fixed number of steps is reached. The index of sensitivity is the stimulus range needed to reach some constant total. To illustrate the procedure, the total count is set at 10 and the stimulus ranges in Table 4.2 (right column) are obtained. A larger stimulus range is required to reach the target count when the Stevens exponent is small as compared to when it is large.

The argument, then, is that a sense organ capable of separating the stimulus dimension into a large number of JNDs is more sensitive than one less proficient in this regard. This is taken to mean that there is a close link between the JND of local psychophysics and the exponent of global psychophysics. The two indices depend on the same underlying sensory event—a neural complex whose compo-

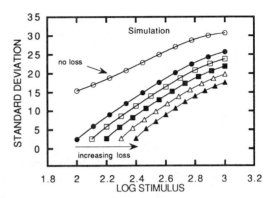

FIG. 4.8. Standard deviation of firing rate as a function of logarithm of stimulus intensity. Data generated by the Sensory Aggregate Model when a cutoff is introduced at different locations along the stimulus (threshold) dimension.

nent neurons are firing at different rates in response to the same stimulus intensity. This matter is discussed further in chapter 6.

## Adaptation and Masking

Figure 4.8 presents the standard deviation of judgments obtained when the lower part of the stimulus scale is incapacitated by stimulus adaptation, masking, or physiological damage. The functions represent the effect of the simulation discussed in chapter 3 (Figure 3.6). A cutoff was introduced there to simulate the impact of adaptation and masking on the steepness of the psychophysical function at the low end of the stimulus scale. Figure 4.8 shows the associated standard deviations produced by the Sensory Aggregate Model along with the function labeled "no loss," which represents simulation data obtained without a cutoff. As the cutoff advances up the stimulus continuum, the standard deviation gets smaller. This occurs because each function essentially does not start until the stimulus exceeds the cutoff. The prediction of the model is clear: The response

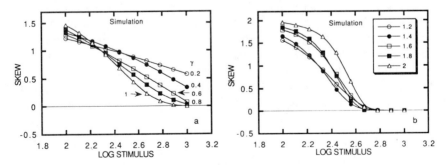

FIG. 4.9. Skew of the firing rate distribution as a function of logarithm of stimulus intensity. Data generated by the Sensory Aggregate Model yielding different Stevens exponents: (a) 0.2 to 1 (b) 1.2 to 2.

variability in empirical studies should be less in the presence of a stimulus masker or adapting stimulus than it is under normal circumstances. This reduced variability should persist throughout the entire function; that is, it occurs well beyond the point where the masker or adapting stimulus is introduced.

## SKEWNESS OF FIRING RATE DISTRIBUTIONS

Figure 4.9 gives the skewness of firing rate distributions generated by the Sensory Aggregate Model for each of the hypothetical data sets. The measure is plotted as a function of the log stimulus intensity for the distributions associated with Stevens exponents ranging from 0.2 to 1 (4.9a), and 1.2 to 2 (4.9b). In all instances, the skew is positive for the weakest intensities and systematically approaches normality (symmetric distributions) for the strongest intensities. The shapes of the functions vary in their details, but the overall trends are the same in all cases. Empirical data on the skewness of magnitude estimation distributions is presented in chapter 10, which considers Ekman's Law.

## OVERVIEW

The functional relation between mean firing rate and stimulus intensity is not exactly a power function (chap. 3). Stevens's Law is a useful approximation, but nonetheless an inexact representation of the facts. For similar reasons, one cannot expect to find a single equation that always describes the trend of variability in the responses, because this variability depends on the details of the neural firing rates making up the ensemble. In general, the variability in the neuronal firing rates increases with increases in stimulus intensity, though the functional relation is sometimes complex.

To recap the basic premises of the model, all the major features of global and local psychophysics can be modeled by assuming a fixed dynamic range for individual neurons, a logarithmic transfer function between stimulus intensity and firing rate of neurons, and a lognormal distribution of absolute thresholds for the aggregate that signals stimulus intensity. The theoretical parameter values of the lognormal distribution determine the empirical parameter values of Stevens functions, Weber functions, and the pattern of skewness in response distributions. Next consider an analysis of reaction time data viewed within the same theoretical framework.

# 5 Piéron Functions

Simple reaction time is the length of time it takes a person to detect a supra-threshold stimulus, such as a light, a sound, or an odor. If the physical intensity is varied over trials, a functional relation is determined between reaction time and intensity. Whereas the details of such experiments are intricate, their broader conceptual basis is not (Luce, 1986). The question is how best to describe and explain the results found in diverse experimental conditions. The Sensory Aggregate Model makes a number of statements about the neural infrastructure of simple reaction time, as well as predictions about the quantitative features to be expected in such data.

The main results of the field have been available for many years. The experimental studies support the conclusion that reaction time to detect a stimulus decreases as its physical intensity increases (for discrete stimuli). Piéron (1914, 1920) proposed a mathematical description of this finding by claiming that the relation between reaction time and light intensity is described by Equation 5.1:

$$MRT = r_0 + \kappa S^{-\beta}, \tag{5.1}$$

where MRT is mean reaction time, and $r_0$, $\kappa$, and $\beta$ are parameters fit to data. Equation 5.1 is referred to as Piéron's Law and any relation between mean reaction time and stimulus intensity is a Piéron function. The exponent, $\beta$, has received the most theoretical attention, and this tradition is continued here for two reasons: First, the Sensory Aggregate Model states that the exponent in Piéron's Law is a consequence of the same averaging process at the neural level that is responsible for the exponent of Stevens's Law. And, second, the model states that the variability in reaction time to a stimulus presented on many occasions depends on the same neuronal aggregate as do Weber functions.

## MEAN REACTION TIME

Figure 5.1a gives an example of empirical data from an oft-quoted study by Mansfield (1973). He tested a dark-adapted subject, who responded as quickly as possible to the appearance of a 30-msec light flash (log intensity on the x axis). For very dim flashes, the reaction time (linear units) is relatively long, on the order of 300 msec, but it changes inversely with flash intensity, reaching an asymptote somewhere in the vicinity of 200 msec. No matter how intense the stimulus becomes, the reaction time is never less than this minimum.

When reaction time itself is the dependent variable, it is cumbersome to actually fit analytic functions to the data, so reaction times are often transformed to allow more convenient estimation of parameters. This transformation is possible because Piéron's Law can be rewritten by taking logs of both sides of the basic equation:

$$log \ (MRT - r_0) = log \ \kappa - \beta \ log \ \mathbf{S}. \qquad (5.2)$$

Equation 5.2 resembles the logarithmic version of Stevens's Law (Equation 3.2), except for two key differences: the slope ($\beta$) of the reaction-time function in log–log coordinates is negative, and there is an additional constant, $r_0$. Confident estimation of this second constant is no trivial statistical exercise, due to the fact that the value settled on for $r_0$ affects the most appropriate value for $\beta$ (Luce, 1986). Despite this complication, Mansfield secured a satisfactory fit of Equation 5.2 by trying out several reasonable values of $r_0$, and then proceeding to determine which of these led to the best estimate of $\beta$.

Figure 5.1b (right) presents the Mansfield data in logarithmic coordinates. The slope ($\beta$) of the function is $-0.33$, which, perhaps fortuitously, is the negative of the slope of Stevens's Law for brightness of a $5^0$ target in the dark (Table 3.1). In most cases, the exponent of Piéron's Law is not the negative of the

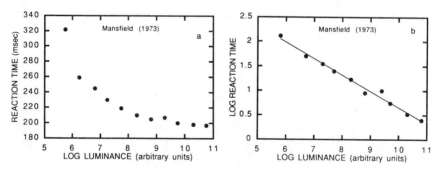

FIG. 5.1.  Mean reaction time as a function of logarithm of stimulus luminance (a) and logarithm of mean reaction time as a function of logarithm of stimulus luminance (b). After Mansfield (1973).

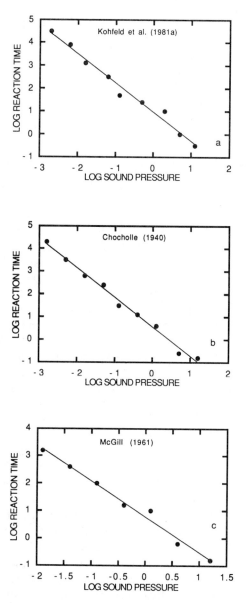

FIG. 5.2.    Mean reaction time as a function of sound pressure (log–log coordinates). From (a) Kohfeld et al. (1981a); (b) Chocholle (1940); (c) McGill (1961).

exponent of Stevens's Law, though, as is argued here, the two laws can be viewed as dual reflections of a common sensory code.

Kohfeld, Santee, and Wallace (1981a, 1981b) reported a substantial body of results on simple reaction time for detection of 1000-Hz auditory signals. Their method of dealing with the constant $r_0$ is to omit it entirely from the theoretical equation by first taking the derivative of Equation 5.1:

$$\frac{dMRT}{dS} = \kappa\beta \; \mathbf{S}^{-(\beta+1)} \, . \tag{5.3}$$

Then, taking the log of both sides yields

$$log \left[ \frac{dMRT}{dS} \right] = log \; \kappa\beta \; - \; (\beta \; + \; 1) \; log \; \mathbf{S} \, . \tag{5.4}$$

The log of the derivative, approximated by using discrete differences along the two dimensions ($\mathbf{S}$ and $MRT$),[1] is then plotted as a function of log intensity in order to estimate the slope ($\beta \; + \; 1$) and y intercept ($log \; \kappa\beta$) of the function, and thereby, secure values for $\beta$ and $\kappa$. Three such plots, together with appropriate parameter values, are presented in Figure 5.2 for the Kohfeld et al. (1981a) data, as well as for data on 1000-Hz tones collected by earlier investigators (Chocholle, 1940; McGill, 1961). All the plots are consistent with Piéron's Law, with a slope of approximately $-0.3$. When subjects give magnitude estimates of sound intensity, the exponent of Stevens's Law is typically in the range of 0.6 to 0.7 (in pressure units), so this is a situation where the exponent of $-0.3$ for Piéron's Law is not just the negative of the corresponding Stevens exponent.

## RESPONSE VARIABILITY

The standard deviation of reaction-time distributions has been fully documented, but the individual studies are somewhat at odds with each other. Figure 5.3 presents a sample of the early work by Chocholle (1940) with 1000-Hz tones. The points are taken from his tabled data for two subjects. The standard deviation is almost a perfect linear function of mean reaction time. The relative error (standard deviation divided by the mean) calculated from several of Chocholle's data sets is discussed more recently by Luce (1986, chap. 2), who noted that it is very close to 10%. This value, calculated from the tabled data, has also been quoted by others, and seems to have been accepted by the field at face value (e.g., Bonnet, 1986, chap. 4). In a personal conversation, however, R. Duncan Luce pointed out that Chocholle's relative errors are amazingly constant throughout the course of intensity change (increases in mean reaction time), and in the

---

[1]This analysis also has problems. The bin size for determining the differences used in Equation 5.4 makes a substantial difference in the outcome.

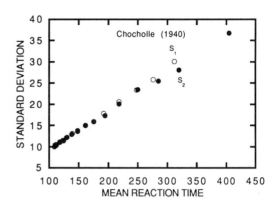

FIG. 5.3. Standard deviation as a function of mean reaction time for two subjects responding to sound intensity. From Chocholle (1940).

context of modern work, the values from his study are comparatively small. This is obvious in Figure 5.3. After consulting the rather lengthy Chocholle article, there is no insight into why these early findings differ so much from those found more recently. Without the benefit of more detailed information about the circumstances surrounding Chocholle's analysis, there is no choice but to accept the data as presented in this classic study.

Green and Luce (1971) reported a nonlinear relation between the standard deviation and the mean, rather than linear functions such as those in Figure 5.3. Figure 5.4 shows their results for detection of the onset of 1000-Hz tones (logarithmic coordinates). For the faster (shorter) reaction times, the variability increases steeply with increases in the mean, but the trend of the points flattens for the slower (longer) reaction times. Over the complete data set there is a visible nonlinearity, which also is apparent when the points are plotted in linear coordinates. These findings imply that the relative error is not at all constant, ranging instead from approximately 0.2 for loud tones (short reaction times) up to 1

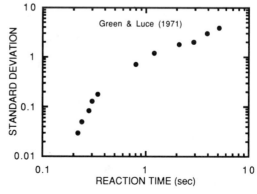

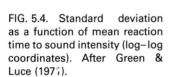

FIG. 5.4. Standard deviation as a function of mean reaction time to sound intensity (log–log coordinates). After Green & Luce (1971).

(standard deviation = mean) for soft ones (long reaction times). Thus, the Luce and Green findings differ from those of Chocholle. Given the notorious variability of reaction times so often mentioned in the literature, the relations reported by Green and Luce are probably closer to the actual situation.

## SKEW OF RESPONSE DISTRIBUTIONS

Another established fact is that the distribution of reaction times for a single stimulus is positively skewed (Luce, 1986; Ratcliff, 1993). That is, the tendency is for most reaction times to be bunched closely around a modal value, but with the intrusion of a smaller number of much longer times. The study by Kohfeld et al. (1981b) indicates that for simple reaction time the skewness is greater for loud sounds than it is for soft ones, after the reaction times are corrected by subtracting out a fixed response component caused by the subject's expectancy concerning the time of signal presentation. Figure 5.5 presents examples of reaction-time distributions published by Kohfeld et al. (1981b) for two frequencies (1000 Hz and 5000 Hz) and intensities (20 phons and 80 phons). The left panel (5.5a) shows that the distributions associated with loud stimuli (80 phons) are positively skewed, whereas the distributions in the right (5.5b) for the soft stimuli (20 phons) are symmetrical about their means. In addition, the response distribution for a loud tone does not seem to depend on frequency, whereas for a soft tone the reaction times for a 1000-Hz tone are much longer than for a 5000-Hz tone. This may have to do with the fact that a 5000-Hz tone must contain more energy in order to match the loudness of a 1000-Hz tone at low levels, but not at high levels. (See the equal-loudness contours schematized in Figure 3.10.)

If reaction time on a single trial deviates substantially from the mean, it

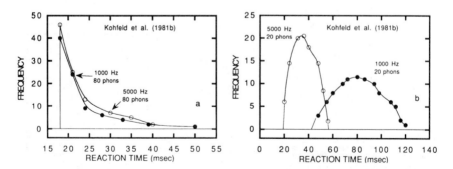

FIG. 5.5.   Frequency of mean reaction times to the onset of 1000- and 5000-Hz tones for loud (a) and soft (b) sounds. After Kohfeld et al. (1981b).

typically falls into the longer tail of the response distribution. Common laboratory wisdom dictates that simple reaction-time distributions should be positively skewed in this manner. Any lapse of attention on the part of the subject would lead to an abnormally long reaction time. Exceedingly short times are also suspect. They may be due to errors of anticipation, so should not legitimately be included in the analysis.

The possible sources of response bias have been enumerated by Ratcliff (1993): "The processes that generate outliers can be fast guesses, guesses that are based on the subject's estimate of the usual time to respond, multiple runs of the process that is actually under study, the subject's inattention, or guesses based on the subject's failure to reach a decision" (p. 510). The confusion arises on the experimenter's side when attempting to distinguish between reaction times influenced by response biases and those that are due to stimulus variables, such as physical intensity. The reason for departures from a symmetric reaction-time distribution has been the focus of much theoretical debate (Luce, 1986).

The response expectations of the subject and related cognitive factors are not incorporated into the Sensory Aggregate Model. Succeeding sections show that skewed reaction-time distributions, as well as several other prominent features of the empirical data base, are consistent on a descriptive level with predictions of the Sensory Aggregate Model. The positive skew in the reaction-time functions is postulated to arise from the operation of neurophysiological mechanisms that are unaffected by response bias. In other words, if an experiment could be purged of all response biases, reaction-time distributions for relatively intense stimuli would still be positively skewed.

## THE SENSORY AGGREGATE MODEL

Because reaction time and most other psychophysical phenomena are based on unobservable processes, their origins in neurophysiology remain uncertain. This may explain why theoretical arguments concerning the neural basis of reaction time can be lengthy and intricate (Link, 1992; Luce, 1986). The present application of the Sensory Aggregate Model, while promising so far as it goes, must be seen as a preliminary step toward a more comprehensive study of reaction time as viewed from the standpoint of this particular model, or from the standpoint of others possessing similar properties.

A decision must first be made between the alternative neurophysiological measures that might be responsible for reaction time. This decision turns on questions about which aspect of the complex neural signal is used in detecting a stimulus. One prime contender is the onset time of neural responses, which is known to be proportional to stimulus intensity. A second possibility is the inverse of the sustained firing rate of a neuron once a stimulus has been present for more than several milliseconds. Because onset time of neuronal firing is proportional to sustained firing rate, either measure will do (chap. 2). Therefore, it is assumed that reaction time is inversely related to the sustained firing rate of individual neurons in the aggregate activated by a stimulus. In short, the discussion here relies on the only dependent measure available in the model: the hypothetical firing rate used in modeling global scaling behavior (chap. 3). This amounts to acceptance of Piéron's (1952) original view: Reaction time is inversely related to stimulus intensity.

A second matter in need of resolution, before moving on to predictions of the model, concerns the supposed link between the firing rate of an individual neuron and reaction time. If a subpopulation of neurons always fires in response to a stimulus, and the firing rate of a single component neuron is the basis for the response on each trial, then what aspect of the neural code actually determines response speed? Two candidates are the amount of time it takes for a fixed number of impulses to occur (timing model) and the number of impulses produced in a fixed time interval (counting model). In the first case, the time to reach a criterion number of pulses is directly related to stimulus intensity. In the second, the number of impulses occurring in a fixed amount of time (average interarrival time) is directly related to intensity. The conditions holding in these models when applied to reaction-time paradigms are discussed by Luce (1986, p. 155) and by Luce and Green (1972). Either a timing or a counting model predicts that increasing stimulus intensity increases neural firing rate. This shortens simple reaction time. The predicted shape of the resulting Piéron function depends on the functional relation between physical intensity and firing rate, as well as on the statistical properties of the impulse train.

Applying the Sensory Aggregate Model in this theoretical context is tantamount to accepting the view already espoused: Mean firing rate is a power function of stimulus intensity (chap. 3), and reaction time is inversely related to the firing rate of the individual neuron being sampled. Theoretically, the neural code behind this process could obey the dictates of either a timing or a counting model, though Luce (1986, p. 156) noted that the timing model does not yield a satisfactory description of the processes underlying simple reaction time.

## COMPUTER SIMULATIONS

The predictions of the Sensory Aggregate Model are implemented by computer simulation. The same parameter values of the model—mean and standard deviation of the lognormal distribution of thresholds, and dynamic range of single neurons—are used as in the simulations leading to Stevens's Power Law (Table 3.2) and Weber functions (Table 4.2). The response time required for each individual neuron to fire is the inverse of its sustained rate, and the Mean Reaction Time (MRT) is the mean of these inverses. This mean was actually calculated as a weighted average: the sum of the standardized probabilities of each inverse multiplied by its numerical quantity. (The unit of this quantity is "frequency per unit time.") The variability and skew measures associated with a single external stimulus are then computed from the distribution of the inverse firing rates. It is important to realize that the inverse of the mean firing rate is not the same as the mean of the distribution of inverses. In particular, the shape and parameter values of the reaction-time distributions are not linked in any simple way to the steady-state distribution of firing rates for subpopulations of neurons responsible for signaling stimulus intensity.

### Piéron Functions

Figure 5.5 presents the simulation results in both linear (left) and logarithmic (right) coordinates. The left panels show the mean of the inverse firing rates as a function of stimulus intensity for the same distributions that produce the Stevens functions in Figure 3.3. The scale units on both axes are arbitrary. The right panels present the same data in logarithmic coordinates in order to assess the adequacy of Piéron's Law. For purposes of exposition, and in accord with the model's predictions, the dependent variable (inverse firing rate) is labeled "reaction time." The model does not include a term for the response constant $r_0$ in Equation 5.1, and so it appears on the graph that reaction time is sometimes equal to zero. This outcome is impossible, short of endowing the subject with extrasensory perception. For actual data sets collected in the laboratory, this constant must be greater than zero, because some behavioral response is required of the subject, and this response always takes a finite time to initiate—pressing a key, blinking an eye, or whatever.

The data in the left two panels all display the characteristic decline in reaction time with increasing stimulus intensity. The steepness of this trend is correlated with the exponent of Stevens's Law (as indicated on the graph). This is true because in the simulations, Stevens and Piéron functions share the same neurological foundation. Reaction times should decline faster with increasing stimulus intensity for attributes yielding the largest Stevens exponents. It is clear from the figures, however, that the exponent of the Piéron function is not just the negative of the exponent of the Stevens function.

The right two panels give the same data in logarithmic coordinates, and straight lines test the adequacy of Piéron's Law. The fits are satisfactory, except for those instances where the exponent of Stevens's Law is especially high. It is implicit in all these fits that $r_0 = 0$ in Equation 5.1.

If both Stevens and Piéron functions depend systematically on stimulus intensity, then one might expect a connection between their respective slopes in log–log plots. A direct comparison of the two laws, arising from the neural aggregate predictions, is possible by consulting Table 5.1,[2] which lists paired values of $\gamma$

---

[2]In chapter 6, these data are graphed in order to facilitate the comparison.

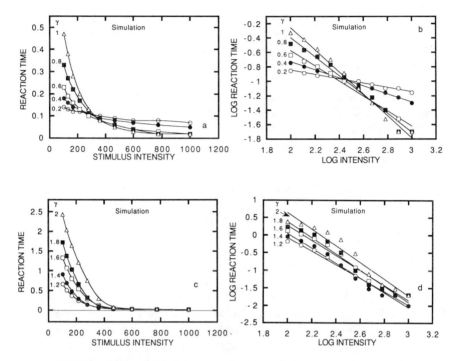

FIG. 5.6.   Mean reaction time as a function of stimulus intensity. The plots on the left are in linear units (a, c). Those on the right are in logarithmic units (b, d). Data generated by the Sensory Aggregate Model yielding Stevens exponents listed to the left of the curves: (top) values from 0.2 to 1, (bottom) values from 1.2 to 2.

(exponent of Stevens's Law) and β (exponent of Piéron's Law) for exactly the same mean and standard deviations of the lognormal distribution of neural thresholds. The rank order of exponents is preserved in the model's predictions: the higher the exponent of Stevens's Law, the lower the exponent of Piéron's Law (taking the sign of the exponent into account). On the other hand, the absolute values of the Piéron functions are all higher than the corresponding exponents in the Stevens functions.

Even if estimates of stimulus intensity and reaction time are inversely related at the level of the individual neuron, one would not expect the ratio of two empirical Stevens exponents (obtained for, say, light and sound) to be identical to the ratio of the comparable Piéron exponents. As previously stated, this is because the reciprocal of the mean firing rate of the population of neurons associated with a stimulus intensity is not the same as the mean of the reciprocal of the individual firing rates.

TABLE 5.1
Exponents for Stevens's Law and Piéron's
Law as Generated by the Sensory
Aggregate Model

| Stevens | Piéron |
|---------|--------|
| 0.2 | −0.29 |
| 0.4 | −0.56 |
| 0.6 | −1.0 |
| 0.8 | −1.3 |
| 1.0 | −1.5 |
| 1.2 | −1.9 |
| 1.4 | −2.1 |
| 1.6 | −2.1 |
| 1.8 | −2.3 |
| 2.0 | −2.4 |

## Attribute Effects

Scant attention seems to have been devoted to the question of possible differences in the slope of the reaction time function (logarithmic coordinates) for a variety of stimulus attributes. The overwhelming number of studies of simple reaction time test either lights or sounds. These attributes typically yield Stevens exponents less than 1. It would prove informative to conduct reaction-time studies with attributes having Stevens exponents greater than 1, if for no other reason than to verify that the same functional relations hold.

The link between these two indicators (magnitude estimates and reaction time) of neural activity is strongly implied by the Sensory Aggregate Model, as well as by some other neurophysiological conceptions of the processes underlying the psychophysics of sensation (e.g., Norwich, 1993, chap. 13). Whether or not such predictions will be borne out in the laboratory must await further study. Experimental tests would best involve a wide range of stimulus attributes for which both the Stevens and Piéron function could be determined with the same group of subjects and stimulus series. Unfortunately, there are very few, if any, laboratories in the world with the facilities and financial resources to conduct such large-scale investigations.

## Response Variability

The standard deviations of the reaction-time distributions produced by the Sensory Aggregate Model were computed and are presented in a format corresponding to that used for the empirical data on response variability (Figures 5.3 & 5.4).

Figure 5.7 presents the standard deviation as a function of the reciprocal firing

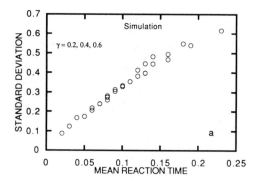

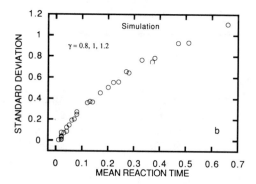

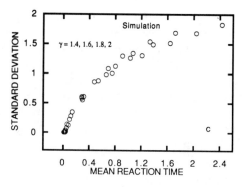

FIG. 5.7.   Standard deviation as a function of mean reaction time. Data generated by the Sensory Aggregate Model yielding Stevens exponents listed: (a) 0.2, 0.4, 0.6, (b) 0.8, 1, 1.2; (c) 1.4, 1.6, 1.8, 2.

rate (linear coordinates) for all 10 Piéron functions. For the small Stevens exponents, the standard deviation is a linear function of the mean (5.7a), just as
Chocholle reported, but the variability produced by the model is more than an
order of magnitude greater than that of Chocholle. The relative error for the
simulation data lies between 3.5 and 4, as compared to a value of 0.1 for the
empirical data.

The middle (5.7b) and bottom (5.7c) panels show how the curvature of the
relation between the standard deviation and mean reaction time increases as the
exponent of the Stevens function increases. The relative error also decreases. A
break in the overall function is clearest in the bottom panel, where the variability
increases rapidly for the shorter reaction times (strong stimuli) and then changes
more slowly over the region of the longer reaction times (weak stimuli). The
course of this trend resembles that seen in the empirical data reported by Green
and Luce (1971) for simple reaction time to a 1000-Hz tone (cf. Figure 5.4),
though the relative error occurring in the simulation is greater. A modification of
the model that generates more realistic relative errors is discussed at the end of
the chapter.

Figure 5.8 plots the standard deviation as a function of the mean in logarithmic coordinates for three of the intermediate Stevens exponents (0.8, 1,
1.2). These axes are the same shown in Figure 5.4 for the empirical data. This
allows more direct comparison with the results of Luce and Green (1971). The
break in the function between fast and slow mean reaction times is evident when
the simulation data are presented in this format, and the agreement with the
empirical data more apparent.

## Skewness

The skewness of the theoretical reaction-time distributions were computed for
the same data sets. Figure 5.9 presents these statistical outcomes, where the

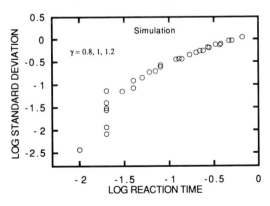

FIG. 5.8. Standard deviation
as a function of mean reaction
time (log–log coordinates).
Data generated by the Sensory
Aggregate Model yielding the
Stevens exponents indicated.

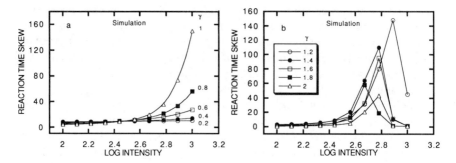

FIG. 5.9.   Reaction time skew as a function of logarithm of stimulus intensity. Data generated by the Sensory Aggregate Model yielding the Stevens exponents indicated: (a) 0.2 to 1 (b) 1.2 to 2.

signature of each curve is the size of the corresponding Stevens exponent. The skewness measure is based on the distribution of the reciprocal firing rates for each intensity and is plotted as a function of the log stimulus intensity. The skewness of each function is close to zero for the lowest intensities, but becomes more positive as intensity increases.

The skewness of the theoretical firing-rate distributions (not their reciprocals) is positive for weak intensities and declines toward zero as intensity increases (chap. 4, Figure 4.8). Because the reaction-time distributions depend on the reciprocal of the firing rates, their skewness is closely tied to the shape of the firing-rate distributions. Firing-rate distributions that are positively skewed correspond to reaction-time distributions that are approximately Gaussian; firing-rate distributions that are symmetric about the mean correspond to reaction-time distributions that are positively skewed.

For the larger exponents, the relation between skew and log intensity is nonmonotonic, as indicated by the fact that the skewness for the most intense stimuli is less than for slightly weaker stimuli. The shape of the reaction-time distributions obviously is connected with the shape of the firing-rate distributions, and vice versa, because one is the inverse of the other.

The finding that the reaction-time distribution for weak stimuli is close to Gaussian, while for strong stimuli, it is positively skewed, agrees with the empirical data reported by Kohfeld et al. (1981b) shown in Figure 5.5. The differences in the theoretical relations associated with different Stevens exponents suggests that experiments be run to determine the shape of the empirical distributions for a wide variety of attributes, instead of only for light and sound.

Figure 5.10 presents illustrative examples of theoretical reaction-time distributions for two stimuli, differing greatly in intensity. The neural firing rates for these two cases are generated by pairs of parameter values for the lognormal distribution leading to a Stevens exponent of 0.6. In Figure 5.10a, the reaction-

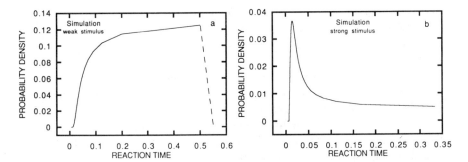

FIG. 5.10.  Probability density for reaction time to the onset of a weak
(a) and strong (b) stimulus intensity. Data generated by the Sensory
Aggregate Mòdel (Stevens exponent = 0.6).

time distribution is for a weak stimulus intensity, and the theoretical curve in
Figure 5.10b represents a hypothetical reaction-time distribution for a strong
stimulus.

The predicted curve for the weaker stimulus fails to reverse direction for the
longer reaction times. This, however, is an unrealistic outcome from an actual
experiment. A value of zero can safely be assigned to the probability of detecting
a stimulus one minute after its presentation. A line (dashed) on the graph represents a decline of the probability of observing very long reaction times. (In a true
density function, the probabilities would sum to 1.) This makes the tails of this
distribution roughly symmetrical, as compared to the strong positive skew in the
reaction-time distribution associated with the stronger stimulus. The two hypothetical distributions then resemble the empirical findings reported by Kohfeld et
al. (1981b), and reproduced in Figure 5.5. The distributions for loud tones are
more skewed than those for soft ones, just as in the simulations.

## TRUNCATED FIRING-RATE DISTRIBUTIONS

One important question regarding the neural basis for reaction time is exactly
what part of the distribution of firing rates over the aggregate subjects sample.
The entire neural distribution may not be sampled when subjects must respond as
quickly as possible to the onset of a stimulus. If the individual neuronal outputs
from the subpopulation are processed in parallel, or if the subject can direct
attention to a particular subset of the population, one might reasonably suppose
that only neurons with the highest firing rates are relevant. The firing rates of
neurons whose thresholds are barely exceeded may be indistinguishable from
background noise (spontaneous firing), and hence, simply ignored.

This suggests that in computer simulations a cutoff (truncation) be applied to the distribution of thresholds, thus excluding the slow-firing neurons from the pool. In other words, one might logically ask why a subject should wait until every neuron in the ensemble reaches some criterion before initiating a behavioral response.

Perhaps a more plausible subject strategy, though of course not one necessarily employed, would be to sample only that part of the neuronal aggregate (thresholds) falling below some adjustable cutoff (thereby including only the faster rates). The rest of the distribution would then be ignored. Without more theoretical elaboration, however, there is no rational way to build into the present model an optimal location for the cutoff. The location selected may be crucial to interpretation, because through computer simulation, it was found that the location has a huge impact on the pattern of the firing-rate distribution. Speaking in favor of a model that includes a cutoff, this procedure would reduce the relative error in the simulated data to values closer to those observed empirically. This would occur because the neurons firing at the slowest rate are responsible for producing the longest reaction times—those occupying the upper tail of the distribution. Eliminating these outliers dramatically reduces the variability of reaction times (see also Ratcliff, 1993).

When the complete theoretical distribution is treated as appropriate for modeling reaction time, as in this chapter, the relative error rates of the Sensory Aggregate Model are in some instances more than an order of magnitude higher than comparable measures obtained in the laboratory. The existence of a cutoff that limits the boundaries of the firing rate distribution would go a long way toward bringing the theoretical predictions in line with the empirical data. Without venturing further in this direction, it is worth mentioning that an adjustable cutoff along the hypothetical axis of neuronal thresholds might also have special advantages in modeling time-accuracy tradeoffs in reaction-time experiments (Link, 1992; Luce, 1986).

## THEORETICAL UPDATE

The main conclusion is that a common neurophysiological code is responsible for the laws and relations of sensory psychophysics, including Stevens functions relating perceived magnitude to physical intensity, Weber functions relating the standard deviation of responses to physical intensity, and Piéron functions relating simple reaction time to physical intensity. This common infrastructure is incorporated into a single theoretical model. All such empirical phenomena are simulated by a model that assumes a logarithmic neural transfer function between stimulus intensity and neuronal firing rate, a limited dynamic range for individual neurons, and a lognormal distribution over the fiber thresholds. An individual neuron's firing rate depends on its position in respect to the stimulus intensity.

These specific assumptions are not written in stone. They can be modified somewhat without materially altering the results.

While acknowledging that the Sensory Aggregate Model runs into difficulties in trying to predict the size and shape of reaction-time distributions, it should be borne in mind that all the simulations leading to the psychophysical laws are carried out with the same parameter values. More impressive matches to particular data sets occur if parameter values are permitted to change when addressing each experimental paradigm and data set. Although this is an appropriate strategy in some circumstances, it is not the one advocated here. The aim here is to present a coherent picture of the psychophysics of sensation, not just a book of snapshots taken through the lenses of different neural models, each tailored to fit the requirements of a single experimental paradigm.

# 6 Unified Sensory Laws?

Three people describe a bird perched on a branch. One person records the song the bird is singing, another estimates the relative size of its body parts, and the third notices the coloring of the feathers. When the three compare notes, they agree that each was referring to the same bird. Similarly, in psychophysics, researchers implicitly understand that the sensory phenomena revealed by local and global psychophysics are the same.

The hope for unifying psychophysical laws under the umbrella of a single theory rests with the adequacy of the premise that different empirical laws are no more than different perspectives on the same sensory phenomena. If this is indeed the case, then we expect that indices of relative perceptual "sensitivity" are independent of the psychophysical methods used in their determination. The consequence of this premise is seen in attempts to unify psychophysical laws by treating them as alternative manifestations of the same underlying principles (e.g., Baird, 1970a, 1970b; Link, 1992; Norwich, 1993; Treisman, 1984). These and other theorists propose that connections exist among Stevens exponents, Piéron exponents, and Weber fractions. Each is an index of perceptual sensitivity. The Sensory Aggregate Model is consistent with this view and provides a theoretical rationale for the belief in a common underlying neural code.

Contrary to this opinion, some researchers claim that apparent links between sensitivity indices and stimulus attributes are only fortuitous. For example, it has been said that the exponent of the Power Law has nothing to do with perceptual sensitivity per se, but merely reflects the fact that subjects use the same range of responses for estimating the intensities of any attribute. Then, because experimenters typically present stimuli over a range of intensities that is proportional to the dynamic range of each attribute (and these ranges differ widely), the exponent varies inversely with the logarithm of the stimulus range (Poulton, 1989).

A number of specific hypotheses have been proposed concerning the potential link between psychophysical indices. This chapter examines the viability of each from the standpoint of the Sensory Aggregate Model. These predictions are discussed in relation to three major conjectures advanced in the literature: (a) The Stevens exponent is inversely related to the logarithm of an attribute's dynamic range. (b) The Piéron exponent is the negative of the Stevens exponent. (c) The Stevens exponent is inversely related to the size of the Weber fraction.

In evaluating each conjecture, the collateral empirical evidence and theoretical rationale are provided, and then the plausibility of the conjecture is examined from the standpoint of the model. The chapter concludes with a discussion of the implications of recent measurement theory results for psychophysical models that attempt to unify empirical laws by restating them in the language of sensory neurophysiology.

## THE RANGE CONJECTURE

Researchers in sensory psychophysics agree that the exponent of Stevens's Law depends on the stimulus attribute, and many would go further and claim that the observed differences in exponent depend on the transducer properties of the sense modality responsible for processing each attribute. Poulton (1967, 1989) challenged the latter claim. Although granting that the exponent depends on stimulus attribute, he argued that the reason has little to do with transducer physiology. Rather, he contended that the size of the exponent is inversely related to the dynamic stimulus range over which the sensory system can process the attribute. A short range implies a large exponent, a long range implies a small exponent. This proposal is referred to as the *range conjecture*.

Teghtsoonian (1971) argued that the exponent is inversely related to the dynamic range of attributes, but not for the reason given by Poulton. He proposed that the exponent of the Power Law reflects differences in perceptual sensitivity and that such differences are confirmed by the fact that the exponent is inversely related to the Weber fraction. He supported this contention by the following logic. Suppose in Magnitude Estimation subjects always use the same range of numbers (say from 1 to 100) in representing a set of intensities, regardless of the stimulus range employed by the experimenter. Then the slope of the psychophysical function in a log–log plot would be the logarithm of this fixed response range (two log units in this example) divided by the logarithm of the stimulus range employed. The choice of stimulus range is left up to the discretion of the experimenter. If experimenters choose stimulus ranges that are a fixed proportion of the actual dynamic range of each attribute, the exponent of the Power Law will be inversely related to stimulus range, as Poulton (1989) suggested. That is, the slope of a linear function in log–log coordinates is by definition:

$$\frac{log\ C}{log\ S_{range}} = \gamma, \tag{6.1}$$

where C is the constant response range and $\gamma$ is the exponent of the Power Law. Under this interpretation, the exponent becomes nothing more than an indicator of subject and experimenter bias. Its status as an unbiased index of perceptual sensitivity is revoked, though it still relates to the Weber function.

### Empirical Justification

Poulton evaluated the face validity of the range conjecture by plotting the exponent as a function of the inverse of the logarithm of the stimulus range for different attributes and seeing if the points fall on a straight line. The data represented by the filled circles in Figure 6.1 were tabulated by Poulton (1967), and the format of the graph follows the one in Poulton (1989). At least to a first order of approximation, it appears that the conjecture is correct at the descriptive level. Attributes with large dynamic ranges (such as loudness and brightness) have the lowest exponents, whereas attributes with short dynamic ranges (such as electric shock and lifted weight) have the highest ones. There are several notable exceptions, however, that are not included in the figure. One such example is odor. The dynamic range of most odorous substances is relatively narrow, yet the exponents for odor tend to be among the lowest ever recorded (B. Berglund, U. Berglund, Ekman, & Engen, 1971). The lack of adequate stimulus control may have been partly responsible for this result in earlier studies (Cain, 1977). On the other hand, most researchers in olfaction would confess that people do not exhibit stellar sensitivity for olfactory stimuli. Special precautions even must be

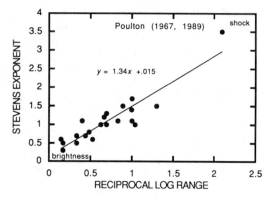

FIG. 6.1. Stevens exponent (Magnitude Estimation) as a function of reciprocal of the logarithm of stimulus range. Each point represents a different attribute. From Poulton (1967, 1989).

taken to insure that subjects detect the suprathreshold stimuli in global scaling tasks (Baird, B. Berglund & Olsson, 1996).

R. Teghtsoonian (1973, 1978) and others (reviewed in Poulton, 1989) also demonstrated that the exponent for a stimulus attribute is affected by the stimulus range over which it is assessed, but the magnitude of this within-attribute effect is less impressive than the between-attribute effect. As noted in chapter 3, a within-attribute effect can be explained from a sensory standpoint. Because the psycho-physical function produced by the Sensory Aggregate Model is not exactly a power function, but depends on the particular section of the function that is examined, the exponent can vary somewhat for different stimulus ranges. This chapter, however, is talking about between-attribute effects that cannot be explained in the same way.

## Theoretical Implications

Although it is true that increasing the range decreases the exponent, the contention that the exponent is entirely dependent on range is a view not shared by most sensory researchers who trust that the Power Law and its accompanying exponent depend on neural physiology, the transducer mechanisms referred to by S. S. Stevens (1975). To these investigators, contextual factors affecting the exponent are more of a nuisance than a serious threat to the validity of the exponent as an indicator of perceptual sensitivity. These researchers might voice the opinion that the relation depicted in Figure 6.1 is an example of a correlated variable leading one astray. The stimulus range is related to the exponent, but in the domain of neural mechanisms responsible for psychophysical functions, this factor is not the crucial one. Range just happens to be correlated with the relative ability of a sense organ to transduce energy according to the Power Law. There is no deeper connection between the two.

The claim that range determines the exponent also has trouble explaining why within-attribute effects are not as strong as between-attribute effects. That is to say, the range of the stimuli should totally determine the exponent, regardless of the attribute or physical range under consideration. This is a major drawback of this view. It is known that within-attribute range effects are markedly less than between-attribute effects (Poulton, 1989).

## RANGE AND SENSORY TRANSDUCTION

The Sensory Aggregate Model allows an evaluation of the range conjecture from an unusual perspective. The model has the advantage that the statistical properties of the firing-rate distribution for each physical intensity is invariant under transformation of stimulus range. The essential parameters in the model are the two endpoints of the stimulus range (in log units), the mean and standard deviation of the lognormal distribution of thresholds, and the logarithm of the dynamic range over which a single neuron fires. Multiplying each of these parameters by a constant leaves the firing-rate distributions unchanged. Because it is possible to alter the stimulus range by scalar multiplication, while maintaining the same mean firing-rate, the slope of the psychophysical function varies inversely with the logarithm of the stimulus range. For example, if the stimulus intensities extend from 1 to 2 log units (range of 1), and a power function is obtained with an exponent of 0.6, then doubling the size of all parameters produces a stimulus range of 2 log units and an exponent of 0.3.

The importance of this feature of the model should be stressed. If a set of parameter values that produces a perfect fit of the Power Law over a specified range of 1 log cycle is chosen, then by multiplication it is possible to obtain a power function over any other range with an identical Goodness-of-Fit.

Because acceptable fits of the Power Law are achieved for exponents extending from 0.2 to 2 over one log cycle (chap. 3), it is possible to find parameter values for the Sensory Aggregate Model that match the range and exponents from the psychophysics laboratory. The slope of the function in Figure 6.1 is 1.34 with a y intercept of 0.15. Therefore, a one log-cycle range yields an exponent in the vicinity of 1.34 (Poulton's evaluation of Equation 6.1 yields an exponent of 1.47 and a y intercept of 0).[1] Because both values are within the region for which the Sensory Aggregate Model produces an acceptable fit of the Power Law, it must be true that transformation of its parameter values can lead to any of the empirical exponents tabulated by Poulton. This feature of the model can be capitalized on to bolster the conjecture that there is only one fundamental relation between perceived magnitude and stimulus intensity. The exponent signifies the stimulus range over which this single relation is manifest.

The same predictions, however, are possible by using more than one "prime" exponent for a one-cycle range, and the extreme case (accepted implicitly by most researchers) is a separate parameter set for each exponent. For instance, a power function with an exponent of 1.0 over a one-cycle range will produce under multiplication of parameters a power function with an exponent of 3 over a stimulus range one third as great. This agrees well with the early estimates of the exponent for electric shock, which for moral and insurance considerations has only been tested over short ranges. On the other hand, this same power function (and its parameter values) possessing an exponent of 1 over a one-cycle range cannot be transformed into an exponent of 0.3 for brightness, which covers six log cycles. This is because the arithmetic gives an exponent of 0.17 = 1/6 for a six-cycle range.

On the other hand, a power function with an exponent of 1.8 over a one-cycle

---

[1]There are some minor discrepancies between the tabled values in Poulton (1967) and the graph in Poulton (1989). I use the data in the original paper.

range can be transformed into a power function with an exponent of 0.3 over a six-cycle range ($0.3 = 1.8/6$). Therefore, two primary power functions and their transformations can also match all the available empirical data, even if the largest exponent is the extraordinarily high value of 3.5 reported by S. S. Stevens et al. (1958) for electric shock. The argument can be extended to show that comparing the relative size of exponents does not necessarily indicate how many sensory blueprints there really are for processing physical intensity.

Other aspects of the model help decide on whether there are one or many psychophysical functions between perceived and physical magnitudes. Because transformations of a single power function by means of multiplication of parameter values does not change the neural firing-rate distributions for different intensities, a single "prime" power function implies that all the statistical properties of the response distributions are identical for all the attributes that have been studied. If the stimulus spacing is fixed (relative to the range), then the mean, standard deviation, and skewness of the output distribution for a particular stimulus in a series (say, the third largest) would be exactly the same, regardless of the stimulus range and its associated exponent.

The place to look, therefore, in assessing the range conjecture, is not in a table of exponents, but in a table of the higher moments of the response distributions (standard deviation and skewness). According to the range conjecture, they should be identical for all attributes. This outcome would be unexpected and, therefore, informative. The variety of psychophysical functions described in chapter 3 were obtained with different parameter values for the mean and standard deviation of the lognormal distribution of fiber thresholds. Therefore, if this is the correct way to view matters, then the response distributions for different attributes should differ (chap. 4).

To the best of my knowledge, no one has ever considered the problem this way. It would involve comparing attributes in terms of variance and the skewness for response distributions obtained by any one of the direct scaling methods, such as Magnitude Estimation or Cross Modality Matching. From observation of a limited number of studies, it seems that a single set of parameter values for the higher statistical moments of the response distribution will not be found, thus disconfirming the range conjecture. It would be surprising to learn that all the senses are equally adept at processing intensity information, but a systematic investigation is necessary before the possibility can be ruled out.

## STEVENS AND PIÉRON EXPONENTS

The Power Law relating perceived magnitude and physical intensity is expressed as

$$R = \lambda S^{\gamma}, \tag{6.2}$$

where $R$ is the mean magnitude estimate and $S$ is stimulus intensity. The exponent ($\gamma$) reflects the attribute being scaled. Piéron's Law relating simple reaction time to physical intensity is expressed as

$$RT = r + \kappa S^{-\beta}, \tag{6.3}$$

where $RT$ is mean reaction time to stimulus onset, $r$ is the minimum reaction time (asymptote of the function), and $\beta$ is the exponent related to the stimulus attribute. It is possible to employ exactly the same set of stimulus intensities in scaling and reaction time experiments, so it should be possible to compare the exponents in Equations 6.2 and 6.3 for the same set of attributes.

There appears to be consensus, despite the absence of much hard data, that the exponent of Equation 6.2 for judged magnitude and the exponent of Equation 6.3 for reaction time are related (Norwich, 1993). Generally speaking, the absolute values of the two exponents tend to be roughly the same (one exponent is the negative of the other), but no careful experimentation seems to have determined a functional relation between these two indices for an assortment of stimulus attributes. The conjecture to be considered is that the absolute values of the exponents for Stevens and Piéron functions are the same.

## Empirical Justification

The bulk of experiments bearing on this issue were conducted in vision and audition, but no study seems to have been done in which exactly the same stimuli were used in reaction time and magnitude estimation tasks.

There is one study reported by Angel (1973) that is tangentially relevant. Instead of measuring reaction time, the mean peak tension of a thumb flick was the dependent variable. The peak tension (force) increases with the intensity of the stimulus, and it is possible to obtain a best-fitting straight line in log–log coordinates whose slope (exponent) can be compared directly with the exponent (from other studies) of the Power Law for the same attribute. Angel employed three types of stimuli: auditory—1000-Hz pure tone, visual—light flash, and tactile—electrical pulse delivered to the middle finger. He conducted the experiment by placing the subject's thumb in a padded metal ring connected to a strain gauge that recorded the force of movement. The subject's task was to initiate a thumb flick as soon as possible after stimulus onset.

The empirical exponents secured by this method were 0.11 for vision, 0.21 for audition, and 1.04 for tactile. These values are far below the exponents reported for these attributes when subjects use magnitude estimation to scale intensity. The Stevens exponents for light, sound, and electrical stimulation listed in Table 3.1 are approximately three times as large: 0.3, 0.6, and 3.5, respectively (though this value for shock is probably on the high side). As Angel pointed out, however, the relative sizes of the reaction time exponents are very similar to the relative sizes of the corresponding Stevens exponents, suggesting that the same underlying neural machinery subsumes both. The differences in absolute values of the exponents in the two methods may occur because of differences in the mapping between the neural signal and the overt response. This mapping is presumably superimposed on the sensory output and would have to be factored out of the data before the pure psychophysical functions could be revealed (a more complete discussion is given by Luce, 1986, Chap. 3; and by Piéron, 1952, chap. 5).

## Theoretical Implications

If the same sensory variables determine the exponents of the two psychophysical laws given by Equations 6.2 and 6.3, and these variables are the only relevant ones, then the Sensory Aggregate Model predicts the relation between the two exponents for the same attribute. The form of this prediction is given in Figure 6.2, which plots the Piéron exponent as a function of the Stevens exponent based on the output of the simulation (data from Table 5.1).

By visual inspection, the two indices appear closely related, but one is not simply the negative of the other. If this were true, the data points would fall on the solid diagonal line. The actual points all fall beneath this line, indicating that the absolute value of the Piéron exponent is greater than the Stevens exponent.

The model's prediction that the absolute values of the Piéron exponents are greater than the Stevens exponents is contrary to what appears in the literature (Norwich, 1993). The absolute value of the Piéron exponent is usually less than that of the Stevens exponent, but this result has not been substantiated for a large number of attributes. In a thorough analysis of reaction-time data, Luce (1986) referred to the difficulties experimenters face in estimating the exponent of Piéron's Law, due to the fact that it is not a simple power function. The size of the exponent determined by some of the analyses reported in the literature can vary by a factor of 2 or 3 simply by changing the size of the additive constant (r

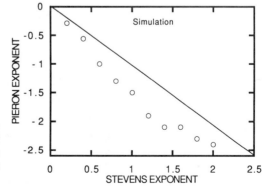

FIG. 6.2. Piéron exponent (re-action time) as a function of Stevens exponent (Magnitude Estimation) according to the Sensory Aggregate Model.

in Equation 6.3), the parameter representing the fastest reaction time. Moreover, Luce reanalyzed several early data sets by modern statistical methods and found a wide range of exponents for audition (Luce, 1986, Table 2.1, p. 62). For example, the exponents based on Chocholle's (1940) observations are in the region of 0.5 to 0.6, whereas more recent studies yield much smaller values (0.1 to 0.15).

Another issue in need of resolution is whether or not subjects base their judgments on the same neural event. As noted in Chapter 5, the response variance of reaction times predicted by the Sensory Aggregate Model is greater than in the empirical data. This might mean that subjects in simple reaction-time experiments are not using the entire output distribution from which individual neural discharges are sampled on a trial-to-trial basis. In particular, they may be ignoring the outputs of the slow-firing neurons.

Everyday logic says that a subject in a reaction-time experiment who could monitor the firing rate of individual neurons would be well served by only trusting the neurons producing the fastest rates (especially if speedy responses are rewarded). Eliminating the slow-firing neurons would shift the means of the output distributions upward. These truncated distributions would produce a lower absolute value of the Piéron exponent for reaction time. If exponents from magnitude estimation studies (direct perception of stimuli) were then compared to the Piéron exponents, their two absolute values would be more alike; that is, the data points in Figure 6.2 would lie nearer the diagonal. It is important, then, to somehow decide about whether the two psychophysical laws are based on the same components of the sensory signal.

At this preliminary stage of theorizing about the sensory basis of psychophysical laws, it is prudent to resist the temptation to formulate explanations for all the available empirical data. There is, after all, an incredible amount to be addressed. About all that can be said from the standpoint of the model is that the Stevens and Piéron exponents are inversely related, but more quantitative tests of their connection must await further experimentation, and no doubt more sophisticated theoretical analysis.


## WEBER FRACTIONS AND STEVENS EXPONENTS

There is a prevailing opinion that the exponent of Stevens's Power Law is inversely related to the Weber fraction. The justification for this conjecture comes from several quarters. R. Teghtsoonian (1971) stated that stimulus attributes with broad dynamic ranges have larger Weber fractions than those with narrow ranges, and because the range is inversely related to the exponent, the Weber fraction should obey the same relation. The unproven assumption here is that there is a fixed amount of sensory discriminability, identical for all attributes, but that it is distributed over different stimulus ranges. Link's (1992) Wave Theory of

Psychophysics also predicts an inverse relation. Baird (1970a, 1970b) came to the same conclusion from quite another line of reasoning. The theoretical foundations for these three approaches differ widely, yet they all concur in calling attention to the same point: Exponents and Weber fractions bear a close kinship.

Perhaps the oldest theoretical view that leads to the inverse relation between the Stevens exponent and the Weber fraction is based on an extension of Fechner's original ideas about integration of local JNDs to produce predictions about global sensation magnitudes. For purposes of illustration, the discussion presented in Baird and Noma (1978, chap. 4) is reiterated here.

There are three main assumptions driving the argument. First, each stimulus attribute, including the number scale used in Magnitude Estimation, obeys Weber's Law, and hence, has a characteristic Weber fraction. Second, any intensive dimension (attribute) can serve as either the stimulus or the response continuum in a magnitude matching task. Thus, Cross-Modality Matching and Magnitude Estimation are just variations on a generic method for obtaining the relative size of the exponents for all attributes. Third, Fechnerian integration can predict the Stevens function from knowledge of the Weber function (a suggestion first made by Brentano, 1874).

The formal argument follows: Let

$$\Delta S = k_s \mathbf{S}$$

be the Weber fraction for the stimulus continuum, and let

$$\Delta R = k_r R$$

be the Weber fraction for the response continuum. According to Fechner, the equation necessary to go from the local to the global level is to treat the relative sizes of the JNDs for the stimulus and response continua as derivatives of the global function. To do this, set

$$\frac{\Delta R}{\Delta S} = \frac{k_r\, R}{k_s\, \mathbf{S}} \, .$$

Then, assuming that what transpires for JNDs holds as well when going to derivatives,

$$\frac{dr}{k_r\, r} = \frac{ds}{k_s\, s}$$

$$\frac{1}{k_r} \int_{R_0}^{R} \frac{dr}{r} = \frac{1}{k_s} \int_{s_0}^{a} \frac{ds}{s}$$

$$\frac{1}{k_r} \, ln \left( \frac{R}{R_0} \right) = \frac{1}{k_s} \, ln \left( \frac{\mathbf{S}}{S_0} \right) \, .$$

Then,

$$\left(\frac{R}{R_0}\right) = \left(\frac{S}{S_0}\right)^{k_r/k_s}$$

And rearranging,

$$R = R_0 \left(\frac{1}{S_0}\right)^{k_r/k_s} S^{k_r/k_s}$$

Then, by letting

$$C = R_0(1/S_0)^{k_r/k_s},$$

we arrive at the Power Law:

$$R = CS^{k_r/k_s}. \tag{6.4}$$

Although Fechnerian integration does not go through smoothly for all forms of Weber functions (e.g., formulation of the near miss), it does hold for the affine versions discussed in chapter 4 (Baird & Noma, 1978, chap. 4; Luce & Edwards, 1958). Therefore, the predicted exponent of the Power Law is the ratio of the Weber fractions for the response attribute in respect to the stimulus attribute. If the same response continuum (e.g., numbers or length of lines or handgrip force) is matched against all others, then the numerator ($k_r$) of the predicted exponent is a constant, which means that the size of the Stevens exponent ($k_r/k_s$) is inversely related to the size of the Weber fraction ($k_s$).

## Empirical Justification

Baird (1970a, 1970b; Baird & Noma, 1978), R. Teghtsoonian (1971), and Link (1992) independently compiled lists of exponents and Weber fractions for a variety of attributes and came to essentially the same conclusion. The summary data compiled by Baird and Noma are presented in Figure 6.3, except that one value has been changed—the exponent for electric shock is taken to be 1.

For this collection of studies (Figure 6.3), the exponent is directly related to the inverse of the Weber fraction (r = 0.82). Realize, however, that these data were compiled from a variety of experiments, not all done in the same laboratory with the same stimulus conditions and method. This introduces a note of caution into the acceptance of the conjecture relating exponents and Weber fractions, even though other compilations of data indicate an even stronger relation of this kind (Link, 1992; R. Teghtsoonian, 1971).

Not all the published data summaries agree with the relation shown in Figure 6.3. For instance, Laming (1989) felt the evidence does not support a connection between Weber fractions and exponents. He referred to a data set collected under comparable experimental conditions in the same laboratory. It is not stated in the published note exactly what these experimental conditions were, but Laming

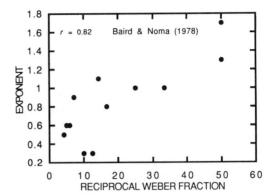

FIG. 6.3.  Stevens exponent as a function of the reciprocal of the Weber fraction. Each point is a different attribute. Empirical data from Baird and Noma (1978).

reported a much weaker relation between the exponent and the Weber fraction than is noted by others. Although he did not give the correlation coefficient between Weber fractions and exponents, from the graph presented the r value appears to be less than 0.5.

## Theoretical Implications

The Sensory Aggregate Model states that each stimulus presentation leads to a unique output distribution of firing rates over a subset of the population of sensory neurons. The neural property coding stimulus intensity is the same as the one coding stimulus difference. Intensity is coded by mean firing rate of the population and is represented at the psychophysical level by Stevens's Law. Response variability is directly related to the variability of firing rates comprising

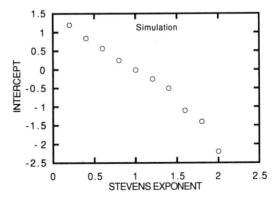

FIG. 6.4.  x axis: Stevens exponent. y axis: Intercept of the function relating logarithm of relative error (standard deviation divided by the mean) to the logarithm of stimulus intensity. Data generated by the Sensory Aggregate Model.

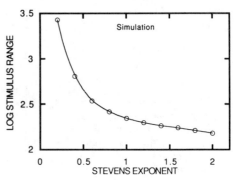

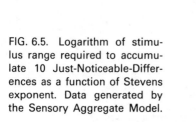
FIG. 6.5. Logarithm of stimulus range required to accumulate 10 Just-Noticeable-Differences as a function of Stevens exponent. Data generated by the Sensory Aggregate Model.

the ensemble. The relation between variability and stimulus intensity is described by a Weber function that is monotonically increasing with increases in stimulus intensity. For large Stevens exponents, however, the Weber function asymptotes at the high intensities (chap. 4).

Figure 6.4 shows the relation predicted by the model between the log of the Weber fraction and the Stevens exponent, from the simulations summarized by Tables 3.2 and 4.1. Small Weber fractions (y intercept of the function relating $log$ $\Delta S/S$ and $log$ S) are associated with large exponents.

Figure 6.5 presents the relation between the stimulus range required to accommodate a fixed number of JNDs and the Stevens exponent (Table 4.2). Consistent with the data in Figure 6.4, the graph indicates that those sensory systems leading to high exponents show high sensitivity to stimulus differences at the local level: the greater the density of JNDs, the greater the local sensitivity, and the higher the Stevens exponent. The relation for the simulation is nonlinear, however. So the overall picture is consistent with Teghtsoonian's proposal of a link between range, exponent, and Weber fraction, but the details are somewhat different.

## MEASUREMENT THEORY QUALIFICATIONS

### Physical Measures

The psychophysicist measures two variables: stimulus intensity and the subject's response. The intensity of the stimulus is measured by physical instruments, such as rulers and sound level meters. The responses may also be measured by physical instruments, such as when determining the size of the JND by the methods of constant stimuli, average error, or limits. Consequently, the conclusions one draws from these measures and their interrelations are limited by the invariance of the measures used in formulating empirical principles or laws. It is tacitly accepted that so long as the experimenter relies on the fundamental measures of physics, the representations of data will be such as to allow conclusions about the underlying neural structures responsible for generating the laboratory data. Chief among these conclusions is that the relative size of indices such as the Weber fraction, the Stevens and Piéron exponents reflect differences in the sensitivity of the sensory mechanisms responsible for processing information for the attributes in question. This view is explicit in the writings of S. S. Stevens (1975), Marks (1974b), and of most other sensory psychophysicists (Baird & Noma, 1978).

A potential problem with accepting these fundamental measures at face value arises because from the standpoint of physics it is possible to define stimulus events in equivalent ways without loss of meaning.[2] The classic example is the measurement of sound intensity. It can be represented either in energy ($I$) or pressure ($p$) units in respect to some standard ($I_0$ and $p_0$). The relation between the two measures is a power transformation:

$$I/I_0 = (p/p_0)^2 \tag{6.5}$$

The difficulty created by alternative physical measures occurs when stating the size of the Stevens exponent or the Weber fraction. The exponent for loudness based on pressure units is 0.6, whereas the value based on energy units is 0.3. This is because in logarithmic units the range for energy is twice as large as for pressure, while the response range is the same for both. Similarly, if the numerator and denominator of the Weber fraction are both squared in going from pressure to energy, the fraction itself changes accordingly. The problem, then, is that the relative size of the sensitivity index for loudness in respect to the other attributes depends on the physical units used to measure the sound. For example, if the exponent is 0.3 for loudness, then the sensitivity of the ear would be equated with the sensitivity of the eye (luminance has an exponent of 0.3). On the other hand, if the "true" exponent is 0.6, then audition actually exhibits greater sensitivity and is closer to the olfactory sense in its processing of airborne chemicals such as heptane (exponent of 0.6 in Table 3.1). The dilemma this poses for psychophysical theory is commented on by several authors (Krueger, 1991; Myers, 1982; Weiss, 1981), and more recently, the measurement issues involved in using physical measures in psychophysical laws is explored by Narens and Mausfeld (1992). They stated that

(a) from the point of view of theoretical physics the stimulus can be characterized in many different but physically equivalent ways, and (b) the physical theory does not depend on which of these equivalent ways are used in the formulation. Thus, from

---

[2] I am grateful to R. Duncan Luce for keeping me apprised of developments in this field.

this point of view, it is only a matter of convention which equivalent way is used to characterize the stimulus in psychophysics." (1993, p. 468.)

Narens and Mausfield went on to show that statements about the relative sensitivity of sensory systems are not meaningful because they depend on the faulty assumption that the physical stimulus for each attribute has just one valid unit of measure (aside from multiplication by a constant, such as in going from meters to centimeters).[3] The only example of this type of measurement issue in the literature concerns sound intensity. Presumably there are others.

By this view, the only valid measure of the relative sensitivity of different sense modalities discussed in previous chapters is the number of JNDs over a fixed stimulus range or over the entire dynamic range of an attribute. Consider an experiment of the following sort. A subject adjusts a comparison to be just noticeably larger than a standard. This comparison then serves as a standard on the next trial and a second JND is determined, and so on, until the stimulus range extends 2 log units. Do this for different attributes and compare the relative density of JNDs. It does not matter how the experimenter chooses to measure the physical values of the stimuli in this experiment. The number of JNDs tallied by this procedure will always be the same, because the subject's decision about a difference does not depend on the experimenter's physical units.

The outcome of such an experiment can be predicted by knowing the Weber fraction. Small Weber fractions indicate a high density of JND steps per unit intensity range and large Weber fractions indicate a low density. Hence, the number of JNDs in a fixed stimulus range relates in a systematic way to Weber fractions, Stevens exponents, and Piéron exponents. According to Narens and Mausfield, it is possible to transform the stimulus measures for different attributes in such a way that the relative size of these indices are rearranged, except for the number of JNDs. Therefore, once the experimenter makes these various transformations of the physical units, the number of JNDs would no longer relate in a systematic fashion to the other sensitivity indices. But then we must conclude that the systematic relation among present-day indices for different sense modalities, though regular (monotonic at least), is entirely fortuitous.

It is important to realize that the Narens and Mausfield argument applies to statements about the relative sensitivity of different sense modalities. The argument does not invalidate conclusions regarding the unification of psychophysical laws in terms of a common underlying physiological code. That is to say, if the same units of measure are used for a single attribute tested with different psychophysical methods (both local and global), then logical inferences can be drawn about whether or not all such data share a common physiological source.

If the experimenter is consistent in measuring the physical stimuli across methods, then the relative ordering of the Weber fractions can be compared with

---

[3]The technical problem is subtle. The Weber fraction, $\Delta S/S$, is inadmissable because it depends on a particular choice of concatenation, but the ratio $(S + \Delta S)/S$ is meaningful.

the relative ordering of Stevens or Piéron functions in order to make inferences about whether or not these laws interrelate in a meaningful way. Nothing need be said here about the relative sensitivity of different sensory modalities in processing stimulus information. For example, the fact that different exponents arise for the loudness of different sound frequencies is evidence that the sensitivity of the auditory system to intensity information depends on frequency.

It seems to me that if it were possible to use exactly the same physical measures (e.g., energy units) for all stimulus attributes, then this measurement issue would disappear. Under these circumstances, theorists could make legitimate claims about relative sensitivity. A distinction, therefore, is necessary between the restrictions of the psychophysical laboratory and the models intended to explain the orderly results observed there. The Sensory Aggregate Model assumes a common measure of physical intensity and a common measure of sensation (neuronal firing rate) for all attributes. If one likes, in terms of theory, the receptor level can be skipped altogether and the stimulus equated with electrical stimulation of nerves, such as the optic (vision) and the VIIIth (audition), and the sensation equated with neuronal firing rate. Because of this commonality, theoretical inferences are admissable about relative perceptual sensitivity. The empirical question is whether the model offers an adequate account of psychophysical results in the light of its assumptions about sensory physiology. Eventually, of course, it would be desirable to know whether the model is supported by the neurophysiological evidence. Granted, we should be prepared to learn that the relative sensitivity for different attributes determined by physiological methods is not identical with the relative sensitivity determined by psychophysics.

In other words, the question posed by measurement theorists about the alternative units for measuring sound and other physical qualities may someday be mooted by the findings of neurophysiology. Is the activity of the auditory system in processing the intensity of a 1000-Hz tone the same in principle as that of the visual system in processing the luminance of a red light, or is it more like the olfactory system's response to heptane? This remains a meaningful question in the context of the Sensory Aggregate Model. A set of neurons signals the brain about a stimulus magnitude. The model makes claims about the organization and relative density of these neurons in different sensory modalities. An empirical test in the physiological domain could in principle determine whether or not this theory is correct.

## Judgment Measures

Another matter often raised by measurement theorists is whether psychophysical judgment involves a matching procedure or whether some ratio operation is always involved. Both Krantz (1972) and Shepard (1978) suggested that subjects in tasks such as Magnitude Estimation and Cross Modality Matching make relational judgments of some kind, either in respect to an explicit or implicit standard. Essentially the same opinion is taken throughout Baird (1970c) on visual space perception. On the other side, Luce (1990) proposed a formal axiomatic model that has subjects in psychophysical tasks matching stimuli rather than estimating their intensities relative to a standard. The distinctions between the two positions are not clearcut. For example, suppose the result of a matching procedure (Method of Adjustment) produces a comparison stimulus that is one JND above a standard stimulus. The ratio of the comparison and standard for different standards might satisfy Weber's Law, which is a ratio invariance.

The Sensory Aggregate Model is consistent with the position that in Cross Modality Matching a subject adjusts the magnitude of one attribute to match the magnitude of another. In the nervous system, this match is represented by equivalent firing rates: one produced by attribute 1, the other by attribute 2. In this sense at least, the model is consistent with the "matching" view of psychophysical judgment.

The opinions of Krantz (1972) and Shepard (1978) are more in keeping with the second part of the Complementarity Theory of Psychophysics. This alternative conception suggests that judgment processes are only loosely coupled to sensory mechanisms and depend heavily on subject strategies. The relativity argument is explored at great length beginning with the discussion of the number preference model in chapter 8.[4]

## OVERVIEW

The Sensory Aggregate Model offers a framework for evaluating conjectures about the connections among psychophysical laws and their associated empirical phenomena. The model makes two clear predictions: There is an inverse relation between the Stevens exponent for global scaling and the Piéron exponent for simple reaction time. And there is an inverse relation between the Stevens exponent and the Weber fraction (details depending on the nature of the Weber function).

This leaves unresolved the conjecture regarding stimulus range and the Stevens exponent. This issue can only be settled by finding out if the response distributions for all Stevens functions are the same. Based on the available data, it does not appear that this is true. If not, then the exponents of the Stevens function most likely depend on the transducer properties of the different sensory systems and are therefore independent of stimulus range. The Sensory Aggregate Model offers a theoretical platform for designing experiments to decide such matters one way or the other.

---

[4]Garriga-Trillo (1995) presented an alternative use of Axiomatic Measurement Theory for examining the connection between the results of local and global psychophysics. She found that results from the two levels are related by an affine transformation.

# 7 Memory Psychophysics

In the early 1960s, the Stockholm psychophysics laboratory, under the direction of Gösta Ekman, conducted preliminary studies concerning the estimation of stimuli not directly viewed at the time of judgment, but experienced at some time in the past. In the first wave of experiments, Björkman, Lundberg, and Tarnblom (1960) had subjects judge the ratio between a stimulus directly perceived and a recalled stimulus designated by a name learned previously. Additional studies tested more unusual stimuli, such as the distance between cities of the world (Ekman & Bratfish, 1965), a paradigm that led eventually to the psychophysical study of "cognitive maps" (Baird, 1979). The experimental situations of interest in this chapter, however, are those in which subjects recall simpler objects such as lines, circles, and balls.

## MEMORY PSYCHOPHYSICS

In 1978, two articles appeared on the estimation of physical stimuli that were not actually presented, but were recalled from previous exposure. Moyer, Bradley, Sorensen, Whiting, and Mansfield (1978) first taught subjects to associate non-sense names with five line lengths until mastery was achieved. Twenty-four hours later, the subject pool was split into two groups who used Free Magnitude Estimation (no modulus) and gave estimates of length relying either on immediate perception of the lines or on recall of their apparent length from the previous learning phase. In the test phase, the experimenter stated the nonsense label for the line and the subject gave a numerical estimate. In two further experiments, estimates from memory were given for visual area (apparent size of states on a map of the United States) and visual volume (familiar spheres, such as a Ping-Pong ball and a beach ball).

The authors summarize their work as follows: "For the one-, two- and three-dimensional objects, power functions fit to the memory data have consistently smaller exponents than power functions fit to the perceptual data" (Moyer et al., 1978, p. 331). The functions referred to are determined by plotting the estimates in the perception and memory conditions against the same set of physical intensities (obtained by physical measurement of these familiar objects). At about the same time, these findings were independently corroborated by Kerst and Howard (1978).

The three panels of Figure 7.1 show the data reported by Moyer et al. (1978). In addition to the fact that the memory exponent is always less than the perception exponent,[1] it is critical to note that each pair of memory-perception functions converges at a point representing a pair of the higher values on the x and y axes. The chief difference between the memory and the perception functions occurs for the weakest intensities. In memory the smallest stimuli are perceived as larger than they are in direct perception. The perception function rotates upward into the memory function with the center of rotation in the vicinity of the largest stimulus.

## The Sensory Aggregate Model

The Moyer et al. (1978) result requiring explanation is that the exponent of Stevens's Law is smaller in memory than it is in perception, and the major discrepancy occurs for the weakest stimuli. This effect does not seem to be caused by an increase in memory variability. In a related study, Hubbard (1991) found no substantial difference in the standard deviation of judgments based on memory and perception. If anything, the variability in the memory condition was less than in the perception condition.

An interpretation of the Moyer et al. data in terms of the Sensory Aggregate Model is grounded on the auxiliary assumption that the neural output distribution is not faithfully represented and/or recalled over time. The original neural ensemble is modified over time such that the slowest firing and/or the fastest-firing neurons are omitted. This loss modifies the mean of the distribution in predictable ways, and leads to data resembling that shown in Figure 7.1.

Suppose first the neurons firing at a slow rate are missing or somehow lost from the stored representation of the output distribution. This could happen because the activation of these neurons in memory is confused with the spontaneous firing of currently active neurons or of those firing in the past. Unless the

---

[1]The slopes of the functions differ somewhat from those in the original study. I probably was not completely accurate in recording the points from the original graphs. The deviations between the original plots and those in Figure 7.1 are minor.

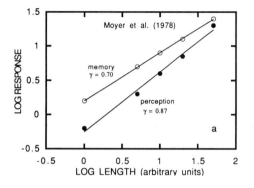

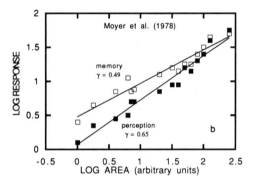

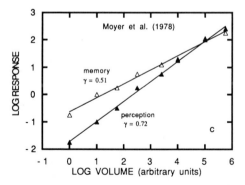

FIG. 7.1.   Mean magnitude estimate as a function of stimulus intensity (log–log coordinates) from perception and memory: (a) visual length, (b) visual area, (c) visual volume. After Moyer et al. (1978).

rate is high enough, the activity of these neurons might not be stored in memory or might be the first to exit memory with the passage of time. With longer time intervals between judgment and the original stimulus presentation, the neural trace of the stimulus is characterized more and more by the memory traces of the faster firing neurons.

Now consider the other end of the firing-rate distribution. The memory representation of the fastest firing neurons may also disappear with the passage of time, depending on the neural code used for maintaining this information in memory. If a disproportionate amount of resources is allocated to the fastest firing neurons, the system may bypass such representations in favor of neurons firing less vigorously.

The easiest way to grasp this conception of the firing-rate distribution (in memory) is to consider the lognormal threshold distribution associated with some arbitrary stimulus. Figure 7.2 depicts a hypothetical threshold distribution for a single stimulus whose location is indicated by the arrow. The probability density below the stimulus characterizes all the neurons whose thresholds are exceeded by the stimulus, and that are active in direct perception. The two vertical lines marking off the section containing the cross-lines are hypothetical boundaries on the neural representation still in memory. The cross-lines specify the part of the perceptual distribution that is still active (represented) after some time has passed. The low cutoff eliminates those neurons with thresholds farthest from the stimulus intensity; that is to say, those with the fastest firing rates. The high cutoff excludes neurons whose thresholds are just exceeded by the stimulus. These are the ones in the ensemble firing at the slowest rate.

What is the impact of each cutoff on the mean firing rate of the entire ensemble? As the low cutoff moves to the right in the direction of the stimulus, the mean firing rate declines. As the high cutoff moves to the left away from the stimulus, the mean firing rate of the ensemble increases. Different shifts in the mean of the memory representation in respect to the perceptual representation is produced by variations in the position of these two cutoffs.

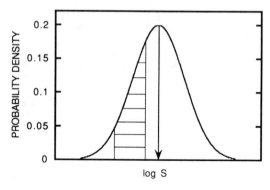

FIG. 7.2. Hypothetical probability density of neuronal thresholds. The arrowhead indicates stimulus intensity. The horizontal lines demark those fibers whose firing rates are represented in memory.

The particular data obtained by Moyer et al. (1978), shown in Figure 7.1, can be mimicked by introducing a high cutoff into each of the threshold distributions of the Sensory Aggregate Model associated with each stimulus intensity. This is a three-parameter model: the mean and standard deviation of the threshold distribution and the high cutoff. Figure 7.3 schematizes the hypothetical situation at the neural level. The left panel (7.3a) depicts the threshold distribution (cross-lines) associated with a weak stimulus, the right panel (7.3b) depicts the corresponding distribution for a strong stimulus. Each attribute has only one full distribution over the stimulus range, but specific stimuli activate neuronal subsets of this distribution. The differences between neuronal representations are signified by the positions of the truncation points delimiting each subsection.

For purposes of illustration, a simulation with a fixed high cutoff of 0.1 log units was conducted. This eliminates the contribution of slow-firing neurons along the stimulus threshold dimension that are within 0.1 log units below the stimulus intensity (log $S - 0.1$). Figure 7.4 shows the results from this simulation for perception exponents of 1 (visual length), 0.8 (visual area), and 0.6 (visual volume). These values are typical for these three attributes (Baird, 1970c).

The filled points are the perception means, without a cutoff. The open points are the memory means with a high cutoff for each section of the threshold distribution appropriate for each stimulus. In all three cases, the memory exponent is less than the perception exponent, and the pivot point is located in the vicinity of the strongest stimulus. For memory, the mean magnitude for the weakest intensity increases more than the mean for the strongest intensity. The means for intermediate magnitudes shift proportionally so that the function remains linear in the double logarithmic plot.

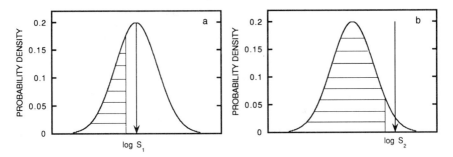

FIG. 7.3. Hypothetical probability density of neuronal thresholds. The arrowhead indicates stimulus intensity. The horizontal lines demark those fibers whose firing rates are represented in memory for stimuli of different intensity (diagrams a & b). The vertical line without an arrowhead indicates the location of the high cutoff along the threshold dimension.

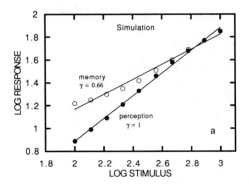

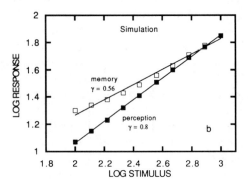

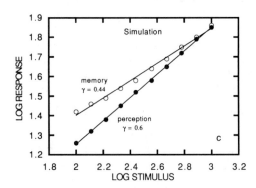

FIG. 7.4.   Mean response magnitude (firing rate) as a function of stimulus intensity (log–log coordinates) from perception and memory.
Simulation data are for perception exponents of (a) 1, (b) 0.8, and (c)
0.6 along with their associated memory data. Results generated by the
Sensory Aggregate Model with a high cutoff of 0.1 log units.

The explanation for the differential shift in the mean for stimuli of different intensity can be appreciated by consulting the two sample distributions in Figure 7.3. For the weak stimulus (left panel), the impact of the cutoff is great. Relative to the entire distribution, the elimination of the slowest firing neurons is significant because they comprise a large proportion of the original threshold distribution for perception. Hence, the memory mean for the weak stimulus increases relative to its perception mean. On the other hand, this same cutoff has practically no consequences for the strong stimulus. Because the bulk of the original perception distribution contains neurons untouched by the cutoff, its impact is minimal. Hence, the memory mean is almost the same as the perception mean for the strong stimulus. The overall result is that the functional relation between the mean firing rate and physical intensity pivots at the strongest intensity. The slope of the memory function is shallower than the slope of the perception function. This is the same pattern Moyer et al. (1978) found (Figure 7.1). No attempt was made to fit the empirical data, though this could easily be done by appropriate choice of a cutoff for each of the three attributes.

## Memory for Other Attributes

After reviewing some 70 studies of memory psychophysics, Wiest and Bell (1985) concluded that the majority of findings are consistent with the initial studies by Moyer et al. (1978) and by Kerst and Howard (1978). The memory exponent is usually less than the perception exponent. Algom (1992a) updated this review by considering work on memory psychophysics for many additional attributes—including brightness, loudness, auditory volume, weight, and haptic extent. This newer research lends some credence to the early studies, while also showing that memory exponents are not always less than perception exponents. For example, Algom and Marks (1989) did not find statistical differences between memory and perception exponents for the perceived taste of sucrose, and Algom and Cain (1991a, 1991b) reported no differences in the exponents for perceived and recalled magnitude of the banana-smelling substance, amyl acetate. The Stevens exponents for odor are relatively small (approximately 0.3) in comparison to other attributes, but those for the taste of sucrose are not exceptional one way or the other (approximately 0.8). In several experiments referred to by Algom (1992a), the memory exponent is even greater than the perception exponent (e.g., roughness of papers). Despite the fact that some of the experiments reviewed by Algom strike me as preliminary, it is clear that matters regarding memory psychophysics are not as simple as the initial studies might lead us to believe.

These recent findings suggest that the passage of time has differential effects on perceived magnitude depending on the attribute. The exponent does not always diminish over time in the manner of the early studies. The Sensory Aggregate Model provides a framework for considering all such findings. Exactly the same high cutoff that generates the data in Figure 7.4 leads to different memory exponents depending on the size of the corresponding perception exponent. Figure 7.5 shows results of a high cutoff (0.1 log units) for two extreme perception exponents of 0.2 and 2. There is a massive drop in the memory exponent when the perception exponent is large, but the decline is barely noticeable when the perception exponent is small. Under laboratory conditions, the variability of psychophysical judgments could easily swamp any effects that might exist for the memory of attributes with small perception exponents. Perhaps this explains why Algom and Cain (1991a, 1991b) did not find a significant difference between the memory and perception functions for amyl acetate. The exponent for this odorous substance is small. This does not explain the fact that Algom and Marks found no differences between the perception and memory of sucrose concentrations. Both taste exponents fall well within the range where differences between perception and memory occur in these particular simulations.

The goal of computer simulation is to show that data patterns produced by the model are similar to those seen in the laboratory. The reason the model generates such different predictions for large and small perception exponents can be understood by reviewing the specific parameter values of the lognormal distribution. Small Stevens exponents are associated with distributions that have a relatively high mean and large standard deviation, whereas large exponents are associated with distributions possessing a relatively small mean and small standard deviation. The position of stimuli relative to statistical landmarks (mean, z scores, etc.) of the distributions depends on the attribute. As shown in Figure 7.3, for large exponents, the weakest and strongest stimuli are located on opposite sides of the mean of the overall threshold distribution. This is not true for the smaller perception exponents. Here, the mean falls at the upper end of the intensity dimension, and hence, all stimuli are situated below the mean in the left tail of the distribution.

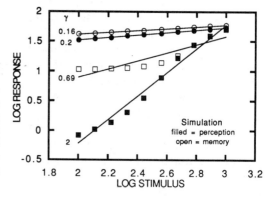

FIG. 7.5. Mean response magnitude (firing rate) as a function of stimulus intensity (log–log coordinates) from perception and memory. Results generated by the Sensory Aggregate Model with a high cutoff of 0.1 log units.

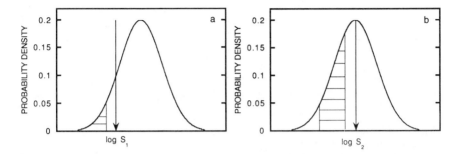

FIG. 7.6. Hypothetical probability density for neuronal thresholds. The arrowhead indicates stimulus intensity. The horizontal lines demark those fibers whose firing rates are represented in memory for stimuli of different intensity (diagrams a & b). The vertical line without an arrowhead indicates the location of the high cutoff along the threshold dimension. Figure 7.6b is identical to Figure 7.3a.

Figure 7.6 schematizes the situation leading to a memory exponent associated with an attribute yielding a small perception exponent. The effect of a high cutoff is quite different than it is in the situation depicted in Figure 7.3. When the Stevens exponent is small, the high cutoff eliminates a substantial part of the probability density function for each stimulus in the series. The probability density is standardized to only include those fibers left in the distribution. Consequently, the slope of the Stevens function in a logarithmic plot does not diminish as much as it does when the perception exponent is large.

There is no reason to believe that the passage of time has exactly the same effect on all attributes. Both the high and low cutoffs may be in different locations at different points in time and for different attributes. The effect of time on the Stevens exponent may be a complex function of duration, stimulus range, and attribute. A four-parameter Sensory Aggregate Model would be required to accommodate all such data. If this model were successful, then the next step might be to seek the neural mechanisms responsible.

## EFFECTS OF TIME ON THE EXPONENT

Most studies of memory psychophysics test subjects after 24 hours have elapsed between learning the codes and estimating the stimuli. It is likely, however, that the exponent declines gradually with time, rather than shifting abruptly to a lower plateau. Hubbard (1991) varied the time between learning the codes for stimuli and estimating magnitude from memory. Figure 7.7 gives a sample of his findings for visual line length, area, and distance. There is a systematic decline

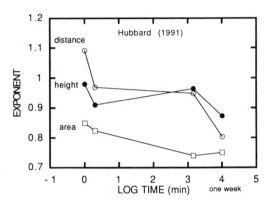

FIG. 7.7. Memory exponent as a function of logarithm of time. Empirical data from Hubbard (1991) for visual distance, height, and area.

in the exponent with time, a trend that is significant in one study, but not in a second. The x axis is the logarithm of the time in minutes, so for example, a log value of 4 corresponds to a time interval of approximately 1 week. From Figure 7.7, it can be inferred that the changes in exponent occur over a span of minutes, perhaps even seconds, rather than over hours or days. In this regard, it seems that a tactical error was made in the selection of time intervals for Hubbard's study. It would be informative to have more extensive data for very short time intervals (minutes, hours). Nonetheless, it is clear that the effects due to temporal interval are not the same for all attributes.

## REGRESSION EFFECTS

In addition to Magnitude Estimation S. S. Stevens pioneered and encouraged the use of several related methods that did not involve numbers as a response continuum. In Magnitude Estimation, subjects assign numbers to stimulus intensity; in Magnitude Production, the procedure is reversed and subjects adjust the intensity of a stimulus to match a number stated by the experimenter. The method of Magnitude Production is the inverse of Magnitude Estimation, but this does not mean that the subject's task in one situation is the inverse of the other.

In Cross Modality Matching, the subject matches the intensities of one attribute to those of another. For example, the brightness of a light is adjusted to match the loudness of a tone. It would be convenient for theoretical argument if the results of these various techniques agreed insofar as the exponents of the power function were internally consistent. Such consistency is not universally achieved (Baird, Green, & Luce, 1980; Mashour & Hosman, 1968).

If the results of Magnitude Estimation and Production are presented in the same graph (identical variables represented by the x and y axes), the slope of the function in logarithmic coordinates is usually steeper for Magnitude Production than it is for Magnitude Estimation. In cross-modality matching, the two slopes (exponents) often differ, depending on which of the two attributes is the independent variable controlled by the experimenter, and which is the dependent variable controlled by the subject.

Figure 7.8 shows an example of these effects from a study by S. S. Stevens and Greenbaum (1966). Subjects either matched numbers to the loudness of a band of noise (magnitude estimation) or they matched loudness to numbers (magnitude production). The values along the x axis represent the sound intensity of the noise; those along the y axis represent the magnitude of the numbers (both are log scales). In Magnitude Estimation, the dependent variable under the subject's control is the number scale (y axis), whereas in Magnitude Production the dependent variable is the sound intensity (x axis). The data are plotted in this way to aid visual comparison between the slopes of the two functions. In the example given, the exponent for Magnitude Production is higher than for Magnitude Estimation.

A discrepancy of this sort also occurs in Cross Modality Matching. J. C. Stevens and Marks (1965) reported an experiment in which subjects adjusted the luminance of a white light to match the loudness of a band of noise and then adjusted the amplitude of the noise to match the brightness of the light. Figure 7.9 gives their results. The linear function in logarithmic coordinates is steeper when the light is matched to the sound than when the sound is matched to the light.

S. S. Stevens (1975) believed that the *regression effects* illustrated in Figures 7.8 and 7.9 occur in all matching experiments, and claimed their cause could be traced to the tendency for subjects to compress the range of whichever variable they adjust (see also Cross, 1974). If the dependent variable under the control of the subject is numbers, then the range of numbers used to convey perceived

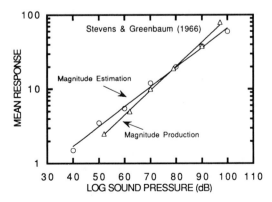

FIG. 7.8. Mean magnitude estimation (open circles) and magnitude production (open triangles) of sound intensity (log–log coordinates). After S. S. Stevens and Greenbaum (1966).

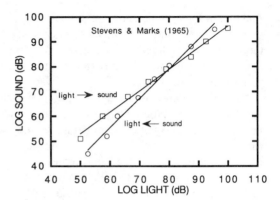

FIG. 7.9. Cross-modality matches of sound to light (open squares) and light to sound (open circles). The axes are log-arithmic. After J. C. Stevens and Marks (1965).

intensity is compressed; if the dependent variable is the intensity of a tone, then its range is compressed, and so forth. The reason for this opinion is as follows.

Consider the two linear functions in Figure 7.9. When the light is adjusted to match the sound (open circles), the range of light intensities is less than the sound intensities. On the other hand, when the roles of the independent and dependent variables are reversed (open squares), the opposite is true. The range of sound is less than the range of light. It is certainly the case that the attribute under the subject's control is compressed relative to the attribute controlled by the experimenter.

Despite its reasonableness, Stevens's interpretation rests on the implicit assumption that the intensity of an attribute is accurately recalled during the interval separating presentation of the target and comparison stimuli.

## SENSORY INTERPRETATION OF REGRESSION

Regression effects by themselves, without the additional assumption of perfect memory, indicate nothing one way or the other about whether the subjects compress the variable under their control. All that can be said is that the relative slopes of the two functions differ when the independent and dependent variables are interchanged. The possibility that the memory of the neural aggregate associated with a stimulus undergoes change over time opens up alternative possibilities for explaining regression effects.

Suppose the independent variable is a light and the dependent variable is the number scale, as in Magnitude Estimation. The stimulus is turned on and off once and the subject states a number. During the time interval between termination of the stimulus and verbalization of the response, the memory representation (trace) of the stimulus drifts in that the traces of the slow-firing neurons drop out of the aggregate. This assumption receives support from the Hubbard data showing that the exponent falls following stimulus offset.

If now the independent and dependent variables are reversed, the subject is told a number and must produce a sound intensity, as in Magnitude Production. Unlike the case with Magnitude Estimation, the independent variable is a number and the neural representation of the number does not change with the passage of time. If the experimenter asks the subject to produce a sound that matches the number "10," it seems unlikely that after a few seconds the memory representation will have drifted up to "11" or down to "9." The number "10" will most probably remain the number "10." Therefore, Magnitude Production is a more valid method for obtaining the exponent than is Magnitude Estimation, because the stimulus representation in memory stays put during the time needed to emit a response. There is no compression of the response scale in Magnitude Production; but, compression occurs in Magnitude Estimation because of changes in the memory representation of the physical stimuli. Magnitude Production may be a more diffcult task for the subject, however, and this complicates interpretation.

In Cross Modality Matching, the differences in exponent from designating one or the other attribute as the dependent variable under the control of the subject might occur because of differences in the relative amount of drift in the mean of the memory representations for the two attributes. Drift occurs regardless of which attribute is designated as the stimulus or response continuum. The shift of the power function, of course, depends on the specific nature of the neural distribution (attribute) and the particular class of neurons leaving the memory store as time elapses.

The viability of this hypothesis concerning the reason for regression effects rests heavily on details of stimulus presentation. For example, if the stimulus is left "on" continuously during the period it takes to produce a response, then one might expect regression effects to disappear. Even here, however, momentary shifts in attention between stimulus and response continua may affect the internal memory representations.

A similar explanation for a shift in category estimates toward the mean of the response scale was proposed in the last century by Leuba (1892). In his study of the perceived brightness of simulated stars, he used a standard at the low end of the stimulus scale and noted:

> We should expect that the lower standard . . . , being a just perceptible star, would assume in the subject's memory a magnitude greater than the real. This very plausible hypothesis received confirmation in the second lot of our experiments, in the fact that the subjects generally designated as equal to the lower limit stars superior to it in intensity. (p. 383)

Such results eventually led to hypotheses concerning the predilection of subjects to compress their response scales for all manner of judgments (Hollingworth, 1910). More recently, Poulton (1989) revived the notion that such tendencies should be treated as "response biases," not attributable to properties intrinsic to the sensory systems. The extension of the Sensory Aggregate Model to explain regression effects in magnitude matching experiments is closer in spirit to Leuba's opinion than it is to Poulton's.

A related phenomenon concerns the effect of interstimulus time on the JND. It has been realized for over 50 years that the JND is critically affected by the time interval separating presentation of the standard and comparison stimuli (LeGrand, 1957). For example, in an experiment involving brightness discrimination, Graf, Baird, and Glesman (1974) employed two interstimulus intervals. In one condition, the standard and comparison lights appeared adjacent to each other and simultaneously for a period of 4 sec, and observers stated whether the comparison was brighter or dimmer than the standard. In the second condition, the standard appeared for 4 sec, followed by a 10-sec delay in the dark, after which the comparison appeared for 4 sec. The experiment was conducted with both a dim and a bright standard. The Weber fractions (JND/standard) averaged over the responses of untrained subjects for the simultaneous condition was 0.14 for the dim standard and 0.09 for the bright one, as compared with results under successive presentation (with a time delay) where the Weber fraction was 0.17 for the dim standard and 0.20 for the bright one.

In discrimination tasks, the subject must recall the "on" states of an entire array of sensory cells that are excited by the standard, and it is this agglomerate that is so hard to recall over time and compare against the "on" states produced by the comparison. The memory store does not contain representations of all the neurons activated in direct perception. The data reviewed in this chapter suggests that stimuli are perceived to be more alike in memory, perhaps more so as time passes. The Stevens exponent declines. This is why the level of performance deteriorates with increasing time separating presentation of the standard and comparison stimuli.

## TIME-ORDER ERROR

A much older finding related to memory psychophysics is the time-order effect (Woodworth & Schlosberg, 1954), also referred to as the time-order error. Fechner (1860/1966) was the first to identify this phenomenon, because it caused him considerable grief in the course of his experimentation with lifted weights. If one presents a standard weight followed by itself, the second weight is not always judged equal to the first. Fechner reported a number of such effects all contingent on either the spatial positions (left and right) of two successive stimuli or on their temporal relation (which came first). Fechner (1966) vented his frustration over attempts to eliminate these errors:

One might regard these results with suspicion and attribute many of these observations to the influence of imagination. However, after one has tried out these methods oneself, he will soon be convinced that he cannot escape these constant errors, try as he may. Since the influence of imagination was practically ruled out in what I observed in this connection, I must admit that this quite unexpected occurrence of constant errors in these experiments was most puzzling to me in the beginning, and before I managed to eliminate them, most embarrassing. Even today, after much work in this area, particularly in the measurement of weight and touch, a great deal is not clear to me about their ultimate cause and only the fact itself is certain. (pp. 75–76)

Since Fechner wrote this, the problem has become more, not less, perplexing. Hellström (1985) presented a bewildering array of findings and conditions related to time-order errors. The two prominent types are identified as negative and positive. If a comparison target follows a standard and is adjusted to match its intensity, there are only three possible outcomes: The comparison equals the standard (as determined by physical measurement) in which case there is no time-order error. The comparison is less than the standard, producing a negative time order error. Or, the comparison is greater than the standard, producing a positive time-order error.

There are two broad perspectives on the cause of these errors. One attributes them to response bias, the other sees them as consequences of actual perceptual or memorial processes taking place during and after stimulus presentation. Hellström (1985) offered a convincing case against most response-bias interpretations and proposed his own perceptual model (Hellström, 1977, 1979). The approach involves differential weighting of the sensations (defined by Stevens's Power Law) associated with the standard and comparison stimuli. The relative weights attached to these successive targets are parameters in a linear equation fit to the empirical data. Hellström's model does quite well at describing the main results in the field.

The aspect of this research of special relevance to the Sensory Aggregate Model and memory psychophysics concerns the direction of the time-order error for standards of different intensity. In one experiment, Hellström (1978) presented 1000-Hz tones in succession and subjects judged the perceived magnitude of one in respect to the other. The main findings are that the time-order error is positive when the tones are soft and negative when the tones are loud. A positive error implies that the remembered loudness of the first tone in the pair is greater than its original perceptual magnitude, as indicated by the fact that the succeeding comparison has to be louder than the standard (as measured physically) in order to be judged identical. The direction of this error is the same as reported by Moyer et al. (1978). The small stimuli in the latter study are recalled as being larger than in perception. The positive time-order error is also consistent with Leuba's (1892) findings concerning the perceived brightness of simulated stars.

Hellström also found, however, that a negative time-order error occurs for loud sounds. This is not consistent with the findings shown in Figure 7.1 because the error for the most intense stimuli there is essentially zero.

What needs to be explained, then, in terms of the Sensory Aggregate Model is a positive time-order error at low intensities that gradually shifts into a negative time-order error at high intensities. Similar findings are reported by others (e.g., Bartlett, 1939; Fraisse, 1948; Needham, 1935). Hellström (1985) gave the details of these studies.

A computer simulation of loudness perception ($\gamma = 0.6$) was conducted with three different conditions regarding the location of the two cutoffs. The first condition was identical to that used earlier to explain the Moyer et al. (1978) data. The low cutoff was set at zero (hence, having no effect) and the high cutoff was set at log $S - 0.1$. This case is included here for comparison purposes only. In the second condition the low cutoff was set at log $S - 0.7$ log units, and the high cutoff was set equal to the stimulus (hence, having no effect). In the third condition, both cutoffs were effective. The low cutoff was log $S - 0.1$ and the high cutoff was log $S - 0.7$, both assessed as a distance in respect to each of the seven stimuli.

Figure 7.10 presents the results from the three conditions. When the slow-firing neurons are eliminated from the memory store by instituting the high cutoff, a positive time-order error occurs for the weak stimuli and this error gradually dissipates to zero with increasing stimulus intensity (Figure 7.10a). This graph is the same as Figure 7.4a. When the low cutoff alone is operational, a negative time-order error occurs for the strong stimuli and the effect declines to zero for the weakest stimulus (Figure 7.10b). Finally, if both a high and low cutoff are operational, it is possible to generate results corresponding to those reported by Hellström (1977, 1978). This is shown in Figure 7.10c. The perception and memory functions intersect at a medium intensity, thus leading to a positive time-order error for stimuli below the pivot and a negative time-order error for stimuli above the pivot.

By adjusting the cutoffs it is possible to achieve a variety of relations between the perception and memory functions. The Sensory Aggregate Model (two parameters), together with two cutoff parameters, provides a framework for investigating time-order errors. One prediction in the spirit of this model is that differences exist among attributes in regard to the relation between stimulus intensity and the direction and extent of time-order errors. Unfortunately, our ignorance concerning the time course of neural loss in memory prohibits us from making quantitative predictions in advance of experimentation. Because of this uncertainty, we should not expect the time-order error to be related in any obvious way to Weber fractions or Stevens and Piéron exponents.

In some ways the analysis of time-order errors is related to one advocated by Köhler (1923), whose empirical results for the attributes of sound and weight are quite similar to those of Hellström (1985). According to Köhler's theory, the first

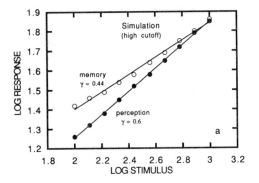

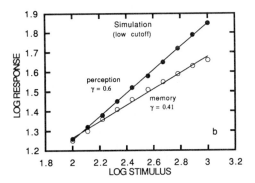

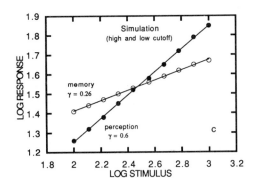

FIG. 7.10.   Perception and memory exponents for a high cutoff (a), a low cutoff (b) and for a high and low cutoff (c). Data generated by the Sensory Aggregate Model.

stimulus leaves a physiological trace in the brain, and it is this trace that is compared with the perceptual impression aroused by the succeeding stimulus. The proposals regarding the gradual disappearance of neural representations with the passage of time might be equated with Köhler's proposals concerning neural traces.

This concludes the sensory analysis of psychophysics. The discussion turns now to the complementary side of the problem and addresses empirical data from the standpoint of a judgment paradigm.

# 8 Number Preference Model

The theoretical argument to this point rests on the shoulders of one giant assumption: Data collected in the psychophysics laboratory faithfully reflect the activity states of sensory neurons that supply the neural code for stimulus events in the external world. The empirical and theoretical results of the last six chapters attest to the power of this assumption in building a model of the sensory foundation for psychophysical laws. At this juncture, however, the Complementarity Theory is only half complete. It is now time to examine the cognitive factors that influence psychophysical results.

The Sensory Aggregate Model's success in predicting psychophysical findings is only accomplished by disregarding cognition's role. Some of these same findings are open to alternative interpretation. This chapter contends that the context effects so prevalent in global psychophysics depend on psychological processes whose neural correlates are in the brain rather than in the periphery.

## JUDGMENT PSYCHOPHYSICS

Restle (1961) discussed the prospects for discovering a single psychophysical law and concluded:

> It seems that the results of a psychophysical scaling experiment depend heavily on the psychophysical method used, and therefore the results may usefully be interpreted not as measures of "perceived magnitude," which lead to an input–output relationship, but rather as *judgments* which lead to an understanding of the process of judging stimuli. (pp. 207–208)

Treating data as tied to judgment processes rather than as direct measures of sensory events leads to consideration of the decision making engaged in by subjects in global scaling tasks. Restle went on to speculate about the strategies used in methods such as Bisection, Fractionation, and Magnitude Estimation, and proposed that differences in strategies depend on whether the attribute is familiar or unfamiliar (a view echoed by Poulton, 1989). Neither Restle nor Poulton offer much in the way of quantitative models, and because of the preoccupation of experimentalists with sensory scales, models highlighting the role of cognition in psychophysics have not received an adequate hearing.

In order to rekindle the spirit of Restle's thesis, this chapter provides a cognitive basis for many psychophysical results. The aim is to identify the psychological strategies subjects use to judge stimulus intensity in global scaling tasks, such as Magnitude and Category Estimation. Although the inclusion of cognition in theories of local psychophysics is commonplace, chiefly through the influence of the Theory of Signal Detectability (TSD; Green & Swets, 1966/1974; Link, 1992; Macmillan & Creelman, 1991), this work is not treated here. Cognitive variables are less prominent in models of global psychophysics. Some years ago a two-factor model for "cognitive psychophysics" was developed, to balance the sensory interpretations that permeated the field at the time (Baird, 1970a, 1970b). Prior to this, Attneave and his colleagues made similar attempts (Curtis, Attneave, & Harrington, 1968), but until recently (Algom, 1992b) such proposals have received little attention. The purpose here is to furnish a more formal treatment of the role of cognitive and stimulus context in psychophysics.

Although no attempt is made to resuscitate the early work, the argument still follows Restle (1961) in claiming that different psychophysical methods yield results that, on the surface, appear incompatible. It then goes beyond this realization to model behavior at a more fundamental level by identifying the variables determining judgments on each trial. The goal is to achieve a unified model of the psychological factors that underlie the means and response variability associated with lawful stimulus–response relations. It is my contention that a rather small set of psychological principles are responsible for all such results. This chapter addresses Stevens functions from the standpoint of a model based on subjects' predilection to use preferred numbers in global scaling tasks. Succeeding chapters focus more on response variability than on the functional relations between stimulus intensity and mean response magnitude.

## NUMBER PREFERENCES

The implicit assumption behind the direct scaling methods is that subjects use numbers in an unbiased manner, obeying the rules of arithmetic. In the absence of an external stimulus, the sampling of values from the number line is presumably a random process. One value taken from this line is as likely as any other, so it is only the stimulus intensities presented for judgment that induce the use of particular numbers. If no stimulus is presented, the frequency histogram of responses should be rectangular over any bounded region of the number continuum. In particular, the Sensory Aggregate Model claims that stimulus intensity is the sole determinant of the numbers given in these experiments, with allowance made for error variance.

Contrary to this view, many investigators (including S. S. Stevens) recognize that subjects give certain response values much more frequently than others when estimating physical stimuli (Baird, Lewis, & Romer, 1970; S. S. Stevens, 1975) or when guessing numbers in the absence of a stimulus event (Baird & Noma, 1975; Noma & Baird, 1975; Ross & Engen, 1959). If someone simply lists a string of 10 numbers ranging from 1 to 100, the outcome will be integers that reflect a dominant round number bias. The choices will likely be multiples of 5 or 10. This tendency surfaces whenever subjects give a numerical response to just about any question involving quantity; such as: "How beautiful is this picture of the campus on a scale of 1 to 100?" or "How long does it take to drive from your home to Boston?" With the exception of a few people who enjoy teasing psychologists, most do not reply by saying things like "6.23 units of beauty" or "2.17 hours." The answer, along with appropriate dimensional units, is more likely to be a common integer, such as 1, 2, 5, 10, 20, 50, or 100.

Figure 8.1 shows an example of this behavior based on data from 26 undergraduates in an environmental psychology course who gave numerical estimates on a scale from 1 to 100 to express opinions about two magnitudes: the relative distances between all possible pairs of 11 buildings in an ideal town (e.g., school, home, factory) and the semantic association between the members of each building pair. (The complete item set is given in Baird, Degerman, Paris, & Noma, 1972.) No physical stimuli were actually presented. All responses concern imagined buildings situated in ideal spaces. Figure 8.1 depicts the frequency

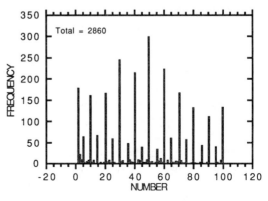

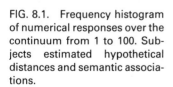

FIG. 8.1.  Frequency histogram of numerical responses over the continuum from 1 to 100. Subjects estimated hypothetical distances and semantic associations.

histogram of responses over the number continuum from 1 to 100. Students use a preponderance of integers that are multiples of 5 and 10.

The type of numbers used when subjects estimate physical stimuli looks much like the pattern in Figure 8.1 (Baird et al., 1970). People favor integers and multiples of 10 and 100, as well as multiples of 5, 50, and 500. They rarely respond with a number such as 37.5 or 0.17. The systematic character of number preferences across subject populations allows the inclusion of such preferences in the output stage of judgment models. It is not necessary to know the unique number preferences of each and every individual, because there is substantial agreement among them.

## Number Preferences and Exponents

A cornerstone of any attempt to interpret psychophysical data in terms of judgment variables is a demonstration that the Power Law and its associated exponent are due to cognitive rather than sensory processes. To be a serious contender, this model must accurately predict the results from direct scaling methods, such as Magnitude and Category Estimation. The model should assume nothing á priori about the relative sensitivity of sensory systems responsible for processing psychophysical stimuli.

The Number Preference Model described here satisfies these prerequisites. The model has two major elements. The first is a list of the preferred numbers in order of magnitude. The second is a list of the preferred numbers in order of importance, defined by their relative frequency of occurrence. The set of preferred numbers comes from asking subjects to generate values in the absence of physical stimuli (Baird & Noma, 1975). From these previous studies, the preferred numbers from 1 to 100 of a typical subject are: 1, 2, 3, 4, 5, 6, 7, 8, 9, 10, 15, 20, 25, 30, 40, 50, 60, 70, 75, 80, 90, 100.

An analytic summary of these preferences is possible, because these 22 values are generated by the mathematical bases 10 and 5 with the inclusion of only one significant digit (Noma & Baird, 1975). If $B$ is the base, n is the integer exponent 0, 1, 2, and so on, and k is an integer ranging from 1 to $B - 1$, then a preferred number ($PN$) can be expressed as:

$$PN = kB^n \qquad (8.1)$$

where $B$ is either 10 or 5. For example, $3 = 3 \times 10^0$, $15 = 3 \times 5^1$, $800 = 8 \times 10^2$. Both bases generate some of the same values, and these are especially favored by subjects expressing judgments; for instance, $10 = 1 \times 10^1 = 2 \times 5^1$ and $50 = 5 \times 10^1 = 2 \times 5^2$. The bases 10 and 5 themselves also occur with great regularity.

Beyond 100, the preferences do not strictly obey Equation 8.1, but instead, duplicate the pattern existing from 10 to 100. For example, in order to predict preferences in the cycle 100 to 1000, we multiply the numbers in the lower log cycle by 10, yielding the values 150, 200, 250, 300, . . . 1000. Although the pattern in higher cycles has not been documented experimentally, assume for purposes of completeness that the same rule holds there as in the cycle from 10 to 100; bear in mind that individuals may be more inclined to depart from this pattern because of personal idiosyncracies in the use of very large numbers. The first part of the Number Preference Model, therefore, is a list of the most common numbers in order of magnitude (cf. the related work by Banks & Hill, 1974.)

The second part of the model concerns the relative importance of the numbers as indicated by usage in an experiment. The most important numbers are those beginning with the integer 1 and ending with trailing zeros (viz. 1, 10, 100, . . . ). The second most important numbers are those beginning with the integer 5 and ending with trailing zeros (5, 50, 500, . . . ). Beyond this, the empirical evidence is sketchy, but in order to reach some closure, assume the set of numbers in the third tier of importance contains values such as 15, 25, 75, 150, 250, and 750. The fourth and final tier contains the numbers 2, 3, 4, 6, 7, 8, 9, 20, 30, and so on. For reference purposes, Table 8.1 gives the list of preferred numbers from 1 to 10,000 in order of importance. An arbitrary 4-point category scale classifies each number as to its qualitative importance: very high, high, low, or very low.

Beyond these dominant values, subjects favor numbers ending in 5 (such as 35, 45, and 55), as well as some repeating digits (such as 22, 33, and 99). They rarely use numbers less than 1, or fractions of any kind, unless forced to do so by experimental constraints. For example, if the experimenter assigns a modulus of "1" to the maximum stimulus, the subject must either use fractions or quit the experiment. Even under the constraint of not surpassing 2, they probably will respond much as they do in the higher log cycles: 0.1, 0.2, 1.15, 1.25, 1.2, . . . , and so on. Another example where subjects use numbers that do not appear in Table 8.1 is when the range of stimuli is very narrow. For instance, in a study of human stereopsis, Youngs (1974) designated a target seen in depth as "100" and subjects estimated the egocentric distance to comparison targets lo-

TABLE 8.1
Preferred Numbers in Order of Importance

| Importance | | | | | | | |
|---|---|---|---|---|---|---|---|
| Very high | 1 | 10 | 100 | 1000 | 10000 | | |
| High | 5 | 50 | 500 | 5000 | | | |
| Low | 15 | 25 | 75 | 150 | 250 | 7500 | 1500 |
| Very low | 2 | 3 | 4 | 6 | 7 | 8 | 9 |
| Very low | 20 | 30 | 40 | 60 | 70 | 80 | 90 |
| Very low | 200 | 300 | 400 | 600 | 700 | 800 | 900 |
| Very low | 2000 | 3000 | 4000 | 6000 | 7000 | 8000 | 9000 |

cated in close proximity to the standard. The responses ranged from 90 to 100 (Gulick & Lawson, 1976, chap. 8). The present model captures only the strongest inclinations of the subject, and must be modified to cover special circumstances such as these.

## COGNITIVE POWER FUNCTIONS

The goal of the Number Preference Model is to give a rationale for the Power Law and the exponents from the Method of Magnitude Estimation.[1] The success of the model rests with its ability to reproduce the essential features of the empirical data (see also Weissman, Hollingsworth, & Baird, 1975).

Poulton (1967) assembled a representative data set. Table 8.2 reproduces his summary for an array of stimulus attributes, ranges, and Power Law exponents (left most columns). This table provides the target data addressed here by the model. The additional columns in the table are explained later.

### Process Assumptions

Two working hypotheses underlie the application of the model: First, the subject selects numerical values from the set of preferred numbers given in Table 8.1 and, second, this selection depends on the relative importance of the numbers bounded by a minimum and maximum value.

A specific test of the model's ability to generate realistic data employed the stimulus range for each attribute listed in Table 8.2. The stimuli were seven intensities, equally spaced in logarithmic units. In the actual experiments reviewed by Poulton, the number of stimuli was, of course, not always seven.

A computer program performed the necessary selections and calculations. The stimulus range of the attribute was initially rescaled so that the smallest intensity in the series was 1. On successive runs of the program, the preferred number assigned to the maximum stimulus was varied from "7" to "10,000," according to the consecutive order of values listed in Table 8.1.

The program began with the number "7" because there always has to be enough preferred numbers to represent the seven stimuli. For each maximum response, the program assigns preferred numbers to the remaining stimuli in the series, starting with the smallest in the most important response cycle—"very high." In other words, the program looks to determine whether 1, 10, 100, 1000, or 10,000 are less than the maximum response, and then puts aside all such

---

[1]Butler and Overshiner (1983) presented an interesting application of number usage to explain certain exponent size. They claimed that exponents for attributes, such as visual area and volume, are lower than for visual line length. According to them, subjects multiply perceived linear extents in estimating stimuli of higher dimensionality. Errors in multiplication are reflected in lower exponents.

TABLE 8.2
Stimulus Range, Empirical Exponent, and Theoretical Exponents

| | Empirical Range | Theoretical | | | |
|---|---|---|---|---|---|
| | | $\gamma$ | $\gamma^*$ | $\gamma^{**}$ | $\gamma^{***}$ |
| Brightness | $10^6$ | 0.3 | 0.23 | 0.28 | 0.27 |
| Brightness of point | $10^3$ | 0.5 | 0.46 | 0.46 | 0.5 |
| Loudness (monaural) | $10^6$ | 0.5 | 0.5 | 0.5 | 0.5 |
| Coffee odor | 80 | 0.6 | 0.73 | 0.58 | 0.62 |
| Loudness (binaural) | $10^7$ | 0.6 | 0.43 | 0.54 | 0.65 |
| Visual area | 188 | 0.7 | 0.6 | 0.73 | 0.71 |
| Tactual hardness | 117 | 0.8 | 0.67 | 0.8 | 0.78 |
| Vibration | $10^3$ | 0.7 | 0.46 | 0.6 | 0.72 |
| Temperature (cold) | 9.2 | 1 | 1.44 | 0.93 | 0.96 |
| Repitition rate | 40 | 1 | 0.86 | 1.04 | 0.99 |
| Visual length | 27.8 | 1 | 0.96 | 0.96 | 1.02 |
| Duration | 16 | 1.1 | 1.15 | 1.15 | 1.11 |
| Skin pressure | 10 | 1.1 | 1.39 | 1.1 | 1.1 |
| Vocal effort | 320 | 1.1 | 1.21 | 0.2 | 1.09 |
| Lightness of grays | 32 | 1.2 | 0.92 | 1.11 | 1.11 |
| Finger span | 27.7 | 1.3 | 0.96 | 1.25 | 1.43 |
| Heaviness | 10.1 | 1.4 | 1.38 | 1.38 | 1.4 |
| Temperature (warmth) | 5.9 | 1.5 | 1.07 | 1.43 | 1.51 |
| Tactual roughness | 13.3 | 1.5 | 1.23 | 1.48 | 0.3 |
| Force of handgrip | 10 | 1.71 | 0.39 | 1.66 | 1.54 |
| Electric shock | 3 | 3.5 | 2.93 | 3.49 | 3.49 |

Note: Empirical values are from Poulton (1967). Theoretical values are from simulations of the Number Preference Model.
$\gamma$ = empirical exponent
$\gamma^*$ = Stevens exponent from the Number Preference Model
$\gamma^{**}$ = exponent with 10% window of acceptance
$\gamma^{***}$ = exponent with additive constant (Equation 8.2)


numbers that satisfy this criterion. For example, if the maximum response is "20," then the numbers "1" and "10" would qualify. Next, the program considers the entries in the "high" category and selects all the numbers fulfilling the criterion of being less than the maximum. For the present example (maximum response of 20), there are two such entries, the numbers "5" and "15." The remaining three numbers are then selected from the next tier of importance (category "low"). For our example, these entries would be 2, 3, and 4.

When there are more numbers in a category than stimuli for which assignment is necessary, the program begins making assignments from the smallest to the largest number. For example, if there is only one remaining stimulus requiring assignment, and the available candidates are 20, 30, and 40, the number 20 is chosen, and so on. If only two stimuli require assignments from this category, the

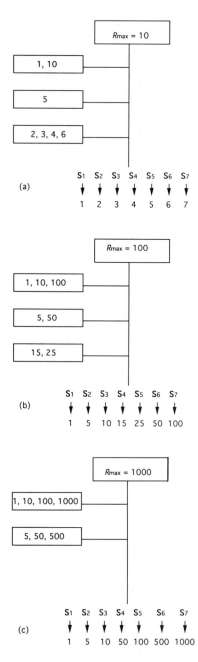

FIG. 8.2.   Three examples showing application of the Number Preference Model. The model assigns preferred numbers to each of seven stimuli with maximum responses of 10 (a), 100 (b), and 1000 (c).

numbers 20 and 30 are chosen. This decision order is arbitrary, starting in the opposite direction (e.g., 30 before 20) does not significantly alter the final result.

Once the computer selects the entire set of numbers, they are assigned in order of magnitude to the stimuli. The smallest stimulus is called "1," the next smallest, "2," and so on. In the example under discussion, the computer would assign the numbers 1, 2, 3, 4, 10, 15, and 20 in a monotonically increasing order to the seven members of the stimulus set. Figure 8.2 gives three further examples of possible decision trees. Each tree has a different maximum response, and hence, contains different integer assignments for each of the seven stimuli.

The logarithms of the responses are then regressed against the logarithms of the stimulus intensities. As usual, the stimulus range is partitioned so as to maintain equal log spacing between stimuli. A linear function is then fit to the data (logarithmic coordinates) to secure the slope (exponent) and y intercept (multiplier) of Stevens's Power Law. The correlation between the predicted and actual responses is the Goodness-of-Fit. Figure 8.3 shows the resulting power functions for the examples diagrammed in Figure 8.2, with a maximum stimulus intensity of 1000 (*log* 1000 = 3). Straight lines fit the data points tolerably well in all three cases.

Application of the model is straightforward when the available numbers below the maximum is equal to or somewhat larger than the total number of stimuli in the series. The more intriguing cases arise when the maximum response is large, and hence, there are many available options. For example, if the maximum were "100," then for seven stimuli the program would first pick the numbers 1, 10, 100, followed by 5 and 50, and then 15 and 25. These values would be assigned to the stimulus intensities in order of magnitude (1, 5, 10, 15, 25, 50, 100). Figure 8.2b diagrams this example. Different upper limits produce different exponents.

An iterative procedure found the power function for each of the successive preferred numbers (7, 8, 9, . . . , 10000) serving as the maximum. Upon com-

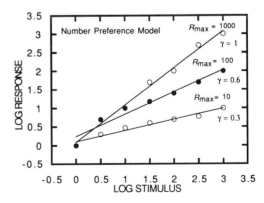

FIG. 8.3. Response magnitude as a function of stimulus intensity (log–log coordinates) for the three examples in Figure 8.2. The slopes (exponents) of the best-fitting straight lines are listed to the right of the functions.

pletion of all 40 iterations (one for each maximum), the program selected the power function and its associated maximum integer yielding the best linear fit for each stimulus range in Table 8.2. In all cases, the highest correlation turned out to be 1. Among the 21 attributes, this procedure resulted in only three ties: two maximum responses leading to a correlation of 1 for the same attribute. Table 8.2 gives the theoretical exponents ($\gamma^*$) generated by the Number Preference Model for each of the attributes listed by Poulton.

Figure 8.4 shows the relation between the empirical and theoretical values. It includes all 21 attributes, as well as the three ties. The close agreement between theoretical and empirical exponents ($r = 0.92$) provides strong support for the model. The graph reveals the ability to predict the exponent of Stevens's Law by knowing the range of stimuli and the preferred numbers representing the minimum and maximum stimuli. It is unnecessary to ask subjects to estimate any of the remaining stimuli in the series. The preferred number yielding the highest correlation is associated with a power function and exponent that is very near the accepted values in the literature.

It is also possible to investigate the implications of this model when the acceptance of the "best" power function is contingent on both the correlation coefficient and the match between the theoretical and empirical exponents. This was determined by repeating the calculation outlined previously, but with the additional stipulation that in order to be considered, the absolute difference between the empirical and theoretical exponent had to be less than 10% of the empirical value. Within this window of acceptance, the program selects the maximum response (preferred number) and associated power function yielding the best fit between stimuli and theoretical responses.

This process determines the smallest difference between empirical and predicted exponents for each of the 21 attributes, where the simulation is based on the maximum stimulus intensity in Table 8.2. It was impossible to find values within the 10% window for the attribute "vibration," so its window was widened

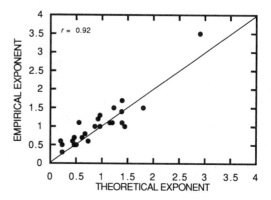

FIG. 8.4. Relation between the empirical and theoretical exponents for attributes and ranges in Table 8.2 ($\gamma^*$). Empirical values from Poulton (1967). Theoretical values generated by the Number Preference Model.

to 15%. As expected, the correlations under these conditions are not always 1. Of the 21 attributes, the correlation is 1 for 7 attributes, 0.99 for 12, and 0.98 for 5. These theoretical values ($\gamma^{**}$), are also in Table 8.2, and Figure 8.5 shows the relation between empirical and theoretical exponents. Perfect predictions would have the points resting on the solid diagonal. The quantitative concordance between theoretical and empirical exponents is almost perfect ($r = 0.99$).

Figure 8.6 shows the resulting psychophysical functions for all 21 attributes, where the coordinates are logarithmic and the functions are shifted along the stimulus axis in order to facilitate viewing. The overall pattern bears a close family resemblance to plots of empirical findings (Figure 3.1) as well as to the predictions of the Sensory Aggregate Model (Figure 3.2).

## Additive Constant

Although the fits of the Power Law are striking, the correlation coefficient does not reflect the systematic nonlinearities in the log–log plot at the low end of the stimulus range of several attributes. The nature of this nonlinearity is a slight downward concavity in the function. Such departures from the strict Power Law are common in psychophysics. As noted in chapter 3, it has been standard practice for some time (Ekman, 1956b) to modify Stevens's Law by subtracting a constant from each stimulus before raising it to a power to achieve a better fit. That is,

$$R = \lambda(S - S_0)^{\gamma}, \tag{8.2}$$

where the constant $S_0$ is usually positive.

It is possible to fit Equation 8.2 to the same simulation results in order to improve what is already a satisfactory fit. Not surprisingly, because of the extra parameter, more stellar linear fits are the rule. Of the 21 attributes, the correlations are 1 for 17 of the attributes, 0.99 for 3, and 0.98 for 1 (binaural loudness).

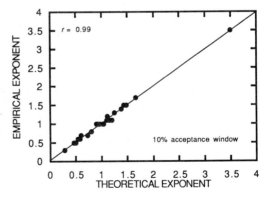

FIG. 8.5.   Relation between empirical and theoretical exponents for attributes and ranges in Table 8.2 ($\gamma^{**}$) when the fit of the power function falls within 10% of the empirical value (15% for "vibration"). Empirical values are from Poulton (1967). Theoretical values generated by the Number Preference Model.

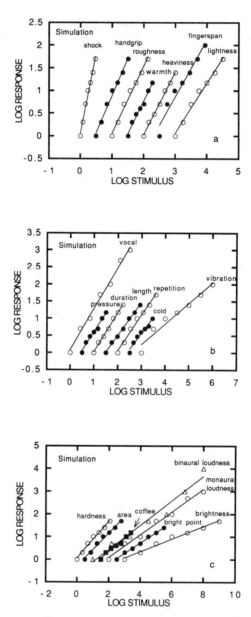

FIG. 8.6.  Response magnitude as a function of stimulus intensity (log–log coordinates) for 21 attributes (a, b, c) in Table 8.2. Each power function falls within 10% of its empirical value (15% for "vibration"). Empirical target values from Poulton (1967). Theoretical points generated by the Number Preference Model.

These theoretical exponents are also listed in Table 8.2 ($\gamma***$) alongside those determined without this extra parameter.

## MAGNITUDE AND CATEGORY EXPONENTS

S. S. Stevens and Galanter (1957) originally raised the question: What is the relation between magnitude and category estimates? The answer since then has been equivocal. Some investigators report that the relation between category estimates and physical stimuli is logarithmic (Eisler, 1962; Helm, Messick, & Tucker, 1961; Montgomery, 1975), and others suggest that a power function provides a better fit (H. J. Foley, Cross, M. A. Foley, & Reeder, 1983). The relation between category and magnitude estimates will depend, of course, on how each relates to the same set of physical intensities. In this respect, if a power function is fit to the data, a rough practical guide is that the category exponent is about half the size of the corresponding magnitude exponent (H. J. Foley et al., 1983; S. S. Stevens, 1975).

### Log Functions

With seven categories, the Number Preference Model assigns them each in increasing order to stimuli that are logarithmically spaced. Therefore, the resulting function is automatically defined as logarithmic between category estimates and intensity. A power function was fit to each set of category responses (1 to 7) distributed over the log range for each of the 21 attributes in Table 8.2. Thus, power functions were fit to known logarithmic relations. Then, the exponents were determined so as to compare them with the values for theoretical magnitude estimates of the same attributes. The correlations for these linear fits are poor (r = 0.96).

Marks (1968) reported it is sometimes possible to obtain more satisfactory fits of the power function for category estimates by adding a constant to each mean estimate before fitting the function. The same could be done here to improve the fits, because all the functions are concave downward. There is no special reason to carry out this least-squares fit, however, in light of the knowledge that the theoretical functions are in fact logarithmic.

Figure 8.7 shows the theoretical category exponent plotted against the theoretical magnitude exponent. A straight line fit to the data points has a slope of 0.49 and a y intercept of 0.03. The category exponent is approximately half the size of the magnitude exponent.

### Power Functions

Subjects tested by S. S. Stevens and Galanter (1957) gave category estimates of the loudness of white noise (ranging from 40 dB to 100 dB in 5 dB steps), where

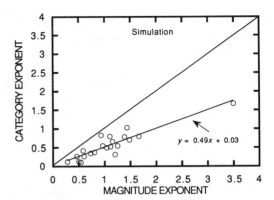

FIG. 8.7. Category Estimation exponent as a function of Magnitude Estimation exponent according to the Number Preference Model.

the categories were either the integers 1 to 7 or the verbal labels: very very soft, very soft, soft, medium, loud, very loud, and very very loud. They then compared the mean category estimates (with the response labels converted to equally spaced integers) with the so-called sone scale for the loudness of a 1000-Hz tone. The sone scale is treated as a summary of the magnitude estimates (linear units) of loudness, though its units need not correspond to the actual numbers given by subjects in any particular experiment. The authors stated that the results for white noise are essentially the same as those for a 1000-Hz tone (J. C. Stevens & Tulving, 1957).

Figure 8.8a (top left) shows the mean category estimates for the experiment involving verbal labels plotted against the sone scale. Both axes are linear. The general trend of the points is concave downward. A logarithmic function (solid line) was fit to the points and, as Stevens and Galanter recognized, the empirical trend is less curved than a log function. These authors reported a similar pattern of results for a variety of other stimulus attributes falling into the class of prothetic continua: duration of time, numerousness of dots, lifted weights, brightness, and lightness of grays.

S. S. Stevens (1975) argued that the relation between the category scale and physical intensity is not logarithmic but, instead, obeys a Power Law. There seems to be widespread agreement nowadays that a power function fits the data from Category Estimation better than a logarithmic function. Because the relation between magnitude estimates and physical intensity is also a power function, it follows that category and magnitude estimates of the same stimulus series must be described by a power function. The same empirical data shown in Figure 8.8a are presented in logarithmic coordinates in Figure 8.8b (top right). A straight line through the data points has a slope (exponent) of 0.44 and a y intercept near zero.

Harder and Baird (1995) recently did an experiment to determine the nature of the relation between category and magnitude estimates in the absence of physical

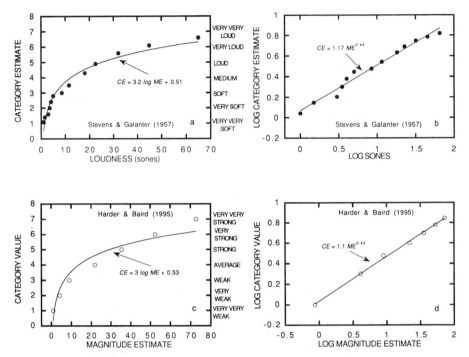

FIG. 8.8.  Category estimates as a function of perceived loudness of white noise (top: S. S. Stevens & Galanter, 1957), and magnitude estimates associated with response categories in the absence of stimulation (bottom: Harder & Baird, 1995). The axes in the left panels (a, c) are linear. The axes in the right panels (b, d) are logarithmic.

stimuli. They gave each subject a sheet of paper containing seven verbal categories: very very weak, very weak, weak, average, strong, very strong, and very very strong. The labels appeared in a column format in different random orders for different subjects. The subjects were told that the labels referred either to the brightness of a light or to the loudness of a sound. The subject then assigned numbers (larger than zero) to characterize each of the verbal labels.

The qualitative response labels were converted into the integers 1 to 7 and plotted against the geometric mean magnitude estimates (48 subjects) in Figure 8.8c (lower left panel). The correspondence between the data of Stevens and Galanter in the left panel and these results is striking. A logarithmic function fit to the data departs from the empirical points in essentially the same places observed in the data of Stevens and Galanter for estimates of white noise. Moreover, the parameters of the best-fitting log function are almost identical in the two plots.

The bottom-right graph (8.8d) shows the associated power function. On a logarithmic plot, the exponent (slope) of the best-fitting power function is 0.43 with a y intercept close to zero. These parameter values are almost identical to those in the top-right panel summarizing the estimates of white noise.

The absolute value of the numerical estimates subjects gave in the experiment by Harder and Baird vary widely from one individual to the next. Some subjects favor a range stretching from 0.0001 to 1, others from 100 to 10,000. The geometric mean across subjects veils these differences in absolute value and indicates that, on average, subjects employ a range of magnitude estimates spanning approximately 2 log cycles (base 10). Because this range would always be constant no matter which attribute was being judged, the predicted exponent of the power function would vary inversely with the stimulus range, in agreement with the views of Poulton (1989) and R. Teghtsoonian (1971).

## Implicit Anchors

G. H. Robinson (1976) reported a study in which a standard stimulus was called "100" and the experimenter gave different examples of response magnitudes for the comparisons. Some subjects were told to say 50 when a stimulus was 1/2 the standard and 150 when it was $1\frac{1}{2}$ times the standard, whereas other subjects were told to say 25 when the stimulus was $\frac{1}{4}$ the standard and 750 when it was $7\frac{1}{2}$ times the standard. The exponent of Stevens's Law was reliably less when the range of response examples was narrow as opposed to when it was wide. This occurred both for estimates of pulse rate and loudness.

An unpublished study by Birnbaum and Mellers (1980), described by Birnbaum (1982), also indicates that the sample numbers given by the experimenter influences the exponent of the Power Law. In their study, subjects evaluated the darkness of dot patterns using Magnitude Estimation. They assigned the number "100" to the lightest pattern, but different pretest numerical examples illustrated potential responses for the darker stimuli. In one condition, the examples went up to "300," whereas in another, they went up to "900." In the ensuing experiment, subjects gave numbers that generally stayed within the implicit boundaries. An additional variation in the study is that the stimulus spacing was skewed such that there was a predominance of light (positive skew) or dark (negative skew) patterns.

The coordinates of the points in the graph published by Birnbaum (1982) were visually estimated. For each stimulus intensity, the results were then averaged under the positive and negative skew conditions. These means are the filled points in Figure 8.9, when the prior example was either "300" (circles) or "900" (squares). The exponent is 60% smaller with the "low" example than it is with the "high" one.

The Number Preference Model generated the open points in Figure 8.9. In the empirical study, the experimenter preassigned the minimum value of 100. If we assume that the subject took the maximum numerical example as a stricture for

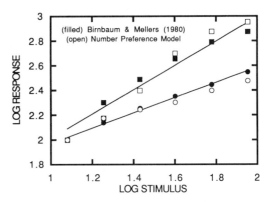

FIG. 8.9. Response magnitude as a function of stimulus intensity (log–log coordinates) when subjects are given a high numerical example (squares) or a low numerical example (circles). Filled points from Birnbaum and Mellers (1980). Open points from the Number Preference Model.

representing the maximum intensity, the model can assign values to the remaining four stimuli falling in-between. For the "900" example, the resulting values for the entire set are: 100, 150, 250, 500, 750, and 900. These numbers follow immediately from the model. A complication arises, however, in predicting numerical responses for the "300" example, because the model is not sufficiently general to handle this particular range and number of stimuli. Therefore, one of the hypothetical response values (see asterisk below) was assigned by invoking the rules of an alternative line of reasoning, embodied in the so-called quarter model (Noma & Baird, 1975). This model states that subjects break a range, which is a multiple of 10, into equal quarters (e.g., 100, 125, 150, 175, 200). The final responses in rank order for the "300" example were then: 100, 150, 175*, 200, 250, and 300.

The open points in Figure 8.9 represent these theoretical responses for the same two empirical examples. There is close agreement between the sets of points, though the theoretical exponents are somewhat more separated than the empirical ones.

## Explicit Anchors

An experiment similar to that of Birnbaum and Mellers was conducted, except that the minimum and maximum response options were both prespecified (Baird, Kreindler, & Jones, 1971). At the time, it was not fully understood why the method produced the result it did. The Number Preference Model offers a more convincing explanation of these results than was possible earlier.

Seven groups (and a control) were run with an identical series of line lengths, presented visually. The experimental groups received different numerical anchors for the largest stimulus, and the smallest stimulus was always called "1." The subjects were told that the experimenter had a certain relation in mind between the lines and the scale used in responding to perceived length. The upper numerical anchor for the maximum stimulus was either 3.14, 5.56, 13.11, 30.92, 97.06, 956.24, or 29,577. All these anchors are uncommon numbers. The idea at the time was to introduce a great variety of maxima, and nothing was known about the Number Preference Model.

The choice of the exact numbers depended on the exponent the study was trying to obtain. If perfect power functions passed through the minimum and maximum stimulus in each case, the expected exponent is the slope in logarithmic coordinates:

$$\gamma = \frac{\log R_{max}}{\log \left(\dfrac{S_{max}}{S_{min}}\right)} \qquad (8.3)$$

Substituting different values for $R_{max}$ into Equation 8.3 yields the predicted exponents.

Power functions provide adequate fits to the mean estimates in each of the groups (except for the two steepest functions), depending on the size of $R_{max}$: the higher the anchor, the higher the exponent. Figure 8.10 reproduces the relevant graph (logarithmic coordinates), adapted from the original study. It is clear that different psychophysical relations are generated for exactly the same set of stimulus intensities. The predicted and empirical exponents are listed to the right of each function.

These are the empirical findings. The Number Preference Model simulates the results with high fidelity. In the laboratory study, the same minimum stimulus was always labeled "1" and the maximum was labeled differently to simulate what would be true in order to produce different exponents. In applying the model, the minimum response was also set equal to 1 and the maximum response was set at the upper boundary assigned by the experimenter for the particular

FIG. 8.10. Response magnitude as a function of stimulus length when the smallest line is assigned the value "1" and the largest line is assigned different values. Coordinates are logarithmic. The empirical exponents are compared with the predicted values (Equation 8.3). From Baird et al. (1971).

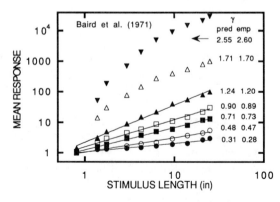

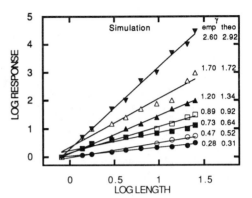

FIG. 8.11. Response magnitude as a function of stimulus length when the smallest line is assigned the value "1" and the largest line is assigned different values. Coordinates are logarithmic. The empirical exponents (Baird et al., 1971) are compared with predicted values from the Number Preference Model.

group in the original study. The model then chose numbers for each of the remaining eight stimuli in accord with the decision rules described earlier in the chapter. Figure 8.11 shows the predictions of response magnitude as a function of stimulus length for each condition. The empirical (based on actual subjects) and theoretical (Number Preference Model) exponents appear to the right of each function.

Excellent fits of Stevens's Law are obtained in each case, and more important, the exponents closely match those found in the laboratory. This agreement can be appreciated by comparing the exponents of the appropriate functions in Figures 8.10 and 8.11. Figure 8.12 accentuates this comparison by indicating with a solid diagonal the perfect match between empirical and theoretical exponents.

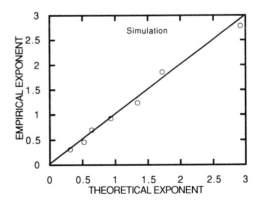

FIG. 8.12. Relation between empirical (Baird et al., 1971) and theoretical exponents (Number Preference Model) generated by varying the magnitude of the number assigned to the maximum stimulus.

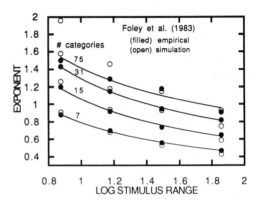

FIG. 8.13. Stevens exponent as a function of logarithm of stimulus range with the number of response categories as a parameter. Empirical data from Foley et al. (1983). Theoretical data from the Number Preference Model.

## Category Estimation

Good fits of the Number Preference Model result when compared with the results of Category Estimation. In this method, subjects usually use the smallest and largest categories for the minimum and maximum stimulus, respectively. Sometimes the experimenter tells them to do so. In one study, H. J. Foley et al. (1983) had subjects give category estimates under conditions where the experimenter provided different numbers of response options (7-, 15-, 31-, and 75-point scales). Subjects estimated line length, number, and sound pressure that varied over different ranges. The exponent of the Power Law depends on the range (larger range, lower exponent).

The Number Preference Model makes explicit predictions about the mean estimates for the stimuli falling between the extremes. The fact that we know the range of stimuli and responses allows us to predict the subject's remaining responses. For each condition, the largest stimulus is assigned the largest category, the smallest stimulus the smallest category, and the remaining stimuli are assigned categories according to the stipulations of the Number Preference Model. This was carried out by assuming there were 7 stimuli in the series, even though the authors actually used 10. This was done because it was not certain how to best handle matters when there were more stimuli than categories.

Figure 8.13 presents the empirical data (filled circles) and the theoretical predictions (open circles), where the solid lines through the points summarize the empirical data for line length. The exponent of the power function is plotted as a function of the logarithm of the stimulus range, with the number of possible categories as a parameter. Except for the case of the smallest range with the 75-point scale, the agreement between empirical and theoretical results is excellent. For this particular data point, the original data are fit poorly by a power function (according to the authors), and therefore, it is not surprising the predictions deviate so much from the empirical value.

# SPECULATIONS FOR SENSORY PSYCHOPHYSICS

If we evaluate Stevens's Power Law from the standpoint of cognition and decision making, then the question is left open as to the nature of the sensory processes activated by presentation of a physical stimulus. The psychophysical relation in the realm of sensory physiology could be one of many possibilities. The success of the Number Preference Model in predicting exponents means that it explains the psychophysical relation without recourse to sensory processing. In this model, the assignment of numerical responses to physical intensities is without regard for the physical spacing between stimuli. This means that any monotonically increasing function between stimuli and sensation magnitude is a viable option.

The simplest, most interesting, and least likely possibility is that the psychophysical relation is linear between sensation and physical intensity. Interest wins out. If the function were linear, then the maximum response and stimulus range for an attribute could be used to determine an index of perceptual sensitivity at the sensory level. For instance, if sensation ($\Psi$) is a linear function of stimulus intensity,

$$\Psi = \alpha S, \tag{8.4}$$

the slope ($\alpha$) is defined as

$$\alpha = \frac{\Psi_{max} - \Psi_{min}}{S_{max} - S_{min}}. \tag{8.5}$$

After the Number Preference Model determines the maximum response yielding the best-fitting exponent of the Power Law, all four terms on the righthand side of Equation 8.5 are known. Substitution in Equation 8.5 yields the slope for each attribute.

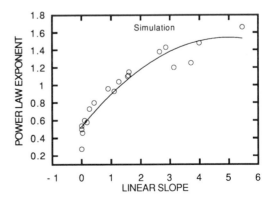

FIG. 8.14. Stevens Power Law exponent as a function of the slope of the linear function (Equation 8.5) between perceived magnitude and stimulus intensity. Each point represents a different attribute in Table 8.2 (from Poulton, 1967).

139

This calculation was made for each of the attributes listed in Table 8.2, where $S_{min} = 1$, $\Psi_{min} = 1$, $S_{max}$ was taken from Poulton's summary, and $\Psi_{max}$ was the response value obtained by applying the Number Preference Model in securing the best-fitting power function (without the additive constant). Figure 8.14 shows the resulting relation between the exponent and the slope of the linear function expressed by Equation 8.4. The solid line is a quadratic function that emphasizes the trend in the data points.

Because the relation is monotonically increasing, theoretical statements can be made regarding the sensitivity of different attributes on the basis of the linear multiplier. It remains to be seen whether thinking about sensory processing as a linear system operating according to Equation 8.4 leads to any further insights into the nature of the link between external stimuli and sensory events. From the available empirical evidence at the sensory level (chap. 2), it seems that linearity might only be a valid representation for very narrow stimulus ranges.

## OVERVIEW

Implicit in the practice of judgment psychophysics is the core belief that all global scaling taps into the same judgment distributions, but that response constraints and subject strategies differ across tasks. Restle's (1961) insight was to suggest that adhering to this belief leads to progress in theoretical psychophysics.

One of the major constraints in the Method of Magnitude Estimation is that subjects prefer to use particular numbers. The spacing of these numbers along the integer scale leads to stimulus–response functions that obey Stevens's Power Law. The next chapter describes a model that explicitly treats judgment variability in a broader framework, including a variety of estimation and adjustment techniques. In this framework, the Number Preference Model defines the representation of the response output for Magnitude Estimation.

# 9 Judgment Option Model

Cognitive approaches to psychophysics give new meaning to variables such as the mean and variance of perceived stimulus magnitude. The aspect of sensory psychophysics reformulated in this chapter is the source of response variability. The Sensory Aggregate Model attributes this variability to the ensemble of neurons involved in coding a single stimulus. Not all the neurons comprising this set are firing at the same rate, and therefore the subject has some leeway (conscious or unconscious) in selecting the neuron or subset of neurons sampled on a given trial. This process is repeated over trials and thereby generates the response variability observed in the psychophysics laboratory.

The complementary side of the picture is fleshed out by putting aside the sensorineural in favor of the cognitive. The observed response variability for repeated presentation of the same stimulus now arises because the subject is uncertain on each trial about exactly which response should be given. Notice that the truth or falsity of either the neural or cognitive approach is not at issue. The idea is to create the minimum number of models to explain the maximum amount of data. Exactly the same experiments must be considered from two different perspectives. So it is the theorists that must change their outlook on the field. The facts themselves are not in question.

First, the class of continuous-response techniques exemplified by Cross Modality Matching and Magnitude Production is examined. Succeeding chapters treat the discrete class consisting of Category Estimation, Magnitude Estimation, and Absolute Identification. Throughout this section, the focus is less on the nature of the sensory scale than on trial-by-trial decision making. These processes are revealed when different procedural constraints are imposed by the experimenter through such variables as instructions, number of response options, and stimulus anchors. I devote no attention to the sensory basis of psychophysical laws or to the "correct" experimental procedures for revealing such laws (Lockhead, 1992). The overarching theme is that the same judgment model can explain data secured by a variety of psychophysical methods.

## THE JUDGMENT OPTION MODEL

Several features of the Sensory Aggregate Model are retained in formulating a judgment model. The first relates to the sensory signal used in estimating intensity. It is assumed that the subject has access to the mean output of the firing-rate distribution aroused by a stimulus, but not to the activity levels of individual neurons. That is, all the psychophysical laws that depend on the mean output of the sensory ensemble are valid, but a new interpretation is given of response variability. In addition, the only information from the sensory signal that is important in the judgment model is rank order. The order of the means of the judgment distributions is the same as the order of the stimulus (sensory) intensities.

A second assumption is derived from the Sensory Aggregate Model: Perceived similarity between stimuli is related to the degree of overlap of their associated neural fiber bands. This assumption is crucial in explaining the sequential effects over trials so prevalent in global scaling. The neural ensemble for a single stimulus is comprised of a set of neurons whose thresholds are exceeded by the stimulus intensity. All sensory neurons are involved in more than one stimulus representation. The degree of overlap between neuron pools in two such representations is defined as the similarity existing between their associated stimuli.

The most critical distinction between the sensory and judgment models concerns the source of response variability. Rather than being due to a variable stimulus or sensory representation, response variability in the judgment model is attributed to the subject's uncertainty regarding response options. This notion has also been entertained by others (e.g., Ward, 1979, 1990a), but the present analysis is more quantitative and specific than its predecessors. The foregoing assumptions, together with more specific ones added later, are the foundation for what is called the Judgment Option Model.

## SPECIFIC ASSUMPTIONS

The model can be broken down into five parts: the mapping between mean judgment and stimulus intensity, the judgment distributions, the trial-by-trial constraints on the judgment distributions, the rules invoked in making a decision within the constraints, and the response transformation (output stage) performed on the judgment selected. Throughout the ensuing discussion, it is important to maintain a distinction between the "hypothetical" judgment distribution and the "observable" response distribution. The empirical data analyzed by experimentalists are response distributions. The hypothetical processes responsible for producing the empirical data are judgment distributions.

## Stimulus–Response Mapping

The stimuli in global scaling consist of intensities that when presented in pairs can be perfectly ordered with respect to their relative magnitudes. The same stimulus always gives rise to the same sensory event, and the mean of this sensory event is the only property utilized by the subject.

The means of the judgment distributions are in the same order as the means of the sensory distributions associated with the physical stimuli. In particular, N sensory magnitudes ranging from small to large are mapped into N consecutive integers. Thus, the intervals between the judgment means are fixed. This mapping is insensitive to the physical spacing between stimuli. For example, sensory magnitudes of 10, 20, and 30 (arbitrary units) might map into the integers 1, 2, and 3 along the judgment continuum, as would members of a set containing magnitudes 10, 11, and 30. Four sensory magnitudes, such as 10, 25, 30, and 50, would map into the integers 1, 2, 3, and 4, and so forth.

Rather than explore the implications of the model for a variety of stimulus–response mappings (e.g., power functions with diverse exponents), there is a description of the performance for a single example of a logarithmic mapping between physical intensity and the mean sensation magnitude. This venerated Fechnerian example is used for purposes of illustration and, more importantly, because the simulation results from this mapping are very much like those seen in the laboratory. Everything said about the influence of cognitive variables on the logarithmic mapping holds just as well for other forms of Stevens function. It is unknown whether the Judgment Option Model would also apply to Piéron functions used to describe reaction-time data, although this is a potentially interesting possibility.

## Judgment Distributions

There are two obvious ways to treat the source of judgment distributions. First, it can be claimed that presentation of the same stimulus on many occasions produces a Gaussian distribution of judgments, with standard deviation constant for each intensity (Thurstone, Case V; Baird & Noma, 1978). This is the standard view and one that has a modern counterpart in TSD (Macmillan & Creelman, 1991). An alternative tack is to postulate that response uncertainty occurs full-blown on each trial; that is, an entire distribution is available following presentation of a single stimulus. In effect, this interpretation implies that a stimulus is presented, and the subject is uncertain about which of many potential responses should signify its perceived magnitude. This uncertainty can also be Gaussian distributed. At some future date, it would be informative to explore other types of distributions, but what follows relies only on the Gaussian.

Although mathematically it does not matter which of the two interpretations of variability is entertained, the second is favored. From this standpoint, it is possible to assess response uncertainty on a single trial, perhaps as a confidence rating or in some related manner, for instance, by having the subject respond with a confidence interval rather than with a point estimate of perceived magnitude (Baird & Szilagyi, 1977).

Historically, there have been different ideas about how to interpret the scale values attributed to hypothetical distributions of this kind. Unlike the interpretation in terms of sensory processes, as implied by TSD, the position described here is closer to that of Thurstone (1927), who considered each point along such a judgment scale as an unknown discriminal process "by which the organism identifies, distinguishes, discriminates, or reacts to stimuli" (p. 368). Thurstone refused to identify a structure in the nervous system where this variability resides. Because there is no compelling reason to identify the place within the organism where these distributions originate, it will suffice to say that the location must be at a higher level in the nervous system than the sense organ.

## Judgment Constraints

The chief constraints on the subject are the stimulus–response pairs that occurred earlier in the experimental session. The influence of a previous stimulus–response pair on the judgment strategy applied to a current stimulus depends on the similarity between what is presented on trial T and what was presented k trials back, where k is usually 1, but can be larger to indicate recall of events further back in time.

The similarity measure is taken from the Sensory Aggregate Model and is defined as the overlap of fibers activated by each stimulus. Considered informally, the assumption is not especially deep: It states that the similarity between stimuli is a function of the difference in their respective intensities. The closer the two are in intensity, the greater their perceived similarity.

The reason a graded measure is needed is that sequential response effects depend on the similarity between successive stimuli. The extent of coupling revealed by statistical tests involving successive responses to similar stimuli is greater than the coupling between responses to dissimilar stimuli (Baird, 1990; Baird et al., 1980; Green, Luce, & Duncan, 1977; Jesteadt, Luce, & Green 1977; Luce, Baird, Green, & Smith, 1980). It is not yet clear, however, if stimulus separation is a determining factor in the Method of Absolute Identification (chap. 14).

A further constraint involves the truncation of the judgment distributions. Because it is unreasonable to assume that a judgment distribution stretches from minus to plus infinity, each is truncated at two standard deviations above and below the mean. Introducing this constraint streamlines the model and leads to more tractable results. In this regard, one of the key questions concerns the extent of truncation and its potential effect on psychophysical functions.

Under some conditions, it is apparent that the judgment distributions are highly truncated at both ends of the range, and this is reflected in the data. For example, in Category Estimation, the judgment distributions are truncated at the means (categories) attached to the weakest and strongest stimuli. A subject is not supposed to respond with a number below the smallest category assigned by the experimenter or with a number above the largest category. As is demonstrated in chapter 12, this alters the psychophysical relation. In methods such as Magnitude Estimation, subjects may impose their own truncation points on the judgment distribution.

The foregoing reasoning leads mathematically to a doubly truncated Gaussian distribution of potential judgments appropriate for each stimulus. The $J$ variable has a probability density function with mean $\xi$, standard deviation $\sigma$, and truncation points L and U (Johnson & Kotz, 1970, p. 81):

$$f(J) = \frac{1}{\sigma\sqrt{2\pi}}\, e^{(-1/2\sigma^2)(J-\xi)^2}\left[\frac{1}{\sigma\sqrt{2\pi}}\int_{L}^{U} e^{(-1/2\sigma^2)(t-\xi)^2}dt\right]^{-1}. \quad (9.1)$$

The term in brackets on the right standardizes the probability density over the region bounded by the truncation. Analytic expressions are available for the expected value and standard deviation of the doubly truncated normal, but these expressions are complex and unwieldy (Johnson & Kotz, 1970). In the present applications, rather than evaluate the equations analytically, it was more efficient to write a computer program to calculate statistical measures for the continuous case by approximations involving discrete steps along the judgment continuum.

## Decision Rules

The major assumption that distinguishes the present approach from a Thurstonian model concerns the decision process on each trial. In a Thurstone model, a judgment is randomly selected from a distribution without regard for what transpired on earlier trials. Contrary to this, the present model says that a subject randomly selects a judgment from the distribution associated with a stimulus, but this choice is not the sole determinant of the response. Before making a final decision, the subject incorporates information on the present trial together with information from previous trials (recalled events). The judgment arrived at on the basis of this amalgamation is then transformed into an overt response. For most applications of the model, the subject only considers the event occurring on the previous trial, but this rule can be generalized to include information from trials further back in the series.

It is possible to modulate the influence of previous trials through instructions and by other procedural steps (DeCarlo, 1992, 1994; DeCarlo & Cross, 1990). By carefully crafting the instructions, one may even succeed in totally negating the influence of previous trials, such as is claimed for the Method of Absolute Magnitude Estimation (Gescheider, 1988; Zwislocki, 1983). If this can be accomplished, then one ends up with a Thursonian model as the best explanation for the data.

For most global scaling tasks, two aspects of the past history of the stimulus sequence are crucial: first, the within-attribute similarity between the current and previous stimuli and, second, the judgment selected on previous trials. The within-attribute similarity between two stimuli, $S_T$ and $S_{T-k}$, is designated as

$$Sim\ (S_T,\ S_{T-k})$$

where T is the current trial and k is the number of trials back.

A slight modification of this term is needed to handle a procedural difference between experiments in which a group of subjects give several estimates of each stimulus and experiments in which a few subjects give many estimates of each stimulus. When subjects render only one or two estimates of each stimulus, the case where $S_T = S_{T-k}$ does not arise. The procedure is to present stimuli in a random order, then provide the subject with a short break, immediately followed by repetition of the same series either in the same or a new order. Different random sequences are presented to each subject, and the data are averaged in order to determine psychophysical functions and measures of response variability.

On those occasions where only a few subjects give many estimates (hundreds), it is accepted practice to allow back-to-back presentations of the same stimulus. It is reasonable to believe on these occasions that the sensory representation drifts a little between trials (chap. 7) and the subject would not perceive the second stimulus as identical in all respects to the first. There are time order effects (Hellström, 1985). In addition, for the two stimuli anchoring opposite ends of the intensity scale, it is assumed they are perceived to be maximally dissimilar. This is a necessary inclusion in the model, because the empirical data show that the connection between responses to successive stimuli is very weak or nonexistent when the members of the pair are widely separated along the intensity scale (Luce et al., 1980).

The similarity measure is arrived at by finding the similarity of the two extreme stimuli and then subtracting this from the value appropriate for each pair of stimuli on a particular trial. That is,

$$\omega = Sim\ (S_T,\ S_{T-k}) - Sim\ (S_{min},\ S_{max}), \tag{9.2}$$

where $\omega$ represents the modified similarity measure. Equation 9.2 is effective for all stimulus pairs, including the case when $S_T = S_{T-k}$. Because the similarity between the two end stimuli is always greater than 0 in the present context (range of one log-unit stimulus intensity), the modified similarity between successive stimuli will always be less than 1. Two successive stimuli are never perceived as exactly the same.

The judgment is then expressed on a given trial ($J_T$) as a weighted average of the judgment on the previous trial ($J_{T-k}$) and the judgment ($J^*$) selected from the doubly truncated Gaussian. Thus,

$$J_T = \omega J_{T-k} + (1-\omega)J^*. \tag{9.3}$$

When considered in terms of physical measures, the closer two successive stimuli are in intensity, the more weight is placed on the previous judgment. If the two stimuli are not at all alike ($\omega = 0$), then the judgment on Trial T is randomly selected and is therefore independent of what happened on previous trials.

In the implementation as a computer program, a matrix of similarity measures was created from the Sensory Aggregate Model for the requisite number of stimuli. Values from this matrix comprised input to the Judgment Option Model. The notion of similarity can be expressed as a proportion of the overlap between neural fiber types subsuming two stimuli. Because these scores can range from 0 to 1, the value of $\omega$ on each trial defines the similarity of the stimulus pair.

Some situations discussed in subsequent chapters assume that subjects consider events further back in the sequence. In such experiments the largest similarity score between the present stimulus and each of the previous ones is found, and that $\omega$ value, along with $J_{T-k}$, is substituted into Equation 9.3. On each trial, only one parameter value and one past judgment determine the current judgment.

An additional adjustment of the decision rule expressed by Equation 9.3 is needed to explain some of the context effects identified by Parducci and others (Mellers, 1983; Parducci, 1965, 1982; Parducci & Wedell, 1986). If the stimulus set is skewed by packing a disproportionate number of stimuli in either the upper (negative skew) or lower (positive skew) half of the stimulus range, the two psychophysical relations bow in opposite directions. To handle these results, it is necessary to assume that subjects keep rank order in their successive responses to match stimulus rank order. That is, response assimilation due to between-stimulus similarity is swamped by a tendency to keep rank order. Details of this version of the Judgment Option Model are given in chapter 12 for Category Estimation.

A rank order rule also does fairly well explaining many results from magnitude estimation (Baird, 1995, Baird et al., 1996). It has since been concluded, however, that such a rule has a circumscribed role in psychophysics, because empirically the rank order among successive responses does not always match that among successive stimuli. Violations of rank order are in fact quite frequent. These violations presumably occur in Category Estimation as well, so skewing of the stimulus distribution might induce a different judgment strategy from the one usually employed.

One may well ask why subjects ever violate rank order if they have access to the means of the sensory distribution and these means are clearly distinguished from each other. Violations can arise in many ways, including simple inattention to the task. Consistency over the course of a session also depends on how many past trials the subject monitors. Suppose there are three stimuli ($S_1$, $S_2$, $S_3$) and that the response options are $S_1$ ($R_1$, $R_2$, $R_3$), $S_2$ ($R_2$, $R_3$, $R_4$) and $S_3$ ($R_3$, $R_4$, $R_5$). Suppose the three are now presented in the sequence $S_2$, $S_1$ and $S_3$. If the subject maintains rank order on successive trials (one trial back), a possible set of responses for the stimuli (in the sequence) might be $S_2-R_4$, $S_1-R_2$ and $S_3-R_3$. This keeps rank order on successive trials but violates rank order two trials back. That is to say, $S_3 > S_2$ but $R_4 > R_3$. Once the subject violates rank order, responses can drift and lead to corrective action on subsequent trials, which results in more violations, and so forth.

## Output Transformation

In all scaling methods, the subject's options are restricted in some way by the experimenter; hence, the actual response observed in the laboratory is a transformation of the underlying judgment. Much has been written on the possible form of this transformation for Magnitude and Category Estimation, with and without the specification of familiar response units (e.g., Birnbaum & Elmasian, 1977; Poulton, 1989). Researchers concur that a single type of transformation does not hold for all the diverse conditions under which subjects estimate magnitudes. The major distinctions made are between the continuous and the discrete class and, within the discrete class, between Magnitude and Category Estimation.

For Magnitude Estimation, the output transformation is between the judgments determined by Equation 9.3 and the numbers typically emitted by subjects. As documented in chapter 8, subjects have preferences for certain numbers, and this influences the form of the results from scaling experiments. The fact that they use a restricted set of numbers leads to Magnitude Estimation being labeled as a discrete method. For Category Estimation, assume that the judgment values map in a one-to-one fashion into the integer categories. More on this in chapter 12.

The least understood output transformation is for the continuous class (Cross Modality Matching, Magnitude Production). In the present application, an exponential transformation is used between judgment and response (cf. Birnbaum, 1982), and a scale factor (called A for arbitrary) brings the response range into the neighborhood of the stimulus range. The output transformation for the continuous class is

$$R = A^{-1} B^J, \tag{9.4}$$

where *J* is the judgment found by evaluating Equation 9.3, and B is a fixed base. The values for these two parameters in the computer simulation to be described next are A = 35 and B = 1.63. These choices yield simulated responses that are close to those seen empirically for the estimation of line length.

This transformation is introduced for convenience, rather than by rational argument. If stimulus intensities are spaced logarithmically, a power function (exponent of approximately 1) results between the stimulus and response magnitudes. This exponent depends on the arbitrary value of B and is therefore devoid of theoretical import. The concern is less with the exact form of this function than with the changes in exponent that occur through changes in the parameter values of the judgment distributions.

## COMPUTER SIMULATIONS

In order to investigate the salient features exhibited by the model, a computer program was written to simulate the behavior of subjects employing a continuous response scale to express the perceived magnitude of each of a set of discrete stimulus intensities—an example of global scaling. The program simulates the behavior of subjects making judgments of seven stimulus intensities, spaced in equal logarithmic steps, spanning a range of one log cycle. The stimulus order is randomized independently for each subject. On the very first trial, there can be no previous judgment, so in this instance, ω is set to zero in Equation 9.3.

In order to ensure that all judgments are positive numbers, taking into account the standard deviation, the mean of each judgment distribution is set equal to the rank integer of the intensity plus 4; that is, stimuli 1, 2, . . . , 7 map into judgment means of 5, 6, . . . , 11. Standard deviation is also expressed in terms of integer units. For example, plus and minus two standard deviations of 1.5 around a mean of 5 produces a doubly truncated distribution stretching from $L = 2$ to $U = 8$ (Equation 9.1).

The values of the parameters are changed to simulate the subject's task under different laboratory conditions. These are noted in each of the appropriate sections. The dependent measures are the mean and standard deviation of the responses. These statistical measures are numerical approximations, obtained by the aid of a computer program written for this purpose.

## SIMULATION RESULTS

### Response Distributions

Figure 9.1 shows the form of the response distribution produced by the simulation. Results are based on 500 subjects. The histograms are for stimulus one (a, top), four (b, middle), and seven (c, bottom). Aside from the fact that the means

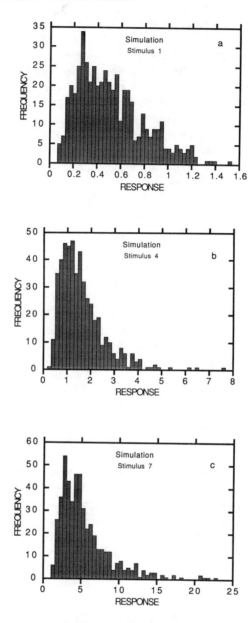

FIG. 9.1.   Frequency histograms for response distributions according to the Judgment Option Model. Histograms represent stimulus one (a), four (b), and seven (c).

maintain the same rank order as the stimuli, the response distributions differ from the associated judgment distributions in two ways. First, the variance of the response distributions increases with the mean, whereas the variance of the judgment distributions is constant. Second, each of the response distributions is positively skewed, whereas the judgment distributions are symmetric about the mean. Both of these facts have a basis in the judgment continuum, which is logarithmic. Because the logarithmically spaced stimuli are mapped into sequential integers, the inverse operation of Equation 9.4 leads to an exaggeration of the righthand tails of the response distributions. The exact form of the response distributions depends on the particular mapping between stimuli and judgments, and subsequently, between judgments and responses.

The next section reviews the detailed performance of the Judgment Option Model for a variety of experimental conditions. This lays the groundwork for explaining judgment behavior in applications of the more common methods of Magnitude and Category Estimation.

## Number of Subjects

In most studies, testing the adequacy of the Power Law, S. S. Stevens (1975) employed a dozen or so subjects, each of whom estimated the magnitude of approximately seven different intensities with several replications. Each subject might only give 14 responses in the entire experiment. The group data were then averaged, usually by taking a geometric mean, and the psychophysical function was displayed by plotting the log of the mean against the log of the intensity. When discussing the simulations of these experiments reference is made to "subjects," but this term should be understood to mean "simulated subjects," unless prefaced by an adjective indicating they had biological rather than electronic ancestors.

The initial point of interest in regard to a computer simulation is whether the constraints of the model distort the Power Law. Because the judgment distributions are constant across subjects, an experiment can be designed in alternative ways; for instance, five subjects giving 5 or 100 estimates of each intensity, or one subject giving 25 or 500 judgments per stimulus. A key aspect of this and all future simulations is that exactly the same number of stimuli and random orders are used for each computer run. Therefore, any variation in results obtained under different conditions cannot be attributed to chance variations in the stimulus order.

The simulations are run with 10, 25, 100, and 500 subjects, where each gives a single response for each stimulus. The standard deviation of each judgment distribution is 1.5, with increasing means of 5 through 11. In analyzing the data, arithmetic means are calculated rather than geometric means, because the former measures are more generally applicable (e.g., for Category Estimation). There is no substantial difference in the pattern of results with the geometric mean.

## Stevens's Power Law

Figure 9.2a shows the logarithm of the arithmetic means plotted as a function of the logarithm of the stimulus intensities. The functions along the y axis were displaced to make viewing easier. A straight line fits each data set very well, and the exponent spans a narrow range (0.96 to 1.1). The exponent for 10 subjects (1.1) is only 10% larger than the one for 500 subjects (1.0). The Judgment Option Model generates data that correspond well to what is observed in the laboratory, and the exponent does not change appreciably as a function of the number of subjects.

## Ekman Functions

Plotting the standard deviation as a function of the arithmetic mean (Figure 9.2b) reveals the response variability. The data are a bit noisy for the small subject pools, but, generally speaking, the standard deviation is a linear function of the mean in accord with Ekman's Law (described fully in chap. 10). The variability increases with the mean because the final output (response) stage of the model is an exponential transformation of the judgment stage. A straight line was fit by least squares criterion to the data for the 500-subject condition. If $sd$ is the standard deviation of the responses and $M$ is the mean, the data are described by the equation

$$sd = 0.65M - 0.09.$$

The relatively large standard deviation (1.5) of the judgment distribution produces considerable response variability. The slope of the function in Figure

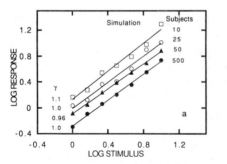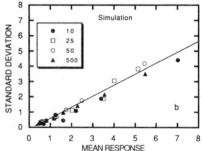

FIG. 9.2. Response magnitude as a function of stimulus intensity (log–log coordinates): left (a). Standard deviation as a function of mean response: right (b). Data generated by the Judgment Option Model from different numbers of hypothetical "subjects." The slopes (exponents) of the best-fitting straight lines are listed to the left of the functions in panel a.

9.2b is of course shallower when the standard deviation of the underlying distribution is smaller.

It is established empirically (chap. 4) that the standard deviation of responses increases with the stimulus intensity, as well as with the mean. The function often bends downward, however, for standard deviations corresponding to the most intense stimuli (Montgomery, 1975). I examine the concavity issue in subsequent chapters. At this stage, it is sufficient to state that the model reproduces the primary data from global scaling methods, and the shapes of both the mean (Figure 9.2a) and variability functions (Figure 9.2b) are stable as the number of subjects varies from 10 to 500. Unless otherwise stated, all future simulations of the model are based on 500 subjects (runs).

## Individual Differences

The aforementioned results are averages for a group. The data are not nearly as systematic for individuals, where log–log plots sometimes exhibit non-monotonicity. As the number of subjects increases, the averages become more in line with the Power Law. So in an actual experiment, asking a subject to give only one judgment for each intensity will result in a function that depends on the particular sequence of stimulus presentations, but, with enough replications using different sequences, the group results should rapidly converge to those displayed in Figure 9.2a. This reduction in variance should not be confused with a reduction due to sheer practice in the task. Even with the same stimulus order, extensive practice can lead to a reduction in response variability. The noisiness in individual functions will also depend on the variability of the judgment distributions. As the standard deviation increases, the Goodness-of-Fit deteriorates, accompanied by an increase in the variability of exponents from a group of participants.

## Judgment Variability

Simulations were conducted with different standard deviations of the judgment distributions to determine possible effects on the Stevens and Ekman functions. These simulations mimic differences in subject uncertainty regarding the appropriate judgment on each trial. Group data were obtained in four conditions with standard deviations of 0.5, 1, 1.5 and 2, respectively. Figure 9.3a shows the psychophysical function (log–log coordinates) for each condition. Judgment variability has virtually no effect on either the Power Law or its exponent, and consequently, only a single function is fit to the data. The best-fitting straight line for each standard deviation has a slope of 1.0. In the continuous response case, at least, changing the variability of the judgment distribution has no remarkable implications for the size of the exponent.

Figure 9.3b presents the corresponding Ekman functions. In all instances, the

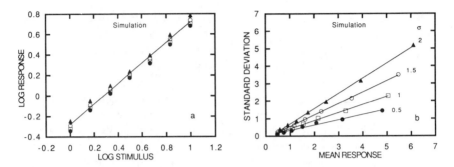

FIG. 9.3.  (a) Response magnitude as a function of stimulus intensity (log–log coordinates) with standard deviation of judgment distribution as a parameter. (b) Standard deviation as a function of mean response. Standard deviations of the judgment distributions are listed beside the functions in the right panel.

standard deviation increases with the mean, and, as would be expected, the overall response variability increases with the standard deviation of the judgment distribution. The only behavioral change that occurs with changes in judgment variability is in the magnitude of the response variability. Otherwise, the shapes of both the Stevens and Ekman functions are relatively unaffected.

## Judgment Truncation

In many experiments on global scaling, a standard is identified at either end of the continuum and serves as a referent, whose response value (modulus) is verbally assigned by the experimenter (Baird, 1970c). This procedure forces all subjects to employ roughly the same span of numerical responses, thus simplifying the collation of their responses into summary statistics. This instruction may also drop the hint, presumably picked up by the subject, that responses should not exceed the modulus when it is assigned to the strongest stimulus, nor be less than the modulus when it is assigned to the weakest one. In Magnitude Production and Cross Modality Matching, the apparatus itself imposes physical limits on the minimum and maximum responses. Subjects also may impose boundaries on how small or large they are willing to go in producing discrete numerical or continuous expressions of perceived magnitude. These limits sometimes depend on subtle cues about acceptable responses that might purposefully or inadvertently be given by the experimenter (Birnbaum, 1982). Whenever the minimum and maximum responses are limited in some manner, the model of the judgment process includes truncation of the appropriate judgment distributions.

A simulation was conducted to explore these issues in which the standard deviation of each judgment distribution is constant at 1.5, but the degrees of truncation at the lower and upper ends of the judgment continuum differ. Four extreme conditions were investigated. In labeling them, reference is made to the truncations of the two judgment distributions associated with the minimum and maximum stimulus intensities. Truncation of these two distributions automatically impacts the remaining ones. If the degree of truncation is expressed in terms of the standard deviation, where $L_{min}$ is the lower truncation point and $U_{max}$ the upper one in respect to the appropriate mean, then the four simulations are $L_{min} = -2$ (smallest distribution mean), $U_{max} = 2$ (largest distribution mean); $L_{min} = -2$, $U_{max} = 0$; $L_{min} = 0$, $U_{max} = 2$; and $L_{min} = 0$, $U_{max} = 0$. In this labeling system, 0 indicates truncation at the mean, 2 indicates truncation at $2 \times 1.5 = 3$ integer steps above the mean, and $-2 \times 1.5 = -3$ steps below the mean.

The results are presented in Figures 9.4a (Stevens functions) and 9.4b (Ekman functions). Turning first to the power function, it is obvious that truncation affects the exponent, which varies from 0.7 when both the lower and upper ends of the judgment scale are truncated at the mean (0, 0) up to an exponent of 1.0 with the least degree of truncation $(-2, 2)$. The implication is that the exponent of the power function will be affected by a procedure that truncates the response distributions: the greater the truncation, the lower the exponent. The reason for this reduction in the exponent is that truncation pushes the means for the extreme stimuli toward the center of the response range. Chapter 12 discusses the quantitative details in regard to the Method of Category Estimation.

Truncation also alters the Ekman functions (Figure 9.4b). As one would expect, response variability is less in the vicinity of the truncation. The judgment

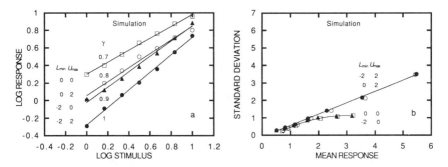

FIG. 9.4.    (a) Response magnitude as a function of stimulus intensity (log–log coordinates) with truncation of the judgment distribution as a parameter. (b) Standard deviation as a function of mean response. $L_{min}$ is the lower truncation point in z-score units for the distribution with the lowest mean. $L_{max}$ is the upper truncation point in z-score units for the distribution with the highest mean. Data generated by the Judgment Option Model.

distributions in the center of the range are less influenced by truncation than those near the ends. A linear function has been fit to the data based on the least truncation ($L_{min} = -2$, $L_{max} = 2$) and a quadratic function to the data based on the most truncation ($L_{min} = 0$, $L_{max} = 0$). The latter function looks very much like that reported by Montgomery (1975) in his investigation of the variability of magnitude estimates under conditions that might well have involved truncation of the judgment distributions.

The influence of truncation will depend as well on the standard deviation of the judgment distributions: the greater the variability, the greater the consequence of truncation. This is an especially important outcome for devotees of the Method of Category Estimation, which by its very nature insures truncation at both ends of the response scale. The Stevens function will change in slope (exponent) depending on the amount of response variability. This is an unwelcomed result if one is trying to infer sensory processes from the slope of the psychophysical function in a log–log plot.

## Trials Back

It may be that subjects sometimes consider trials further back in the sequence than just the previous one. To examine the implications of this, a simulation was conducted in which the standard deviation was 1.5 and the truncation $L_{min} = -2$ and $U_{max} = 2$. The number of previous trials considered by the subject was varied. In what might be called the control condition (trials back = k = 0), the subject randomly selects judgments from the appropriate distributions, and these are the sole basis for the overt responses (Thurstone model). In the other three conditions, the number of trials back in the sequence was either k = 1, 3, or 6.

Note one minor technicality. Because each subject only makes one estimate of each intensity, it is not possible to consider trials k steps back unless the requisite number has already occurred. For example, in the condition in which the number of trials back is six, it is only possible to consider the maximum of six previous trials on the very last trial, because a subject only estimates seven stimuli. In the event that an insufficient number of previous trials has occurred, the subject considers only so many as possible. No other assumption makes any sense!

The previous trial entering into Equation 9.3, in which between-stimulus similarity is a parameter, is determined by finding the similarity between the stimulus on the present trial and each of the stimuli on previous trials (within the constraints set by the condition) and then selecting the judgment value associated with the stimulus yielding the maximum similarity. In other words, assume that the subject searches electronic memory banks to find a previous stimulus representation that is as close as possible to the current one. The associated judgment from the past is then entered into Equation 9.3; that is, the equation is only evaluated once on each trial.

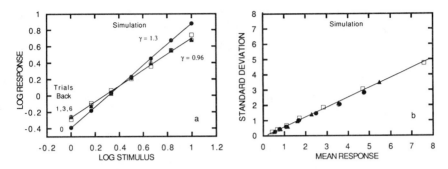

FIG. 9.5.   (a) Response magnitude as a function of stimulus intensity (log–log coordinates) with trials back (considered by the "subject") as a parameter. (b) Standard deviation as a function of mean response. Data generated by the Judgment Option Model.

The results relevant to the Stevens and Ekman functions appear in Figure 9.5. The exponent is steepest for the pure Thurstone model ($\gamma = 1.3$) in which the subject does not utilize information from any previous trials. This is what would be predicted for the Method of Absolute Magnitude Estimation, if subjects actually followed the instructions given by the experimenter (Gescheider, 1988; Zwislocki, 1983). The exponent is approximately constant ($\gamma \approx 1$) for the other three conditions in which the number of trials back is 1, 3, or 6. The corresponding Ekman functions are linear for all four conditions. Therefore, changes in the number of previous trials (greater than zero) recalled by the subject does not unduly influence either the means or standard deviations of the overt responses.

## RECAP AND PREVIEW

In the next five chapters, the Judgment Option Model confronts empirical facts that implicate cognitive processing beyond what is required to perform a one-to-one mapping between sensory events and observable responses. The ability to model such results successfully rests with identifying the source of response variability. If one wishes to investigate sensory psychophysics, it is best to assume that response fluctuations arise from activity in the neural infrastructure of the sense organs themselves. If one is interested instead in central psychological processes, it is more advantageous to view response fluctuation as a reflection of the subject's uncertainty regarding exactly which of the potential responses should be given on each trial.

The manipulation of experimental procedure has different consequences as seen through these two lenses. In the Sensory Aggregate Model, procedural variables have no special influence on the outcome, whereas in the Judgment Option Model this influence can be pronounced. According to the thesis, both conceptions are required if we are to explain all the available psychophysical data. In this regard, the two conceptions of response variability are "mutually completing." The next chapter gives a more in-depth account of the response variability produced by the Judgment Option Model.

# 10 Ekman Functions

The theme of this chapter concerns the statistical properties of response distributions from global scaling tasks of a discrete character. Special attention is paid to the relation between the standard deviation and the mean (Ekman functions). First, empirical data are presented on Stevens's Law and on the variability of judgments that accompany this law. The next section describes computer simulations of trial-by-trial scaling behavior as seen through the lens of the Judgment Option Model. Finally, the outcomes from these simulations are compared with the empirical results and conclusions drawn about the viability of the model in the light of its performance.

## STEVENS FUNCTIONS

The Power Law fares somewhat better in describing average data from a group than data from individuals. There are several plausible reasons for this advantage. One is that subjects have idiosyncratic biases in their use of numbers, and perhaps even in their use of other response continua. This bias may only be evident when many responses are given to a large number of stimuli (R. Teghtsoonian, M. Teghtsoonian, & Baird, 1995). Whatever might be the drawbacks of using individual data, this is the only source available for checking the adequacy of the Judgment Option Model at the level of the single trial.

A prototypical experiment was conducted by Green, Luce, and Duncan (1977).[1] The stimuli were 1000-Hz tones of 500-msec duration distributed over a

---

[1]The authors kindly provided me with the original data for these analyses and for those described in chapter 13.

range of 40 dB to 80 dB in 2-dB steps. Five subjects were given 600 practice trials in estimating the ratio of successive loudnesses. Afterward, they gave either 1200 or 2400 magnitude estimates over the course of several 2-hr sessions. All trials within a session were randomized, so in advance of stimulus presentation, the subject could not narrow the pool of candidates that might subsequently be presented. Magnitude estimates were registered by typing integers into a specially designed response box.

A second experiment that figures prominently in the discussion of response variability in this chapter is a more recent one by Baird et al. (1996) on the estimation of pyridine odor intensity. The stimuli were seven supra-threshold concentrations and a clean-air blank. Subjects were first preadapted to clean laboratory air in a climate chamber and were given 10 min of practice trials. Four subjects then gave 105 "free-number" (no modulus) magnitude estimates of each stimulus, whose presence was detected by a single sniff.

Figure 10.1 gives four examples of Stevens functions from these two studies.

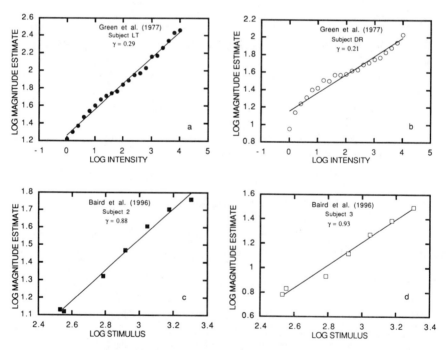

FIG. 10.1. Geometric mean magnitude estimates as a function of stimulus intensity (log–log coordinates). Panels a and b: loudness estimates from Green et al. (1977). Panels c and d: odor estimates from Baird et al. (1996). Straight lines fit by least squares solutions to obtain the slopes (exponents).

The top two panels (a, b) present data from two subjects who estimated loudness (Green et al., 1977); the bottom two panels (c, d) present data from two subjects who estimated the strength of pyridine odor (Baird et al., 1996). Straight lines are fit to the points, and the slope (exponent) is given in each panel. Neither the exponents for loudness nor odor fall very close to those recorded in Table 3.1. It is evident that such tabled values are not always representative of the functions generated by individuals. The concern here is not with the Stevens functions themselves, however, but with the response variability associated with such functions. The next section concerns this aspect of the findings and explains its relevance for the Judgment Option Model.

## EKMAN FUNCTIONS

The dependent measure in a Stevens function is the mean response to stimulus intensity. The variability of responses associated with each mean does not follow quite so predictable a course as the Stevens function. This has been known since the late 1950s when Gösta Ekman and his colleagues at Stockholm University developed analytical and graphical methods for determining the relation between the mean and standard deviation of Stevens's Law (Björkman, 1958, 1960; Ekman, 1956a, 1959; Ekman & Künnapas, 1957). Their initial approach relied on two empirical relations: that between mean magnitude estimates and physical intensity (Stevens functions) and that between stimulus JNDs and physical intensity (Weber functions). Both relations were examined for the same stimulus attribute, though each pair of databases came from independent studies conducted by different investigators.

The theoretical procedure was to mark off equal stimulus JNDs on the x axis and graphically determine the corresponding response JNDs on the y axis. This was accomplished as follows. From the Weber function, define the JND at stimulus $S_1$ as

$$\Delta S = S_2 - S_1, S_2 > S_1$$

From the Stevens function, define the mean magnitude estimates of $S_1$ and $S_2$ as

$$R_1 = S_1^\gamma$$
$$R_2 = S_2^\gamma$$

The response JND for $R_1$ corresponding to the stimulus JND for $S_1$ is then,

$$\Delta R = R_2 - R_1.$$

The response JNDs are then plotted against the mean magnitude estimates for different stimulus intensities in order to reveal a functional relation. That is,

$$\Delta R = f(R). \tag{10.1}$$

Equation 10.1 is referred to as an Ekman function. The foregoing approach is similar to one described earlier by Harper and S. S. Stevens (1948), the main steps of which are given by Gescheider (1985).

According to Ekman, it was critical that the exact form of the Stevens function must not automatically be taken as a power law, and the exact form of the Weber function must not automatically be taken as linear (Weber's Law). His concern was whether or not a graphical technique results in a systematic relation between perceived magnitude and response variability, indexed as a JND along the response continuum relative to the mean at which it is determined. These values can always be found empirically even if their variation with physical intensity is not well behaved. The final results of Ekman's efforts were mixed, because they depended on the stimulus attribute (Ekman, 1956a). A constant measure of response variability resulted for brightness and pitch over changes along the stimulus dimension. An affine, linear relation held for lifted weights (a generalization of Weber's law), whereas for the taste of salt, the function was nonlinear.

In further work (Ekman & Künnapas, 1957), the relation between what was referred to as the subjective JND (standard deviation of responses for a single stimulus) and its mean ($R$) was formulated as a mathematical hypothesis (Olsson, Harder, & Baird, 1993). If $\Delta R$ is equated with the standard deviation, then the proposal is that

$$\Delta R = \kappa R^\delta + \xi. \tag{10.2}$$

Equation 10.2 is identical in form to the generalized version of Weber's Law given in chapter 4 (Equation 4.5). Ekman and Künnapas then proceeded to define special cases holding for different attributes. For example, setting $\delta = 1$, they described the variability of responses for visual line length as

$$\Delta R = \kappa R + \xi. \tag{10.3}$$

When $\xi = 0$, there is a situation on the response side that parallels the stimulus side (Weber's Law):

$$\Delta R = \kappa R. \tag{10.4}$$

In brief, the Stockholm researchers admitted that the relation between the standard deviation and the mean did not always satisfy Weber's Law, but it was similar in form to a generalized Weber function. However, S. S. Stevens (1975) avoided any reference to the general formulations and only commented on the implications of Equations. 10.3 and 10.4. He referred to these as Ekman's Law, a practice that has continued in the literature (Baird & Noma, 1978; Gescheider, 1985; R. Teghtsoonian, 1971, 1974).[2]

It seems clear we should distinguish between Ekman's Law and Ekman func-

---

[2]Gösta Ekman told me he had an uneasy feeling about having a law named after him. He appreciated the honor but would have felt better if the law was true.

tions. The latter are more generic and refer to the relation between the standard deviation (or some other measure of response variability) and the mean, as described by Equation 10.1 or related formulas. If the definition is generous enough, the empirical data can always be described by Ekman functions but the particulars do not always follow Ekman's Law.

It is also necessary to distinguish between Weber and Ekman functions. The former is the relation between a discrimination measure and the physical intensity of a standard. The latter is the relation between variability and the mean. On a similar note, the term *Weber function* applies to results expressed in stimulus units and collected by the classical Fechnerian methods of local psychophysics (Limits, Adjustment and Constant Stimuli), whereas the term *Ekman function* applies to results expressed in response units and collected by the methods of global psychophysics (Magnitude Estimation, Category Estimation, and Cross Modality Matching). Whereas it might be reasonable within another theoretical framework to treat Weber and Ekman functions as one and the same (Baird & Noma, 1978, chap. 4), for purposes of the present analysis, they are interpreted differently. The source giving rise to Weber functions resides in sensory physiology; the source behind Ekman functions is cognitive uncertainty.

## STANDARD DEVIATION

The early Stockholm studies were preliminary. Montgomery (1975) reported a more complete investigation of the variability arising in direct scaling methods. He found that the standard deviation is a nonlinear function of the mean for a variety of experimental procedures (e.g., instructions to judge stimulus differences or ratios, stimulus range, and the number of response categories). His dependent measure is the average across the standard deviations obtained from individual subjects. This measure is then related to the group mean in order to reveal the shape of the Ekman function (although Montgomery does not refer to it as such).

Figure 10.2 presents several such functions, based on the graphs in Montgomery's article. For each data set, a parabola (quadratic equation) offers a satisfactory description, with different weights of the parameters for different experimental conditions. That is, in all cases,

$$\Delta R = \kappa_1 + \kappa_2 R - \kappa_3 R^2 \qquad (10.5)$$

provides a good description of the Ekman function, where the coefficient for the square term is larger in Category Estimation (limited response options) than in Magnitude Estimation. The depression of variability at the ends of the stimulus scale for Category Estimation is due to the boundaries set by the smallest and largest categories. This issue is thoroughly explored in chapter 12. Equation 10.5 is yet another rendering of Equation 10.1 to accommodate empirical data. Its

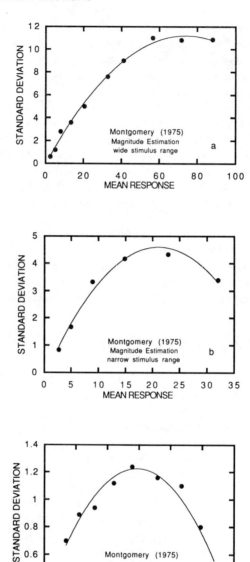

FIG. 10.2.   Standard deviation as a function of mean response (Ekman function) for Magnitude Estimation with a wide stimulus range (a), Magnitude Estimation with a narrow stimulus range (b), and Category Estimation (c). From Montgomery (1975).

most salient feature is the negative sign of the square term. This is responsible for the nonmonotonic behavior of the function; response variability does not continuously increase with increases in the mean. This is in marked contrast to Weber's Law, which is monotonic throughout most of its course, with occasional deviations near the lower absolute threshold (chap. 4, Laming, 1986).

Montgomery's functions depend on rather sparse data, but additional evidence from other studies indicates that his findings are indeed representative and regularly occur for individual subjects who give many estimates of the same stimulus intensity. Figure 10.3 gives four examples of Ekman functions for individual subjects run for a substantial number of trials with Magnitude Estimation (at least 100 estimates of each stimulus). Each panel shows the standard deviation as a function of the mean for a single subject, whose accompanying Stevens function is depicted in Figure 10.1. The top two panels (a, b) give summary data based on magnitude estimates of loudness (Green et al., 1977). The bottom two panels (c, d) present comparable data for estimates of pyridine odor (Baird, 1995; Baird et al., 1996). Equation 10.5 is fit to each data set, merely to highlight the quadratic trends evident to the naked eye.

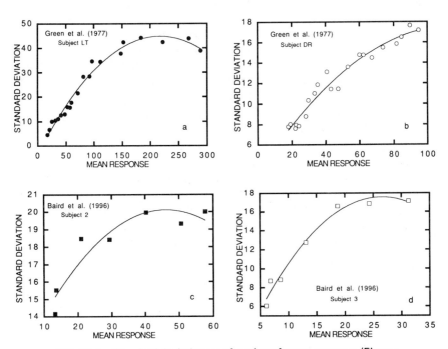

FIG. 10.3.    Standard deviation as a function of mean response (Ekman function). Panels a and b: loudness estimates from Green et al. (1977). Panels c and d: odor estimates from Baird et al. (1996). Quadratic functions are drawn through the points to emphasize the trends.

Not all subjects in these two studies produced such nonlinearities. The data of several show a linear relation between the standard deviation and the mean, a result that is described by substituting the appropriate parameter values into Equation 10.5. It is nevertheless true that a negatively accelerated curve is the rule for the Ekman functions for most individuals, thus lending support to Montgomery's conclusions based on average standard deviations across individuals.

## RELATIVE ERROR

An alternative way to represent variability is to plot the relative error (standard deviation divided by the mean) as a function of the mean (Baird et al., 1980; Green et al., 1977). Figure 10.4 presents examples of such functions for the four subjects whose Stevens functions appear in Figure 10.1. The relative error declines as a function of the mean, which is what must occur if the standard deviation is a negatively accelerated function of the mean (seen in Figure 10.3).

Relative errors for groups are similar to those for individuals. For example, a recent study (Nordin, 1994) tested groups who judged the attributes of odor, loudness, and brightness. Subjects estimated intensities along each stimulus dimension by using a common numerical response scale. The unusual aspect of the study is that values of different stimulus attributes are intermixed within the series, so, for example, a sound might follow an odor or a light might follow a sound. There is little or no influence of one attribute on the reliability of judgments obtained for the others. The points in Figure 10.5 are relative errors for each attribute analyzed separately.[3] The label at the top of each graph indicates the physical attribute being judged, either by itself, or in the context of the other two attributes noted in the legend.

The relative error declines with the logarithm of the mean, just as in the data plots for individuals (Figure 10.4).[4] Similar findings were reported for Magnitude Estimation and Cross Modality Matching of loudness and visual area (Baird et al., 1980). This pattern of results is frequent in global psychophysics, both for individuals who give many estimates of each stimulus and for larger groups whose members only give one or two estimates of each stimulus.

## SKEWNESS

Another measure of potential relevance in isolating the cognitive factors at work in global psychophysics is the skewness of the response distributions. Although

---

[3]The author kindly provided me with the summary statistics.

[4]The relative error for individuals is usually plotted as a function of the logarithm of the mean response. I only want to demonstrate here that the relation is monotonically decreasing for individuals and for groups.

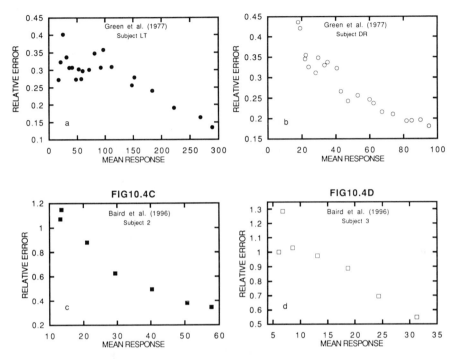

FIG. 10.4.   Relative error (standard deviation divided by the mean) as a function of mean response. Panels a and b: loudness estimates from Green et al. (1977). Panels c and d: odor estimates from Baird et al. (1996).

this measure is seldom mentioned in published reports, the existing data for individuals are consistent. The response distributions typically seen in Magnitude Estimation are positively skewed for the weakest intensities and approach normality, or negative skew, for the strongest ones. Figure 10.6 presents data from the four individuals used for purposes of illustration.

Within each set of response distributions, skewness decreases with increases in stimulus intensity, but the trend is more pronounced for the two subjects judging odor than it is for the two judging loudness. The marked negative skew for the loudness distributions associated with intense stimuli is almost certainly due to the fact that subjects in this study, who were run for more than 1000 trials in multiple experimental sessions, eventually settled on a single upper numerical response for assignment to the maximum stimulus. This was especially true for subject LT, whose response scale became firmly anchored at the top by an explicit preference for the number "290" (a fact revealed by examining the raw data). For purposes of setting the stage for comparison of empirical data with computer simulations, remember that the response distributions associated with

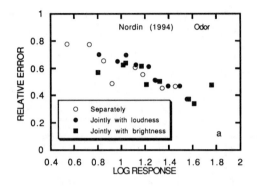

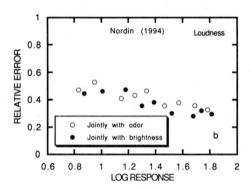

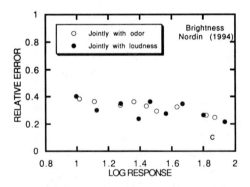

FIG. 10.5.   Relative error (standard deviation divided by the mean) as a function of mean response (logarithmic units). The attribute is in the upper righthand corner of each panel: odor (a), loudness (b), brightness (c). Judgments given under conditions noted in the enclosed captions. From Nordin (1994).

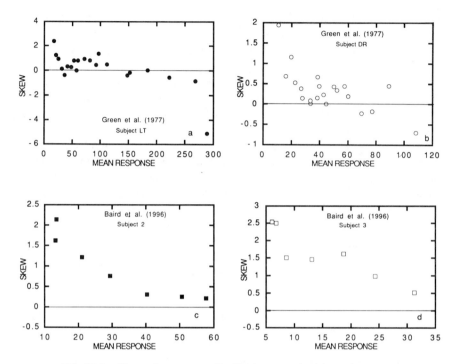

FIG. 10.6.   Skew of response distribution as a function of mean response. Panels a and b: loudness estimates from Green et al. (1977).
Panels c and d: odor estimates from Baird et al. (1996).

the Method of Magnitude Estimation tend to be positively skewed, less so for the
more intense stimuli.

## SIMULATION RESULTS

The same kinds of computer simulations described for the continuous case (chap.
9) for Magnitude and Category Estimation were conducted. The data are based
on the Gaussian distributions of potential judgments, and on the same equations
for determining response assimilation in terms of the similarity between successive stimuli. While leaving open, for the time being, the possible relevance of
events occurring several trials back in the series, assume here that subjects only
consider events one trial back.

The major modification that must be made in the Judgment Option Model for
Magnitude Estimation is that the response options become discrete values arrayed along the number continuum in accord with subjects' tendency to use
certain numbers much more frequently than others. Such biases are described by

the Number Preference Model (chap. 8). There are several ways to handle the transformation between the hypothetical judgment continuum and the observed responses. The approach assumes that the subject only selects integers from the judgment distribution, and these values are transformed into preferred responses. It relies on the assumptions of the Judgment Option Model and the Number Preference Model and then computes probabilities for each of the discrete judgments available within each of the distributions associated with each stimulus intensity.

As noted earlier, the x variable along the judgment continuum has a probability density function with mean $\xi$, standard deviation $\sigma$, and truncation points L and U (Johnson & Kotz, 1970, p. 81). Unless otherwise stated, the default truncation points for each judgment distribution are plus and minus two standard deviations from the mean:

$$ f(J) = \frac{1}{\sigma\sqrt{2\pi}} e^{(-1/2\sigma^2)(J-\xi)^2} \left[ \frac{1}{\sigma\sqrt{2\pi}} \int_L^U e^{(-1/2\sigma^2)(t-\xi)^2} dt \right]^{-1} . \quad (10.6) $$

## Standardization of Categories

Upon presentation of a stimulus, only discrete judgments are available, so it is necessary to standardize the probability for each by first employing Equation 10.6 to find the probability density for each option. Next, standardized (discrete) probabilities are determined by dividing each $f(J)$ by the sum of all such probabilities for the available set of judgments (Baird, 1995; Baird, Harder, & Preis, 1996).[5] The standardized probability $pr(J_i)$ for a judgment is defined within the boundaries of the lower ($L$) and upper ($U$) truncation points:

$$ pr(J_i) = \frac{f(J_i)}{\displaystyle\sum_{i=1}^{N} f(J_i)}, \quad U \geq J_i \geq L . \quad (10.7) $$

The similarity between the stimulus presented on trials T and T−1 influences the eventual response on trial T. From now on, judgments and stimuli are indexed by trial number instead of by magnitude; so $J_T$ is the judgment of $S_T$ on trial T. The same weighted average formula is used as for the continuous case; that is,

$$ J_T = \omega J_{T-1} + (1 - \omega) J^*, \quad (10.8) $$

where $J^*$ is selected from the Gaussian distribution, and the similarity between successive stimuli is determined by the Sensory Aggregate Model. The weighting factor is then defined in the manner explained in the previous chapter:

$$ \omega = Sim\ (S_T, S_{T-1}) - Sim\ (S_{min}, S_{max}). \quad (10.9) $$

---

[5]See Huttenlocher, Hedges, and Duncan (1991) for a related argument on the effects of truncation.

One additional change from the continuous model is necessary, because of the discrete character of the judgments. Equation 10.8 produces noninteger values of $J_T$ because the weighting factor is graded. Therefore, an adjustment is required to negate this problem. The solution is to round the value of $J_T$ to the nearest integer (among the available judgment options). The actual value of $J_T$ is then defined as

$$J_T = round \, [\omega J_{T-1} + (1 - \omega)J^*], \, J_{min} \le J_T \le J_{max}, \qquad (10.10)$$

where $J_{min}$ and $J_{max}$ are the minimum and maximum judgment allowed for a particular stimulus.

Magnitude Estimation is simulated by changing the output stage from what holds in the continuous case. The discrete judgment options are now converted into preferred numbers. For example, if the judgments for a set of three stimuli are 1, 2, 3, then the output for Magnitude Estimation might be 1, 5, 10, depending on the maximum stimulus intensity.

For Category Estimation, the transformation between judgments and responses is one to one; that is, judgments 1, 2, and 3 convert directly into categories 1, 2, and 3. More details about these transformations and the exact numbers in the computer simulations are discussed in what follows.

## Preferred Numbers

There is some leeway in choosing the numerical responses used in computer simulations, because not all subjects exhibit exactly the same preferences. Different choices result in somewhat different results, although the general outcomes of the simulations are the same for most reasonable choices. In order to make specific predictions, however, the responses corresponding to the means of the judgment distribution for the seven stimuli are taken to be 15, 20, 25, 50, 75, 100, and 150. This particular series does not start at 1, because magnitude estimates in the absence of truncation of the judgment distributions can extend below and above these boundaries. Response options added to the ends of the range are 1, 2, 5, and 10 (lower end) and 200, 250, 500, and 750 (upper end). These 15 preferred numbers correspond to integer values along the judgment continuum that extend from 1 to 15. That is, if the mean of the judgment distribution for the weakest intensity is "5," and the standard deviation is 2, then plus and minus two standard deviations stretches from 1 to 9. Thus, it is necessary to have nine preferred numbers to cover the response options for the weakest stimulus. The same principle is adhered to in deciding on the available options for all other stimuli.

The essential point in regard to the significance of the output phase of the model is that the determination of the probabilities assigned to each response alternative depends on the standard deviation of the underlying Gaussian. A greater abundance of response options exists with large standard deviations than with small standard deviations.

The simulated judgment strategy is the same as for the continuous case. The only difference is that at the output stage the judgments are transformed into preferred numbers, and are not subjected to the exponential transformation employed for the continuous case. Subsequently, all data analyses are performed on the preferred numbers. In brief, Magnitude Estimation is identical to a continuous response method insofar as the judgment process is concerned, but this process leads subsequently to a discrete representation of perceived magnitude, modulated by a preferred number bias. The model for Category Estimation does not include these biases; the mapping is one-to-one between discrete judgments and category responses.

## Discrete Judgment Distributions

Figure 10.7 shows response histograms for a weak, medium, and strong intensity without the influence of assimilation from previous trials. The judgment distributions underlying these histograms each have a standard deviation of 1.5. The Thurstone Model generates hypothetical probabilities for each response option available under each of three conditions:

1. Truncation of each judgment distribution at plus and minus 2 standard deviations (2 × 1.5 = ± 3 integer steps). This is the default situation for Magnitude Estimation.

2. Truncation at minus 2 standard deviations for the distribution associated with the weakest intensity, but truncation at the mean of the distribution associated with the strongest intensity. This represents a frequent case in which the judgment options are truncated at the top of the response continuum.

3. Truncation at the means of the distributions associated with the weakest and strongest stimuli. This simulates the method of Category Estimation, but also is appropriate for some Magnitude Estimation conditions (discussed in chap. 11).

The truncations apply to all distributions; that is, no judgment options exist outside those enclosed by these boundaries.

## Statistical Measures

The statistics for evaluating predictions for Magnitude and Category Estimation are calculated by the usual methods. The mean response is expressed by Equation 10.11:

$$\bar{R} = \sum_{i=1}^{N} pr\,(R_i)\,R_i \tag{10.11}$$

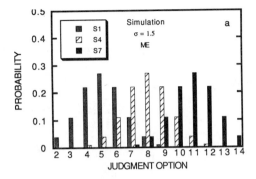

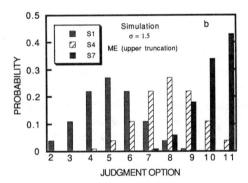

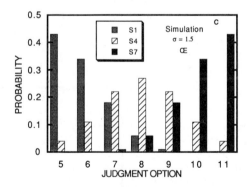

FIG. 10.7.  Discrete probability histogram for stimuli one, four, and seven: Magnitude Estimation (ME) (a), Magnitude Estimation with truncation at the mean judgment for stimulus seven (b), Category Estimation (CE) with truncation at the mean judgment for stimulus one (lower) and at the mean judgment for stimulus seven (upper) (c). Data generated by the Judgment Option Model.

with variance,

$$var\ (R) = \sum_{i=1}^{N} pr\ (R_i)\ (R_i - \overline{R})^2 \qquad (10.12)$$

and standard deviation,

$$sd = \sqrt{var\ (R)} \qquad (10.13)$$

The skew of the distribution is defined as:

$$Sk\ (R) = \frac{\sum_{i=1}^{N} pr\ (R_i)\ [R_i - \overline{R}]^3}{sd(R)^3} . \qquad (10.14)$$

Computer simulations were conducted to explore the implications of the model for the response distributions associated with Magnitude and Category Estimation. In all cases, seven stimuli were employed and 500 subjects gave one estimate of each. The data were then pooled across the group and measures calculated to compare the relation between the predictions of the model and the data from actual experiments. As has been the practice throughout this book, no attempt is made to achieve best fits to empirical results, being content at this juncture to show that the model predicts the same patterns seen in the laboratory.

### Simulation Exponents

Figure 10.8 presents the Stevens functions for each of the three conditions. The exponent for the magnitude estimation condition is the largest ($\gamma = 0.81$); the exponent is somewhat less for the truncation condition ($\gamma = 0.72$) and is signifi-

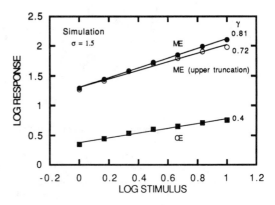

FIG. 10.8. Response magnitude as a function of stimulus intensity (log–log coordinates). Data generated by the Judgment Option Model for magnitude estimation (ME), Magnitude Estimation with upper truncation, and Category Estimation (CE). Parameter values of the simulation are listed on the graph.

cantly smaller for Category Estimation ($\gamma = 0.4$). The difference in the y intercept of the magnitude and category estimation functions occurs because of differences in the two output functions; category estimates can only vary from 1 to 7.

## Standard Deviation

In order to evaluate the match between the simulation and empirical data, the standard deviation of the response distributions was determined for each of the three hypothetical conditions. Figure 10.9 shows the results, where the standard deviation is plotted as a function of the mean. The left panel (a) shows the results for the two Magnitude Estimation conditions, the right panel (b) gives comparable data for Category Estimation.

The Ekman function is linear (Equation 10.4) for Magnitude Estimation without truncation (filled circles), but when truncation is present (open circles), the standard deviation levels off for the highest mean responses. In this case, the Ekman function is a parabola (Equation 10.2). For Category Estimation, the standard deviation is highest in the middle of the scale and sharply lower at both ends. When compared with the results displayed in Figures 10.2 and 10.3, it is apparent that the trends are the same in the simulation as in the empirical data. The fact that empirical magnitude estimates show a decline in the standard deviation for the highest stimulus intensities suggests that subjects in these experiments are limiting their responses by imposing boundaries on the acceptable response options. That is to say, the results lie somewhere between the simulation results for Magnitude Estimation (with truncation at the upper end) and Category Estimation.

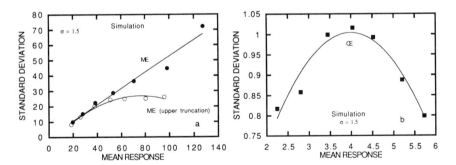

FIG. 10.9.   Standard deviation as a function of mean response. Data generated by the Judgment Option Model for Magnitude Estimation (ME, filled circles) and Magnitude Estimation with upper truncation (open circles) (panel a) and for Category Estimation (CE, panel b). The standard deviation of each judgment distribution is 1.5.

## Relative Error

Figure 10.10 shows the relative error (standard deviation divided by the mean) as a function of the mean responses for the sample power functions generated by the Judgment Option Model. Data are presented for three conditions: Magnitude Estimation, Magnitude Estimation with truncation at the top, and Category Estimation. Consistent with the result that the standard deviation is a negatively accelerated function of the mean, the relative errors decline as the mean increases. This pattern is evident for both individuals (Figure 10.4) and groups (Figure 10.5).

There are nonetheless interesting differences in the shape of the simulation functions under the three conditions. Magnitude Estimation without truncation (filled circles) is nonmonotonic and relatively constant over changes in the mean. On the other hand, when truncation is present, the function is initially nonmonotonic and then declines in a regular fashion (open circles). For Category Estimation (Figure 10.10b), the function declines monotonically with increases in the mean. If truncation occurs at both the bottom and top of the judgment continuum, the function for the relative error of simulation data for Magnitude Estimation (not shown here) looks more like that for Category Estimation.

In sum, empirical and simulation data for Magnitude Estimation all show a general decline of relative error with increases in the mean. This suggests that subjects in psychophysical experiments render estimates based on a strategy that lies somewhere between the two "ideal" strategies simulated here for Magnitude and Category Estimation.

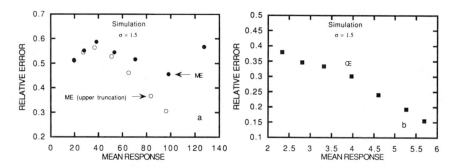

FIG. 10.10.   Relative error (standard deviation divided by the mean) as a function of mean response. Data generated by the Judgment Option Model for Magnitude Estimation (ME, filled circles, panel a) and Magnitude Estimation with upper truncation (open circles, panel a) and for Category Estimation (CE, panel b). The standard deviation of each judgment distribution is 1.5.

## Skewness

Figure 10.11 presents the skew of each response distribution for the three conditions as a function of the mean. As with the empirical data (Figure 10.6), the skewness for Magnitude Estimation (Figure 10.11a) is highly positive for low intensities (small means) and declines as the mean increases. Neither of these two relations are monontonic and they appear to be leveling off at the highest means. The relation for the truncation condition (open circles) asymptotes at a lower level than it does for Magnitude Estimation without truncation (filled circles). The skew for the most intense stimulus is abnormally high. Without truncation at the upper end of the response scale, the approximately logarithmic spacing between response options leads to high positive skew. The fact that this does not occur in the empirical data suggests that subjects there are truncating their responses at the upper end of the scale.

The skew for Category Estimation also declines with increasing mean, but actually becomes negative for the largest values. This is an obvious result of the truncation automatically imposed by the method. For the weakest stimulus intensities, the response distributions must be positively skewed and for the strongest intensities negatively skewed. These simulations suggest that subjects using Magnitude Estimation are inclined to truncate their responses at one or both ends of the judgment continuum. Negative skew is seen for the largest means in the loudness data of subjects DR and LT (Figure 10.6a,b).

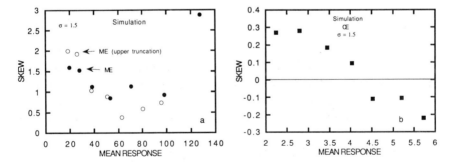

FIG. 10.11.   Skew of response distribution as a function of mean response. Data generated by the Judgment Option Model for Magnitude Estimation (ME, filled circles, panel a) and Magnitude Estimation with upper truncation (open circles, panel a) and for Category Estimation (CE, panel b). The standard deviation of each judgment distribution is 1.5.

## INTERPRETING EKMAN FUNCTIONS

In summarizing his own efforts to specify a theoretical connection between the standard deviation and the mean of magnitude estimates, Ekman (1956a) proceeded with caution: "No obvious conclusions can be drawn from our survey of experiments. We have found three different types of relations between difference limen and position on the subjective continuum. . . . It is quite clear that difference limens and scale values ought to be determined within the same investigation" (p. 9).

If the problem of perceptual discrimination is treated just in terms of the psychophysical method, it is justifiable to say that classical methods—such as the Method of Limits, Adjustment, and Constant Stimuli—yield results consistent with a generalization of Weber's Law, at least over the range of stimulus intensities tested in the psychophysics laboratory (chap. 4). Therefore, when a stimulus and response dimension are both selected from among the perceptual attributes commonly used in psychophysics (e.g., line length, brightness, loudness), a generalization of Weber's Law applies to the stimulus side on the local level and a generalization of Ekman's Law applies to the response side on the global level.

This conclusion does not imply, however, that the local source of variability is identical to the global source. According to the Sensory Aggregate Model, the neural code responsible for Weber's Law is the firing-rate distribution over a population of neurons that respond characteristically to each stimulus quality and intensity. In contrast, the source of variability behind Ekman's Law is another matter. According to the Judgment Option Model, it depends on the subject's uncertainty as to exactly which response to give.

## OVERVIEW

This concludes the presentation of the fundamentals of the Judgment Option and Number Preference Models. The cognitive approach inherent in these formulations provides explanations for Stevens's Law and its exponent (chap. 8), as well as for the detailed shape of response distributions arising from the use of global scaling methods.

These same empirical phenomena are explained equally well by the complementary viewpoint actualized in the Sensory Aggregate Model. The two approaches are alternative, equally valid perspectives on the same set of facts. The next three chapters address psychophysical phenomena that create more perplexing problems for a sensory model. In many, but not all, such cases a cognitive orientation still helps to formulate satisfactory explanations.

# 11 Context and Magnitude Estimation

Ever since direct scaling gained currency in the 1960s, a criticism has been voiced that results critically depend on stimulus and response context. Variables such as the stimulus range, the number of response alternatives, and the position of the standard have all been singled out as important determinants of results. The unspoken opinion behind some of this criticism is that a sufficiently clever experimenter could arrange conditions so that context effects are nonexistent. Researchers who champion the use of scaling methods, though not all of their critics, believe it is possible to identify a set of conditions that is "bias free," and therefore, capable of producing scale values that faithfully reflect the operation of sensory processes.

This line of reasoning implies that context is something added to an otherwise pristine method, which left unsullied, can be trusted to yield unbiased results. There is no unequivocal evidence to support this contention. The accepted validity checks for Magnitude Estimation, such as Cross Modality Matching, are susceptible to the same contextual constraints as the method they are supposed to validate. It seems likely that Cross Modality Matching would be influenced by the position of a standard in the series or by the particular examples used in practice trials. As Mashhour and Hosman (1968) demonstrated, even the choice of whether or not an additive constant is included in fitting the power function can spell the difference between excellent and poor validation of Magnitude Estimation by transitivity tests using Cross Modality Matching.

Within the framework of the Judgment Option Model, it is impossible to devise a psychophysical method that validates another scaling method if both tap into the same level of information processing—that is, the level of behavioral judgments based on external stimulus inputs. The question of validity can only be answered by transferring the experiments into an entirely different realm. S. S. Stevens (1970, 1971a, 1975) reviewed a considerable body of sensorineural data he believed validated the Power Law, but this law is not validated definitively by showing it describes the relation between external stimulation and neural discharge of a single neuron or of an entire nerve bundle. A more impressive result would be to discover that the same exponent of the Power Law occurs electrophysiologically and psychophysically, or that the same form of response variability exists at both levels of analysis. This can only be accomplished by comparing a variety of dependent measures from different sensory systems. It would be especially informative if one could show that all the psychophysical laws, including those describing response variability and reaction time, share the same neurophysiological substructure. The potential understanding that would follow a unification of psychophysical laws is hinted at by the predictions of the Sensory Aggregate Model, which is but one example of what is needed to unify the laws of psychophysics by tracing their origin to a common neurophysiological source (another is provided by Norwich, 1993).

Even if unification could be achieved, context effects, so prevalent in direct scaling methods, are best understood by adopting a cognitive slant on the source of response variability. The Judgment Option Model assumes that such variability arises because of uncertainty on the part of the subject about exactly which of many responses is appropriate to express perceived magnitude. There is no such thing as a context-free psychophysical method. All one can say in this regard is that results depend on the details of the method employed, and a theoretical model is required to clarify exactly why such details are critical. The results of direct scaling methods are "conditional" on the circumstances under which they are obtained, both with regard to the stimuli, instructions, and procedure.

This chapter and the succeeding two review some well-known facts concerning the nature of context effects, while providing new theoretical reasons for their existence. The starting point is the Judgment Option Model, but variations on the core model are required to deal with all the phenomena.

## STIMULUS–RESPONSE FUNCTIONS

The initial inquiry addresses possible distortions of the psychophysical relation that might creep in when going from the continuous to the discrete case. With this possibility in mind, performance of the model is examined for several standard deviations of the judgment distributions (constant within each condition for all seven means).[1] Two key equations from previous chapters are worth

---

[1]Some of these analyses duplicate or are similar to those presented in the previous chapter. They are necessary to set the stage for the analyses that follow.

reiterating here. On any given trial (T) the judgment is a weighted average of the judgment on the previous trial and the judgment selected from the Gaussian distribution:

$$J_T = \omega J_{T-1} + (1 - \omega)J^*, \tag{11.1}$$

where the weighting factor, $\omega$, is the similarity between successive stimuli

$$\omega = Sim\ (\mathbf{S}_T, \mathbf{S}_{T-1}) - Sim\ (\mathbf{S}_{min}, \mathbf{S}_{max}). \tag{11.2}$$

Figure 11.1a shows typical simulation results. The log mean response is plotted as a function of the log stimulus intensity for two standard deviations of the judgment distributions (0.5 and 2). The linear functions offer excellent fits to the data, and the exponents for these two conditions are similar (0.84 and 0.80). Both are less than for the continuous case with the same parameter values, but it should be recalled that the values of the parameters of the exponential transformation between the judgment and response continua for the continuous case affects the exponent. In other words, the two cases are not directly comparable. Intermediate standard deviations yield exponents that fall between the two values shown in Figure 11.1a, but for these conditions as well, the fits of the linear function are excellent. Stevens's Law describes the simulation results, and the exponent does not change appreciably with changes in the variability of the judgment distributions.

Figure 11.1b (right panel) gives parallel data pertaining to Ekman's Law. The standard deviation is plotted as a function of the mean for the same two standard deviations of the judgment distributions. Linear functions are fit to highlight the trends. Ekman's Law offers reasonable summaries of the trends in both instances, though a slight curvilinearity is noticeable (bowing in opposite directions for the large and small standard deviations). The quadratic generalization of

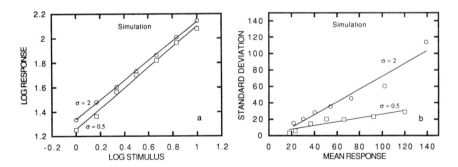

FIG. 11.1.  (a) Mean response magnitude as a function of stimulus intensity (log–log coordinates) for two standard deviations of judgment distributions (0.5 and 2). (b) Standard deviation as a function of the mean. Data generated by the Judgment Option Model.

Ekman's Law would incorporate these curvilinearities better than linear functions. The patterns are comparable to those for the continuous case, and also agree with the pattern in sets of empirical data collected in the laboratory (chaps. 3 & 10). The following addresses the results arising from procedural variations on the Method of Magnitude Estimation that impact on the exponent of Stevens's Law.

## STIMULUS RANGE

An obvious prediction of the Judgment Option Model concerns the effect of stimulus range. As reviewed in chapter 6, some research implies that subjects have a fixed response range and this "subjective" range is mapped into different stimulus ranges associated with different attributes (Poulton, 1989; R. Teghtsoonian, 1971). This mapping might be responsible for producing the diverse Stevens exponents.

The Judgment Option Model generates outputs that can be well fit by a power function, but because the model is impervious to stimulus spacing, the exponent is at the mercy of the stimulus range. The exponent does not depend exclusively on range because responses assimilate to those from previous trials, and the amount of assimilation depends on stimulus similarity. Therefore, doubling the range reduces the exponent, but the reduction is less than half the starting value.

### Empirical Exponents

R. Teghtsoonian (1973) reported several experiments in which the stimulus range is varied and the exponent of the power function determined. His findings are depicted in Figure 11.2 for the attributes of loudness and visual distance (along

FIG. 11.2. Stevens exponent as a function of logarithm of stimulus range for magnitude estimates of loudness (squares) and distance (circles). Filled points represent empirical data. Open points represent the cases where the exponent varies inversely with logarithm of stimulus range. After R. Teghtsoonian (1973).

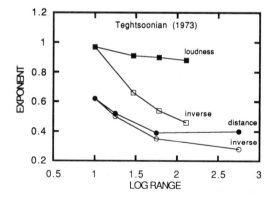

the ground). The open points indicate predictions under the assumption that the inverse of the stimulus range is the sole determiner of the exponent. Neither of the empirical trends (filled points) fall as rapidly as the inverse function.

## Computer Simulation

A simulation of range effects is based on two considerations. First, with the number of stimuli held constant, exactly the same response options are available for each stimulus regardless of its magnitude—response options are independent of range. Second, assimilation depends on the sensory similarity between the present stimulus and the one that occurred on the previous trial. The absolute amount of assimilation across all trials depends on stimulus range. The greater the range, the less the interstimulus similarity, and the weaker the assimilation over successive trials. The key theoretical decision concerns exactly how the weight ($\omega$) placed on the previous judgment should change as a function of stimulus range. This problem is resolved by employing a simple definition of the weighting factor ($\omega$) as it relates to stimulus range ($S_{max}/S_{min}$). On each trial its value is defined as

$$\omega = \frac{1}{2 \, log \, (S_{max}/S_{min})} \, . \tag{11.3}$$

This expression is different from Equation 11.2. The strength of assimilation in the present simulation decreases inversely with range, but the degree of assimilation is independent of stimulus separation. This definition of the weighting factor is introduced in lieu of a full understanding of the way changes in stimulus range actually affect the assimilation occurring over successive trials for different stimulus separations. The multiplier $1/2$ in Equation 11.3 is arbitrary. It establishes a reasonable value for $\omega$ when the range is one log unit.

Figure 11.3 shows the results produced by this model ($\sigma = 1.5$). The expo-

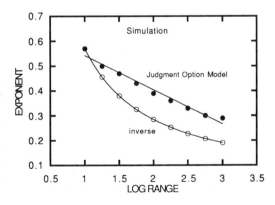

FIG. 11.3. Stevens exponent as a function of logarithm of stimulus range. Filled circles represent predictions of the Judgment Option Model. Open circles represent the case where the exponent varies inversely with the logarithm of stimulus range.

nent (filled circles) decreases as a function of stimulus range, but not at the same rate as the inverse of the range (open squares).

To recap, then, the Judgment Option Model predicts that two factors are at work when stimulus range increases. The exponent decreases because response options are impervious to stimulus range, while the exponent increases because of the weakened pull of assimilation. The exponent is a function of the comparative strengths of each factor. It should also be noted, however, that other studies do not always find a monotonic relation between the exponent and stimulus range (Ahlström & Baird, 1989; H. J. Foley et al., 1983). This complicates the explanation of range effects and raises doubts about the universality of the explanation offered here in terms of the Judgment Option Model. Some of these effects may in fact have a sensory origin (chapter 3).

## Response Variability

The Judgment Option Model minus the assimilation module is a Thurstone model. The latter predicts that the entire response distributions are invariant under transformations of stimulus range. In other words, the response variability for stimulus "1" in a set of 7 is identical for all ranges. This is in contrast to the Sensory Aggregate Model, which predicts a variety of exponents by assuming that the parameter values of the distribution of neuronal thresholds are not the same for all attributes. Response variability in that model depends on the properties of the particular distribution for an attribute, so the variability for stimulus "1" depends on which attribute is at issue.

It would seem at first glance that a critical test between the Thurstone, Judgment Option, and Sensory Aggregate Models is possible. An experiment could employ the same number of stimuli, with several different attributes. According to the Thurstone Model, the Ekman function is the same for all attributes; but, according to the Sensory Aggregate Model, the Ekman function depends on the attribute. This is not a very discriminating test in regard to the Judgment Option Model, however, because it includes assimilation processes that depend on range. This model is also sensitive to differences in the standard deviation of the judgment distributions. If response uncertainty depends on stimulus attribute, the Ekman functions will vary. It may prove difficult after all to make an unambiguous choice among these three models in this instance.

## POSITION OF THE STANDARD

The position of a standard in respect to the stimulus series is a major context effect in Magnitude Estimation (Poulton, 1989). The exponent is lowest when the standard (assigned a modulus value such as "100") is at either end of the stimulus series, and highest when the standard is in the middle. Among the earliest studies of this phenomenon are those of Engen and Levy (1955) and Engen and Ross (1966), who investigated the influence of the numerical value assigned to the standard. These authors noted a change in exponent as a function of the position of the standard in respect to a series of line lengths that were magnitude estimated by different groups. Sufficient data for drawing a summary function through the points exists only for the unusual condition in which the modulus was assigned the value "14." Nonetheless, the relation is clearcut. As seen in Figure 11.4 (filled circles), the highest exponents occur when the standard is in the middle of the range. When the standards are the smallest or largest in the series, and are not even presented for judgment, the exponents are smaller.

The other data set (open circles) in Figure 11.4 was generated by a simulation of Magnitude Estimation derived from the Judgment Option Model. The stimulus range is identical to that of Engen and Ross, and results were obtained with a standard deviation of the judgment distributions fixed at 1.5. In separate simulation runs, subjects made estimates with the modulus assigned to each of the seven stimuli.

In order to simulate laboratory performance, it is assumed the subject never assigns the value of the standard to any of the other stimuli. That is, a constraint is imposed on each judgment distribution such that the value of the modulus is only available as an option in response to the standard. In effect, imposing this constraint means that rank order is roughly preserved between responses to the other stimuli in respect to the standard. Errors in rank order can still be made, however, because the judgment distributions of neighboring stimuli extend beyond the value of the standard. That is to say, the response options for some of the stimuli larger than the standard extend below the modulus assigned to the standard, and some stimuli smaller than the standard have response options that extend above the modulus.

The rationale is that subjects in such experiments usually recognize the standard and generally call it by the modulus assigned by the experimenter (Baird,

FIG. 11.4. Stevens exponent as a function of position of the standard stimulus (logarithmic units). Filled circles from Engen and Ross (1966). Open circles from the Judgment Option Model. Open triangles from the Judgment Option Model where lower truncation is at the mean of the lowest judgment distribution and high truncation is at the mean of the highest judgment distribution.

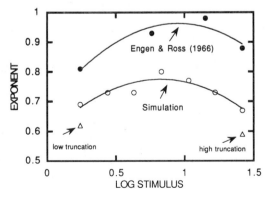

1970c). As with the empirical data, the exponent from the simulation (summarized by the solid line in Figure 11.4) is highest when the modulus is assigned to a stimulus in the middle of the range and is much less when the standard is at either end.

The two open triangles below the line represent other simulations in which the modulus is a truncation point for the judgment distributions—at the mean of the lowest distribution when the modulus is the smallest in the series, and at the mean of the highest distribution when the modulus is the largest. The diminished size of the exponent indicates that this procedure exaggerates the differences between exponents obtained when the modulus is located at the ends of the series in comparison to when it is in the middle.

The reason these effects occur in the simulation is because responses are pushed away from the modulus on either side of the standard when it is located in the center of the series, and only from one side when it is located at the end. The quantitative result is of similar magnitude to the one reported by Engen and Ross (1966).

## TRUNCATION EFFECTS

When a standard is at one end of the stimulus series, it serves as a barrier that apparently inhibits the subject from giving a response beyond the limit defined by the modulus. For instance, if the experimenter labels the strongest stimulus "100," then it is unlikely that many responses greater than 100 will be given to any stimulus. In this respect, the standard bounds the region of the judgment continuum available for selecting judgments. If two standards are used, one at either end of the series, the situation becomes one in which the response distributions are truncated at the minimum (lower modulus) and maximum (upper modulus) values designated by the experimenter. This should result in a much lower exponent. Such double truncation (simulation) produces the two psychophysical functions shown in Figure 11.5a. The nontruncated case is shown as well for purposes of comparison. The exponent is 0.81 without truncation and 0.64 with it.

The right panel (Figure 11.5b) gives the parallel relation between the standard deviation of the responses and the mean (Ekman functions). A linear function fits the data tolerably well for the condition without truncation, but a quadratic function is a better choice when truncation is present. The negative curvature of this latter function is very similar to the empirical data (chap. 10) for certain types of Magnitude Estimation procedures, as well as for Category Estimation. Such negatively accelerated functions are seen empirically for groups (Montgomery, 1975), as well as for individuals (Baird et al., 1980; Jesteadt, Luce, & Green, 1977).

Whenever the Ekman function bends over in the manner shown in Figure

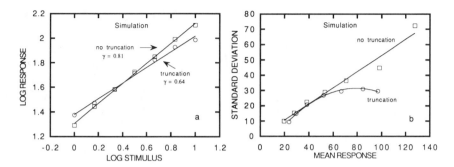

FIG. 11.5. (a) Mean response magnitude as a function of stimulus intensity (log–log coordinates). (b) Standard deviation as a function of mean response. Data generated by the Judgment Option Model for Magnitude Estimation with and without truncation at the mean of the highest judgment distribution.

11.5, it should raise suspicions that subjects for some reason or other are truncating their judgment (response) distributions at one or both ends of the continuum. In fact, it is doubtful if further progress will be made in understanding the strategies employed in Magnitude Estimation unless experimenters pay close attention to the detailed shape of response distributions.

## STIMULUS ORDER EFFECTS

If the only outcome of an experiment using Magnitude Estimation is a set of means, then a wealth of valuable information has been lost. The variability and shape of the response distributions provide important clues regarding the judgment strategies on a trial-by-trial basis. But even if one considers only the mean responses, much can be learned about the conditions responsible for psychophysical judgments by noting the relation between responses given to pairs of stimuli presented successively. The exponent of the Power Law, for example, is a summary index that does not reveal any nuances that might exist in the relations within subsets of stimuli.

When mathematical functions are fit to empirical data, the parameter values of the function are the indices that are supposed to hold at all levels of scale. For example, when the slope of the linear function in logarithmic coordinates is an overall index, the unspoken assumption is that this practice does not conceal systematic differences among responses to successive stimuli depending on the location of particular intensities within the series.

This presumption is often unjustified. The order of stimulus presentation does make a systematic difference in the response magnitude, and most critically, the effect of stimulus order over successive trials is asymmetric. The response ratio associated with the order "stimulus A followed by B" is not always the inverse of the response ratio associated with "stimulus B followed by A." This has been known for some time (Svenson & Åkesson, 1967). Admitting the existence of order effects leads to an examination of the trial-by-trial behavior in an experiment, and reinforces the view that the usual statistical measures are first orders of approximation, distant and cloudy reflections of the subject's behavior on a single trial.

## Empirical Results

Figure 11.6a illustrates a stimulus order effect. The data are from a study conducted by Baird, B. Berglund, U. Berglund, and Lindberg (1991). Twelve subjects employed Magnitude Estimation (with a standard called "100" at 68 dB) and estimated the loudness of a 1000-Hz tone (three repetitions of each of 12 intensities). Back-to-back presentations of the same stimulus were prohibited. Each point on the graph indicates the pair exponent based on the two responses given to physically adjacent stimulus intensities, with trials categorized into ascending and descending orders. The location of the point along the x axis is coded by the stimulus intensity on the current trial (T). The strength of the effect diminishes as successive stimuli are spaced further and further apart (not shown here).

Each "local" exponent is computed by isolating particular stimulus pairs from the random series and averaging their successive response magnitudes over the group. Specifically, the local exponent is defined as

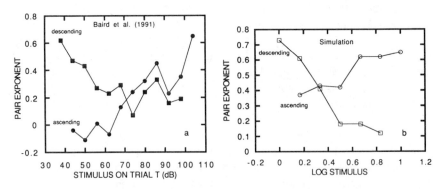

FIG. 11.6. Momentary exponent for adjacent pairs of stimuli as a function of log intensity on trial T for empirical data (a) (Baird et al., 1991) and for simulation data (b) generated by the Judgment Option Model. Ascending: $S_T > S_{T-1}$. Descending: $S_T < S_{T-1}$.

$$\gamma = \frac{|log\ R_T - log\ R_{T-1}|}{|log\ S_T - log\ S_{T-1}|} \tag{11.4}$$

where the successive stimuli ($S_T$ and $S_{T-1}$) are adjacent in relative magnitude and separated by 6 dB. The label "ascending" indicates that $S_T > S_{T-1}$, and "descending," that $S_T < S_{T-1}$.

It is obvious the pair exponent depends on the absolute stimulus intensities involved and on the relative intensities of successive stimuli. On ascending trials for weak intensities, the exponent hovers around zero, whereas for exactly the same pair of intensities presented in the opposite order (descending trials), the exponent is between 0.4 and 0.5. The effect is not as pronounced at the upper end of the stimulus dimension, where ascending trials produce higher exponents than do descending trials. These findings indicate that when the second of two successive stimuli is closer to the ends of the stimulus series, the exponent is higher than in the reverse situation in which the second stimulus is closer to the center.

## Computer Simulation

A simulation was conducted by employing the same default conditions of the Judgment Option Model used to produce the data in Figure 11.1. The standard deviation is 1.5 for each of the judgment distributions. The stimuli are presented in different random orders to hypothetical subjects who mindlessly follow the rules expressed by Equation 11.1.

Figure 11.6b gives the simulation results. The order of stimulus presentation and location within the series has a marked effect on the exponent. The direction of these effects is identical to that found in the laboratory. For exactly the same stimulus pair, the exponent depends on the order in which the two stimuli occur in the sequence. Whenever the intensity of the stimulus on the current trial is situated at the end of the series, the exponent is relatively high in comparison with its value for the opposite situation.

The reason the Judgment Option Model reproduces these findings so well is because the current judgment depends on the previous one (Equation 11.1). This in turn depends on the amount of stimulus separation (Equation 11.2). This can be understood by noting the relative sizes of the judgment means associated with stimuli of different intensity and presented in different orders. To elaborate on this point, consider two new terms. First, a *Thurstone mean* is the judgment value associated with a stimulus intensity without the influence of previous trials. This is the mean of the $J^*$ values in Equation 11.1. Second, a *transformed mean* is the mean of the judgments ($J$) arrived at by evaluating Equation 11.1 ($\omega > 0$).

Figure 11.7 shows the relation between these two types of means. The solid diagonal indicates a match between the Thurstone means and the transformed means. The filled points indicate the transformed means ($\omega > 0$ in Equation 11.1) and demonstrate an assimilative influence of the previous judgment on the

FIG. 11.7. Transformed mean (assimilation, Equation 11.1, $\omega$ > 0) as a function of Thurstone mean (no assimilation, Equation 11.1, $\omega$ = 0). Sample differences between the two types of means are indicated by the lines without arrowheads (pointing upward) and the lines with arrowheads (pointing downward). The direction indicates the difference in mean response by moving from trial T-1 to trial T. Data generated by the Judgment Option Model.

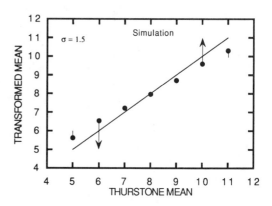

present one. The key result is this: The transformed means are calculated over all possible pairs of intensities (successive presentations of two stimuli). The transformed means associated with the strongest and weakest intensities are shifted toward the center of the judgment range, whereas the transformed mean for the center stimulus ("4" in the series of seven) is unaffected.

Now consider one possible stimulus order: $S_{max,\ T-1}$ followed by $S_{max-1,\ T}$, where the first subscript refers to rank order intensity and the second refers to trial number. The filled point at the very top of the graph in Figure 11.7 shows the transformed mean = 10.3 for $S_{max,T-1}$. The tiny line extending down from the filled point indicates the distance between this value and the Thurstone mean = 10 for $S_{max-1,T}$. With this particular order (stronger to weaker), the two means are almost the same (difference of 0.3), and therefore, the average of the set of ratios (over many trials) between successive responses taken from the two distributions is close to 1. This results in a very small exponent for this stimulus pair, as seen in Figure 11.6b. The data point of interest there is the open square (descending trial) located at the highest point along the x axis.

Now consider what happens when the same two stimuli are presented in the opposite order: $S_{max-1,T-1}$ followed by $S_{max,T}$. In Figure 11.7, the solid arrow starting at the transformed mean = 9.6 for $S_{max-1,T-1}$ designates the distance between this mean and the Thurstone mean = 11 for $S_{max,T}$. This implies that pairs of judgments taken from the two distributions will be relatively distant (difference of 1.4) from each other, and hence, their ratios produce a large exponent (Equation 11.9). This is indicated in Figure 11.6b by the open circle (ascending trials) furthest out along the x axis.

The same effect occurs at the bottom of the stimulus scale, as shown on the diagram (Figure 11.7), and as reflected in the exponents given in Figure 11.6b. On these theoretical grounds, the size of such effects would approach zero as the pair of successive stimuli came closer and closer to the middle of the series.

## LOCATION OF STIMULUS RANGE

### Empirical Results

Marks (1993) demonstrated in an intricate series of experiments that the location of the stimulus range defined by a set of sound intensities (of the same frequency) influences the level constant (y intercept) of the power function relating mean magnitude estimates to stimulus intensity.[2] In one illustrative experiment (Marks, 1993, exp. 1), seven 500-Hz tones are presented in each of three sets of ranges (25–55 dB, 40–70 dB, and 55–85 dB). Subjects use Free Magnitude Estimation (no modulus specified) and estimate the loudness of the tones within each set; the different sets are interspersed in blocks of trials over the course of the experiment.

Figure 11.8a shows the results pooled over 16 subjects for the two extreme ranges. The slopes of the two functions in the logarithmic plot are similar, but the level constants differ inasmuch as the lower set is associated with a smaller y intercept than the higher one. This implies that the loudness of a 500-Hz tone embedded in a set of high-intensity tones is greater than the loudness of exactly the same tone (same physical intensity) embedded in a set of low-intensity tones. The tones common to both sets are the four values occupying the center of the total range defined by combining the two sets. Marks interprets his findings as indicating that an assimilation occurs between the response on trial T and the response on trial T−1. The results are consistent with the notion that the estimates tend to move in the direction of the estimate on the previous trial.

### Computer Simulation

The Judgment Option Model elucidates why this happens. The results shown in Figure 11.8b were generated by running simulated subjects who gave one estimate for each of seven stimulus intensities spread over each of two stimulus ranges (on separate runs of the program). The standard deviation of the judgment distributions was fixed at 1.5 and three stimuli overlapped each other in the two ranges (as seen on the graph).

Because slight differences in the spacing between preferred numbers appropriate for representing stimuli over different ranges might influence the exponent of the power function, the simulation with the seven preferred numbers (monotonically mapped onto the stimuli) used in previous simulations in this chapter (Figure 11.1) was run first. The stimulus range was one log unit. The second stimulus set was arrived at by adding the same constant (in log units) to each of the intensities in the first set so as to create a shift upward in range. In order to

---

[2]The author kindly provided me with the mean data from many of these experiments.

insure that the exponent for this second set did not differ from the exponent of the first, a constant of the same magnitude (logarithmic value) was added to the log responses generated for the first set.

The key factor in the simulation is that the judgment on trial T assimilates toward the judgment on trial T−1 depending on the similarity between the two relevant stimuli, as determined by the Sensory Aggregate Model (Equations 11.1 and 11.2). Assimilation is permitted for only one trial back. Speaking figuratively, the "pull" of assimilation is strong when successive stimuli are close together along the stimulus dimension, and weak when they are spaced far apart.

The pattern of simulation results in Figure 11.8b is identical to that of the empirical results in Figure 11.8a. The reason the model generates this pattern is that for both conditions assimilation reduces the slope of the psychophysical function over what it would be if only a Thurstone process were operating. That is, the influence of assimilation is to raise the responses given to the weaker stimuli and lower those given to the stronger ones. This serves to rotate the psychophysical function in a clockwise direction, and coincidentally causes the two level constants to part company.

An intuitive grasp of why this happens is achieved by conducting an informal experiment. Draw a straight line on a graph with a slope of 45°. Place a paper clip aligned with the diagonal such that the bottom of the clip touches the origin of the graph. Now rotate the paper clip in a clockwise direction (say about 20°) around a pivot at its center. The result is that the bottom of the clip rises and the top falls in respect to the diagonal. Note the point at which the clip, if extended, would intersect the y axis. Next, position a second paper clip on the diagonal, but

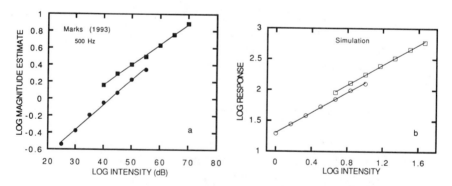

FIG. 11.8. Mean magnitude estimate as a function of stimulus intensity for a 500-Hz sound (log–log coordinates) for two sets of stimulus range (25 dB–55 dB, 40 dB–70 dB). Subjects estimated the loudness of tones within each set. The different sets were interspersed in blocks of trials over the course of the experiment. (a) Empirical data from Marks (1993). (b) Simulation data from the Judgment Option Model.

with the bottom of the clip slightly above the origin of the graph. Rotate this second clip the same amount as the first. If both clips are left in their rotated positions, it is evident they have the same slope, but different y intercepts. If the experiment is repeated with the clip moved farther and farther up the diagonal, the height of the y intercept systematically rises. Hence, the differences in level constant between locations of the two stimulus ranges is a mathematical necessity due to the fact that assimilation flattens the slope of the psychophysical function over what it would be for a sheer Thurstonian process.

## SLIPPERY CONTEXT EFFECT

### Empirical Results

An extension of the experiments mentioned earlier yield results whose implications for judgment models are not as easily understood. Marks (1988, 1993) had subjects estimate the loudness of a set of low-intensity tones of 2500 Hz interspersed with a set of high-intensity tones of 500 Hz (or the reverse arrangement of frequency and intensity). Therefore, successive trials could involve either tones of the same or different frequency. Under these conditions, the results are quite different from those in Figure 11.8. Specifically, although the slopes of the loudness functions remain almost the same for the two sound frequencies, the relative positions of their level constants are reversed from what they are when only one stimulus set is presented. The y intercept for the low-intensity sounds is larger than that for the high-intensity sounds. Marks and Warner (1991) referred to this phenomenon as the "slippery context effect." Figure 11.9 gives illustrative

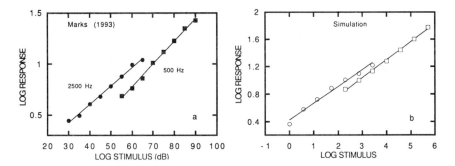

FIG. 11.9.   Mean magnitude estimate as a function of stimulus intensity for a set of low-intensity tones of 2500 Hz interspersed with a set of high-intensity tones of 500 Hz. (a) From Marks (1993). (b) From the Judgment Option Model. Results in both graphs indicate a "slippery context effect."

data (Marks, 1993, exp. 12). Marks and Algom (1996) reviewed similar results for several other attribute pairings, including those of taste intensity for different gustatory qualities (Rankin & Marks, 1991) and the estimation of visual length when the members of two sets of lines are at different orientations (Potts, 1991).

Whatever the difference between the two qualitative attributes, it is clear that it must be noticed by the subject in order to secure a slippery context effect (Rankin & Marks, 1991). For example, if the task is one of estimating taste intensity of NaCL and sucrose (two qualities), the subject must be able to distinguish between salt and sucrose. Otherwise, no effect occurs.

An explanation of the slippery context effect has proven elusive. The results may be due to judgment processes, sensory adaptation, or both. Schneider and Parker (1990, 1994) argued for a sensory interpretation. They had subjects decide between two tone pairs as to which had the largest within-pair intensity difference. The tones within a pair differed in both frequency (500 Hz or 2500 Hz) and intensity in the manner employed by Marks. But in the Schneider and Parker experiments, no numerical estimates were actually given, only judgments of relative magnitude. Through the use of nonmetric scaling techniques (Baird & Noma, 1978, chap. 10), Schneider and Parker found that the slippery context effect still appears. This suggests a sensory origin, though the exact mechanisms remain obscure. Whereas this may turn out to be the correct interpretation, the following sketches several alternative approaches that might be used in an attempt to explain this effect within the rubric of the Judgment Option Model. None of these attempts has proven totally convincing, but each serves a purpose by highlighting the variables and constraints involved. Yet another theoretical tack is suggested in chapter 15.

## Theory and Computer Simulation

The most puzzling feature of this problem is that on a purely descriptive level it appears that subjects assimilate their responses for one attribute (say the 500-Hz tone) toward the responses given to an earlier occurrence of the second attribute (say, the 2500 Hz). That is, the shift in y intercept in Figure 11.9 implies that the estimated magnitude of the set of low-intensity tones (500 Hz) has shifted in the direction of the estimates for the high-intensity tones (2500 Hz), and vice versa.

Within the strictures of the Judgment Option Model, the implied process can be represented by assuming that the judgment on the present trial is influenced by two types of assimilation, one dependent on the similarity of successive stimuli, the other dependent on the difference in the geometric means of the two stimulus sets. Hence, we can write a formula that includes both factors in the same equation:

$$J = \omega_1 J^* + \omega_2 J_{T-1} + \omega_3 (log\ GM_{T-1} - log\ GM_T) \qquad (11.5)$$

where $J*$ is the judgment selected from the Gaussian, and $\omega_1 + \omega_2 + \omega_3 = 1$. This model is the same as the one expressed by Equation 11.1, but with the addition of a term to specify that the judgment depends as well on the separation between the stimulus ranges of the two sets of qualitatively different stimuli. For example, on any given trial, the geometric range of the intensities at 500 Hz might be defined as $GM_{T-1}$ and the geometric range of the intensities at 2500 Hz defined as $GM_T$. When successive stimuli are the same, this term is zero.

Therefore, the first term in the model emphasizes the Thurstonian contribution, the second emphasizes the contribution of the previous judgment, without regard to stimulus quality, and the third emphasizes the importance of the separation between the two ranges. As the weight of the range factor increases, the judgment shifts toward the mean of the responses given to the other attribute. This creates the slippery context effect. Despite its welcomed simplification, this model is purely descriptive in character and does not really tell us much about the judgment processes responsible for creating the effect.

A variation of Equation 11.5 that comes somewhat closer to a bona fide theoretical explanation is given by Equation 11.6:

$$J_{A,T} = \omega_1 J* + \omega_2 J_{B,T-k} \tag{11.6a}$$

$$J_{B,T} = \omega_1 J* + \omega_2 J_{A,T-k} \tag{11.6b}$$

The subscripts A and B refer to the attribute (e.g., 500 or 2500 Hz), and the subscript $T-k$ indicates that the subject searches k trials back in memory to retrieve the most recent appearance of the alternative attribute. Assimilation depends as usual on the amount of stimulus separation (along the intensity dimension). This model was instantiated in a computer simulation using the conditions discussed earlier for the case producing the data in Figure 11.8. Figure 11.9b presents the outcome. The slippery context effect appears. Aside

FIG. 11.10. Mean magnitude estimate as a function of stimulus intensity (log–log coordinates). Data generated by the Judgment Option Model when the stimulus ranges of the two stimulus sets are identical.

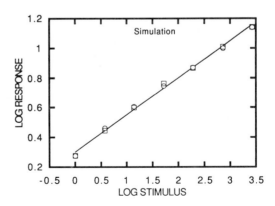

from its rather implausible, though possibly true, assumption that subjects are assimilating responses to the alternative attribute, this model also assumes that assimilation is a function of similarity based only on stimulus intensity, independent of quality. The Judgment Option Model assumes something that is incompatible with this: Namely, the similarity between stimuli depends on the degree of overlap between neural fibers underlying their representation in the sensory domain. It is difficult to see how this view can be held in cases where each stimulus is qualitatively different. So there are difficulties here as well.

An alternative model of the effect could proceed by assuming that the subject treats the experiment somewhat like one in absolute identification (chap. 14), and tends not to repeat responses that have been previously given for the same stimulus attribute. This constraint would have the net effect of pushing down the responses given to the set of strong intensities, and pushing up those given to the set of weak intensities. Simulations show that this model produces a slippery context effect. Without actually having the trial-by-trial data of a laboratory study available, however, it is difficult to decide on the viability of these various models.

One prediction made by all such variations on the Judgment Option Model is that the slippery context effect should disappear when the ranges of the two stimulus sets are identical. This can best be appreciated by consulting Equation 11.5. When the geometric ranges of the two attributes are identical, the equation reduces to the Judgment Option Model, and this alone cannot yield a slippery context effect. Simulations confirm this prediction for Equation 11.6, which assumes assimilation to the response given most recently to the alternative attribute. Pertinent data are displayed in Figure 11.10, where it is evident that the two data sets are indistinguishable when the stimulus ranges are the same.

An alternative explanation of the slippery context effect is outlined in Chapter 15. The distinguishing feature of this alternative is its definition of between-stimulus similarity. The similarity between two qualitatively different stimuli is their rank order positions within each qualitative dimension. This definition is contrary to the assumption of the Judgment Option Model. It is too early to tell which, if any, of these alternative approaches will eventually lead to a solution. On this uncertain note, attention is now shifted to context effects in Category Estimation.

# 12 Context and Category Estimation

The functional relation between stimuli and responses rendered by Magnitude Estimation is not linearly related to comparable functions rendered by Category Estimation. In the latter technique the subject uses only a relatively small number of integers (or word descriptors) in order to express perceived magnitude. Montgomery (1975) remarked on the differences between these two methods:

1. In Category Estimation, an upper and lower limit are defined by the end categories and subjects assign integers to reflect perceived differences among stimuli, whereas in Magnitude Estimation the subject assigns numbers to reflect perceived ratios.

2. In Category Estimation, the set of responses is fixed and relatively small, whereas in Magnitude Estimation the highest and lowest numbers are at the discretion of the subject.

3. In Category Estimation, the responses are discrete, whereas in Magnitude Estimation the number scale is theoretically continuous.

Despite these apparent differences, Montgomery concluded, that based on results from 13 experiments, the instructions for assignment of responses to stimuli (ratios or differences) has no influence on the psychophysical function. He also found that the discreteness or continuity of the response scale is relatively unimportant. This latter outcome may be a consequence of the fact that subjects in Magnitude Estimation favor the use of a restricted set of whole numbers, making their estimates resemble those when the experimenter prespecifies the response options. On the other hand, the nonlinearity between magnitude and category estimates depended on the range and openness of the response scale. When the two methods are used over the same range and are closed in the sense that a minimum and maximum response value is specified, they yield the same result. R. H. Gibson and Tomko (1972) also reported that the results of Category Estimation approach those of Magnitude Estimation when the number of categories is large. In this respect, then, Category Estimation is a limiting case of Magnitude Estimation, a limit reached when the response categories are evenly spaced and their number is small relative to the number of stimulus intensities.

## SIMULATING CATEGORY ESTIMATION

In order to predict category estimates, two modifications are necessary in the Judgment Option Model. First, the means of the judgment distributions are defined as the integers 1 to N, where N is typically, but not always, the total number of stimulus intensities. Second, all judgment distributions are truncated at the means associated with the weakest and strongest intensities (see the histogram in Figure 10.7c). Therefore, there are fewer response options for the end stimuli than there are for those located in the center of the series.

In the simulations, the probability of each judgment option is determined in the manner described in chapter 10. The judgment distribution surrounding each mean is kept discrete so as to determine the probabilities for each of the options associated with each stimulus intensity. The response categories are in one-to-one correspondence with the judgment options. This latter assumption is relaxed somewhat at the conclusion of the chapter when situations are considered in which the number of response categories is not the same as the number of stimulus intensities.

According to the model, on the very first trial, the subject selects a judgment from the appropriate distribution (contingent on the stimulus), converts the judgment into a category, and emits a response. On all subsequent trials, a value is selected from the appropriate judgment distribution and modified by the similarity between the current stimulus and the one that preceded it. The assimilation module is functional.

The initial computer simulation provides a comparison of Magnitude and Category Estimation with exactly the same stimulus and judgment parameters. The standard deviation of each judgment distribution (before truncation) is varied ($\sigma = 0.5$, 1, 1.5, and 2) in separate runs, and 500 "subjects" make magnitude and category estimates of each of seven stimuli presented in a random order, different for each subject.

### Exponents

Figure 12.1 presents the psychophysical functions (logarithmic coordinates) based on the geometric mean for Magnitude Estimation and on the arithmetic

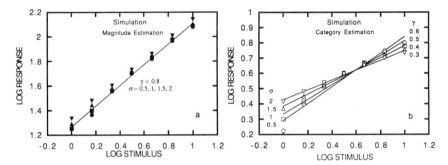

FIG. 12.1.   Mean response estimate as a function of stimulus intensity (log–log coordinates) for different standard deviations of the judgment distributions: (a) Magnitude Estimation (b) Category Estimation. Data generated by the Judgment Option Model.

mean for Category Estimation. The line drawn through the magnitude estimation points (left panel) is a least squares solution for the single function generated by a standard deviation of 1. Linear fits for the category estimates (right panel) depend on the standard deviation of the judgment distribution and are less satisfactory than for Magnitude Estimation.

The major comparison of interest is between the size of the slopes (exponents of the power law) for different standard deviations. The most obvious difference is that exponents for Category Estimation are roughly 40% to 70% as large as those for Magnitude Estimation. A second critical finding is that changing the standard deviation has virtually no impact on the exponent for Magnitude Estimation, but has a profound impact on the exponent for Category Estimation. For Magnitude Estimation, the rounded exponent is 0.8 for all standard deviations of the judgment distributions; for Category Estimation the exponent varies twofold (from 0.3 to 0.6).

## Response Variability

Figure 12.2 shows the corresponding Ekman functions. The left panel is a plot of the standard deviation as a function of the mean for Magnitude Estimation. The right panel shows comparable data for Category Estimation. The curved lines are quadratic functions fit to each data set to summarize the trends. In both instances, the variability increases with increases in the standard deviation of the judgment distributions, but the methods produce different shapes of Ekman functions. The relation is monotonic for Magnitude Estimation, but nonmonotonic for Category Estimation. In the latter instance, the truncation of the distributions at the ends of the judgment continuum leads to a sharp reduction in the response variability.

This initial simulation highlights essential differences between the two chief methods employed by global psychophysics. Differences in the subject's re-

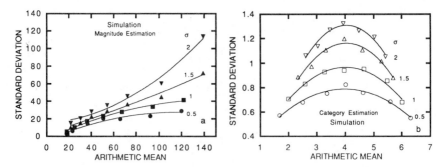

FIG. 12.2.    Standard deviation as a function of mean response for different standard deviations of the judgment distributions: (a) Magnitude Estimation (b) Category Estimation. Data generated by the Judgment Option Model.

sponse uncertainty have no effect on the mean magnitude estimates but have a marked influence on category estimates. It seems that nobody has done research to decide whether or not this holds true in an actual experiment.

Judgment truncation is an unavoidable property of Category Estimation. Researchers should be aware that with this method the slope of the Stevens function varies inversely with the standard deviation of the judgment options. This signals a serious flaw in a psychophysical method that might be enlisted to assess sensory processes. The link between judgment uncertainty and mean responses poses difficulties in the interpretation of category estimates as direct measures of perceived magnitude in both field and laboratory settings (Baird, Harder, & Preis, 1996). A second distinction between the results of the two methods occurs in the Ekman functions, where truncation creates a very different relation between the standard deviation and the mean.

The Judgment Option Model produces a substantial range of exponents simply by altering the standard deviation of the judgment distribution. This implies that such a parameter is critical in determining the exponent of the Power Law whenever subjects constrain their response options by truncating the relevant judgment distributions at either end of the continuum. If response variability depends in turn on the stimulus attribute, then, rather than being an expression of differences in sensory transduction, the exponent for Category Estimation is mostly an indication of decision uncertainty.

Subjects using Magnitude Estimation may also impose operating limits at both the lower and upper end of the response continuum, in which case the results will come to more closely resemble those of Category Estimation. In Magnitude Estimation, subjects seldom use fractions, and thereby impose a default boundary of 1 on their response options. At the upper end of the scale, a subject may also restrict the response range by idiosyncratic preferences: for example, not wanting to give a number beyond 100, or, in a production task, not wanting to extend the setting on a knob that pushes the response indicator beyond some point (Baird & Noma, 1975; Poulton, 1989). The proclivity to do this leads to a truncation of the judgment distributions at both the lower and upper ends of the response scale.

In this regard, the approximate logarithmic nature of the spacing between response options in Magnitude Estimation means that the impact of truncation at the top end of the continuum is greater than at the bottom; one obtains almost the same outcome when the top of the judgment range is truncated as when both ends are truncated.

## WHY THE MEAN DEPENDS ON THE VARIANCE

The judgment distributions located near the ends of the category scale are truncated at the mean for the distributions of the weakest and/or strongest stimulus. This has quantitative implications worth further elaboration.

Suppose subjects rate the intensity of an odor by assigning one of seven verbal labels to each stimulus. These response options might be predefined as "very very weak," "very weak," "weak," "neutral," "strong," "very strong," and "very very strong." Suppose further that two different groups are tested. One is comprised of a sample taken from a class of college sophomores enrolled in introductory psychology. The second is a sample taken from the population of fans at a high school sporting event. Assume that the mean rating of each stimulus is the same in both groups. Because the sports fans differ in age, educational backgrounds, and states of physical and psychological health, it is reasonable to expect that their estimates would be more variable than those from the more homogeneous sample of college students.

The hypothetical situation involving a 7-point category scale is diagrammed in Figure 12.3, where the minimum category (1) corresponds to "very very weak"

FIG. 12.3. Hypothetical probability density functions over category responses. Means of the two judgment distributions are the same. Standard deviations are different (1, 2). The resulting mean of the category estimates is effected such that the mean for the larger standard deviation is less than the mean for the smaller one. This is due to truncation at the maximum response category (7).

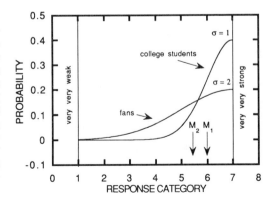

and the maximum category (7) to "very very strong." The judgment distributions for the maximum stimulus are depicted for the two groups, where both distributions are truncated at the mean of 7, but with different standard deviations ($\sigma = 1$ and 2).

Now consider the response distribution for the maximum stimulus. As the standard deviation increases, the probability of choosing category "7" decreases, and in fact, the means of the distributions associated with the estimates of the two groups will be different (indicated by the arrows on the diagram). Because the sports fans as a group are more variable, their mean response to the maximum stimulus will be less than that of the college students. The estimates of the weakest intensity will also migrate toward the middle of the response scale. In short, as the uncertainty expressed by a group (or a single subject for that matter) increases, the mean response associated with the weakest stimulus increases and that associated with the strongest stimulus decreases.

The extent of response migration will diminish as the stimulus intensity is located closer and closer to the center of the series. This creates an overall reduction of the slope of the psychophysical function relating the logarithm of the response to the logarithm of the stimulus. From the example, it would be concluded erroneously that the sports fans are less responsive to stimulus magnitude than the college students. Unlike the typical case for Magnitude Estimation, proper interpretation of data from category scaling must take into account both the mean and the variance of the response distributions. Failure to do so can mislead efforts to relate the parameters of psychophysical functions to stimulus parameters.

The interdependence of the mean and variance in this method detracts from its usefulness in evaluating the behavioral correlates of sensory processing. Of course, this in no way detracts from the method's usefulness in studying the influence of contextual variables on estimates of perceived magnitude, though some researchers have claimed this feature is also a weakness (S. S. Stevens & Galanter, 1957).

## ORDER OF STIMULUS PRESENTATION

### Empirical Results

Most psychophysical experiments present stimuli in a random order, and subjects give numbers to express perceived intensity. It has been known for some time, however, that with many judgment techniques the order of presentation influences the outcome. This is especially true with Category Estimation and related methods in which the experimenter prespecifies the response options (S. S. Stevens, 1975), but it probably occurs as well with Magnitude Estimation (Baird et al., 1991). The psychophysical function on descending trials commonly bows downward while the comparable function on ascending trials bows upward. This is well illustrated in a study by Bevan, Barker, and Pritchard (1963), who used the Newhall Scaling Method (described later) to test for differences between estimated lifted weight as a function of the order in which stimuli were presented, from light to heavy (ascending) or from heavy to light (descending).

Their procedure is somewhat unorthodox. The subject is given a piece of graph paper, visibly marked to show 10 equally spaced values on the y axis and 7 on the x axis. The experimenter preassigns the extreme weights to the minimum and maximum categories, and the task is to indicate on the graph paper the appropriate category for each of the remaining five weights, ranging from 150 g to 300 g in alternate steps of 20 g and 30 g. The crucial methodological variation is that subjects lift the weights in either ascending or descending order. Figure 12.4a shows the results from one such experiment, where bowing is evident for both stimulus orders, but in opposite directions. Bevan et al. related their findings to possible predictions of adaptation-level theory (Helson, 1964).

## Theory and Computer Simulation

The Judgment Option Model suggests an explanation of stimulus-order effects that applies with equal force to Category and Magnitude Estimation. Before discussing the model's predictions, however, consider a simpler explanation in the service of emphasizing the essential aspects of the judgment process. In the Bevan et al. task, there are 10 available response categories, and the experimenter denotes the heaviest weight as "10" and the lightest as "1." One might expect

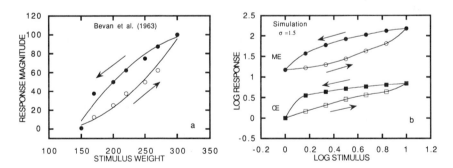

FIG. 12.4. Mean response magnitude as a function of stimulus weight. The experimenter designated the lightest weight as "1" and the heaviest as "10." On ascending trials (open circles), the weights were presented in order from lightest to heaviest. On descending trials (filled circles), the weights were presented in order from heaviest to lightest. (a) From Bevan et al. (1963). (b) From the Judgment Option Model.

that on ascending trials the subject would elect to give integers in an orderly progression beginning with 2. If this happened, the response series would read: 1, 2, 3, 4, 5, 6, 10. On descending trials, the integers might be selected in succession beginning with 10, so the response series from heavy to light would read: 10, 9, 8, 7, 6, 5, 1. This efficient solution to the task at hand produces two data sets that bend in opposite directions, depending on the presentation order. The functions resemble the empirical findings (Figure 12.4a).

If the direction of stimulus change is always the same, subjects might just be trying to keep the rank order of their responses in correspondence with the rank order of the stimuli. Because the direction of stimulus change from trial to trial is obvious, only the most perverse subject would violate rank order in assigning integer categories to the highly predictable relative magnitudes. Within the framework of the Judgment Option Model, this decision rule is formalized more carefully in a simulation.

To do this, the standard deviation is fixed at 1.5 and the assimilation module is tuned off. This is done because the rank-order rule for successive trials would overpower any assimilation that might exist anyway. The hypothetical subject maintains rank order between categories assigned to successively increasing or decreasing stimulus intensities and only samples values from that portion of the judgment distribution satisfying rank order among judgments contingent on rank order between consecutive stimuli.

Figure 12.4b (lower two curves, CE) shows the simulation results for Category Estimation. The top two curves are the consequence of applying the same rule for Magnitude Estimation (ME), where the smallest judgment mean was arbitrarily assigned the number 10 and, the maximum assigned the number 100. On ascending trials, the means of the responses are 10, 15, 20, 25, 30, 40, and 100. On descending trials, the means are 100, 90, 80, 75, 70, 60, and 10. As with Category Estimation, the two stimulus orders bow the psychophysical functions in opposite directions, just as in the empirical data.

This model of the judgment process implies that subjects' intentions in the Bevan et al. study were to maintain rank order as the stimulus weights were successively incremented or decremented over trials. In attempting to understand the empirical findings, it is unnecessary to claim that sensory or judgment adaptation plays any role whatsoever. In fact, the "simple model" sketched previously provides ample rationale for the results, without even resorting to the variability assumed by the Judgment Option Model.

## SKEWED STIMULUS SETS

### Empirical Results

One of the most reliable findings in the field of psychophysics is that the category rating of a stimulus depends on the number and frequency of stimuli included in the full stimulus set. For some years now, Parducci and his colleagues have been publishing evidence that the stimulus context defined in these ways affects judgments of the magnitude of a single stimulus when the subject is restricted to the use of a relatively small number of integer categories for expressing responses (e.g., Parducci, 1965, 1982; Parducci & Wedell, 1986). The contextual variable manipulated most often is the relative frequency with which different stimulus intensities are presented. If the series is a set of discrete values, its skewness, or degree of asymmetry, can be computed and then manipulated experimentally.

In a prototypical experiment, Parducci and Wedell (1986) presented subjects with five squares (optically on a screen) for them to categorize according to size. Different groups assign a value along a 2-, 5-, or 9-point scale. Under the positively skewed condition, the squares are presented in a random order but with different frequencies, as indicated in parentheses: $S_1(20)$, $S_2(14)$, $S_3(8)$, $S_4(4)$, and $S_5(4)$. Under the negatively skewed condition, the same squares are presented with frequencies $S_1(4)$, $S_2(4)$, $S_3(8)$, $S_4(14)$, and $S_5(20)$. The skew of these two sets is identical, except for the direction of the distribution's tail (right or left). In other experiments, the number of stimulus and response categories varies, whereas the chief independent variable remains the direction of skew.

Before making any estimates, subjects preview the stimuli in order to familiarize themselves with the series and to iron out any problems they might have in performing the task. Each subject then estimates each of the stimuli in the full series twice.

Figure 12.5 gives mean results, where the open circles represent the positively skewed distribution, and the filled circles represent the negatively skewed distribution. Three major effects emerge. First, subjects recognize the ends of the stimulus series very well and consistently assign them the extreme categories. The skew of the series has no influence on these estimates. Second, skewing the distribution so that the smaller squares are presented more often than the larger ones (positive skew) results in higher overall ratings than when the larger squares are presented more often than the smaller ones (negative skew). The trends of the data points for the two skew directions curve in opposite directions. Third, the relative effect of skewing the stimulus distributions depends on the number of categories. The differences between the curves for positive and negative skew diminish as the number of categories increases.

## Theoretical Explanations

Parducci and Wedell (1986) interpreted their findings in terms of a range-frequency model that has been undergoing renovation for three decades (Parducci, 1992; Parducci, Calfee, Marshall, & Davidson, 1960). The general idea is that the mean category rating for a stimulus is a weighted average of its range value (obtained by dividing the response range into subjectively equal, rank-ordered subranges) and its frequency value (obtained by allocating the same number of

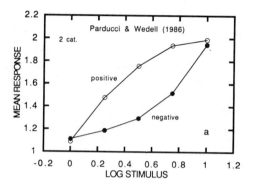

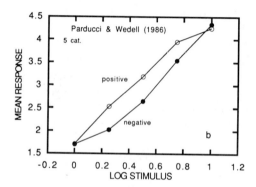

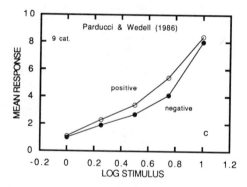

FIG. 12.5.   Mean category response as a function of logarithm of the size of stimulus squares. The squares were presented with different frequencies, depending on the skew (positive or negative) of the stimulus distributions: (a) 2 categories, (b) 5 categories, (c) 9 categories. From Parducci and Wedell (1986).

stimulus presentations to each response category). The subject supposedly partitions the response range into equal intervals (one for each stimulus) and assigns each of the response categories with equal frequency. The relative weight placed on these two factors determines the eventual selection of a category on a particular trial.

Haubensak (1992a) pointed out weaknesses in the Range-Frequency Model and proposed an alternative way to explain the results in Figure 12.5. He saw the difficulties with the Range-Frequency Model as connected with the unreasonable processing demands it places on the subject. According to the assumptions of Parducci's model, subjects must somehow keep track of what they said on all previous trials in order to satisfy the requirement of equal assignment of response categories. Haubensak noted, however, that context effects are evident after only a few trials. Such an early appearance of the effect implies that subjects at this point in the experiment would not have adequate experience to assess the relative frequency with which the different stimuli would be presented, or the frequency with which different categories would be used.

Haubensak believed that the entire response scale is shifted up or down according to where the most frequent stimuli are located. Because the frequent stimuli are likely to occur on the early trials, the subject shifts the mean of the response scale in their direction. For example, if many small stimuli occur on the early trials, then the scale shifts down, and the subject is inclined to assign the later stimuli to higher categories, whereas the opposite occurs when a preponderance of larger stimuli occur on the early trials. This "consistency" model accounts quite well for the available results. The pros and cons of both positions are aired in a lively exchange between Haubensak (1992b) and Parducci (1992).

## SKEWING AND THE JUDGMENT OPTION MODEL

The Judgment Option Model provides yet another interpretation for these results, much along the lines used to explain stimulus order effects (Bevan et al., 1963). The heart of the argument is that subjects attempt to maintain rank order among the response categories that match the perceived rank order among the stimulus intensities on successive trials. If subjects have to estimate a disproportionate number of small squares, then on the rare occasion when a large one is presented, they must assign it a response category greater than what was given on the previous trial to the smaller square. In other words, the subjects try to express a perceived difference between successive stimuli, and the only way to do so is to switch response categories whenever the perceived magnitude changes.

One of the given primitives of the Judgment Option Model is that subjects have the information necessary to utilize the mean of the neural aggregate aroused by a stimulus in order to determine whether the stimulus on trial T is less than, equal to, or greater than the stimulus presented on trial $T-1$ (chap. 9). This does not necessarily mean that rank order is always preserved in the category ratings, because it is possible for a particular sequence of stimuli and responses to paint subjects into a corner where they find it impossible to keep rank order.

This response strategy has definite consequences. With a positively skewed distribution, there is a lopsided number of small stimuli that precede (on any trial) the rather infrequent occurrence of a larger stimulus; therefore, the responses to the latter are pushed upward. By the same reasoning, with a negatively-skewed distribution, the preponderance of large stimuli depresses the scale values (categories) assigned to the smaller stimuli. Whether subjects are trying to keep rank order over more than one trial back in the series is not clear. The major trends reported by Parducci and Wedell (1986) are mimicked by assuming that subjects insure the category assigned to the current stimulus bears the correct magnitude with respect to the category assigned to the previous stimulus.

## Simulations

The computer modeling of such a strategy is straightforward so long as the number of response categories matches the number of stimulus intensities. Difficulties arise if there is a mismatch between the number of stimuli and the number of response options. For example, when the number of categories is small (say two) relative to the number of stimuli (say seven), the theorist must decide where the cutoff should fall between the two response options. Should the boundary be at the arithmetic mean of the stimulus series, at its geometric mean, or at the mean of the perceived intensities over the full series? No matter what the decision, one must bear in mind that an odd number of stimuli cannot be evenly divided into two categories. Such choices also are called for when modeling a condition in which the number of response options is greater than the number of stimuli.

As in dealing with stimulus order effects, the assimilation module of the Judgment Option Model is disconnected for all simulations involving the effects of stimulus skewing. The rank-order rule would overwhelm such effects. Disconnecting this module permits a better assessment of the model's performance without having to deal with additional complexity.

## Two Categories

In the first simulation, subjects employ two categories to express the perceived magnitude of five stimuli, each presented with the frequencies (listed earlier) for the two skew conditions of Parducci and Wedell (1986). The means of the judgment distributions range from 1 to 5 in integer steps, with a constant standard deviation of 1.5. Each subject renders a single estimate on each of 50 stimulus presentations (sum of the frequencies for all stimuli). One group estimates the stimuli in the positively skewed set, another group estimates those in the negatively skewed set.

On the first trial of each run, the subject selects a value from the appropriate judgment distribution and maps it into one of the two categories. The two smallest stimuli are mapped into category 1, the two largest into category 2, and the middle stimulus is randomly mapped into 1 or 2. On all subsequent trials (2 through 50) the decision rule is the paragon of simplicity:

$$\text{If } S_T = S_{T-1} \text{ then } R_T = R_{T-1}$$

$$\text{If } S_T > S_{T-1} \text{ then } R_T = 2$$

$$\text{If } S_T < S_{T-1} \text{ then } R_T = 1$$

Figure 12.6a (top left) shows the mean category rating as a function of the logarithm of stimulus intensity. The open squares represent the positive-skew condition, the filled squares, the negative-skew condition. Except for the end stimuli (which are given the same ratings in both conditions), the positive skew produces higher category ratings than the negative skew. This finding is in agreement with the empirical results for a 2-point scale (Figure 12.5a).

The data in the top-right panel (Figure 12.6b) are measures of the associated response variability. The standard deviation is plotted as a function of the logarithm of the stimulus intensity. Both skew conditions show the familiar quadratic relations, but the peaks of the two functions are shifted relative to each other. Parducci and Wedell did not present variability data, so it is not possible to tell whether or not this aspect of the Judgment Option Model produces output in agreement with laboratory results. Neither the Range-Frequency nor the Consistency Model makes any predictions concerning response variability, so it is not surprising that these statistics are never reported.

## Five Categories

On the first trial, a value is randomly selected from the appropriate judgment distribution and mapped into the response category having the same integer value (1 through 5).

On all subsequent trials, the decision rules are identical to those already listed for the two-category condition, with two additional constraints to deal with the potentially disabling situation where the subject cannot maintain rank order because the previous stimulus has been assigned one of the extreme categories. These two constraints are dealt with as follows:

$$\text{If } S_T < S_{T-1} \text{ \& } R_{T-1} = 1 \text{ then } R_T = 1$$

$$\text{If } S_T > S_{T-1} \text{ \& } R_{T-1} = 5 \text{ then } R_T = 5$$

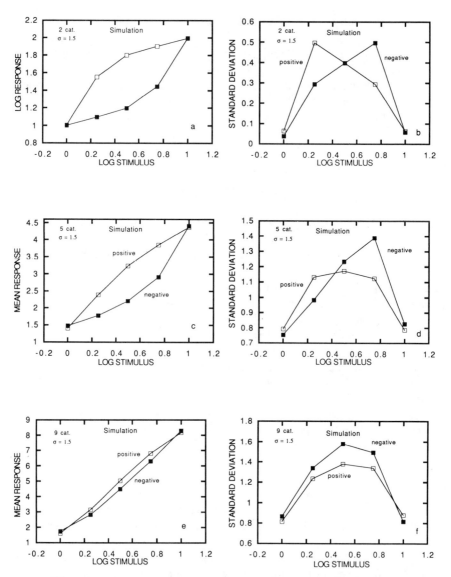

FIG. 12.6.    Mean category response as a function of logarithm of stimulus intensity with different numbers of response categories (left panels: a, c, e). Standard deviation as a function of logarithm of stimulus intensity (right panels: b, d, f). The particular stimuli were presented with different frequencies, depending on the skew (positive or negative) of the stimulus distributions. Data generated by the Judgment Option Model.

The left-middle panel (Figure 12.6c) shows the mean results. The effect of skewing is less than it is with two categories, just as in the empirical data (Figure 12.5b). The right-middle panel (Figure 12.6d) presents the associated variability predictions. The shape of the functions resemble those for two categories, though there is no pronounced peak in the standard deviation for the positive-skew condition.

## Nine Categories

A linear transformation maps the means of the five judgment distributions into values along a 9-point scale. If $J*$ is the value along a 5-point scale and $J$ the corresponding value along a 9-point scale, then the transformation between the 5-point and 9-point scales is obtained by the linear equation:

$$J = 2J* - 1, \ 1 \le J* \le 5$$

The resulting means of the judgment distributions in terms of the 9-point scale then become: 1, 3, 5, 7, and 9. Based on the truncated Gaussian, probabilities are calculated for all judgment options on the 9-point scale for each of the five stimuli. The subject's strategy for selecting values from among these options follows the same rules as when the number of judgment options equals the number of stimuli (5-point scale).

The bottom-left panel (Fig. 12.6e) presents the mean results of the simulation and the bottom-right panel (Fig. 12.6f) gives the associated response variability. The impact of skewing the stimulus distributions in opposite directions is smaller here than it is for either the 2-point or 5-point scales, and the shapes of the variability functions are more alike.

## The Category Effect

In both the simulation and the empirical data, the effects of skewing decrease as the number of categories increases. Parducci and Wedell called this the *Category Effect*. They interpreted it in terms of a memory retrieval notion in which the subject presumably makes decisions based on the relative frequency of particular stimulus–response events from the past.

In contradistinction, the Judgment Option Model sees the Category Effect as due to a procedural constraint with no special theoretical import. This conclusion arises from the fact that the smaller the number of categories, the greater the proportion of the total response scale occupied by each. When keeping rank order on a 2-point scale, the subject must move from a response of "2" to a response of "1" (or the opposite), always traversing the full extent of the response scale. On the other hand, when there are many response categories, the subject can always keep rank order by moving a smaller fraction of the response scale. That is, suppose a 100-point scale is employed and the subject adjusts a response up one category in order to maintain rank order in respect to the previous stimulus–response pair. Then, if the response on trial $T-1$ was "23," and the stimulus on trial T is judged to be larger than the previous one, all the subject need do is increment the previous response by 1 unit to "24." In support of this contention, consult the Parducci and Wedell report showing that minor differences exist between skew conditions with a 100-point scale. In the limiting case of a truly continuous scale, it is possible, though exceedingly unlikely, to maintain rank order by saying "23.000000001." Under these circumstances, the effects of skewing would be vanishingly small.

In all such examples with different numbers of categories, the Judgment Option Model employs probabilities for each judgment/category. Hence, the argument should not be interpreted to mean that subjects maintain rank order by simply moving one category unit away from what was said on the previous trial. The special case mentioned earlier points out that the leeway provided the subject depends on the number of categories allowed by the experimenter. The Category Effect in such tasks has no more significance beyond recognition of this procedural fact. This conclusion holds just as well in regards to Haubensak's Consistency Model.

## The Stimulus Effect

Parducci and Wedell reported a second effect, less dramatic than the Category Effect; namely, that the magnitude of the difference between category ratings for positively and negatively skewed distributions is greater when there are relatively many stimuli than when there are relatively few. By adjusting the frequency with which different stimuli are presented, it is possible to secure roughly the same skewness for sets containing different numbers of stimuli. The so-called Stimulus Effect appears when the same number of response categories are used for both sets. Sample results are presented in Figure 12.7. Admittedly, it takes a certain amount of courage to argue on the basis of this graph that the effects of skew are greater for 9 stimuli than for 5 stimuli. The authors' conclusions are based on more data sets than these samples, but in any event, the effect is not very impressive.

Because of ignorance concerning the rules actually used by subjects in assigning categories, it is difficult to decide whether the Stimulus Effect is due to the number of stimuli, or rather, to a change in the strategy by which stimuli are assigned to categories when the number of stimuli and categories do not coincide. One plausible explanation is that it occurs because the judgment variability increases with stimulus set size.

In order to flesh out the implications of this hypothesis, a simulation was run in which hypothetical subjects estimate five intensities by using a 5-point category scale. As before, the stimulus distributions are positively and negatively skewed in two separate conditions, but here the parameter under investigation is the standard deviation of the judgment distributions. The simulation was run with three such values: 0.5, 1, and 2.

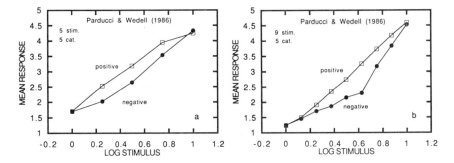

FIG. 12.7.    Mean category response as a function of logarithm of stimulus square size. The squares were presented with different frequencies, depending on the skew (positive or negative) of the stimulus distributions: (a) 5 stimuli and 5 categories (b) 9 stimuli and 5 categories. From Parducci and Wedell (1986).

The results are shown in Figure 12.8. The standard deviation of the judgment distributions obviously affects the magnitude of the difference between mean ratings for the two skew conditions (left panels). With a standard deviation of 0.5 there is no difference to speak of, but as the variability of the judgment distribution increases, the differences become more pronounced.

With small judgment variability the occasion hardly ever arises where rank order is violated. The means of the resulting response distributions could be calculated directly by applying the formula for finding the expected value of a truncated normal distribution (Johnson & Kotz, 1970). As the judgment distributions overlap more and more, the rank-order rule must be invoked with greater regularity, causing a shift of the mean response depending on the direction of the skew.

The means within a skew condition also depend on the standard deviation, because, as demonstrated earlier, the mean of a truncated Gaussian will shift away from the boundary as variance increases. This is apparent in the simulation results but not in the empirical data (Figure 12.7). The biological subjects are prone to assign the extreme categories to the extreme stimuli, regardless of differences in the variance of the judgment distributions. The computer subjects have no such compunctions, though this too could be changed.

An empirical test of the Judgment Option Model, as applied to conditions giving rise to the Stimulus Effect, would be to examine the standard deviations of the response distributions associated with different set sizes. According to the present working hypothesis, the Stimulus Effect occurs because the judgment variance increases with increasing numbers of stimulus intensities. With this possibility in mind, Figure 12.8 (right panels) shows the standard deviations from the simulation. The quadratic shape appears when the standard deviation of the responses is plotted as a function of log intensity. There is little difference

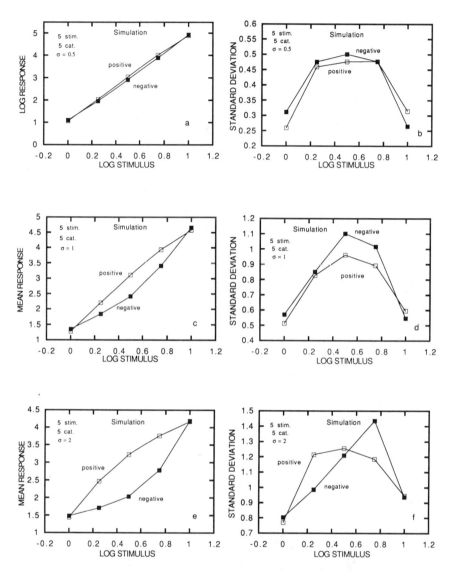

FIG. 12.8.   Mean category response as a function of logarithm of stimulus intensity (left panels: a, c, e) with 5 stimuli and 5 categories.
Standard deviation as a function of logarithm of stimulus intensity
(right panels: b, d, f). The particular stimuli were presented with different frequencies, depending on the skew (positive or negative) of the
stimulus distributions. The parameter responsible for differences in
the data plots is the standard deviation of the judgment distribution
(top, 0.5; middle, 1; bottom, 2). From the Judgment Option Model.

between the variability for positive and negative skew, but the amount of re-sponse variability does depend in the expected manner on judgment variance.

The unanswered question is whether or not biological subjects act in the same way as electronic ones. Response variability is not reported in Category Estima-tion studies. Hence, a rich lode of important information is being thrown away or at the very least, ignored. Measures of central tendency and variability are both critical in distinguishing between theoretical models, and should receive equal attention.

## Magnitude Estimation and Rank Order

Subjects may also adopt a strategy of keeping rank order over successive trials when using Magnitude Estimation. The data in this regard are sparse. J. C. Stevens (1958) ran several experiments tangentially related to this issue. Subjects gave loudness estimates for stimuli spaced differently along the intensity dimen-sion. When the stimulus distribution is skewed in either a positive or negative direction, local perturbations of the psychophysical function appear. The local slope of the function increases in the region where the stimuli are bunched together. Subjects perceive (estimate) a greater difference between stimuli packed closely together in intensity as compared to what one would predict from the function when stimuli are more separated.

According to J. C. Stevens, this exaggeration of differences among closely spaced stimuli might represent two intentions on the subject's part: "(a) to esti-mate the apparent loudness of the stimulus, but also (b) to communicate the fact that he heard a difference between stimuli of nearly equal loudness" (J. C. Stevens, 1958, p. 249).

Unlike the findings with Category Estimation, however, the perturbation of the psychophysical relation for Magnitude Estimation is confined to the bunched stimuli. The remainder of the function is unaffected by skewing the stimulus set. From the findings in additional experiments, J. C. Stevens concluded that stimu-lus spacing has a much greater impact on category estimates than it does on magnitude estimates.

A powerful context effect can be observed in all global scaling methods: the sequential dependencies between the current response and responses given ear-lier in the stimulus series. The next chapter considers this issue more thoroughly.

# 13 Sequence Effects

When people estimate the intensity of a stimulus by methods such as Magnitude and Category Estimation, their responses depend not only on the value presented, but also on the psychophysical events that occurred earlier in the series. The patterns exhibited by such sequence effects are complex and, as such, pose challenges for existing theory. The motivation to answer these challenges comes from the promise of securing a deeper understanding of the judgment processes engaged in by subjects when using such methods.

Most experiments in global psychophysics are conducted with groups of participants. One disadvantage of such experiments involving individuals who only render a few estimates of each intensity is that once a stimulus is presented, the subject may think it will never be presented again. They may be reluctant to use the same response value twice in a single session and so resort to a strategy of keeping rank order among successive stimuli.

In order to study the finer details of the judgment process, it is necessary to collect a large number of repetitions on the same stimulus intensities. Only in this way can summary statistics reveal the strongest effects inherent in the data. For this reason, the experiments reviewed and simulated in this chapter typically employ a small number of subjects who give many responses to the same stimulus set.

The key element of the experiments with a small number of subjects is that within each session all the stimuli are randomized over trials. This means each intensity can follow each of the others, including itself, and the subject is unable to discern a pattern in the series. The procedure also permits longer runs of stimulus repetitions. Thus, subjects are not inhibited from repeating response values over trials. They cannot infer the stimulus magnitude by a process of elimination based on those stimuli that have already been presented. Such experimental procedures yield data suitable for the analysis of sequential dependencies.

## EMPIRICAL RESULTS

The empirical examples presented here are taken from Green et al., (1977), whose experimental procedure is outlined in Chapter 10. Subjects gave many magnitude estimates of the loudness of a 1000-Hz tone. The original statistical analyses (chap. 10) for this study were for the estimates by individuals, but averages are presented for all five subjects, along with individual data chosen to make a point about how subject strategies may differ in exactly the same task.

### Stevens Functions

Figure 13.1a presents average responses over five subjects in logarithmic coordinates. The means follow a sinuous course, but a straight line nonetheless provides an adequate description of the trend, indicating that Stevens's Law is upheld. The exponent is 0.21. The sinuosity present in the overall function may be related to the fact that subjects employ a small set of preferred numbers (chap. 8; Baird, 1986; R. Teghtsoonian et al., 1995).

### Computer Simulation

In order to determine the viability of the Judgment Option Model, a computer simulation was created in which one hypothetical subject gave 500 estimates of

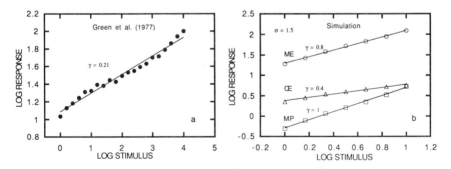

FIG. 13.1.  Mean response as a function of stimulus intensity (log–log coordinates). (a) Averages for five subjects estimating the intensity of a 1000-Hz tone (Green et al., (1977). (b) Mean results from the Judgment Option Model simulating Magnitude Estimation (ME), Category Estimation (CE) and Magnitude Production (MP) with a constant standard deviation of 1.5 for the judgment distributions.

each of seven stimuli distributed over a single log cycle. All 3500 trials were randomized. The standard deviation of the judgment distributions was fixed at 1.5, and the simulation run for Magnitude Estimation, Magnitude Production (continuous case), and Category Estimation. Other details of the simulation, including trial-by-trial assimilation based on sensory (stimulus) similarity, were the same as in chapter 9. Figure 13.1b presents the average results to allow side-by-side comparison with the empirical data.

In all three scaling methods, the trend of the data points is linear in the log–log plot, and hence, Stevens's Law is upheld with the exponents indicated on the graph. No attempt was made to equate the exponents generated by the simulation with those in the empirical data, though this could be done by manipulating the size of the stimulus range in the simulation. It is clear, however, that the Judgment Option Model based on a single subject making many magnitude estimates produces essentially the same outcomes as when the simulation is run for groups of subjects, each of whom gives only a single estimate of each stimulus (chaps. 9 and 11).

## Ekman Functions

Figure 13.2 displays the average response variability produced by the five subjects in the Green et al. study. The standard deviation is plotted as a function of the mean in order to evaluate the Ekman function. A quadratic trend is apparent, though the data for several individuals (not shown) are more appropriately characterized as linear.

Figure 13.3 shows the corresponding results from the computer simulation for each of the scaling methods. The three patterns differ from each other. For Magnitude Estimation (13.3a) the data follow a quadratic trend, though not as pronounced as the empirical data. For Magnitude Production (13.3b), the relation is linear, and for Category Estimation (13.3c), the relation is characterized

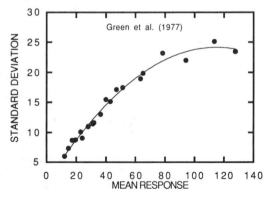

FIG. 13.2. Standard deviation as a function of the mean. Averages for five subjects estimating the intensity of a 1000-Hz tone (Green et al., 1977). The solid line is the best-fitting quadratic function.

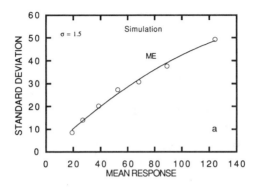

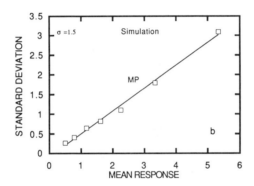

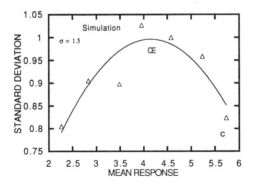

FIG. 13.3.  Standard deviation as a function of the mean (linear coordinates) from the Judgment Option Model for Magnitude Estimation (a), Magnitude Production (b), and Category Estimation (c).

by an inverted U function. The outlier (third largest mean) in the latter plot is apparently due to a quirk in the stimulus order. It does not occur when the simulation is run with other stimulus orders. The results are not presented from a substitute order because it is more important that exactly the same order exist in all the simulations than it is to rectify a single recalcitrant point.

Figures 13.1 through 13.3 are intended to assure the reader that the Judgment Option Model is not limited to applications involving large groups. The model is just as effective for individual subjects, who also give data in compliance with Stevens and Ekman functions. The next section examines the predictions of this model in regard to sequence effects that can only be evaluated when subjects give many responses to the same stimulus set.

## THE TRIANGLE PATTERN

The instructions in global scaling methods are to preserve ratios among stimulus intensities over trials. If subjects obey these instructions to the letter, and if the stimulus on the previous trial $(T-1)$ serves as a referent, a high correlation would be expected between responses on the current and previous trial (Luce & Green, 1974). Such correlations should be independent of stimulus separation over successive trials. In the empirical data, however, this independence is not attained.

The calculation necessary to determine correlations between successive responses proceeds as follows. Because each of N stimuli can occur on trials T and $T - 1$, the domain of possible sequences is represented by the $N \times N$ matrix of stimulus pairs. Then compute the correlation between $log\ R_T$ and $log\ R_{T-1}$ for each cell of the matrix, and average the results across stimulus pairs of the same log intensity separation (in linear terms, the same stimulus ratios).

Figure 13.4a presents the correlation results from Green et al. (1977). The correlation coefficient is plotted against the rank stimulus separation between successive stimuli. A quadratic function is fit to the points to emphasize the trend. This summary trend is referred to as the triangle pattern—in some publications it is called the inverted V pattern (Baird et al., 1980). The critical result is that the correlation is positive and large when successive stimuli are highly similar and is close to zero when successive stimuli are highly dissimilar. This implies, for example, that a relatively low evaluation of a 40-dB tone would be followed by another low evaluation if a tone in the vicinity of 40 dB were presented on the next trial. If, instead, the succeeding tone was 80 dB the two estimates would be independent. The previous stimulus serves as a referent when it falls in the neighborhood of the current stimulus, but the usefulness of this referent dissipates rapidly with increasing stimulus separation.

The point here is not just that the subject assigns a small (in absolute terms) numerical response to the second stimulus. The subject's estimate on trial $T-1$ is

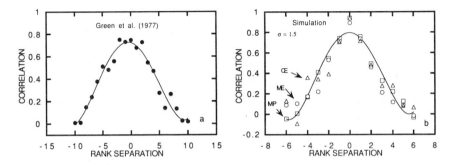

FIG. 13.4. Correlation between responses on successive trials as a function of stimulus rank separation. (a) Averages for five subjects estimating the intensity of a 1000-Hz tone (Green et al., 1977). (b) Simulation from the Judgment Option Model for Magnitude Estimation (open circles), Magnitude Production (open squares), and Category Estimation (open triangles).

low relative to its entire response distribution, and the following estimate is low relative to the entire response distribution associated with the stimulus on trial T. This is why the correlation is positive.

Figure 13.4b shows the simulation results for Magnitude Estimation, Magnitude Production, and Category Estimation. All three methods yield the same triangle pattern in concordance with the pattern of the empirical data. The reason the Judgment Option Model is able to reproduce these data with such fidelity is because the amount of assimilation of a judgment to the one occurring on the previous trial depends on between-trial stimulus similarity. In fact, the original motivation for including this factor in the model was because the triangle pattern has been observed with such a wide array of stimulus attributes (Baird et al., 1996; Baird et al., 1980; Green et al., 1977; Jesteadt, Luce, & Green, 1977; Luce et al., 1980; Ward, 1979).

## V-SHAPE

Another consequence of the hypothesized link between judgments on successive trials is in response variability. Baird (1970c, especially chap. 5) reported that for many kinds of visual stimuli (lines, areas, volumes) the relative error (standard deviation divided by the mean) of responses from the methods of Magnitude Estimation and Production depends on the physical separation between the standard and comparison stimulus. When the two are in close proximity, the relative error is small; increasing stimulus separation leads to an increase in relative error. When the relative error is plotted against stimulus separation, the pattern resembles that of a butterfly with its wings extended. Because more recent studies find that the tips of the wings do not always bend downward, the butterfly has lately been demoted to the less aesthetic V shape. This shape is ubiquitous in global scaling studies, appearing across a large number of methods and attributes (Luce et al., 1980).

The way to reveal the V shape is to determine the mean and standard deviation of the response ratio $(R_T/R_{T-1})$ for each stimulus ratio. Instead of employing a metric measure, a more generic index of response variability is used, one-half the interquartile interval within the distribution of response ratios. This measure is calculated for each pair of stimulus ratios (entries in the $N \times N$ matrix) and then averaged across the same ratio values. In Figure 13.5a this variability index is plotted against stimulus separation for the data collected by Green et al. The V shape is evident. The lowest variability occurs when the same stimulus is presented on successive trials; increased stimulus separation in either a positive or negative direction is associated with increased variability.

Figure 13.5b shows results from the computer simulation. The V shape is obtained for all three scaling methods, though the trend is less regular in the case of Category Estimation. According to the Judgment Option Model, these results are caused by exactly the same processes responsible for the triangle pattern. When successive stimuli are close in intensity, the assimilative force is strong, and therefore, the judgment on the current trial is pulled in the direction of the judgment on the previous trial. As similarity decreases, the assimilative force weakens, resulting in more variability of response ratios over successive trials.

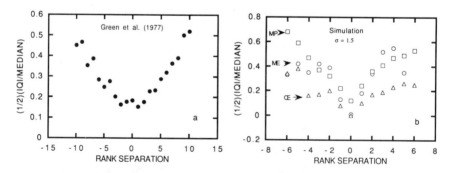

FIG. 13.5.   One-half the interquartile interval divided by the median as a function of stimulus rank separation. (a) Averages for five subjects estimating the intensity of a 1000-Hz tone (Green et al., 1977). (b) Simulation data from the Judgment Option Model for Magnitude Estimation (open circles), Magnitude Production (open squares), and Category Estimation (open triangles).

# RANK-ORDER VIOLATIONS

In global scaling tasks the spacing between stimuli is such that a subject would almost always recognize the rank-order intensity within any pair in the set, if this pair was presented in isolation. This is not the case when many stimuli are presented in a random order. Stimulus pairs whose members are perfectly discriminated in isolation are not always properly rank ordered when the subject estimates them within the context of a larger stimulus set. Violations of rank order depend on stimulus separation. Fewer violations occur for stimuli spread far apart in intensity than for pairs whose members are closer. A violation of rank order occurs when successive responses satisfy one of two conditions: If $S_T >$ $S_{T-1}$, then $R_T < R_{T-1}$; or, if $S_T < S_{T-1}$, then $R_T > R_{T-1}$.

Figure 13.6a presents the percent of violations for the empirical data collected by Green et al. The histogram only encompasses a subset of pairs comprised of the most similar stimuli. The highest number of incorrect assignments falls between 20% and 25% and occurs for stimuli separated by the smallest amount (2 dB). As one might expect, the closer together two successive stimuli, the more difficult it is to recognize their rank order. The percentages decline with increasing stimulus separation, but even for rather large separations, the incorrect responses are all between 5% and 10% of the total. A rank separation of 6 on the graph corresponds to a 12 dB stimulus separation.

Figure 13.6b displays comparable data from the Judgment Option Model. The results for Magnitude Production are most like the empirical data, though for all three methods, there is a reduction in violations for the larger separations. It is

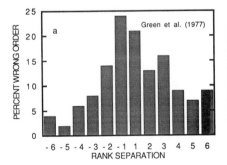
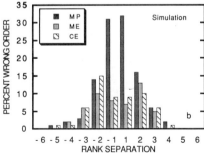

FIG. 13.6. Percent incorrect rank orders over successive trials as a function of rank stimulus separation. (a) Averages for five subjects estimating the intensity of a 1000-Hz tone (Green et al., 1977). (b) Simulation data from the Judgment Option Model for Magnitude Estimation, Magnitude Production, and Category Estimation.

much easier to violate rank order when judgments are chosen from overlapping continuous distributions. For reasons that are not clear, the violations for Magnitude and Category Estimation are higher for stimuli with rank separation 2 than they are for rank separation 1. This appears to be a fault of the model, perhaps a result of the discrete and limited nature of the response set. It would be surprising to find such a reversal in empirical data.

## INDIVIDUAL DIFFERENCES

The Green et al. data presented so far consists of averages over five subjects. There are individual differences within the group for all of the foregoing data plots. One subject (FS) in particular departed from the average in an interesting way that may shed light on subjects' judgment processes in such tasks. Next consider this individual's data more carefully, with special emphasis on the triangle pattern and the rank-order violations.

The power function for FS has an exponent of 0.12, which is 57% of 0.21, which is the average across all five subjects. More detailed consideration of the correlations of successive responses indicates that FS does not show a triangle pattern and has more violations of rank order than the other subjects. Pertinent data for the triangle pattern are given in Figure 13.7 (filled circles). The correlation between successive responses is high and unsystematic. Moreover, it does not drop to zero for any separation, including the extremes.

The open circles in Figure 13.7 represent the results of a computer simulation of the Judgment Option Model, but with one change in the way in which the similarity measure is determined. Instead of computing the similarity between the stimulus on trials T and T−1, it is assumed here that the subject employs a single similarity measure on all trials, regardless of the stimulus separation between the present stimulus and that occurring on the previous trial. A single

FIG. 13.7.  Correlation between responses on successive trials as a function of rank stimulus separation. Subject FS (filled circles) from Green et al. (1977). Simulation data from the Judgment Option Model (open circles).

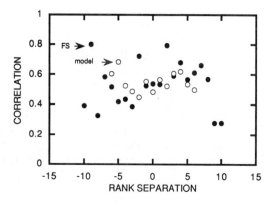

value of 0.5 is the average similarity measure for every separation. On each trial (T > 1), this value is the weight the subject gives to the previous judgment—that is, they place equal weight on the current judgment selected from the Gaussian distribution and on the judgment from the previous trial (see chap. 9 for details). Implicit in this version of the model is the assumption that the subject considers the general similarity between stimuli that have occurred recently in the series and the current stimulus. If many such averages are computed for different numbers of trials into the past, the values gradually approach a constant.

The results (open circles) in Figure 13.7 indicate that the triangle pattern disappears with this judgment strategy, just as it is absent in the data of FS. Moreover, the exponent of Stevens's Law is 0.56, which is 70% of the value of 0.8 when assimilation is based only on the similarity between consecutive stimuli (Figure 13.1b).

Figure 13.8a presents a comparison between the empirical data of subject FS and that of all five subjects tested by Green et al. regarding rank-order violations. On balance, FS has roughly twice as many violations as the group, and it appears that most occur when the stimulus on trial T is more intense than the one on trial T−1. Why this asymmetry occurs is unclear. It does not appear in the simulation that follows.

Figure 13.8b shows data for the simulation of FS's strategy (as described previously), as well as for a strategy that only considers stimuli one trial back in the series (ME). The simulated FS has many more violations of rank order when stimulus separation is small (plus or minus one), but no such difference occurs for larger separations. It is rather curious that the overall pattern of the violations for the simulation corresponds more closely to that of the average empirical data (Figure 13.8a, Group) than it does to the simulation data when the "subject" only

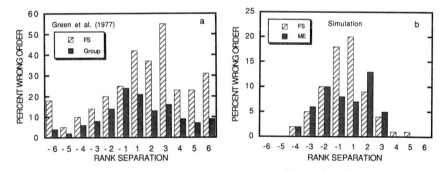

FIG. 13.8.  Percent incorrect rank orders over successive trials as a function of rank stimulus separation. (a) Subject FS (cross hatch) and average data for five subjects (dark bars) from Green et al. (1977). (b) Comparable data from the Judgment Option Model.

considers the psychophysical event occurring on the previous trial (Figure 13.8b, ME).

The performance of FS, together with the appropriate simulation results, suggests that at least some subjects in experiments involving many estimates of the same stimulus set are considering stimulus–response events occurring more than one trial into the past. This apparently happens despite the fact that subjects are instructed to render a ratio estimate of each stimulus in respect to the one presented on the preceding trial. Before considering the possibility that some subjects ignore or are unable to follow this instruction, consider a situation that at first glance also implies that subjects use information from several trials into the past, whereas in fact, they are only influenced by the event on the preceding trial.

## IMPULSE PLOTS

An alternative way to describe sequence effects is to examine the average response on trial T as a function of the specific stimulus or response presented k trials in the past (Holland & Lockhead, 1968; Ward & Lockhead, 1970). This type of analysis is referred to by Lockhead (1984) as an "impulse plot." In discussing impulse plots, the term *lag* is used to designate the number of trials separating the current stimulus from the contingent stimulus preceding it. So a lag of 1 indicates that the mean response on the current trial is contingent on a specific intensity having occurred on the previous trial. A lag of 2 indicates that the current mean is contingent on a stimulus that occurred two trials back, and so forth.

Figure 13.9 presents results collected by Ward (1973) for magnitude estimation of the loudness of 10 tones. The function labeled "loud" represents the average of all responses (irrespective of stimulus intensity) following stimulus 9 or 10 (k trials into the past). The function labeled "medium" represents the

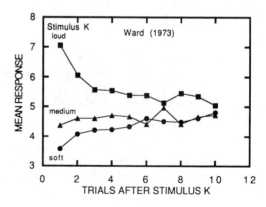

FIG. 13.9. Mean response on Trial T as a function of intervening trials since stimulus **K**. Category estimates of loudness: stimulus **K** soft (circles), medium (triangles), and loud (squares). From Ward (1973).

average of the responses following stimulus 5 or 6. And the function labeled "soft" represents the average following stimulus 1 or 2.

A strong assimilation effect is evident at lag 1 inasmuch as the mean response on the trial after a loud tone tends to be high relative to the mean response on the trial after a soft tone, and vice versa. The mean response on the trial after a medium tone falls between these two extremes. The large differences between the means contingent on loud and soft tones persist out to lag 9.

Jesteadt, Luce and Green (1977) reported similar results for group data but their assimilation effects only extend three trials back. These data are important when addressing the topic of contrast effects. On the basis of additional regression analyses, Jesteadt et al. concluded that all such assimilation effects only extend to lag 1. The diminishing impact observed further back in the series occurs because of the initial large shift in response magnitude immediately following a loud or soft sound.

To appreciate this argument, suppose for the moment that a very soft tone is presented on trial 100. It receives a relatively small response magnitude. Because of assimilation, the response on the next trial (101) will be less than average. If the response on trial 102 assimilates to the response on trial 101, then it too will be relatively small. This propagation of assimilation traced back to the original soft tone will continue for several trials, until eventually the mean response on trial T tapers off to the average value over the entire stimulus series. The apparent assimilation effect beyond lag 1 is entirely artifactual. It depends only on the original presentation of the soft tone and does not reveal the operation of a judgment process whose strength wanes as the number of trials increases.

This version of the Judgment Option Model generates data that supports the Jesteadt et al. position. Continuing with the example of a subject who only considers a single trial into the past, impulse plots were determined for both

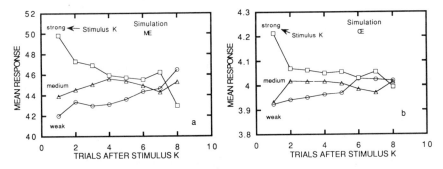

FIG. 13.10. Mean response on Trial T as a function of intervening trials since stimulus **K**: weak (circles), medium (triangles), and strong (squares): (a) Magnitude Estimation (b) Category Estimation. From the Judgment Option Model.

Magnitude and Category Estimation with the parameters stated for the earlier simulations. Figure 13.10 presents the relevant findings.

Both data sets agree substantially with the empirical patterns in Figure 13.9. Assimilation to the response given on the previous trial is strong and gradually loses strength as the contingent stimulus is located further and further in the past. Assimilation has disappeared completely by lag 8. Because there is absolutely nothing in the internal workings of the model that permits the hypothetical subject to consider events beyond one trial, the propagation referred to by Jesteadt et al. must artifactually produce the apparent assimilation seen for earlier trials. It seems likely that exactly the same propagation is responsible for the empirical results in Figure 13.9.


## CONTRAST EFFECTS

Figure 13.11a shows an impulse plot for a Category Estimation experiment conducted by Ward and Lockhead (1971). The y axis is the average deviation between the category given and the rank order of the stimulus. It is unclear why this task produced such a marked negative deviation, but this aspect of the data is not relevant to the point concerning sequence effects. Assimilation is evident for lags 1 and 2, but for greater lags the relative heights of the curves for the responses following loud (stimuli 9 & 10) and soft (stimuli 1 & 2) tones reverse positions. The mean response on the current trial now contrasts with the response given to the stimulus presented k trials in the past. That is to say, the mean response across all stimuli following a soft tone tends to be larger than the mean response following a loud tone.

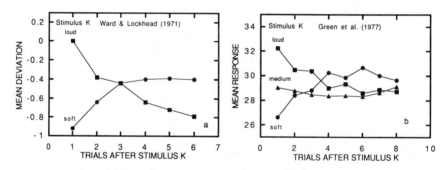

FIG. 13.11.   Mean error on Trial T as a function of intervening trials since stimulus **K**: soft tones (circles), medium tones (triangles), loud tones (squares). (a) Category estimates from Ward and Lockhead (1971). (b) Magnitude estimates from Green et al. (1977).

Ward (1975, 1990a) reported comparable findings for Magnitude Estimation and Cross Modality Matching. One of his frequent results is that assimilation occurs at lags 1 and 2, but that contrast occurs when the target stimulus is farther back in the series. Details of the experimental conditions are important in determining the exact form of the sequential dependencies. These findings differ from those shown in Figure 13.9 for Magnitude Estimation. Some additional factor must be at work in the studies of Ward and his colleagues that is not captured by the version of the Judgment Option Model allowing the subject to consider only events one trial into the past.

Figure 13.11b gives average data for the five subjects in the Green et al. (1977) study, which serves as our main example of sequence effects. Assimilation exists for lags 1 to 3, but beyond this point the responses following loud and soft tones reverse their positions, indicating contrast. Careful examination of the Jesteadt, Luce, and Green data (1977, Fig. 2, right panel) reveals the same trend. The discrepancies between studies that do and do not yield contrast effects require explanation.

The pattern in Figure 13.11 cannot be generated by the Judgment Option Model if the subject considers events extending only one trial into the past. For some unknown reason, subjects in these experiments do not all rely on the same judgment strategy. The data for one subject (FS) in the Green et al magnitude estimation study departs in significant ways from the group norm. The behavior of this subject can be modeled if we assume judgments are influenced by stimulus–response pairs occurring at lags greater than 1. In the context of the findings shown in Figure 13.11, it is clearly possible that FS is not an exception after all.

An impulse plot was made from a simulation comparable to the one for subject FS, except, instead of assuming a constant degree of assimilation for each stimulus pair, an average similarity was computed based on the present stimulus and its similarity with stimuli from the previous 7 trials. As the number of trials back increases, the present simulation approaches that in which the similarity measure is a constant. The outcome of the simulation is shown in Figure 13.12 for Category and Magnitude Estimation.

Assimilation occurs out to lag 3, but the functions for the two extreme cases (contingent on strong and weak stimuli) exchange places beyond that point and show contrast rather than assimilation for lags 4 to 8. At least modest contrast effects result from assuming the subject considers the overall similarity between the most recent stimuli and the present one. The subject uses an average similarity to weight the judgment on trial $T-1$ in arriving at an estimate on trial T. The eventual response on the current trial, therefore, is a weighted average of two factors: the judgment selected from the Gaussian distribution of options and the judgment on the previous trial based on an average similarity between the stimulus on trial T and the subset of stimuli that occurred several trials back.

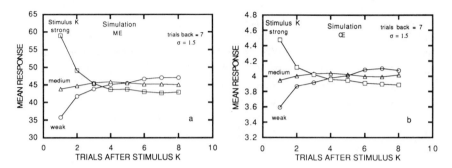

FIG. 13.12.   Mean response on Trial T as a function of intervening trials since stimulus **K**: weak (circles), medium (triangles), strong (squares). Simulation data from the Judgment Option Model for Magnitude (a) and Category (b) Estimation.

## REGRESSION EQUATIONS

The use of the impulse plot as the format for revealing sequence effects suggests that a regression equation could quantify the relative contribution of the stimulus on trial T and the stimuli and responses on trials T−k, where k is the lag representing stimulus–response events extending back 7 or 8 trials. For reasons associated with the nature of Stevens's Law, as discussed in chapter 3, the appropriate terms for such an equation are logarithmic values. Cross (1973) used this approach and Jesteadt, Luce, and Green (1977) generalized it by proposing a formula that took into account both previous stimuli and responses:

$$log\ R_T = \gamma\ log\ \mathbf{S}_T + \sum_{i=1}^{N} \alpha_i\ log\ \mathbf{S}_{t-1} + \sum_{k=1}^{M} \beta_k\ log\ R_{T-k} + \delta + \epsilon\ , \quad (13.1)$$

where $\gamma$, $\alpha_i$, and $\beta_k$ are regression coefficients, $\delta$ is a constant related to the response scale, and $\epsilon$ is the error term. Jesteadt et al. reported that virtually all the variance in the responses on trial T can be accounted for by including only the stimuli and responses on the immediately preceding trial. In other words, Equation 13.1 can be reduced to the case where both N and M equal 1:

$$log\ R_T = \gamma\ log\ \mathbf{S}_T + \alpha\ log\ \mathbf{S}_{T-1} + \beta\ log\ R_{T-1} + \delta + \epsilon \quad (13.2)$$

On the other hand, Ward (1990a) reported that the general form (Equation 13.1) is necessary to describe his data because of the significant influence of events earlier in the stimulus series. These effects of previous events are not always reliable, however, and are open to alternative interpretations. A variety of other regression equations are tested by DeCarlo and Cross (1990), whose work is discussed momentarily.

If error terms are ignored, Equation 13.2 can be reduced to either of two simpler forms that emphasize the influence of previous stimuli or responses.

$$log\ R_T = \gamma\ log\ \mathbf{S}_T + \alpha\ log\ \mathbf{S}_{T-1} \tag{13.3a}$$

$$log\ R_T = \gamma\ log\ \mathbf{S}_T + \alpha\ log\ R_{T-1} \tag{13.3b}$$

Cross (1973) employed Equation 13.3a to describe his original results on sequence effects in Magnitude Estimation.

Stimulus and response values are usually closely related in scaling experiments—the psychophysical function is monotonically increasing—so a choice between Equations 13.3a and 13.3b must be made on theoretical grounds. This holds for the more general formula (Equation 13.1) as well. Within the context of the Judgment Option Model, it seems that Equation 13.3a is appropriate for Magnitude Estimation, and Equation 13.3b is appropriate for Magnitude Production. This follows from the model, because it appears that the sequential effects in scaling studies are due to the perceived similarity between the present stimulus and those stimuli that occurred on earlier trials. The grounds for this similarity lies in the sensory representations of the physical stimuli. If the stimulus is defined as the value under the control of the experimenter and the response as the variable under the control of the subject, Equation 13.3a is appropriate for Magnitude Estimation (stimulus similarity) and Equation 13.3b for Magnitude Production (response similarity). This would be the way to proceed if one believes that the regression analysis provides the best way to analyze the results on sequence effects. However, under most circumstances, the regression equation is an inadmissable way to analyze sequence effects.

The crucial question is not whether to include previous stimuli or responses in the equations, but whether the regression approach itself yields meaningful results when it comes to the analysis of these particular sequence effects. The difficulty arises in trying to reconcile the assumptions underlying linear regression with the empirical fact that sequential effects depend on stimulus separation. As the triangle pattern demonstrates, the correlational link between successive responses depends on the separation between successive stimuli. When the members of a stimulus pair are of like intensity, the correlation is high; but when stimulus separation is great, the correlation drops to zero. The linear regression is blind to these distinctions and lumps all stimulus pairs together. As far as Equations 13.1 to 13.3 are concerned, the contribution of a stimulus or response on trial T−k is independent of its distance (in terms of intensity) in respect to the present stimulus.

The interpretation of the impulse plot runs into the same problem for the same reason. The mean response on trial T contingent on a specific stimulus having occurred on trial T−k is computed over the entire response domain, without regard for the separation between each of these different stimuli and the target stimulus on trial T−k (soft, medium, loud). An analogy would be if someone were to add a sine and a cosine function together, obtain a straight line, and then proceed to model the linear function by ignoring the manner in which it was produced. At best, the impulse plot only reveals an approximate picture of the sequential dependencies influencing a subject's response. For this reason, Jesteadt, Luce, and Green (1977) rejected this type of analysis as an appropriate model. DeCarlo and Cross (1990, p. 387) also recognized the difficulties raised by the triangle pattern for regression analysis, though their theoretical models are not designed to cope with this problem.

## ALTERNATIVE JUDGMENT REFERENTS

### Global Methods

The existence of sequence effects implies that subjects are making comparisons between the stimulus to be estimated and a contextual referent from the past. Baird (1970c) argued that in visual perception all estimates of intensity are relative in the sense that the comparison stimulus is assessed in respect to some standard. In this work, the stimulus and response variables in Stevens's Power Law are all expressed in terms of ratios between a comparison (stimulus or response) and a standard (usually designated by the experimenter). A similar notion of perceptual relativity is proposed more recently by DeCarlo and Cross (1990) and DeCarlo (1992, 1994). They apply it to an analysis of sequence effects for a variety of stimulus attributes.

The latter studies contain two major empirical findings. First, the assimilation effects between the current response and that given on the previous trial can be controlled by instructions (DeCarlo & Cross, 1990). Two types of instructions are given: "free" Magnitude Estimation in which the subject must make all judgments in respect to a stimulus referent of their own choosing, and a "prior reference" condition in which the task is to estimate the stimulus in respect to the previous one in the series. The two instructions have a differential impact on the assimilation effects in the manner one might expect. Assimilation is strong in the direction of the previous response when subjects are instructed to use the prior psychophysical event as a referent, whereas assimilation to the previous response is less substantial when the subject is allowed to choose any referent from the series.

The reason this study is important for the tenets of the Judgment Option Model is its implication that alternative referents are available in global scaling tasks, and in the absence of explicit instructions, different subjects may well use different referents. The resulting individual differences among subjects greatly complicates the formulation of judgment models that apply to averages across subject populations, because it is necessary to take into account the particular referents being used by each subject. This knowledge is usually lacking when instructions do not explicitly state a referent. The earlier example of FS clearly illustrates this complication.

The second finding of importance from the standpoint of the Judgment Option Model is that assimilation effects decline with an increase in the intertrial interval (DeCarlo, 1992). If a subject utilizes the previous stimulus–response event as a referent, its effectiveness depends on how long ago it was presented. Although by no means a startling result, it does suggest that either memory for the stimulus, for the response, or for both, are critical in producing assimilation. Because it seems likely the subject can recall the previous response (at least when it is a number), regardless of the intertrial interval, the weakening of assimilation has more to do with failure to recollect the previous stimulus accurately. This implies that the assessment of the perceptual similarity between the current stimulus and that from the past will suffer as the intertrial interval becomes large. The current stimulus will be judged less like the previous one, regardless of their physical similarity in terms of relative intensity.

## Local Methods

Sequential dependencies also occur when using the classical psychophysical methods such as the Method of Limits and Adjustment (Figure 4.1 gives an example.) In one use of the Method of Limits the experimenter presents a standard followed by a comparison whose magnitude is obviously less than or greater than the standard. The subject acknowledges this fact and so the experimenter increases (ascending trials) or decreases (descending trials) the magnitude of the comparison. This stepwise procedure continues until the subject indicates that the comparison matches the standard. The procedure is similar in the Method of Adjustment, but the subject controls the changes in the magnitude of the comparison instead of the experimenter. Variations on both methods exist (Békésy, 1947; Cornsweet, 1962) and these modifications have seen extensive use in clinical settings where people come to have their hearing and vision evaluated.

From the very beginning of psychophysics it has been recognized that these methods introduce "errors" into the assessment of an absolute or difference threshold. Two types of errors are frequently identified. Most texts refer to the first as an error of anticipation (expectation) and to the second as an error of habituation (Engen, 1972; Gescheider, 1985). The first occurs when the subject decides too soon that the comparison matches the standard and therefore halts the change in the comparison at a magnitude less than the standard on ascending trials and greater than the standard on descending trials. The second occurs when the subject decides too late in the series that the two stimuli are equal and therefore halts the change in the comparison when it is greater than the standard on ascending trials and less than the standard on descending trials. This judgment behavior is only labeled an "error" if it occurs consistently over the entire course of the experiment.

Most texts state the aforementioned facts and then go on to offer advice as to how an experimenter can take precautions to avoid the errors either through procedural or statistical fixes. Curiously, nobody has much to say about the conditions under which each error is observed, and no one has remarked on the judgment processes responsible for the subject's behavior.

This text ventures the guess that both types of errors are intimately connected with assimilation effects and in particular, with the referent subjects use to render their judgment on each trial. A specific hypothesis can be proposed concerning these two types of errors by relying on the experimental results of DeCarlo and Cross (1990).

The two potential referents in local judgment tasks are the standard stimulus and the comparison presented on the previous trial. If the subject uses the standard as a referent then the comparison will assimilate toward it, and the subject will halt the change in the magnitude of the comparison before it equals the standard. This is an error of anticipation: On ascending trials, the comparison is set to be less than the standard and on descending trials it is set to be greater than the standard. On the other hand, if the subject uses the previous value of the comparison as a referent, the apparent magnitude of the comparison will always lag behind its actual physical magnitude. Even when the comparison is physically equal to the standard, it will be judged as too small on ascending trials and as too large on descending trials. The subject continues to change the comparison until it surpasses the level of the standard, making the comparison too large on ascending trials and too small on descending trials. This is an error of habituation.

An experiment in which one changes the availability of the standard and the previous comparison stimulus might test this hypothesis. This could be arranged either through physical procedures (such as exposure time) or through instructions directing the subject to attend to one or the other target. The goal of such manipulations is to induce the subject to utilize one or the other stimulus as a referent, and then to determine whether or not this leads in the predicted manner to errors of anticipation and habituation.

## OVERVIEW

The following are the major results on sequence effects from individual subjects: (a) The relation between the arithmetic mean and stimulus intensity approximates Stevens's Power Law, though some of the individual functions are sinuous on a log–log plot. (b) The standard deviation is a quadratic or linear function of the mean, in accord with a generalized version of Ekman's Law. (c) Sequence effects are present in that the response on trial T depends on the stimulus and response magnitudes on trial $T-1$. There are three varieties of effects.

*Assimilation:* Using the grand mean response over all stimuli and trials as a comparison, the mean following a relatively weak stimulus tends to be less than the grand mean; the mean following a relatively strong stimulus tends to be greater than the grand mean; whereas, the mean following medium stimuli tends to be near the grand mean.

*Triangle pattern:* The correlation between responses on trial T and trial $T-1$ is highly positive when stimuli on successive trials are close in intensity, whereas the correlation approaches zero as the separation between successive intensities increases.

*V-shape:* The relative error of the ratio of responses on successive trials is low when stimuli on successive trials are similar in intensity, whereas it increases as separation between successive intensities increases.

*Rank-order violations:* Responses over successive trials violate rank order more frequently for small stimulus separations than for large ones.

*Individual differences:* Not all subjects engage the same judgment strategies. Some consider only the preceding psychophysical event in deciding upon a response, while others extend consideration to events embedded further back in the series.

Variations on the Judgment Option Model provide explanations for most of these empirical facts. The advantage of the model rests with its generality; applications are not confined to sequence effects. The success of the analyses presented in the previous four chapters attests to the model's wide range of application.

The absolute identification of stimulus intensities are considered next. Many of the judgment strategies incorporated into models of context effects are even more prominent when modeling subjects' attempts to identify absolutely each of a small number of unidimensional stimuli.

# 14 Absolute Identification

One of the enduring tasks of psychophysics is to provide models concerning the ability of perceptual systems to transmit and accurately code information from the surrounding world. One experimental technique used extensively to determine the amount of information transmitted is the Method of Absolute Identification (Baird & Noma, 1978), formerly referred to as the *Method of Absolute Judgment* (Wever & Zener, 1928). The procedure is deceptively simple. The subject must assign a unique response label to each of a set of stimuli distributed along a physical dimension. The labels are usually the integers 1 to N, where N is the total number of stimuli. The physical values are typically separated by equal logarithmic steps, and following each response, subjects receive feedback as to the correct label for that trial.

Many of the judgment principles raised in regard to the Judgment Option Model find expression in Absolute Identification, and results are difficult to fathom without taking into account the potential influence of all such principles. Instead of starting out with a full-blown model of how these judgment principles apply to specific data, this chapter approaches the problem from several directions by proposing a series of approximations, each of which highlights the influence of only one or two relevant factors. These approximations are also referred to as *hypotheses*, reserving the term *model* for the final and most complete view of the problems addressed in this chapter. The hypotheses build on one another, and the model incorporates the major factors that effect limitations on a person's attempt to label absolutely each member of a set of unidimensional stimuli. The chapter concludes by suggesting how one might explain the results of studies specially designed to investigate the trial-by-trial behavior of subjects.

# CHANNEL CAPACITY

As the number of alternatives in the stimulus set increases, performance keeps pace up to some level, but then tapers off with larger stimulus sets, inasmuch as the subject is unable to uniquely identify each of the stimuli without making errors. In the language of information theory, a channel capacity is reached (Garner, 1962; Miller, 1956). Increasing the number of stimuli beyond channel capacity does not lead to any further improvements in the amount of information transmitted. The values typically reported in the laboratory fall between 1.5 and 4 bits. A "bit" is the power to which 2 must be raised to equal the number of stimulus alternatives. The puzzle created by this limitation on information processing is that it seems to fly in the face of everyday experience. Most people can perfectly recognize thousands of objects in the environment without error. Why is the limit so small in psychophysical experiments involving unidimensional stimuli? This question remains in the forefront throughout this chapter.

The experimenter computes information measures based on the confusion matrix giving the number of times each response alternative is assigned to each stimulus (Baird & Noma, 1978). Several measures are possible, but the one yielding the clearest insight into the judgment process expresses information transmitted $(I_t)$ as a function of the average uncertainty of the response set $[U(R)]$ and the average uncertainty of the response set conditional on the stimulus set, $U(R|S)$:

$$I_t = U(R) - U(R|S) \qquad (14.1)$$

Details of how to evaluate the terms of Equation 14.1 are available in many sources (e.g., Attneave, 1959; Garner, 1962; Luce, 1960). The crucial point is that the two terms on the right side of the equation are nonmetric measures of variance. Response uncertainty is a function of the logarithm of the probability (empirically interpreted to mean relative frequency) of giving each response summed over each member of the total response set (M):

$$U(R) = - \sum_{j=1}^{M} p(r_j)\, log_2\, p(r_j) \qquad (14.2)$$

This measure is computed without distinguishing among stimuli. The conditional response uncertainty refers to the average variability in assigning responses contingent on the stimulus:

$$U(R|S) = - \sum_{i=1}^{N} p(s_i) \sum_{j=1}^{M} p(r_j|S_i)\, log_2\, p(r_j|S_i) \qquad (14.3)$$

This is a nonmetric index of the subject's errors in assigning labels, where the data substituted into Equations 14.2 and 14.3 are entries in the stimulus–response confusion matrix. In studies of sequence effects reviewed later, metric measures are employed. This practice has advantages in some situations and drawbacks in others. Mori (1989) extended traditional information-theoretic measures to describe some of these effects. Nonmetric measures are reported for computer simulations, though this is not always reasonable when discussing the empirical studies already in the literature, especially those indicating that metric stimulus properties are of some relevance.

## AN EMPIRICAL EXAMPLE

Figure 14.1 shows the outcome of a classic experiment by Pollack (1952) in which the stimulus set was a series of tones, logarithmically spaced over a frequency range from 100 Hz to 8000 Hz (metathetic dimension). In the left panel (14.1a), the information transmitted in bits is plotted as a function of the stimulus uncertainty available in the stimulus set, each of whose members was presented equally often. Perfect matches between the available stimulus information and the transmitted information would occur if all the data points fell on the diagonal line. The transmitted information begins to fall below the theoretical maximum in the vicinity of 1.5 bits of stimulus uncertainty, and beyond this, it gradually climbs to a maximum of approximately 2 bits.

One critical implication of a channel capacity is that the conditional response uncertainty increases at the same rate as the response uncertainty. Beyond some point, the potential information contained in the larger response set is offset by the increased variability in the assignments—even for stimuli to which no errors

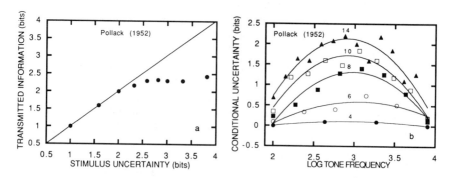

FIG. 14.1.    (a) Information transmitted as a function of stimulus uncertainty for auditory tones. The solid diagonal indicates perfect transmission. (b) Conditional response uncertainty as a function of logarithm of tonal frequency (position in the stimulus series). The parameter is set size (4 to 14). After Pollack (1952).

are made when the set size is smaller. The problem, then, is to explain why the conditional response uncertainty increases as a function of stimulus alternatives.

Figure 14.1b depicts a different side of the data collected by Pollack. The conditional response uncertainty is plotted as a function of the logarithm of the tone frequency with set size as a parameter. The variability of response assignments is a function both of the location of a tone in the frequency series and of the number of tones in the set. There is less variability at the ends of the series as compared with the center locations, and the overall conditional uncertainty increases with set size. This bow-shaped function has motivated almost as much theoretical debate as the channel capacity (e.g., Lacouture, 1994; Luce & Nosofsky, 1984; Luce, Nosofsky, Green & Smith, 1982; Marley & Cook, 1984; W. Siegel, 1972). More is said about this later.

In the literature, four judgment factors, or some subset thereof, are deemed responsible for the data trends in Figure 14.1: *attention, memory, assimilation,* and *contrast*. Substantial reference is made only to the last three because of their central role in model building here. Each is sometimes referred to as though they were "real" psychological processes, whereas each term is an operational definition bereft of theoretical import until rational argument pinpoints their source. What follows attempts to provide this rationale through discussion of each factor acting alone, then by combining the three into what is called the *Identification Model*. This chapter considers the source of response variability from the standpoint of the Judgment Option Model, rather than from that of the Sensory Aggregate Model. Nevertheless, much of the material in chapter 7 regarding changes in stimulus representations in memory bear on the issues raised here. In particular, if the memory exponent is less than the perception exponent, then the stimulus representations become more alike with the passage of time. This should reduce channel capacity.[1]

## FACTOR I: MEMORY

### Empirical Findings

One theory about why the channel capacity is so low for unidimensional attributes is that the stored representation of the stimulus deteriorates over time and the number of stored representations of the same stimulus increases precipitously with increases in set size. Implicit in this explanation is the notion that the subject in an absolute identification task recalls previous occurrences of the stimulus together with the correct feedback attached to this stimulus by the experimenter.

---

[1]These results are not incorporated into the present discussion because the chapter is already long and the general connections to be drawn are transparent. The details are not transparent, but they are best left for future investigations.

Two variables may cause the subject to be less certain of response assignments as the stimulus set size increases. The first possibility is that the subject forgets the stimulus representation as it fades into the past (increased retention interval). The second possibility is that recent stimuli stored in memory interfere with attempts to recall an earlier stimulus. W. Siegel (1972) tested these two hypotheses with definitive results.

The stimuli were seven tones ranging from 500 Hz to 560 Hz, and the subject tried to label each tone with the correct integer from 1 to 7. The parameter of interest is the time between each presentation: 0, 0.5, 1, 3, or 6 sec (in different blocks of trials). The dependent measure is the percent correct for each of the delay conditions. The number of intervening trials since the last occurrence of the same stimulus is a parameter, extracted from the trial sequence after the experiment. Figure 14.2 presents Siegel's findings.

Both the retention interval and the number of intervening items (excluding the target stimulus) influences the outcome. As retention interval increases, the percent correct decreases, and the level of retention for a stimulus also declines with the number of intervening items (0, 1, or 2). Accepting the percent correct as a satisfactory correlate of the conditional response uncertainty, the results imply that limitations on channel capacity reflect limitations on the subject's ability to recall stimuli over time under conditions in which other items in the series play a disruptive role. In a companion review paper, J. A. Siegel and W. Siegel (1972) proposed that this comparatively poor showing results from the pristine quality of the stimulus attributes. The authors contended that attributes, such as pure tones and lights, are "ultra meaningless" in comparison with objects encountered in the everyday environment. The idea, raised originally by Miller (1956), is that subjects have difficulty chunking subsets of these meaningless items into packages that can later be recovered as single entities. If efficient chunking were possible, then upon retrieval, each entity could be unpacked to

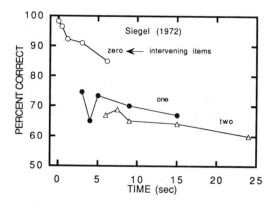

FIG. 14.2. Percent correct identification of auditory tones as a function of intertrial interval with the number of intervening items since the stimulus' last occurrence as a parameter. After W. Siegel (1972).

reveal the constituent items. This would assist the subject in making correct identifications.

## A Memory Hypothesis

The initial theoretical approach has a Thurstonian flavor designed to accent the influence of the sheer number of intervening items on channel capacity. In a computer simulation, the standard deviation of the judgment distributions is fixed at 1.5. The set of judgment options is truncated at the lower end by the mean of the distribution for stimulus 1 and at the upper end by the mean of the distribution for stimulus N. So far this simulation is the same one used for Category Estimation, but without a term to represent the sensory similarity between stimuli. This approach, therefore, can not produce sequence effects.

The simulation's main parameter is the number of previous stimulus–response pairs the subject recalls in attempting to identify the current stimulus. It is optimistically assumed that the subject has superb memory and can recall events that occurred 10 trials back in the series. If the current stimulus is recovered from memory during this search, the accompanying response label is also retrieved and given as the correct response. Identification is perfect so long as the same stimulus occurred within the last 10 trials.

Simulations were run under these hypothetical conditions: a single "subject" made 500 estimates of each of N stimuli, where N varied in different simulations from 3 to 15 in steps of 2. Therefore, the stimulus uncertainty ranged from 1.58 to 3.91 bits.

Equations 14.2 and 14.3 are used to analyze the confusion matrices in the standard way. Equation 14.1 determines the information transmitted. Figure 14.3a shows the amount transmitted as a function of stimulus uncertainty, where it is assumed the subject would be errorless in identifying one or two stimuli. The transmitted information produced by the simulation increases up to a value somewhat greater than 1.5 bits and begins to level off as stimulus uncertainty extends beyond this. The reason for this trend is the lowered likelihood of finding a stimulus representation in memory within the window of the previous 10 trials. For small set sizes, it is often true that the current stimulus falls within this window, hence, a high percentage of "hits" accumulate. For the larger set sizes, a fruitful search of memory happens less often, given that the subject can only solicit information 10 trials into the past. Therefore, the information transmission does not keep pace with the increased stimulus uncertainty. In terms of Equation 14.1, the conditional uncertainty (degree of response equivocation) increases progressively as stimulus–response uncertainty increases, and the potential gain in the amount transmitted is offset by the mere fact that the subject finds the critical item less often in what might be called "working memory" (Baddeley, 1994). This is essentially the same argument Siegel (1972) put forth to explain his results.

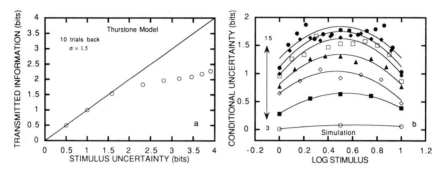

FIG. 14.3.   Data from a Thurstone model assuming the subject recalls stimulus–response events 10 trials back in the series. (a) Information transmitted as a function of stimulus uncertainty. (b) Conditional response uncertainty as a function of logarithm of stimulus intensity. The parameter is set size (3 to 15).

Figure 14.3b has the same format Pollack used (Figure 14.1b) and shows the specific character of the conditional response uncertainty for different set sizes. Response equivocation is lowest at the ends of the stimulus scale and highest in the middle. These end effects have nothing whatever to do with stimulus discriminability or sequence effects because there is nothing built into the simulation to produce such effects. The bowing of the function occurs because the judgment distributions are truncated at the means of the weakest and strongest stimuli. The number of response alternatives for the extremes are smaller than those in the middle because the ends are more affected by truncation. Therefore, the subject makes fewer errors when attempting to identify the end stimuli because the experimental procedure constrains the type and number of errors that can be made. A response of N + 1 in a set size of N is impossible, because this option is disallowed by the experimenter.

It is true, however, that the bowing in Figure 14.3b is not as marked as it is in the empirical data collected by Pollack (Figure 14.1b). This may be related to the degree of learning that occurs in Absolute Identification and/or to the nature of that learning in respect to particular stimuli. These learning effects were investigated by Cardello (1970). He used absolute identification for line lengths with different mappings (rank order or random) between the response labels and the stimulus lengths; he discovered that subjects first learn the ends of the series, then master the stimuli adjacent to the ends, and finally learn those in the center locations. Both response times and percent correct judgments reveal the same learning pattern (see also Lacouture, 1994). Hence, in any experiment concerning absolute identification, the end stimuli generate less response equivocation by dint of the fact that they are associated from the beginning with fewer numbers of response options. This is why they are quickly learned.

The memory constraints of an absolute identification task are important con-
tributors to the limitations on the amount of information transmitted, but they are
not the only relevant factors.

## FACTOR II: ASSIMILATION

As documented in chapter 13, sequence effects exist with methods such as
Category and Magnitude Estimation. It should come as no surprise, therefore,
that similar effects occur with Absolute Identification (Lockhead, 1984; Luce &
Nosofsky, 1984).

An adequate model of a subject's judgment processes must address the problem of sequence effects, and this requires special assumptions beyond those
underlying the memory hypothesis. According to the latter, the response given
for a particular stimulus depends on the associated judgment distribution
(Thurstone in character). In addition, the subject presumably receives assistance
by searching memory and retrieving an earlier representation of the same stimulus together with its appropriate label. Such a judgment strategy generates no
sequence effects.

One empirical indication of sequence effects is the difference in the amount of
information transmitted when stimuli are distributed over different physical
ranges.

### Empirical Results on Range

If the number of stimuli is constant and the logarithm of the overall range is
varied, the information transmission is greatly affected (Luce et al., 1982).
Figure 14.4a shows typical results reported by Braida and Durlach (1972). Rather than use information measures as indicators of sensitivity, they employed the
cumulative sum of $d'$ values for two adjacent stimuli (as per application of the
Theory of Signal Detectability, Green & Swets, 1966/1974; Macmillan & Creelman, 1991).

$$\Delta' = \sum_{i=1}^{N-1} d'_{i,i+1} \tag{14.4}$$

In this special application, the $d'$ measure between two adjacent stimuli is
inversely related to the response uncertainty associated with each. That is, as the
variance of response assignments increases (as seen in the confusion matrix), $d'$
declines. In most instances, this calculation leads to the same pattern of results
revealed by an information-theoretic analysis (Luce & Nosofsky, 1984; Luce et
al., 1982). High total sensitivity ($\Delta'$) is equated with high information transmission, and in fact, Luce et al. (1982) replicated in all essential respects the
findings in Fig. 14.4a.

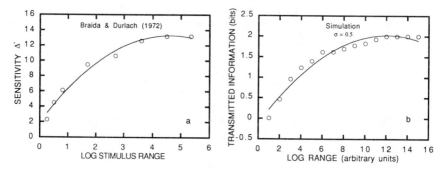

FIG. 14.4.  (a) Cumulative sensitivity (Equation 14.4) as a function of logarithm of stimulus range. After Braida & Durlach (1972). (b) Information transmitted as a function of logarithm of stimulus range. Theoretical predictions of an assimilation hypothesis (Equation 14.5).

There are two aspects of these data of special interest. First, the conditional uncertainties when the range is narrow are larger than when the range is broad. This means the total sensitivity (information transmitted) is smaller for narrow ranges as compared with broad ranges. Second, the relation is negatively accelerated and levels off for the most expansive ranges. Each phenomenon requires explanation, and each has been the target of modeling efforts (Lacouture & Marley, 1991; Luce & Nosofsky, 1984; Marley & Cook, 1984, 1986). The approach described here is a further extension of this tradition, but one consistent with the Judgment Option Model.

## Range Effects and Sensory Similarity

According to the Judgment Option Model, the sensory similarity among stimuli determines the strength of assimilation between the present judgment and those occurring on previous trials. Therefore, as the members of the stimulus set are compressed into a smaller and smaller region, the total amount of assimilation increases. This stimulus packing increases the conditional response uncertainty and thereby reduces the amount of information transmitted. The change in information transmission seen in Figure 14.4a is therefore due to sensory effects linked to stimulus spacing along the physical dimension.

As this spacing continues to increase, the similarity among stimuli approaches zero, and, at this turning point, judgments are driven solely by the Thurstonian distributions. There is no assimilation between successive trials. Recall that the means of the judgment distributions are equally spaced and represent the rank order of stimuli. As the physical spacing between stimuli becomes large, the degree of assimilation goes to zero, and the information transmission tends to a constant value that is independent of stimulus range. This is why the function in Figure 14.4a does not continue to increase with further increases in range.

In order to model the judgment process already described, it is necessary to decide on a relation between stimulus spacing and sensory similarity. There are several alternative ways to do this and most have been tried with roughly the same outcome in terms of a computer simulation. The final approximation is very simple. A single similarity measure is used for all stimulus pairs and this measure is the inverse of the stimulus range. This is a sure-fire way to achieve a desired mean similarity across all stimulus pairs, though its ultimate validity is questionable. It implies that the amount of assimilation is independent of stimulus separation over successive trials, and this is certainly not true in Magnitude Estimation, as indicated by the triangle pattern (chap. 13). This reservation is disregarded in what follows.

In the present simulations, the stimulus range varies from 1 to 15 (arbitrary units), and, hence, the sensory similarity varies from 1 to 0.067. Each similarity value enters the model as a fixed quantity ($\tau$), which is added to or subtracted from the judgment ($J*$) selected from the Thurstone distribution so as to bring the final judgment closer to the feedback on the previous trial.

### The Assimilation Hypothesis

The process is simulated by building feedback into the program. The idea is that the subject adjusts the value selected from the judgment distribution according to the feedback. The amount of this adjustment is defined as $\tau$, and $FB$ designates the correct response label for a particular stimulus. Hence, $FB_{T-1}$ is the appropriate label for $S_{T-1}$. Two cases for determining the final judgment ($J$) are defined in terms of $J*$ and $FB_{T-1}$.

$$\text{Case I: } |J* - \tau| < \tau$$

$$\text{If } J* = FB_{T-1} \text{ then } J = J* \tag{14.5a}$$

$$\text{If } J* - FB_{T-1} < 0 \text{ then } J = J* + \tau \tag{14.5b}$$

$$\text{If } J* - FB_{T-1} > 0 \text{ then } J = J* - \tau \tag{14.5c}$$

$$\text{Case II: } |J* - \tau| \geq \tau$$

$$J = FB_{T-1} \tag{14.5d}$$

Each version of Equation 14.5 creates assimilation by an amount less than or equal to $\tau$. Equation 14.5d is necessary in case $\tau$ is greater than the separation between $J*$ and the feedback on the previous trial ($S\, T_{-1}$). This ensures that the subject does not overshoot in shifting toward the feedback.

The important difference between the assimilation hypothesis and those variations on the Judgment Option Model used for Magnitude and Category Estimation is that assimilation here is to the previous feedback rather than to the previous judgment (response). A second difference is that the amount of assimilation is independent of the separation between successive stimuli. Figure 14.4b shows the simulation results produced by adopting these assumptions.

As stimulus range increases, the transmitted information (Equation 14.1) increases at a decelerated rate and eventually asymptotes at two bits. This is the value generated by a pure Thurstone model with no between-trial assimilation. The solid line drawn through the points has no deeper theoretical meaning. It only summarizes the trend of the data points, a trend that bears a close resemblance to the empirical data in Figure 14.4a.

## Empirical Data at Channel Capacity

Studies carried out in the early 1950s establish that the stimulus range has little impact on the channel capacity, so long as this range is sufficiently large to allow for adequate discrimination among stimuli (e.g., Pollack, 1952). On the other hand, as already noted, more recent experiments indicate that an extreme compression of range does reduce channel capacity. The assimilation hypothesis states that the reduction in channel capacity under these latter conditions is due to an increase in the sensory similarity among stimuli, leading to the assimilation of the judgment on trial T to the feedback on trial $T-1$.

Now consider this question: Do sequential effects exist when stimuli are separated enough so that channel capacity is reached, and any additional separation does not much change the information transmitted? This issue has been addressed in independent work by a number of laboratories, and Shiffrin and Nosofsky (1994) and Luce (1994) provided concise overviews of the literature. The experimental procedures used by various laboratories differ somewhat from each other, and the findings differ as well. To make matters even more challenging, not all researchers use exactly the same data analyses, nor the same theoretical models in discussing the implications of their findings. Because the models are quite technical, it is not always easy to distinguish between times when the researchers are talking about data and when they are talking about theoretical parameters inferred from the data. Despite these interpretive difficulties, there has been some success in simulating the major findings.

## Asymmetric Assimilation Errors

Luce et al. (1982) determined sequence effects over successive trials by estimating the probability of making two types of error. An error is said to occur whenever the subject gives a response that is one step above or one step below the correct one, contingent on the stimulus presented on the previous trial. These probabilities are expressed as

$$P[R_{(i+1,T)}|S_{(i,T)},S_{(j,T-1)}] \text{ and } P[R_{(i-1,T)}|S_{(i,T)},S_{(j,T-1)}], \qquad (14.6)$$

where $S_{(i,T)}$ is stimulus i on trial T. In the experiment, subjects try to identify each of 11 sound intensities with feedback provided after each response. Figure 14.5(a, c) shows the results averaged over stimuli 3 to 9 and over three subjects. The conditional probability of moving one integer down in the response assignment (14.5a, top) and one integer up (14.5c, bottom) is plotted as a function of the stimulus occurring on the previous trial ($S_{j,T-1}$).

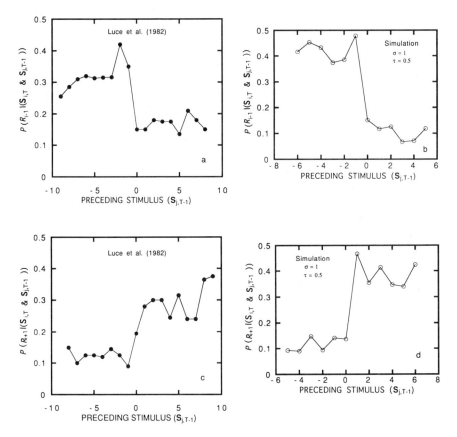

FIG. 14.5.   Results of the sequential one-step response error analysis. The probability (y axis) of giving a response that is one step below (top panels) or one step above (bottom panels) the correct one, contingent on the stimulus presented on the previous trial. Probabilities from Equation 14.6. Panels a and c from Luce et al. (1982). Panels b and d: Data generated by the assimilation hypothesis (Equation 14.5) with parameters indicated on the graphs.

Reading the axes of this graph requires some care. The two parts of Equation 14.6 are plotted (top and bottom) on the y axis. A value of zero on the x axis indicates that the same stimulus was presented in succession. Stimuli (j) presented on the preceding trial that are greater than the present stimulus are arrayed along the right half of the x axis; those presented on the preceding trial that are less than the present stimulus are arrayed along the left half. The units along the stimulus axis are integer steps of separation, not metric units.

The results imply an assimilation effect that is independent of the intensity difference between two successive stimuli. When the previous stimulus is small relative to the current one, there is a sharp increase in the probability of giving a response one step below the correct value (Figure 14.5a); and when the previous stimulus is relatively large, there is a comparable increase in the probability of a response one step above the correct value (Figure 14.5c). One implication is that assimilation does not depend on stimulus separation, suggesting that the judgment rules in Absolute Identification are not exactly the same as those in estimating stimuli when no feedback is provided (Magnitude and Category Estimation). It should be recalled, however, that the extreme stimuli are excluded from this analysis. It is possible that these extremes are impervious to influence from preceding stimuli that are distant in terms of intensity (sensory similarity), and their probabilities for asymmetric errors (according to the analysis in Figure 14.5) would therefore be relatively low.

A simulation was conducted with seven stimuli, a standard deviation of 1 for each of the judgment distributions, and $\tau = .5$ (when a judgment fell half way between two response options, one of them was selected at random). The results are shown in Figures 14.5b and 14.5d (right panels), where the format is the same as for the empirical data on the left. A clear assimilation effect is evident and it resembles the pattern in the empirical data. The "subject" adjusts the response given on trial T in the direction of the feedback given on trial $T-1$. This is not surprising, given that an adjustment of this very sort was incorporated into the model. It remains unclear as to exactly why an assimilation in an actual experiment would occur that is independent of stimulus separation.

## Conditional Response Uncertainty

Luce et al. (1982) also computed a $d'$ measure to assess the sensitivity of the subject to adjacent stimulus intensities. The calculation is somewhat different from the one employed by Braida and Durlach (1972), but its interpretation is comparable. It is described in greater detail in a later section of the chapter. For now, it is enough to know that the smaller the $d'$, the greater the variability in assigning response labels to the stimuli and the lower the percentage of correct judgments. In some approximate sense, $d'$ corresponds to the inverse of the conditional response uncertainty. Figure 14.6a displays the empirical data. The overall trend is consistent with the pattern exhibited by Pollack's (1952) data on

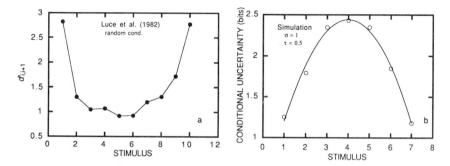

FIG. 14.6. Judgment sensitivity as a function of stimulus position within the series. (a) $d'$ measure from the Theory of Signal Detectability. (b) Conditional response uncertainty generated by the assimilation hypothesis (Equation 14.5).

absolute identification of tones (Figure 14.1b). The results for the end stimuli imply the most agreement in the use of a small number of response labels, whereas stimuli in the center of the series induce the highest uncertainty.

Figure 14.6b presents the simulation results in terms of conditional response uncertainty. The inverted U shape is as it should be if the simulation captures the same judgment processes that produce the U-shaped empirical data in the left panel. It is also true that the depth of the bowing in the simulation is greater than predictions of the memory hypothesis (Figure 14.2b).

## Conditional Variance

In an early absolute identification experiment, Holland and Lockhead (1968) computed the variance of responses for each of 10 stimulus tones, contingent on the preceding tone being very soft ($S_{T-1} = 1, 2$), very loud ($S_{T-1} = 9, 10$), or of medium intensity ($S_{T-1} = 5, 6$). The data are shown in Figure 14.7a, which reveals that the maximum response variance depends on the intensity of the prior tone. The peak shifts somewhat above the midpoint of the intensity scale when the prior stimuli are soft, and somewhat below the midpoint when the prior stimuli are loud. No such shift appears when the prior stimuli are of intermediate intensity, though all three curves indicate that the smallest variance occurs at the extremes. Braida and Durlach (1972) replicated these results.

Figure 14.7b presents simulation results based on the same computer runs that produced the sequential effects in Figure 14.5b. The simulation pattern is strikingly similar to the empirical data. The reason the Judgment Option Model captures such effects is purely a function of the assimilation occurring on each trial. At the extremes of the stimulus scale, variance is small because the response options are truncated at the means of the softest and strongest tones. After

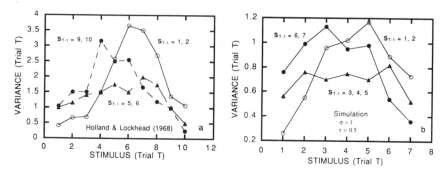

FIG. 14.7.    (a) Response variance for estimates of each of 10 stimulus tones, contingent on the preceding tone being very soft, very loud, or of medium intensity. After Holland and Lockhead (1968). (b) Response variance for each of seven stimuli, contingent on the preceding tone being very weak, very strong, or of medium intensity. Data generated by the assimilation hypothesis (Equation 14.5).

a soft tone, all responses shift downward, but the response usually does not fall below the integer assigned to the previous stimulus, so the variance is reduced for stimuli near the lower end of the scale. For stimuli far enough away from the soft stimuli (say 5 and 6), the shift also occurs, but the previous feedback is never a limiting factor in determining how far this movement can extend. Hence, the variance is greater than it is for stimuli closer to the soft tones. The opposite tendency occurs when the prior tone is strong.

In summary, assimilation of the response to the value given on the previous trial accounts for range effects, response variance, and asymmetric error patterns. These particular assimilation effects appear to have a sensory origin.

## FACTOR III: CONTRAST

A set of results reveals a weakness of the foregoing theoretical approximation because of its failure to describe another aspect of the data that has so far been ignored.

Most would grant that the response given on the current trial shifts in the direction of the response given on the previous trial. But this is not the only sequence effect observed. In the same study that led to the data in Figure 14.7a, Holland and Lockhead (1968) found that the response given on the current trial also contrasts with the average responses given over recent trials, up to lags of eight trials. This contrast effect is not as powerful as the one connecting the response to the immediately preceding feedback, but it nonetheless is reliable.

Lockhead (1984) reviewed the relevant data, and Lacouture (1994) replicated the major results.

## Empirical Data on Contrast Effects

To reveal contrast effects one takes the average response (or error) in respect to the correct value on the present trial as a function of the intensity of the stimulus given on the previous trial, treated separately for lags (trials back) 1 to 8. This type of analysis appears in chapter 13 where sequence effects are discussed for the Method of Category Estimation, in which feedback is not provided. The data from Absolute Identification with feedback are presented in an "impulse plot." Figure 14.8a gives an example adapted from Holland and Lockhead (1968). If there were no sequence effects, all the points would cluster around zero (no errors). They clearly do not.

The graph indicates that when stimuli follow a soft tone (1, 2), the mean responses are relatively small (negative errors), and that when stimuli follow a loud tone (9, 10) the means are relatively large (positive errors). This is assimilation. On the other hand, when the responses being averaged on the current trial depend on a soft or loud tone having occurred two trials back in the series, the opposite effect occurs. Now the mean on the current trial is relatively large after the soft event and relatively small after the loud one. This is contrast. Though not as pronounced as assimilation, contrast phenomena are robust inasmuch as they persist up to eight trials back in the series.

It should be noted that the apparently larger effects attached to trials following presentation of the end stimuli are due to the fact that errors are only possible in

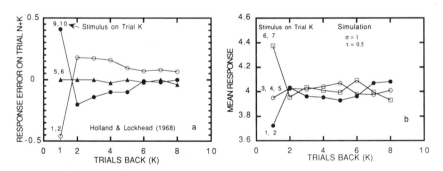

FIG. 14.8.   Mean error on trial T as a function of intervening trials since stimulus **K**: soft tones (open circles), medium tones (triangles), loud tones (filled circles). (a) Category estimates from Holland and Lockhead (1968). (b) Data generated by the assimilation hypothesis (Equation 14.5).

one direction for these cases. If stimulus "1" is presented on trial $T-1$, it is likely to be called either 1, 2, or perhaps 3. On the next trial it is impossible to give a response less than "1," so the bulk of the assimilation will be in the direction of lowering the average response. (Data are averaged over all responses to all stimuli on trial T, including instances where the same stimulus is presented twice in a row.) The same thing happens at the upper end of the scale. Assimilation operates just as strongly for the middle stimuli as it does for the ends, but the experimental conditions are such that effects arise in the impulse plot only for the extremes.

Figure 14.8b presents the assimilation data using the same parameter values that generated the data for Figure 14.5b. The simulations mimic the empirical data in regard to assimilation at lag 1, but do not generate contrast effects at lags greater than 1. Some other factor must be implicated, and contrary to earlier thinking on this matter (Wagner & Baird, 1981), this additional factor is extremely important in helping us understand the judgment processes of subjects using the Method of Absolute Identification. Before elaborating on this view, Lockhead and King's (1983) and Lockhead's (1984) explanations for contrast effects are summarized.

According to these authors, both assimilation and contrast depend on memory for prior events. Assimilation occurs because, for some unspecified reason, the response on the current trial moves toward the memory of the response on the previous trial; contrast occurs because the response on the current trial moves away from the mean of the responses given on the most recent trials (up to eight trials back). Although the authors make no attempt to explain assimilation, their explanation of contrast is that the subject strives to recalibrate the response scale that has been thrown off by assimilation.

Memory is certainly the culprit behind both effects, but it is hypothesized in a moment that the judgment processes involved are not those discussed in the literature. Before addressing this matter, however, consider sequence effects that cannot be attributed to physical stimuli, because none are present. Such studies are important in formulating an all-inclusive explanation of contrast effects, even though the determining factors in these special experiments may not directly apply to sensory stimuli.

## Guessing Studies

Ward and Lockhead (1971) conducted an experiment, replicated by Wagner and Baird (1981), in which subjects anticipate which of N numbers will be presented on an ensuing trial (see also Mori, 1988). No physical stimuli are actually presented, just integers to represent the imaginary stimuli after the subject has responded. In the Wagner and Baird study, subjects were told they were participants in an extrasensory perception (ESP) experiment and they had to guess which of the integers from 1 to 9 would appear next on the computer screen.

After each response, a randomly selected integer (1 to 9) was presented. The subject was to assume that this integer was the correct value (feedback) for the preceding trial.

Figure 14.9a shows the impulse plot for a single subject in this type of study with five response–stimulus options (Lockhead, 1984). The average response on trial T is shown as a function of what occurred (feedback) k trials preceding that response. Strong assimilation to the previous feedback occurs at lag 1 (trial $T-1$), and a small, but visible contrast effect between the smallest and largest stimulus (1 & 5) occurs for lags of 2 or more (though the middle stimulus 3 does not differ from 1 in this region).

Figure 14.9b gives the results of a computer simulation designed to address the ESP experiment. It uses two weighting parameters and one other that is critical later for understanding the results of Absolute Identification when stimuli are actually presented. The weights are called $\alpha_1$ and $\alpha_2$ ($\alpha_1 + \alpha_2 \leq 1$). The critical term is the number of trials back in the sequence the subject considers in coming to a response selection. This is called the "Omit" factor and is designated by the symbol, $\Phi$. The subject excludes with a specific probability the use of the integer responses given on the last k trials. The reason for making this assumption becomes plain in a moment. For now, the goal is to demonstrate that a simple model can account for the ESP data, and can help formulate a more realistic model of contrast effects.

The following describes the subject's decision rule in an ESP experiment, where the possible responses are the integers 1 to 7. If $J^{**}$ is a value chosen from among seven alternatives, and x is a random number from 0 to 1,

$$R_T = J^{**}, \quad x \leq \alpha_1. \tag{14.8a}$$

If $J^{***}$ is a value chosen from the alternatives not used on the previous $\Phi$ trials, then

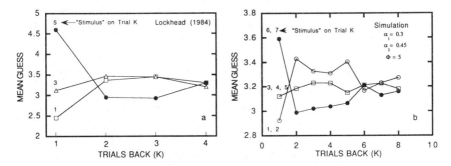

FIG. 14.9.   Mean guess of an integer, contingent on the appearance of a small, medium, or large integer "stimulus" on trial K. (a) From Lockhead (1984). (b) Theoretical predictions from Equation 14.8.

$$R_T = J^{***}, \alpha_1 < x \leq \alpha_2. \qquad (14.8b)$$

Otherwise, the previous feedback is repeated:

$$R_T = FB_{T-1}, \alpha_2 < x \leq 1. \qquad (14.8c)$$

Figure 14.9b presents the results of the simulation. (Parameter values are listed on the graph.) The pattern of results resembles the empirical data in the left panel (Figure 14.9a), and is even more similar to the findings of Wagner and Baird (1981).

The main point is that subjects exhibit a tendency not to use response values that were given in the recent past. A slightly different interpretation would be that they are inclined to give responses that have not occurred as feedback over the previous few trials. A rationale is offered next as to the advantage this strategy bestows on a subject attempting to identify physical stimuli.

## MEMORY, ASSIMILATION, AND CONTRAST

The foregoing approximations implictly assume that subjects make errors, and, therefore, channel capacity does not match the information available in the stimulus set. One of the complications in modeling data on Absolute Identification is that the analyses are conducted over a large number of trials. At the same time, this ignores the very real possibility that judgment strategies in the early learning phase of the experiment (even after practice trials) are not the same as those in the later stages. These two phases are separated here and somewhat different views are offered concerning the nature of the judgment strategies in each.

Whatever subset of the database is analyzed, the pertinent question is this: What strategy does the subject use in learning the response labels associated with the stimuli? In this regard, two working hypotheses are proposed. First, assimilation occurs because the subject perceives a sensory similarity between successive stimuli and concludes that the response on the current trial should bear some resemblance to the feedback on the previous trial. Assimilation only occurs one trial back. There is no hard evidence that assimilation in these tasks depends on stimulus separation, and so tentatively, and somewhat hestitantly, the discussion carries on as if it were a fixed amount on each trial. Second, the subject sees the task as one of recalling information from previous trials in order to render a judgment concerning the response for the current trial. This hypothesis is close to, but not the same as W. Siegel's (1972) view.

There are two important types of information available (in a cognitive processing sense). If the subject queries memory and finds a previous occurrence of the current stimulus, then the associated label is given on the present trial. Moreover, in performing this memory search (it could be either serial or parallel), the subject will also find a number of stimulus representations that do not match the current stimulus. But discovering a nonmatch is valuable as well, because it means that the associated label (feedback) should not be a response for the current stimulus. It makes sense for the subject to use a label that had been correct in the past for the same stimulus, while at the same time, it is equally logical to avoid using those labels the search indicates are attached to other stimuli. If a label was assigned by the experimenter to some other stimulus, this same label cannot be appropriate for the current one. This, then, is the reason for contrast effects.[2]

## THE IDENTIFICATION MODEL

Thousands of trials are routinely run in absolute identification tasks, and it is likely that subjects learn something about the stimulus–response mapping over this long series of judgments. This means that a model designed to accommodate data collected early in the experiment may not be adequate to describe data collected later. In the absence of a dynamic model of learning over the course of the experiment (see Lacouture & Marley, 1995), it will suffice to develop a simulation model whose parameters are designed to accommodate two extreme situations: performance on early and late trials.

It can be hypothesized that the subject assimilates the previous feedback in the manner already described, but further, that the subject considers the stimulus–feedback pairs on a number of prior trials. For each such pair, the subject decides whether the previous stimulus is the same or different from the present one. If the answer is "same" for any of the pairs, then the associated feedback is given as a response on the current trial. If the answer is "different" for every pair examined from the past, then their attached feedback values are dropped from the list of candidates for the current response. The subject then makes a selection from among the remaining options, by weighing their respective probabilities.

### Early Learning Trials

A simulation was conducted in which assimilation occurs on each trial, but then, with fixed probability (0.7 for this example), the subject goes on to consider earlier trials in the series. The standard deviation of the judgment distributions was 1, the $\tau$ value indicating the amount of assimilation was 1, and the Omit factor ($\Phi$) was a lag of 6.

The simulation results are presented in Figure 14.10. Assimilation is evident in respect to the trial immediately preceding, but contrast is the rule for trials further back in the series. The amount of contrast is fairly constant up to six trials

---

[2]I arrived at this conclusion after analyzing some unpublished identification data kindly furnished to me by Yves Lacouture.

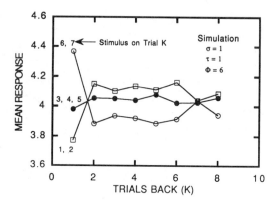

FIG. 14.10. Mean guess of an integer, contingent on the appearance of a small, medium, or large integer "stimulus" on trial K. From theoretical predictions of the Identification Model.

into the past, whereas the empirical data in Figure 14.8a imply a degradation of contrast as events fade further into memory. Such graceful degradation of the memory representation could easily be included in the theoretical model, but it is of secondary importance.

## Late Learning Trials

Conditions for the later trials are optimum in the sense that subjects reach their peak identification performance. These conditions are treated here as representing those existing at channel capacity.

The foregoing simulations of memory, assimilation, and contrast suggest two conjectures: First a channel capacity exists because the variance of the underlying judgment distributions increases as a function of the stimulus set size. Also, the size of the channel capacity depends on the ability of subjects to recall stimulus–feedback pairs from the past.

Small channel capacities arise when the subject cannot recall events from many preceding trials. Large channel capacities arise when the subject can recall and gainfully use events further back in memory. This implies that relatively many trials are recalled for stimulus attributes yielding high channel capacities, such as visual hue (Miller, 1956), whereas fewer previous trials are recalled for attributes yielding low channel capacities, such as coffee odor (Engen & Pfaffman, 1960).

These two conjectures imply that the information transmitted depends first on the stimulus set size, which in turn determines the standard deviation of the judgment distributions, and second on the number of trials back the subject can recall.

If the subject recalls events 9 trials back in the series (an optimistic value), Figure 14.11 shows the result of varying both the set size (2 to 15 in increments of 2) and the standard deviation (.5 to 2 in increments of 0.05). In this three-

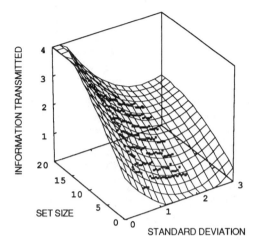

FIG. 14.11. (a) Information transmitted as a function of set size (2 to 15 in increments of 2) and (b) standard deviation (0.5 to 2 in increments of .05) of the judgment distributions. Theoretical predictions from the Identification Model. A quadratic surface emphasizes the overall shape.

dimensional plot, the dependent measure is the information transmitted, which is a joint function of set size and standard deviation. A quadratic surface is fit to the data in order to reveal the overall shape (Wilkinson, Hill, & Vang, 1992). As the set size increases, the information transmitted increases, but this is offset to some extent by a concomitant increase in the standard deviation. The plots look much the same for other numbers of trials back.

One can consult (with computer assistance) these data and extract a constant channel capacity across different set sizes. To do this, different standard deviations of the judgment distributions are selected for different set sizes such that the channel capacity is constant. Three examples are given in Figure 14.12a (for recall of 1, 5, and 9 trials back). The data for 1 trial back is selected from the

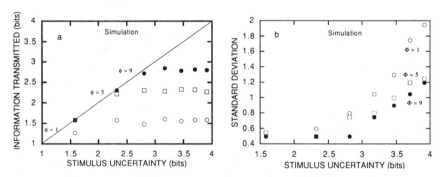

FIG. 14.12. (a) Information transmitted as a function of stimulus uncertainty. The parameter is the number of trials back recalled by a hypothetical subject. (b) Standard deviation as a function of stimulus uncertainty. Theoretical predictions from the Identification Model.

appropriate three-dimensional diagram such that the information transmission is as near as possible to 1.58 bits (3 stimuli), the data for 5 trials back are for information transmission as near as possible to 2.32 bits (5 stimuli), and the top set of data are as near as possible to 2.81 bits (7 stimuli). Each of the three data sets corresponds rather well to the empirical findings on channel capacity.

It is also of interest to consider the standard deviation associated with each of the points in Figure 14.12a, and then to inquire as to the trend of these values in respect to stimulus uncertainty. The results in Figure 14.12b indicate that once a channel capacity is attained, each of the curves for different numbers of trials (recalled) increases with set size.

## FURTHER SEQUENTIAL EFFECTS

A substantial number of experiments have been conducted to sort out the sensory and judgment processes responsible for errors in absolute identification tasks. Luce and Nosofsky (1984) summarized this work. In several ways, each of these studies is unique, and, therefore, none can be immediately woven into the discussion without more elaboration. Three of these experiments are used as examples of the general approach to take within the framework of the Judgment Option and Identification Models.

### Stimulus Range and Stimulus Repetition

Nosofsky (1983a) conducted an experiment (Exp. 2) in which he ran subjects in two range conditions with four sound intensities in each. In the narrow-range condition, the intensities were 65, 67, 69, and 71 dB; in the wide-range condition, the intensities were 53, 67, 69, and 83 dB. The two center signals were the same in both ranges (67 dB and 69 dB), which is important in comparing performance between the two conditions.

An unusual twist to this study concerns the repetition of signals on the same trial. Rather than receive a single presentation, the subject listened to the same sound four times in a row with a 2-sec interstimulus interval. On a single trial, after each stimulus presentation the subject attempted to identify the stimulus with an integer response. Therefore, within each trial the subject gave four estimates of the same intensity. The subject realized it was always the same stimulus on each of these within-trial presentations, and after the fourth response, was told the correct integer label.

The analysis examines the discrimination performance on the two middle stimuli (67 dB and 69 dB) as a function of judgment order (1 through 4) and range (narrow and wide). The degree to which subjects discriminate between the two stimuli is evaluated in terms of a $d'$ measure in the spirit of the Theory of Signal Detectability (Green & Swets, 1966/1974; Macmillan & Creelman,

1991). The author estimates $d'$ for the pair of middle signals (ordinal position 2 and 3). The analysis itself is somewhat unorthodox (see Nosofsky, 1983b). With the presentation of stimulus 2, a response of 1 or 2 is called a "correct rejection," whereas a response of 3 or 4 is called a "false alarm." If stimulus 3 is presented and the response is either 3 or 4, it is registered as a "hit," whereas a response of 1 or 2 is a "miss." By converting these response frequencies into probabilities, a $d'$ measure is determined in the usual way. This measure depends on the relative sizes of the "hit" and "false alarm" probabilities (Baird & Noma, 1978, chap. 8). The starting point for this type of analysis is summarized by the diagram in Figure 14.13. The value of $d'$ is a positive function of the separation between the "hits" and "false alarm" probabilities—high hit rates and low false alarm rates are reflected in large $d'$ values.

With regard to stimulus repetition, Nosofsky found that $d'$ increases as a function of judgment order. That is, within a single trial, subjects exhibit better discrimination on their fourth estimate than they do on their first. With regard to the range variable, $d'$ is larger for the narrow-range condition than for the wide-range condition.

Nosofsky interpreted the repetition effect as due to an integration of sensory information occurring when the same stimulus is presented many times in a row. According to the argument, on each stimulus presentation the subject is sampling from a relevant array of sensory events and the sum of four such samples will yield a better estimate of the event being assessed than will a single sample. [The

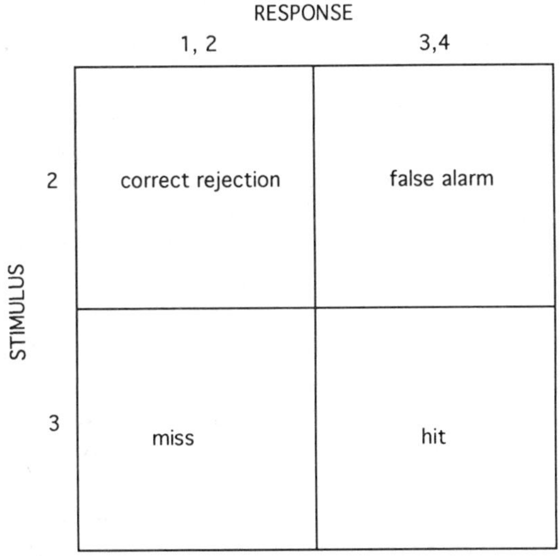

FIG. 14.13. Matrix representing stimulus–response conditions (Nosofsky, 1983a) for applying the Theory of Signal Detectability.

multiple observation task, as well as the analysis in terms of the Theory of Signal Detectability, were introduced to the field originally by Swets, Shipley, McKey, and Green (1959) and by Swets and Birdsall (1967).]

The Judgment Option Model makes a similar prediction from the samples the subject takes from the Gaussian distribution of judgments, instead of from a distribution of sensory events (or liklihood ratios). If the subject is combining the judgment options of each stimulus repetition together with those that occurred previously (on the same trial), and computing some kind of central tendency, then this measure will be closer to the mean (correct value) than any of the individual samples. Except in the case of stimuli near the ends, where the mean of the judgment distribution is in one-to-one correspondence with the correct response label, discrimination will improve with the number of judgment samples included in the average. Therefore, $d'$ will increase with the number of repetitions. Unlike this analysis, however, the present model predicts a tapering off in improvement as the number of observations increases beyond four or five. This performance plateau would occur because the number of judgment/response options are discrete and limited for each stimulus.

Nosofsky explained the range effects in terms of two theoretical models, the full description of which would take us too far afield. The general notion is that performance on the wide range is poorer than on the narrow range for either of two reasons: (a) The variability of boundaries separating response categories increases with stimulus range (Durlach & Braida, 1969; Gravetter & Lockhead, 1973). (b) A limited attention band has more territory to cover with a wide range than it does with a narrow one, and is therefore less likely to be in the right place at the right time (Luce, Green, & Weber, 1976).

The Judgment Option Model provides an interpretation of the range effect, if it is granted that end stimuli in the wide range are more identifiable than those in the narrow range. This should be true because there are so few stimuli and the extreme tones are sharply separated in similarity (intensity) from the two middle tones. This, however, seems like an inauspicious start to an explanation, inasmuch as the wide-range condition leads to poorer performance in terms of discrimination. It should be recalled, nonetheless, that this inferior performance is only seen for the two middle stimuli. Nosofsky presented no data concerning performance on the extremes.

In what follows it helps to refer to Fig. 14.13. The inferior performance in the wide-range condition implies that the false alarm rate is higher than in the narrow-range condition, or that the hit rate is lower, or both. That is, $FA_w > FA_n$ and/or $HIT_w < HIT_n$. Assume that the viable response options are equally likely and that errors are only made plus and minus one step from the correct value. The range conditions then modify these probabilities. Consider first the two hit rates for stimulus 3. For the wide range, the subject is aware that the answer is not likely to be either 1 or 4 (the labels for the ends are obvious), so the viable options are responses 2 and 3. For the narrow range, the subject realizes the answer cannot be 1 (distant possibility), but does not rule out the remaining three options (2, 3, 4). Therefore, the probability of a "hit" in the wide range condition is $1/2$ and the probability of a "hit" in the narrow range condition is $2/3$. Thus, $HIT_w < HIT_n$.

Consider next the two false alarm rates calculated for stimulus 2. For the wide range, responses 1 and 4 are excluded, leaving options 2 and 3. For the narrow range, the options do not include 4, but do include 1, 2, and 3. Again, if we make the simplifying assumption that all options are equally likely, the probability of a false alarm for the wide range is $1/2$ and for the narrow range, $1/3$. Thus, $FA_w > FA_n$.

This explains why the wide-range condition leads to worse performance than the narrow-range condition when based on this special definition of $d'$. The same conclusion can be reached if a Gaussian distribution of options is assumed (centered on the correct value), instead of the equal-probability assumption, though naturally the quantitative details will differ.

The conclusion concerning the relative sensitivity of the subject in the two range conditions is quite different in the previous example if the transmitted information is calculated for the entire stimulus set. The response uncertainty resulting from Equation 14.2 is 2 bits for both the narrow and wide ranges. The conditional response uncertainty found by Equation 14.3 is 0.25 bits for the wide range and 0.82 bits for the narrow range. Using Equation 14.1 to find the information transmitted, the value for the wide range is $2 - 0.25 = 1.75$ bits and that for the narrow range is $2 - 0.82 = 1.18$ bits. Depending on perspective, the implications of the range results are very different. This analysis states that subjects are more sensitive to stimulus differences in the wide range than in the narrow range, as opposed to Nosofsky's conclusions from an analysis of responses for the two center stimuli.

## Sequential Clustering

Another variation on the absolute identification task is to introduce sequential dependencies such that judgments are rendered after different trial histories with regard to the difference in intensity between the current stimulus and earlier ones. Luce et al. (1982) referred to two such methods as the "small-step" and "large-step" procedures. The small-step procedure involves a dependency of the following kind. In Absolute Identification with N stimuli (11 sounds in this experiment), labeled by the integers 1 to N, if i designates the signal on trial $T-1$, then the signal on trial T must fall within the cluster containing $i - 1$, i, or $i + 1$ with equal probability (special accommodation is made for the end stimuli). In the large-step procedure the trio of possibilities are still adjacent intensities, but the preceding stimulus is relatively distant from the cluster. The investigators also ran a standard identification condition in which they presented stimuli in a random order.

The small-step procedure produces superior performance in the task, as assessed by a $d'$ measure or by a probability correct measure, when compared with results of either the large-step or random conditions. The relative performance levels of the latter two conditions depend on the data analysis ($d'$ or probability correct), but both are clearly inferior to that of the small-step condition.

In order to understand these findings within the framework of the simulation models in this chapter, it is necessary to examine the trial history for both the small-step and large-step procedures. the Identification Model claims that subjects search memory and utilize information on previous stimulus–response pairs to decide on the viable options for expressing an estimate of the current stimulus. In the small-step procedure, if subjects search memory, they will retrieve events bearing on the decision required on the current trial. The stimuli in the recent past will all be in the neighborhood of the current stimulus, and hence, response options are reduced. Suppose the current stimulus is $S_T = 4$. If the subjects realize that $S_{T-2} = 5$ and $S_{T-1} = 3$, and that neither of these stimuli is the same as $S_T$, then they can be certain that the answer is neither 5 nor 3. So it must be 4. This pruning of relevant response options is not possible when the previous stimulus is always far from the one being estimated on the current trial. Knowing that $S_{T-2} = 6$ and that $S_{T-1} = 1$ does not help in deciding on the response options for $S_T = 10$, even if the experimenter limits the available choices to 9, 10, and 11. The labels of neither of the previous stimuli fall among the set of reasonable options for the current stimulus.

The "random" condition is comprised of a mix of histories, some of which are helpful and others not in arriving at a decision concerning the response assignment for the current stimulus. As such, this condition would probably not result in as good performance as the small-step procedure, but better than the large-step procedure. On the other hand, in the "random" condition, the response alternatives on each trial are not limited to three. This would further detract from performance. In fact, the random procedure yields the worst performance in terms of the $d'$ analysis, but not in terms of the probability correct analysis.

This interpretation does not say the subject merely tries to keep rank order over successive trials, and this strategy is more successful in the small-step procedure than it is in the large-step procedure. What is proposed instead is that subjects utilize the immediate trial history as a means to limit the response options. Indeed, an incidental consequence of this strategy is that rank order will be preserved more often when the number of response options is small. An additional experiment by Nosofsky (1983b) rules out the possibility that a simple discrimination strategy (keeping rank order) leads to the differences in performance for the small- and large-step procedures.

## Lag Effects

In an attempt to test the notion that subjects compare the current stimulus and the most recent stimulus that is close to it in intensity, Luce et al. (1982) conducted an experiment in which the stimulus on trial T was "near" the stimulus on trial T − k and "far" from those on intervening trials, T − 1, . . . , T −k + 1. The experiment was run with lags of k = 1 to 4. The results are that $d'$ is markedly higher when the "near" comparison is presented on the immediately preceding trial, but that the subject seems not to utilize the information from the same event occurring farther back in the series. It is as though the information that might have been gained from the feedback of a "near" stimulus is totally ignored if it occurred in the marginally distant past. This is an unexpected outcome in terms of the Identification Model because it claims that subjects process information several trials back in the series.

Although these results are damaging to the model, one can imagine possible reasons for such an outcome. First, the only information the subject could possibly gain from searching further back in memory is this single event. All other trials in the immediate past contain stimuli that are far away (in intensity) from the current one. Perhaps the payoff is simply too small to justify the effort to retrieve information beyond that received by searching one trial back. In other words, the unusual conditions of this experiment may change the subject's judgment strategy. The resolution of this matter is vital for the Identification Model, as well as for any other model contending that subjects pay heed to events that transpire more than one trial back in the series.

# 15 Unified Judgment Principles?

There are no established "laws" instantiating judgment principles that repeatedly surface in the course of laboratory study. Indeed, there has been very little theoretical work of any kind to identify invariances that transcend psychophysical methods and stimulus attributes. Because the necessary foundation is unsteady, the ensuing proposals of links across methods and attributes must be treated as prospective.

In order to provide structure for the discussion, two opposing views are outlined for each of four potential "principles." Two sides of each of the following issues are presented as bipolar extremes in order to encompass the entire range of possible opinions:

*Response Options:* (Side 1) Response options for each stimulus depend on the attribute and increase as a function of the number of intensities. (Side 2) Response options are independent of both stimulus attribute and the number of intensities.

*Attribute Effects:* (Side 1) The success in recalling previous stimulus–response events over a series of trials depends on the attribute. The subject recalls intensities of attributes yielding higher exponents and channel capacities better than those attributes yielding lower indices. This implies that the exponent of Stevens's Law is positively related to the channel capacity. (Side 2) The subject's memory processes are not responsible for attribute effects. They arise because the sensory transducers are not the same for all stimulus attributes.

*Assimilation Effects:* (Side 1) Response assimilation is a function of the overlap of sensory fiber types. The more fibers two stimuli share, the greater their perceived similarity. (Side 2) Response assimilation is a function of the relative

264

ranks of two stimuli in the set. These ranks have nothing to do with overlapping fiber types.

*Contrast Effects:* (Side 1) Response contrast is a stand-alone judgment process. It is a byproduct of the subject's attempt to stabilize the response scale by correcting for response drift due to assimilation. (Side 2) Response contrast occurs because the subject tries to maintain a rank order among responses that matches the rank order among stimuli. At the same time, contrast arises from the subject's reluctance to give response values that were recently assigned to other stimuli.

## RESPONSE OPTIONS

### Side 1

In Absolute Identification the number of response options increases with the size of the stimulus set. In addition, at channel capacity the conditional response uncertainty increases with the number of stimuli to be identified. The question is whether this also occurs when subjects choose their own response values, such as in Magnitude Estimation. To answer in the affirmative is to accept a judgment principle that transcends method; namely, subjects increase the abundance of their response options in accord with the richness of the stimulus set. Estimates of a single stimulus depend not only on intensity, but also on the other stimuli in the series. Enriching the context in which a stimulus is embedded leads to a parallel enrichment of the response set.

### Side 2

R. Teghtsoonian (1971) and Poulton (1989) suggested that subjects employ a constant response range in Magnitude Estimation that is independent of stimulus range. If true, the exponent of Stevens's Law should vary inversely with the logarithm of the stimulus range (chaps. 6 & 11).

The empirical results on number preferences encourage a bolder stance on this issue, while still leaving open the possibility that response range is a constant. Subjects use a limited set of integers in Magnitude Estimation, and these preferences tend to be integers and multiples of 5, 10, and 100 (chap. 8). Another question is how many different values are used and how often? In methods such as Category Estimation and Absolute Identification, the number of response options is small and predefined by the experimenter. The interesting variation occurs when the experimenter leaves the selection of response options up to the subject, such as in Magnitude Estimation.

A typical instruction with this method is to "assign numbers to stimuli so as to reflect perceived magnitude. You are free to use any number you wish, including fractions." Actual results indicate that subjects do not exercise their freedom to use many response values. Instead, they restrict themselves to a relatively small set of integers.

## Assessing the Evidence

At the second International Meeting of the Society of Psychophysics (Baird, 1986) data were presented from the study by Green et al. (1977) involving many magnitude estimates of the loudness of each of 21 sounds (discussed in chaps. 10 and 13). One of their unusual results is that subjects generated a small set of "preferred" integers—one individual gave only 14 different response values over the course of 2400 trials!

Table 15.1 summarizes the number behavior engaged in by subjects in this experiment and by those tested in a comparable study by Baird et al. (1996). The

TABLE 15.1

Number of Response Options, Response Uncertainty, and Exponents of Stevens's Law for Magnitude Estimates of Loudness (top) and Pyridine Odor (bottom)

| | *Loudness (Green et al., 1977)* | | | | | |
|---|---|---|---|---|---|---|
| | *Percentage* | | | | | |
| | 25 | 50 | 75 | 100 | *U (R)** | *Exponent*** |
| LT | 3 | 10 | 19 | 56 | 5.10 | 0.29 |
| JU | 6 | 15 | 34 | 115 | 6.00 | 0.29 |
| DR | 2 | 6 | 13 | 69 | 4.79 | 0.20 |
| WC | 1 | 2 | 3 | 14 | 2.79 | 0.17 |
| FS | 1 | 4 | 7 | 46 | 4.10 | 0.12 |
| MEAN | 2.6 | 7.4 | 15.2 | 60 | 4.56 | 0.21 |
| | *Odor (Baird et al., 1996)* | | | | | |
| | *Percentage* | | | | | |
| | 25 | 50 | 75 | 100 | *U (R)** | *Exponent*** |
| $S_1$ | 4 | 11 | 21 | 59 | 5.24 | 0.66 |
| $S_2$ | 3 | 7 | 13 | 41 | 4.64 | 0.88 |
| $S_3$ | 2 | 5 | 11 | 40 | 4.34 | 0.93 |
| $S_4$ | 1 | 3 | 7 | 28 | 3.83 | 1.06 |
| MEAN | 2.5 | 6.5 | 13 | 42 | 4.51 | 0.88 |

*response uncertainty in bits
**Stevens's Power Law

latter study collected 105 magnitude estimates of the perceived intensity of each of eight (including a blank) olfactory stimuli (pyridine). Chapter 10 presents the Stevens and Ekman functions for two of the four participants in this experiment.

The response preferences were analyzed as follows: Taking the database for each subject, it was parsed into categories indicating the frequency each number was used across all trials. Next, the numbers were sorted according to relative frequency and cutoffs were imposed to classify 25%, 50%, 75%, and 100% of the total. The values in the leftmost columns of Table 15.1 show the number of response values employed by each subject below each cutoff. For example, the value "3" appearing in row 1, column 1 indicates that subject LT gave three different numbers on approximately 25% of the trials ("approximate" because the cutoffs are not exactly coincident with an empirical frequency).

It becomes clear from the table that each subject used a small number of values in estimating a large number of stimuli. This is especially apparent in the Green et al. study, which involved 21 sounds. Twenty five percent of the time these subjects gave (on average) 2.5 different integers, and the mean only reaches 13 at the 75% cutoff. The same pattern is present in the bottom half of the table for estimates of pyridine odor. The means for each of the cutoffs for an 8-stimulus set are almost identical to those obtained for a 21-stimulus set (above). Subjects in both studies apparently chose their responses from a restricted pool of candidates.

These findings may occur because in everyday life the processing demands placed on people are impossible to meet. Human beings are surrounded by a welter of sensory information, most of which they cannot process thoroughly. In an effort to compress this information down into manageable "chunks," individuals categorize the perceptual world by relying on a small number of semantic quantifiers. This categorization may carry over into the psychophysics laboratory, thus leading to the outcomes summarized in Table 15.1.

An alternative measure of response variability is the entropy or uncertainty (in bits) of the entire response set. Chapter 14 introduced the equation for calculating this quantity:

$$U(R) = -\sum_{j=1}^{M} p(r_j) \, log_2 \, p(r_j) \, . \qquad (15.1)$$

The relative frequency (equated with a probability) of each numerical response was determined and then substituted into Equation 15.1 to compute the response uncertainty. These results are also listed in the table. The individual means range from a maximum of 6 bits ($2^6 = 64$) for subject JU to a minimum of 2.79 bits ($2^{2.79} = 6.9$) for subject WC. The average response uncertainty of 4.56 bits across subjects estimating loudness is remarkably close to the average of 4.51 bits for subjects estimating odors. This occurs even though there were almost three times as many sound stimuli as there were odor stimuli. In both experiments, subjects used a small number of response types regardless of the number of stimulus intensities, and regardless of the stimulus attribute (though only two were tested).

The rightmost column in Table 15.1 presents the individual exponents of Stevens's Law. In the loudness study, there is a weak positive relation between the size of the exponent and the amount of response uncertainty, but if anything, the direction of this relation is reversed for olfaction. The evidence does not give much credence to the view that response uncertainty is related to the exponent.

It is not known whether the same response pattern occurs in the continuous tasks of Magnitude Production and Cross Modality Matching. The possibility was once raised that a bias exists in using both discrete and continuous response scales (Baird, 1975a, 1975b). But apparently nobody has ever done an experiment to ascertain the viability of this hypothesis. It would involve asking subjects to generate a random set of response values along a continuous scale, then determining whether the responses over a group of subjects bunched together at common points along the continuum.

The chief message from Table 15.1 is that response options actually used by subjects in Magnitude Estimation are extremely limited in comparison with what might be expected from the instructions. This outcome is at odds with the Sensory Aggregate Model and with all models of psychophysics that assume subjects are unbiased in selecting values from a continuous response scale. The Judgment Option Model explains data such as those in Table 15.1 more effectively.

## ATTRIBUTE EFFECTS

### Side 1

Sequential effects in global scaling suggest that, before giving an estimate, subjects recall and take into account previous stimulus–response events. In addition, memory is obviously important in Absolute Identification, where the source of both assimilation and contrast are related to the subject's ability to recall events that took place several trials back.

Despite these advances, it is not fully understood exactly how memory influences the parameter values of empirical functions for different attributes. The implication is that both the exponent of Stevens's Law and the channel capacity depend on the subject's ability to recall psychophysical events over an experimental session. The relative effectiveness of this ability depends on the stimulus attribute. Instead of assigning the leading role to sensory processes, this argument claims that memory is the crucial factor. Perceptual sensitivity varies with stimulus attribute because memory storage and/or retrieval capabilities vary with the attribute.

The translation of this claim into a research paradigm might proceed by asking how far back in the stimulus series a subject is able to recover relevant information. The expectation is that higher sensitivity (exponent and channel capacity) occurs when the subject recalls fairly distant events in the series, and conversely, low sensitivity occurs when the subject recalls only the most recent events.

## Side 2

A sensory orientation to psychophysics implies that memory plays a minor role in determining the parameters of psychophysical laws. Different parameters for different attributes reflect the sensory transduction properties of the underlying sensorineural structures. These are unaffected by the subject's memory of prior events. The only thing that matters is the stimulus quality and intensity currently being judged. Even if one admits that contextual variables involving memory influence experimental outcomes, this does not imply that these variables are responsible for the parameter values for different attributes. For instance, increasing the stimulus range reduces the exponent of Stevens's Law, but because this occurs to the same extent for all attributes, the relative sensitivity among attributes remains the same.

## Assessing the Evidence

In reviewing the ability of humans to transmit stimulus information, Miller (1956) proposed that only seven, plus or minus two, unidimensional intensities could be absolutely identified (chap. 14). By characterizing the findings in this manner, Miller may have inadvertently overlooked reliable differences in channel capacities.

Hake and Garner (1951) reported a channel capacity of 3.25 bits for the visual position of a point on a line, and Engen and Pfaffmann (1959) reported a channel capacity of 1.5 bits for odor. In the world of small integers, these two are similar, until one realizes they are logarithmic measures. When we convert them to equally likely stimulus alternatives, the interval between the two is more outstanding. Because $2^{3.25} = 9.5$ and $2^{1.5} = 2.8$, there is more than a threefold span between the number of points on a line and the number of odor intensities that can be identified without error. Data such as these originally led to the conjecture that the channel capacity is related to the size of the exponents in Stevens's Law (Baird, 1970b), but this conjecture has not been verified by direct experimental test.

Figure 15.1 presents the channel capacities and exponents for a variety of attributes, taken from the tabled values in Baird and Noma (1978, chaps. 5 & 12), but using an exponent of 1 for electric shock, instead of the extraordinary value of 3.5 noted by S. S. Stevens (1975). The graph indicates that exponents and channel capacities are weakly associated (r = 0.41).

It is possible that the general trend in Figure 15.1 depends on the relative rates

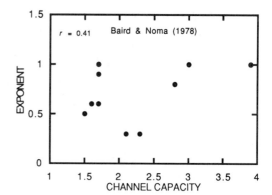

FIG. 15.1. Stevens exponent as a function of channel capacity. Each point represents a single attribute. After Baird and Noma (1978).

of decline in memory of the neural representations of stimuli for different attributes or on the ability to retrieve these representations. If the rate of deterioration (or memory retrieval) of the neural representation over time is a function of the attribute, then we might see evidence of this decay in the results of both Magnitude Estimation and Absolute Identification. Therefore, exponents and channel capacties should be related. This coupling is by no means assured, however. Memory factors probably have a more pivotal role in Absolute Identification than they do in Magnitude Estimation, and the relative rates of decay for different attributes may change their respective positions as the number of prior trials accumulates. If this is true, the relative sizes of the exponents of Stevens's Law will not be the same as the relative sizes of the corresponding channel capacities.

A direct evaluation of this thesis might be possible through a memory paradigm that tested for the forgetting of a single stimulus, while simultaneously controlling or eliminating interference from other intensities. Such a paradigm enjoyed some popularity toward the end of the last century (Baldwin & Shaw, 1895; Leuba, 1892; Warren & Shaw, 1895).

Another experimental tack is to adopt some of the familiar methods of memory research, for instance, a technique for disrupting short-term memory storage (L. R. Peterson & M. J. Peterson, 1959) or one that increases stimulus interference among trials (Keppel & Underwood, 1962). For example, suppose a light is flashed together with a three-digit number. The subject counts backward by threes until a cue indicates that the brightness of the light should be estimated. The experimenter varies the time between the stimulus and the cue. Would this procedure reduce both the channel capacity and the exponent of the Power Law? And if it hampered performance, would the relative degradation be the same across attributes?

The psychophysical method, through its instructions, may also influence the number of trials into the past examined by the subject before rendering an estimate. For instance, in so-called Absolute Magnitude Estimation, the subject attaches numbers to the stimuli without considering the broader stimulus context (Zwislocki & Goodman, 1980). If subjects obey these instructions, there will be no sequence effects, no assimilation or contrast. A second example is when a standard is designated in the method of Magnitude Estimation. Here a subject gives all estimates relative to the standard, in which case memory for the standard is the relevant past event. If subjects follow this instruction, assimilation and contrast will be a function of the distance of the comparison from the standard (DeCarlo & Cross, 1990). And if the subject produces response ratios for successive stimuli that match the corresponding stimulus ratios, there will be large sequence effects one trial back (Green et al., 1977). Less explicit instructions may lead the subject to consider more trials before coming to a decision (Ward, 1987), and so forth. In sum, the extent to which memory is a factor in psychophysics is closely tied to the subject's understanding of the task requirements.

It is not enough, however, to say that storage and retreival processes are important in psychophysics. One must go on to show exactly how they affect the performance in a specific task. In addressing this problem, it is also critical to do the proper data analysis to reveal any subtle differences. The common reliance on correlation measures (triangle pattern) and the impulse diagram (chaps. 13 & 14) may be inappropriate for determining the role of memory in psychophysics. At this stage of theory development it is safe to say that subjects query the past in judging the present, but it is an inexact science when it comes to predicting exactly how this information from the past is integrated with stimulus information available on the current trial.

## ASSIMILATION EFFECTS

### Side 1

The Judgment Option Model contends that assimilation of responses over successive trials is a function of the degree of sensory similarity between successive stimuli. Most of the discussion in the last four chapters rests on this contention.

### Supporting Evidence

The explanation of range effects in Magnitude Estimation presumes that increasing stimulus range leads to a decrease in the sensory similarity among stimuli (chap. 11). This in turn implies that assimilation over successive trials is weaker with wide stimulus ranges than it is with narrow ones. Because a decrease in assimilation raises the exponent of the power function, the exponent does not simply decline inversely with stimulus range. The reduction in assimilation tends to offset the influence of an increased range. This argument is the only one to date that explains the available data on stimulus range. Its success rests on the presumption that the cause of assimilation is sensory similarity.

The triangle pattern provides auxiliary evidence. Stimulus separation affects the amount of assimilation over successive trials inasmuch as the correlation between successive responses is high when two consecutive stimuli are of similar intensity and falls to zero as stimulus separation widens. This argument is stronger if assimilation is a positively increasing function of stimulus (sensory) similarity.

Other consistent evidence is seen in the type of errors made in judgment tasks. In his undergraduate thesis, Cardello (1970) conducted an absolute identification experiment of line lengths in which different couplings were imposed between the stimulus lines and the "correct" responses. In one condition, the integers 1 to 10 were mapped onto the set of lines in order of magnitude, while in another condition, the 10 integers were assigned randomly. In the latter situation the stimulus–response mapping was "incompatible."

In examining Cardello's confusion matrix, it is obvious that errors occur as a function of stimulus, and not response, similarity. For example, suppose in the random condition the response "6" is the correct value for stimulus "3," the response "1" is correct for stimulus "4," and the response "7" is correct for stimulus "10." In the early phases of the experiment the subject makes frequent mistakes by assigning the response "1" to stimulus "3." This error most likely happens because stimulus "4" is similar to stimulus "3." On the other hand, response "7" is almost never used for stimulus "3," even though this integer is similar to the correct value of "6." This is so because stimulus "10" is far from stimulus "3."

## Side 2

In its present form, the nexus of the Judgment Option Model is a mix of sensory and judgment factors. The sensory part concerns the definition of stimulus similarity, the judgment part is everything else. A more internally consistent model would be one in which the sensory indicator of similarity was replaced by a context-dependent one.

A straightforward way to do this is to define the similarity between two stimuli as their rank positions in the stimulus series. The closer the ranks of two stimuli, the greater their similarity, and therefore, the greater the response assimilation when they are presented on successive trials. The stimulus context of the experiment, indicated by the number of different stimuli, determines similarity rather than some process intrinsic to sensory representations.

## Supporting Evidence

Some data raise problems for the hypothesis that sensory information is the force behind assimilation. Ward (1990a) reported several studies in which two stimulus attributes are intermixed in a random sequence and subjects use the method of Magnitude Estimation with a common response scale. These so-called mixed modality experiments still produce assimilation that appears to be the same as that found when only a single attribute is tested. For example, assimilation occurs when a sound follows a light, and the amount of assimilation depends on stimulus separation (in terms of relative intensity)—that is, the triangle shape results. If assimilation comes from the overlap of sensory fiber types, then why does it occur when successive stimuli are qualitatively different?

A second fact that causes difficulties for the Judgment Option Model comes from the experiments by Marks (1992) on the slippery context effect (chap. 11). Here, the responses for stimulus set A, say the one containing the softer sounds at 500 Hz, assimilate upward toward the responses for stimulus set B at 2500 Hz, containing the louder tones. It would seem that a set of soft 500-Hz tones and a set of loud 2500-Hz tones would not share many fiber types. This is problematic because the Judgment Option Model claims it is the degree of overlap between fiber types that determines the amount of response assimilation.

A change in the definition of stimulus similarity may help sort out some of these perplexing results. Perhaps the crucial factor in the mixed-modality experiments is the rank position of a stimulus within the context of all stimuli possessing the same quality. In other words, the softest tone is considered similar to the dimmest light and dissimilar to the brightest light, the loudest tone is similar to the brightest light, and so forth.

Looking at the experiment in this way suggests two post-hoc predictions: First, the triangle pattern should appear in experiments such as Ward's, even if successive stimuli are qualitatively different. This is because assimilation depends on the separation of stimulus ranks, regardless of whether or not the stimuli are the same quality. Second, in the experiments producing the slippery context effect, the weakest member of the "loud" stimulus set (say 2500-Hz tones) is perceived as similar to the weakest member of the "soft" stimulus set (say 500-Hz tones). Rank order within an attribute class is critical, not absolute intensity. Therefore, the response to a soft 500-Hz tone may assimilate to the response to a loud 2500-Hz tone that preceded it, and vice versa.

The outcome of this judgment strategy was calculated for a hypothetical situation involving two sets of seven stimuli. The "lower" set consists of judgments ranging from 1 to 7 in integer steps (in the absence of a sequential effect), and the "higher" set consists of judgments ranging from 4 to 10. The rank values of the seven members of the lower and higher sets are identical, both ranging from 1 to 7.

If assimilation occurs one trial back, there is an influence of $S_{T-1}$ on the response given to $S_T$. Consider a single stimulus, $S_{i,T}$, associated with judgment $J_i$ and rank $K_i$. Over the experimental trials, this stimulus will be preceded equally often by all 14 stimuli in the series, including itself. The index j is used to designate the stimulus presented on the previous trial. Therefore, the previous stimulus is associated with judgment $J_{j,T-1}$ and rank $K_{j,T-1}$. Assimilation is now defined in terms of the ratio of the ranks for $\mathbf{S}_i$ and $\mathbf{S}_j$, where

$$\text{Case 1: } \omega = \frac{K_{j,T-1}}{K_{i,T}}, \; K_{j,T-1} \leq K_{i,T}$$

$$\text{Case 2: } \omega = \frac{K_{i,T}}{K_{j,T-1}}, \; K_{j,T-1} > K_{i,T} \; .$$

Then, the mean response $(M_i)$ for $\mathbf{S}_i$ is

$$M_i = \sum_{j=1}^{14} \omega \, J_j + (1 - \omega) \, J_i \; . \tag{15.2}$$

Equation 15.2 was evaluated for $i = 1$ to 14, and the results appear in Figure 15.2. The means (Equation 15.2) are plotted against the original judgments (devoid of the influence of sequential dependencies). The "low" set of responses is above that of the "high" set, indicating a slippery context effect.

This theoretical approach is promising, but at present writing there is no empirical evidence to uphold the view that stimulus similarity is a function of stimulus rank order. Therefore, until we learn more about the trial-by-trial strategies in global scaling tasks, it may be impossible to decide whether a sensory or a context-bound definition of stimulus similarity yields the deepest revelations about judgment principles.


## CONTRAST EFFECTS

### Side 1

From his extensive studies of assimilation and contrast in scaling tasks, Lockhead (1984) suggested that the response on trial T is a function of three variables.

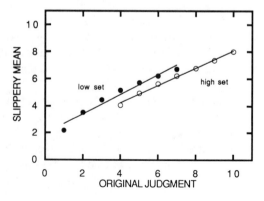

FIG. 15.2. Mean response to stimuli in a low and high set of intensities as a function of their original means (no sequential dependencies) in the "slippery context" paradigm. Data computed according to Equation 15.2.

First and foremost, is the stimulus intensity presented on that trial. The second factor is the memory representation of the stimulus on trial $T-1$; that is, its recalled magnitude in respect to stimulus T. The third factor is the difference between two memory representations: the average value of all stimuli presented to that point in the session and the average value of the stimuli occurring on the preceding trials (perhaps up to 6 trials into the past). The essential aspect of the model is that the subject's recall of the previous stimulus determines assimilation and that memory for all stimuli subtracted from the aggregate memory of the immediately preceding events determines contrast. This last statement has implications for the present discussion.

Lockhead (1984) explained contrast in terms of the subject's resolution of dissonant memories:

> The suggestion is that the subject adjusts the response scale by comparing the memory pool, which is a running average of the previous few memories, with the average of all memories from the experiment and adjusts the response in terms of how these differ. If the memory pool is larger than average then the response will be smaller than when the dynamically changing memory pool is small. This produces contrast, on average, to each prior trial that participates in the pool. (p. 44)

The gist of the argument is that the subject is aware of the range of responses that should be given in the experiment (accumulated over time in the session) and that contrast occurs because local (in time) responses are recognized as perturbations from this long-term average. Contrast between the present response on trial T and recent responses happens because the subject attempts to "correct" the perturbation by adjusting the response magnitude on trial T away from the responses given on the most recent trials.

By converting these hypothetical memory concepts into observables (measured stimuli and responses) a regression model predicts responses in an actual experiment using Absolute Identification (Lockhead, 1984; Staddon, King, & Lockhead, 1980). The fits of the model to their data are good. This, of course, does not prove that the theoretical interpretation of the variables in the regression are the ones proferred by the authors.

## Side 2

The term *contrast* conveys valid information when used in a descriptive sense. It is misleading, however, to think of contrast as a psychological process—that is, as some kind of judgment strategy subjects employ in scaling tasks. Alternative views of the empirical facts are equally plausible and more in keeping with the spirit of the Judgment Option Model.

One situation in need of clarification is that in which a contrast appears between responses on trials T and $T-1$. Such a case was described in chapter 11 when discussing the exponent's dependence on the position of the standard in the stimulus series. Another instance arose in chapter 12 concerning the effects of skewing the stimulus series on the shape of the psychophysical function. A third instance is reported in the Baird et al. (1996) study on the magnitude estimation of pyridine odor.

In all instances, the most plausible model states that subjects strive to maintain rank order among responses that match the rank order among stimuli (Baird, 1995; Baird et al., 1996). It is not at all obvious, however, what it is in the experimental situation that promotes contrast instead of assimilation. When subjects do keep rank order over trials it is also true that the response on trial T contrasts with the response on trial $T-1$.

Another circumstance under which it appears that subjects exhibit contrast is when they drop response options from service, apparently because they recently used them for other stimuli. The explanation offered for this effect in regard to Absolute Identification (chap. 14) is that subjects are reluctant to give a response that in some sense "goes with" some other stimulus. If each stimulus demands its own response label, the subject avoids using the same response for more than one intensity. Therefore, recently emitted responses will only be given again if the subject believes that the same stimulus is being repeated on the present trial. Otherwise, recent responses will have a lower probability than will those appropriate for stimuli that have not occurred for awhile. This omission of response values makes matters look as though the subject is contrasting the present response with those immediately preceding it. The mistake of theoreticians is to conclude that this signals a deliberate attempt by the subject to recalibrate the response scale.

Comparable effects may also occur in Magnitude and Category Estimation when no feedback is given after each trial. Here too, subjects may behave as though each stimulus should have its own assigned response. Though less salient in these methods than in Absolute Identification, the tendency here may be to attach particular responses to particular stimuli.

Judgment strategies leading to contrast effects are more likely when the number of response options is small or equivalent to the number of stimulus values. This would certainly include Category Estimation and any ratio technique that induced subjects to use a constrained set of responses. The strength of this effect may be related to the response uncertainty—the smaller the response uncertainty, the greater the probability of contrast effects. By this line of reasoning, such effects should be less evident in Magnitude Production or Cross Modality Matching, because the subject should have more trouble recalling the exact responses from earlier trials.

## COMPARING JUDGMENT MODELS

Most models of psychophysical judgment are more abstract than the one developed in this book. The theorist places heavy processing demands on the "idealized" subjects and imbues them with a remarkable talent to retain detailed information over long periods of time. This complexity is evident in the Theory of Signal Detectability (Green & Swets, 1966/1974; Macmillan & Creelman, 1991) and its applications (Treisman, 1984), as well as in the models of Lockhead (1984) and Parducci and Wedell (1986), to mention a few.

The distinction between previous models and the philosophy behind the Judgment Option Model can be illustrated by comparing a lottery to a poker game. In playing the lottery, the number of opportunities in the hypothetical "jar" are very large and a random process decides the winning number on each day. As a player, it is of no use whatsoever to know what the winning number was on the previous day, or on the day before that, and so on. But suppose in a variation of the game the player is told that subtle, statistical biases exist in the distribution of numbers in the "jar." The clever player in possession of a physical memory device may register the outcomes of daily drawings over a long period of time (maybe years) and then use this information to devise a model for predicting the next winning number. The more the player knows about the biases, the better the chance of success. Even with this knowledge, however, the probability of winning in the short run remains low, because there are so many possibilities.

The options in card games are more finite. In poker, a relatively small number of cards (perhaps 7) are dealt to each player from a deck of 52. As the game proceeds, the experienced player keeps track of the various cards, whether they have been played, if so, by whom, and so forth. Enlisting the aid of memory for determining the whereabouts of cards already played greatly improves the chances of winning, though admittedly, most amateurs are not very proficient at this.

Most judgment models in the literature are analogous to the lottery metaphor. Theorists presume that subjects know a good deal about the statistical properties of the stimulus set and have access to its neural representation. Further, they are supposed to recall prodigious amounts of information, and put such information to good use in deciding on the most appropriate response. On the other hand, the Number Preference and Judgment Option Models in this book imply that psychophysical experiments are more analogous to playing poker than they are to playing the lottery. The response options are really very limited, and it is likely that the cards (responses) played on earlier trials hold the key to determining which card the subject plays at any point in the game. To take advantage of such information requires the accurate recall of stimulus–response events. This task is finite and doable without a substantial memory storage and a sophisticated retrieval strategy. The danger in theory construction, therefore, is to endow the subject with too much power. The human memory system does have its practical limits, and subjects may wisely choose to stay within them.

## PERCEPTION OF PSYCHOPHYSICAL METHODS

By now it is clear that an unexplored territory in judgment psychophysics concerns the extent to which different methods impose the same processing demands on the subject. One way to investigate this issue is to ask subjects to rate the similarity of different methods (Baird & Szilagyi, 1977; Baird, Weissmann, & McHugo, 1977).

This research program looked at ways in which subjects perceive the similarities among psychophysical tasks. The original rationale was to gain an alternative source of information for theory construction concerning the relations among the judgment processes in different tasks. The experimental outcomes were quite different from those usually seen in the psychophysics laboratory and, therefore, informative.

The target tasks were Absolute Identification, Category Estimation, Magnitude Estimation, Method of Constant Stimuli, and Binary Choice. One group participated briefly in each procedure where the stimulus attribute was a light presented in a dark room. A second group received instructions for each task, but made no actual judgments. During each procedure subjects took notes to help them encode the requirements of the task, each of which was identified by a letter of the alphabet (A through E). After an informal recall test certified that they were able to keep the methods straight, they rated each pair as to its within-member similarity on a scale from 1 to 10. Four criteria for the similarity rating were used in this phase: memory, learning, visual discrimination, and general similarity. The ratings were then entered into a proximity matrix, and Multi-dimensional Scaling placed the tasks along a single dimension. Cluster Analysis determined hierarchical groupings (for descriptions of these analysis techniques, see Baird & Noma, 1978, chaps. 10 & 11).

Figure 15.3 presents the findings for the condition in which subjects actually performed the tasks. There were no important differences among the scale values of the tasks based on the four criteria. In addition, subjects who received instructions, but no opportunity to participate, gave approximately the same judgments as those who did participate. As seen in Figure 15.3, the methods are ordered along a single dimension, with Absolute Identification at one end and Binary choice at the other. Hierarchical clustering indicates that Absolute Identification, Magnitude Estimation, and Category Estimation are perceived to go together, as are the methods of Constant Stimuli and Binary Choice. The tree diagram depicts the pattern of clusters for each of the judgment criteria.

It appears from further work (Baird & Szilagyi, 1977) that subjects base their similarity judgments on how much accuracy they deem necessary in order to comply with instructions. For example, the perceived accuracy demand is greatest for the Absolute Identification task in which subjects uniquely identify each intensity, whereas, the demand is less severe in those cases where two stimuli are to be distinguished (binary choice) or one stimulus is to be judged as greater or less than another (constant stimuli).

An interesting finding here is that the subject perceives Category Estimation as closer to Absolute Identification than to Magnitude Estimation. This suggests that if subjects use a small number of categories and the number of stimuli is

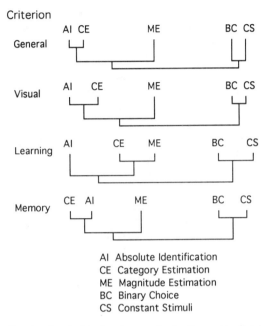

AI  Absolute Identification
CE  Category Estimation
ME  Magnitude Estimation
BC  Binary Choice
CS  Constant Stimuli

FIG. 15.3.  Psychophysical tasks along a single dimension (horizontal) for each of four judgment criteria. Relative positions of the tasks determined by Multidimensional Scaling. Tree structures represent Hierarchical Cluster Analyses. After Baird et al. (1977).

correspondingly small, they will assume there is a necessity for assigning categories so as to reflect rank order. If this is true, then plotting quantitative relations between category and magnitude estimates is inappropriate (Baird & Noma, 1978; Gescheider, 1985; S. S. Stevens & Galanter, 1957). That is, if subjects in Category Estimation are really making absolute identifications, while trying to be consistent in their rankings, and subjects in Magnitude Estimation are producing ratio judgments, there is a mismatch between the measurement level of the two types of data. Therefore, plotting category estimates against magnitude estimates is synonomous to plotting perceived ranks against perceived ratios, a practice of dubious validity. It may be argued of course that subjects in neither task are actually "scaling" the magnitude of the stimulus beyond its ordinal value (cf. Laming, 1984, 1991), in which case the entire enterprise is suspect from the standpoint of measurement theory (Falmagne, 1986).

Another experimental result suggesting that different methods induce different judgment strategies comes from an unpublished study (briefly described in Baird, 1989a). The Method of Constant Stimuli was used with one standard and eight comparisons to obtain a JND for line length. The obtained size of the JND is unimportant in this context (see Ono, 1967, for a more complete investigation

of the JND for line length). A different group of subjects gave magnitude estimates (with the standard called "100") of the same eight comparisons. After
some 200 judgments, this phase of the experiment (Magnitude Estimation or the
Method of Constant Stimuli) ended, and subjects stated how many different line
lengths were seen over the entire session. There was no doubt the subjects
correctly understood the question. The answer was surprising and depended on
the previous experimental condition. Most subjects who had used Magnitude
Estimation stated there were between 7 and 10 lines, whereas most of those who
had used the Method of Constant Stimuli stated there were only 3 to 5 lines. This
occurred despite the fact that each group was exposed to exactly the same
stimulus series. The results are consistent with the view that subjects using the
two methods employ different judgment strategies that influence their recall of
selected aspects of the stimulus conditions.

The next chapter addresses the psychophysics of multidimensional stimuli,
and concludes the presentation of hard data and soft simuluations pertaining to
the Complementarity Theory of Psychophysics. The final chapter recaps the
main arguments of the book and links the theory to the broader topics of sensation and perception.

# 16 Multidimensional Psychophysics

The vast majority of psychophysical studies involve unidimensional stimuli, but experimenters devote some attention to the perception of stimuli that vary along two or more dimensions. This research is referred to as "multidimensional psychophysics." Olfaction and taste are ideal testing grounds for revealing the intricacies of multidimensional psychophysics. Most empirical examples are taken from these two systems and they are interleaved with theoretical explanations derived from the models described in earlier chapters.

## CHANNEL CAPACITY

As the number of dimensions increases along which stimuli vary, the channel capacity increases, and the information transmitted (chap. 14) exceeds that for the unidimensional case. For instance, Pollack and Ficks (1954) employed auditory stimuli that varied on eight dimensions dichotomously (e.g., frequency, intensity, range, duration). They reported a maximum information transmission of seven bits out of a possible eight ($2^8$ alternatives). With overlearned stimuli (numerals, colors), the transmission figures can go as high as 15 bits (Anderson & Fitts, 1958; Garner, 1962). Two generalizations are often drawn from this research with multidimensional stimuli (reviewed by Garner, 1962).

First, the maximum information transmitted by a stimulus that varies along two or more component dimensions is less than the sum of the transmitted information when the components are tested alone. This implies there is an underlying correlation, or at least an interaction of some kind, between the components when they are members of the same set.

Second, a gain in transmitted information from combining stimulus dimensions depends on whether the components maintain their independence in the composite. For some attributes, independence is the rule, for others it is not. This distinction leads to a twofold classification of attributes: *integral* and *separable*. Stimulus integrality occurs when subjects perceive combinations of stimulus dimensions as an altogether new compound (Garner, 1974; Lockhead, 1966). Stimulus separability occurs when subjects still perceive individual components when they are presented in combination.

An example of two dimensions that maintain independence when combined to form a single object is visual length and brightness. These two stimuli combine orthogonally, thus producing lines in which brightness and length do not interact to form an entirely new percept, depending on the particular brightness–length combination. A very bright, short line is perceived as "very bright" and "short" and not as some entirely new quality such as a "gleaming chopstick." On the other hand, in olfactory research, airborne chemicals do not always retain their independence when sniffed in combination (B. Berglund, U. Berglund, & Lindvall, 1971; B. Berglund & Olsson, 1993a, 1993b, 1993c). When certain chemicals are mixed, the perceiver has difficulty separating the relative contributions of the components. Stimulus integrality holds for many, but not all, chemicals (Olsson, 1994).

If stimulus independence is complete, the subject decides on the intensity status of a dimension in the compound without interference from the other dimensions. In this instance, information transmission for the compound approaches the sum of the measures for each dimension alone. On the other hand, if the subject perceives an entirely new attribute when dimensions are combined, then information transmission for the compound is the same as transmission for the components in isolation.

The data usually lie somewhere between these extremes. This suggests that intensity is not the only property subjects evaluate in absolute identification experiments. If it were simply a matter of the nervous system processing intensity information from multiple sources (different attributes), then there should be no difference between the results with integral and separable dimensions. Instead, the channel capacity for multidimensional objects becomes less than the maximum attainable, because the subject processes patterns of stimulation as unique compounds.

An assessment of this previous research leads to the conclusion that multidimensional objects are compared to each other in terms of the complex patterns formed by the joint action of their separable and integral contributions. Now, multidimensional psychophysics is discussed and, in particular, the composition rules that determine how a pattern of stimulation produces a unified percept in the mind of the subject.

## COMPOSITION RULES

In extending either a sensory or a judgment model to complex stimuli, two considerations are foremost: First, it must be decided whether the analysis should focus on the "stimulus" side or on the "perceptual" side; second, composition rules must be derived to predict the joint outcome produced by the simultaneous presentation of two or more attributes.

The first issue is resolved by considering the total outcome arising from presentation of a multidimensional stimulus. It is the perceptual/neural representations of the individual attributes that are combined, and not the stimuli themselves. Although under some conditions, such as mixed tastants, it may be true that component stimuli combine to form entirely new physical compounds, this possibility is not entertained here.

The selection of composition rules is more problematic, and, given our current state of ignorance, it seems prudent to mention more than one viable candidate. Consider this problem along the following lines, restricting the argument to the case of two attributes presented in combination (generalization to multiple dimensions is straightforward). The first factor is the degree to which the two compete for the same neural sites. It is not necessary to specify the place in the nervous system where this competition occurs. It could be peripheral or central; it could arise from a sensory or cognitive source. One candidate for a central source is the superior colliculus, which is a gathering place for sensory interactions (Stein & Meredith, 1993). Although physiologists are making progress in assessing the firing rates of neurons driven by different sensory inputs (light and sound, for example), it may be premature to tailor quantitative models to these particular experiments until more details are forthcoming. For now a more general approach is preferred.

A convenient way to illustrate neural competition is by set theory notation. Imagine a two-dimensional diagram of neural sites, occupied by attributes A and B. For any given pairing of stimulus values from the two attributes, a Venn diagram represents the sites for each (Figure 16.1).

Two aspects of this diagram are relevant: the overlapping (interactive) and nonoverlapping (separable) portions. The intersection of A and B are those sites

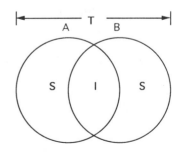

FIG. 16.1. Venn diagram of the composition rule for two attributes (A & B), whose union is T. The separate portion of the composite is indicated by S. The interactive portion is indicated by I.

occupied by both. In this regard, it is important that attribute A is perceptually distinct from attribute B, when each is presented alone. This is necessary because in some of the models described later it is not possible to predict the addition of two responses for the same attribute. In some instances, this can be done if, instead of the raw responses, the logarithm of the responses is the independent variable. All the models described here operationally define percepts as the combination of component raw responses.

## Formalization

Let intersection **I** stand for the "interactive" portion of the compound. The remainder are those sites for which there is no competition between A and B. Define this as **S**, for "separate." The amount of overlap between the neural sites occupied by attributes A and B is the degree of interdimensional similarity (Melara, 1992).

## The Averaging Model

Assume that the relative contributions of regions **S** and **I** depend on their respective proportions in the compound. Hence, a weighted average predicts the influence of both regions acting together, thereby arriving at the final outcome (**T**):

$$T = w_s\, S + w_i\, I \tag{16.1}$$

where $w_s + w_i = 1$. Equation 16.1 is a simple composition rule for predicting the relative contributions of the separable and integral aspects of the perception of a compound.

Next regions **S** and **I** are expressed in terms of hypothetical neural firing rates of the two attributes. To expedite communication and provide a more intuitive understanding, assume that responses in a psychophysical experiment directly reflect firing rates. The symbol $R$ refers to both response magnitude and to neural firing rate.

If there is no competition for neural sites, the outputs of two attributes are additive. If $R_a$ is the firing rate for attribute A in the absence of competition from B, and $R_b$ is the firing rate for attribute B in the absence of competition from A, then the joint firing rate, denoted by **S**, is

$$S = R_a + R_b. \tag{16.2}$$

Within the intersection, where there is competition between A and B, several possibilities are equally plausible, but this chapter elaborates on just one: The relative importance of an attribute in the pair depends on its strength in respect to its competitor. The joint firing rate of A and B together is then defined as a weighted average,

$$I = \frac{R_a}{R_a + R_b} R_a + \frac{R_b}{R_a + R_b} R_b \,, \tag{16.3}$$

which reduces to

$$I = \frac{R_a^2 + R_b^2}{R_a + R_b} . \tag{16.4}$$

Assuming $R_{ab} = T$, and substituting Equations 16.2 and 16.4 into Equation 16.1, the total firing rate is defined as

$$R_{ab} = w_s(R_a + R_b) + w_i \left( \frac{R_a^2 + R_b^2}{R_a + R_b} \right). \tag{16.5}$$

Equation 16.5 is referred to as the Averaging Model. It expresses the total firing rate generated by attributes A and B when they form a compound. The predicted firing rates of each of the mixture's components acting within the compound are given by solving for $R_a$ and $R_b$:

$$R_{a|ab} = w_s R_a + w_i \left( \frac{R_a^2}{R_a + R_b} \right) \tag{16.6a}$$

$$R_{b|ab} = w_s R_b + w_i \left( \frac{R_b^2}{R_a + R_b} \right). \tag{16.6b}$$

Equation 16.6 predicts judgments when subjects estimate the intensity of single elements of a complex mixture. The generalization of Equation 16.5 to the case where there are more than two attributes in the compound is straightforward:

$$R_{ab} = w_s(R_a + R_b + \ldots r_N) + w_i \left( \frac{R_a^2 + R_b^2 + \ldots R_N^2}{R_a + R_b + \ldots R_N} \right). \tag{16.7}$$

When the firing rate produced by one attribute is conditional on the firing rates of two or more additional attributes, Equation 16.6 generalizes to

$$R_{a|ab\ldots N} = w_s R_a + w_i \left( \frac{R_a^2}{R_a + R_b + \ldots R_N} \right). \tag{16.8}$$

## The Dominance Model

There are stimulus combinations where the Averaging Model does not fare very well in describing empirical data. When the dominant intensity in a pair determines the response to the compound, a winner-take-all rule is in effect. For this situation, the interactive region has a new function, where dominance is defined as

$$\text{If } R_a \geq R_b, \text{ then } \mathbf{I} = R_a \tag{16.9a}$$

$$\text{If } R_b \geq R_a, \text{ then } \mathbf{I} = R_b \tag{16.9b}$$

The composition rule is then applied by evaluating Equation 16.1, but Equation 16.9 is taken as the interactive term. The final result is a prediction of the perceived intensity of the compound. Following McBride's (1989) lead, this formulation is referred to as the *Dominance Model*.

## INTEGRATION PSYCHOPHYSICS

In an impressive series of theoretical and empirical studies, Anderson (1981, 1982, 1992) argued that a deep understanding of psychophysics will only occur when more research is conducted with multidimensional stimuli. The consideration of joint firing rates (responses) as a weighted average of the separable and interactive components is very much in the spirit of Anderson's "functional measurement" approach. Composition rules underlie the effects accruing from the presentation of objects comprised of two or more attributes. The empirical data Anderson treats, however, cover a substantial range of topics, including personality, person perception, and hedonics. The more parochial concerns here are with data pertaining to the joint effect of two or more sensory attributes on the perception of total intensity. Toward this end, Anderson's graphical format is used to show how the theoretical approach of the previous section applies to psychophysics.

### Additivity

Anderson presented intensity values for each of two attributes in a complete factorial design, and the subject estimated on a linear scale either the total intensity of each pair of values, or the intensity of one attribute in the compound formed by each pair. Figure 16.2a (left) shows a typical data plot. These results are from an unpublished experiment by McBride, described by McBride and Anderson (1990). Subjects rated the perceived total intensity of mixtures of sucrose (sweet taste) and orange (orange odor) presented in a 3 × 3 factorial design. The rating of the total intensity is plotted as a function of the sucrose level with "orange" as a parameter (indicated by the different lines). The x axis and the parameter on the graph represent physical values, the y axis represents the judgment of total intensity. Because experimenters working in the functional measurement tradition often assume a linear relation between judgments and physical values (transformed, e.g., by taking logarithms), the discussion pro-

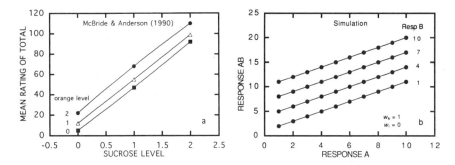

FIG. 16.2.   (a) Mean rating of total intensity as a function of sucrose level with orange as a parameter. After McBride and Anderson (1990). (b) Averaging Model simulation of total perceived intensity (AB) as a function of the perceived intensity of A, with the perceived intensity of B as a parameter. Best-fitting parameter values of Equation 16.5 as indicated.

ceeds as if the same graphical picture would arise when subjective ratings are substituted for physical variables. The composition rules predict the outcome achieved from combining two attributes without specifying the way in which the dependent variables are measured. Returning to the data in Figure 16.2a, it appears that additivity occurs between the two attributes: Perceived total intensity is a direct function of the sum of the components.

The Averaging Model (Equation 16.5) obviously accommodates such results. Figure 16.2b (right) shows hypothetical results of an evaluation of this equation. No attempt was made to equate units of measure with the empirical data in the left panel. In the model, all the weight is attached to the separable (additive) portion of the compound ($w_s = 1$, $w_i = 0$).

## Mixture Suppression

McBride and Anderson (1990) discussed another variation on the theme of stimulus integration under the heading of "mixture suppression." In an experiment on gustation (McBride & Johnson, 1987) with a sugar-lemon mixture, the stronger concentrations of sugar decrease the perceived intensity of lemon. A comparable experiment is reported by McBride (1989), whose results are shown in Figure 16.3a (left). The perceived intensity of citric acid is plotted as a function of the physical acid level (with sweetness as a parameter). Each curve represents a different level of sucrose. The highest such level leads to the lowest amounts of perceived acid strength, but all curves converge toward a common point at the low end of the scale. (A logarithmic transformation of the x axis produces less curvature, but I want to show the values at zero.)

McBride and Anderson claimed these results imply the operation of a "sub-

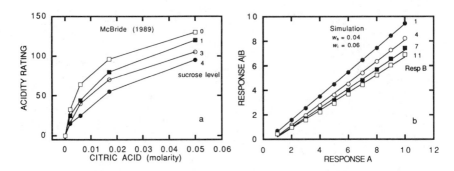

FIG. 16.3.    (a) Mean acidity rating as a function of citric acid level, with sucrose as a parameter. After McBride (1989). (b) Averaging Model simulation (Equation 16.6a). Results indicate mixture suppression. For more details, see Figure 16.2b.

traction rule," because an increase in the amount of sucrose induces a decrease in the perceived intensity of the acid. The averaging model predicts the same fan pattern when subjects judge only one component of a mixture. The data in Figure 16.3b (right) were generated by evaluating Equation 16.6a, with weights of $w_s =$ .4 and $w_i = .6$. Whether one wishes to treat McBride's empirical findings as due to subtraction or averaging seems to be purely a matter of taste.

## Averaging and Dominance

McBride (1986) gave results from additional experiments concerning intensity ratings of mixtures of similar tastants, where the functions converge at the top of the intensity scales. Figure 16.4a shows this outcome, where subjects' ratings of

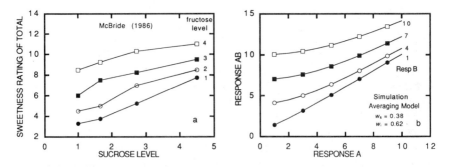

FIG. 16.4.    (a) Mean sweetness rating as a function of sucrose level, with fructose as a parameter. After McBride (1986). (b) Averaging model simulation (Equation 16.5). Results indicate a dominance of the strongest member of a pair of stimuli.

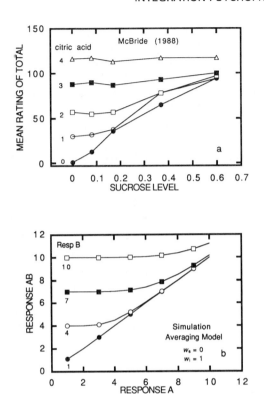

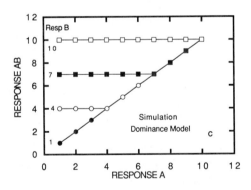

FIG. 16.5. (a) Mean intensity rating as a function of sucrose level, with citric acid as a parameter. After McBride (1988). (b) Averaging model simulation (Equation 16.5). (c) Dominance Model simulation (Equations 16.2 & 16.9).

total intensity is plotted for combinations of sucrose and fructose. The slight convergence of the curves indicates that the dominant intensity in a pair has more influence on the combination than in the simple additive case. Figure 16.4b (right) gives hypothetical results generated by the Averaging Model. The parameter values are also listed on the graph. The visual similarity between the data patterns in the left and right panels is apparent.

In further experiments, McBride (1988) presented results in which the empirical functions converge more definitely at the top end of the intensity scales. In a 5 × 5 factorial design involving different levels of sucrose and citric acid, he reported the outcome in Fig. 16.5a (top), where the strong dominates the weak. To better appreciate this, consider first the top curve representing the maximum amount of citric acid (4). As the level of sucrose changes from weak to strong, the total intensity along the citric acid curve stays the same, indicating that the dominant factor is the level of citric acid. When this is fixed at its weakest level, however, the perceived total intensity increases systematically with increases in the amount of sucrose. For each stimulus condition, the rating of the intensity of the compound depends primarily on the strongest member of the pair.

Figure 16.5b shows results of the Averaging Model, where the weight of the separable contribution is 0 and that of the interactive contribution is 1. The pattern parallels that of the empirical data, though the Averaging Model cannot produce data in exact conformity with a winner-take-all rule. In the Averaging Model, the weaker component always donates something to the overall complex (Equations 16.3 & 16.4).

Figure 16.5c (bottom) gives predictions of the dominance model for these same data, where the pattern corresponds less well to the empirical findings than does the Averaging Model. Except in the case of extreme dominance, the Averaging Model provides an adequate characterization of data collected within the tradition of information integration.

## MINKOWSKI METRICS

The Minkowski metric often describes dissimilarity ratings among stimuli that vary along several dimensions (Baird & Noma, 1978). The critical distinction researchers make is between attributes that when combined are either perceptually "separable" or "integral." Garner (1974) favored this dichotomy by claiming that attributes such as saturation and brightness of colors combine to form an integral percept, whereas subjects perceive attributes such as size and color as separate entities even when presented together as a compound. One of the oft-quoted differences between these two types of composition rules, and one also emphasized by Garner, is that the dissimilarity between pairs of intensity values taken from separable dimensions is best described by the "city-block metric," whereas the dissimilarity between pairs of values taken from integral dimensions is best described by the "Euclidean metric" (Melara, 1992; Shepard, 1991). The general form of the Minkowski metric yielding positive, real values is

$$d_{ab} = \left[ \sum_{k=1}^{N} |x_{ak} - x_{bk}|^r \right]^{1/r}. \qquad (16.10)$$

The dissimilarities ($d_{ab}$) between two objects are the distances ($x$) along each of k dimensions. The power ($r$) specifies the appropriate metric defining the coordinate location of one object in respect to others. When $r = 1$, the city-block metric defines the distances between points; when $r = 2$, the Euclidean metric applies. As $r$ approaches infinity, Equation 16.10 becomes the supremum metric, when the distance between two objects is the largest difference along any one of their shared dimensions. Explicit formulation of these three cases is given by Equation 16.11.

$$\text{city-block} \quad d_{ab} = \sum_{k=1}^{N} |x_{ak} - x_{bk}| \qquad (16.11a)$$

$$\text{Euclidean} \quad d_{ab} = \sum_{k=1}^{N} [|x_{ak} - x_{bk}|^2]^{1/2} \qquad (16.11b)$$

$$\text{supremum} \quad d_{ab} = \max_{k=1}^{N} |x_{ak} - x_{bk}| \qquad (16.11c)$$

Other values of $r$, including nonintegral ones, define other metric spaces. For example, some stimulus objects are located in a space where the power of the Minkowski metric is less than 1 (Tversky & Gati, 1982). The stimulus objects in this particular study are impossible to classify in terms of scales of intensity. They include such items as house plants, parallelograms, and schematic faces. These studies are not discussed here because they imply that the less intense member of a pair of dimensions controls the overall reaction to the combination. This strikes me as an unlikely occurrence at peripheral or cortical sites that underlie the processing of perceptual intensities. Factors of a more cognitive nature must be responsible for the Tversky and Gati results, and most probably, these factors are only tangentially relevant to psychophysics.

## COMPOSITION RULES AND MINKOWSKI METRICS

In the psychophysical context, Minkowski metrics predict the outcome of combining inputs from all the defining properties of an object. The question then arises as to how data obeying the Minkowski metric would look if plotted in the format of information integration (Figure 16.2). First, it is necessary to rewrite the Minkowski metric to clarify the meaning of the variables and their relation to those in the Averaging and Dominance Models. Changing the terms in Equation 16.10 yields an equation whose variables have the exact meaning of those in the two composition models:

$$R_{ab} = \left[ \sum_{k=1}^{N} |R_{ak} - R_{bk}|^r \right]^{1/r} \tag{16.12}$$

For purposes of illustration, the discussion is restricted to the two-dimensional case (N = 2 in Equation 16.12).

Several calculations are necessary before comparing the representation of objects (stimuli) in a Minkowski space with the results predicted by the composition models. First, data are generated for a hypothetical situation involving two dimensions whose intensity levels vary in integer steps from 1 to 10. The predicted value for each cell of the $10 \times 10$ factorial matrix is then found by evaluating the Minkowski metric with different powers (Equation 16.12). In other words, a range of combinations $(R_{ab})$ are secured by inserting different $r$ values into Equation 16.12 to produce matrices of hypothetical percepts.

Next, the Averaging Model (Equation 16.5) was fit to the set of points in each of these output matrices by an iterative technique. This was done by incrementally changing the weights in the model and finding the highest correlation between the predicted and obtained data sets. Other Goodness-of-Fit measures give comparable results. The adequacy of the model in predicting data that are in fact distances in a Minkowski space is assessed by examining the two sets of points in the same plot.

Figure 16.6 presents data for six different values of $r$, noted on each panel. The best-fitting value of the weighting factors for the additive and separable portions in Equation 16.5 are also given. The format is the same shown previously to represent judgments of total intensity based on combinations of two attributes. That is, the dependent variable $(R_{ab})$ corresponding to the stimulus compound is plotted as a joint function of the independent variable $(R_a)$ for one attribute (x axis), with the second independent variable $(R_b)$ serving as a parameter.

A perfect fit of the Averaging Model must occur for the city-block metric (Figure 16.6a) when the weight for the additive portion equals 1. This means that the two attributes maintain their distinctiveness in the compound, and hence, all the weight in the Averaging Model rests with the additive portion. As the power $(r)$ of the Minkowski metric increases, the pattern of results undergoes systematic transformation. The data points for these metrics (including the Euclidean) converge more and more for the stronger intensities of the components. The distance between two points in this joint space is increasingly less than the sum

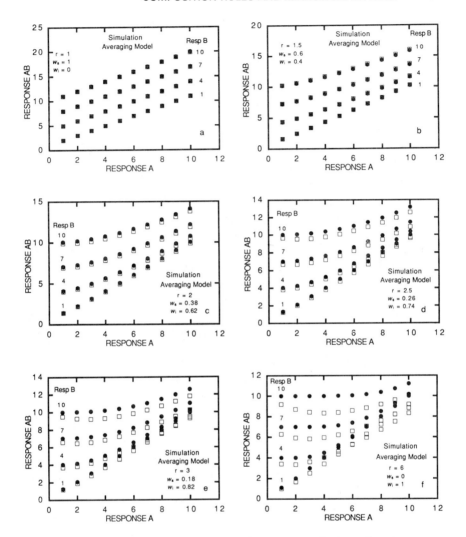

FIG. 16.6.    Response to pairs of attribute values (A & B) as a function of Response A, with Response B as a parameter. Data (filled points) generated by evaluating the Minkowski metric (Equations 16.12) with different powers ($r$). Panels a through f show Averaging Model simulations (open points) for six $r$ values. Best-fitting functions acheived by iterating the weights of the separate and interactive terms in Equations 16.5.

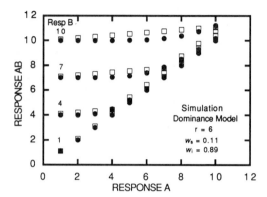

FIG. 16.7. Data (filled points) generated by evaluating the Minkowski metric (Equation 16.12) with a power of $r = 6$. Dominance Model simulation (open points).

of their components. This outcome leads some investigators to conclude this pattern implies "subadditivity" (Townsend, 1992).

The fit of the Averaging Model is adequate for all metrics up to and including $r = 2.8$ (not shown), but more substantial deviations between the predictions of Equation 16.5 and the hypothetical data occur for the larger $r$ values of 3 and 6. This happens because the averaging rule cannot perfectly duplicate the rules inherent in the Dominance Model. In the latter, the strongest component of a pair characterizes the perceptual outcome from presenting values of both attributes. For large $r$, the Dominance Model (Equations 16.1 & 16.9) is more appropriate. This is shown in Figure 16.7. The hypothetical results compare favorably with McBride's empirical data (Figure 16.5c, bottom).

The data arising within the framework of functional measurement and within the Minkowski framework are part and parcel of the same theoretical structure. As the exponent of the Minkowski metric increases, the weight of the interactive portion of the composition rule increases. The two approaches provide alternative ways of viewing the same data sets. In regard to the Minkowski metrics, there is really no rationale given in the literature as to why one or the other metric applies, whereas for the Anderson approach, the averaging rules are too limited to embrace all the types of data patterns possible within the Minkowski framework. The more complete composition rules of the Averaging and Dominance Models handle the full scope of data pertaining to judgments of a compound based on the relative contribution of their components.

## VECTOR MODELS

A vector notation offers another means to characterize the joint perceptual effect of two or more attributes. The rationale here parallels the one in physics to clarify the concept of "force." When several forces are simultaneously applied at a point, the same effect is produced by a single force of the proper magnitude and direction. This single force is modeled as the resultant addition of the constituents.

For the psychophysical analogy, the perceived total magnitude (resultant) of a compound stimulus is the sum of the perceived magnitudes of the components. Figure 16.8 illustrates the concept of vector addition by the parallelogram method. An algebraic representation of the resultant is found in terms of the component vectors and the angle ($\theta$) separating them. From the diagram,

$$x = R_b cos\ \theta$$

$$y = R_b sin\ \theta.$$

By the pythagorean theorem, the square of the resultant ($R_{ab}$) is the square of the total extent in the $x$ and $y$ dimensions:

$$R_{ab}^2 = (R_a + x)^2 + y^2. \tag{16.13}$$

Substituting for $x$ and $y$ and rearranging,

$$R_{ab}^2 = R_a^2 + 2R_aR_b\ cos\ \theta + R_b^2\ (cos^2\theta + sin^2\theta). \tag{16.14}$$

Because $cos^2\theta + sin^2\theta = 1$, the square root of both sides of Equation 16.14 yields the form for psychophysical applications:

$$R_{ab} = (R_a^2 + R_b^2 + 2R_aR_b\ cos\ \theta)^{1/2}. \tag{16.15}$$

Several restricted versions of this equation are worth special mention. When $\theta = 90°$, $cos\ \theta = 0$ and Equation 16.15 reduces to the Euclidean metric. When $\theta = 0°$, $cos\ \theta = 1$ and Equation 16.15 reduces to the city-block metric.

## Detection Tasks

During the early days of the Theory of Signal Detectability (TSD), Tanner (1956) predicted detection rates for multidimensional targets. Two years later, Green (1958) successfully predicted detection of a multidimensional stimulus from the

FIG. 16.8. Illustrative diagram of vector addition by the parallelogram method. An algebraic representation of the resultant in terms of the component vectors and the angle ($\theta$) between them.

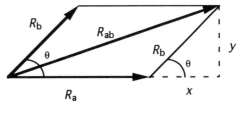

detection rates of the components. He compared detection rates $(d')$ for single sinusoids of different frequencies with the detection rates when two sinusoids were simultaneously presented as a multidimensional signal. A Euclidean model predicted the detection of the multidimensional stimulus very well, where $d'$ for the complex equalled the Euclidean distance between the component $d'$s for the sinusoids presented in isolation. The Minkowski metric had a power of $r = 2$ (Equation 16.12). In terms of the vector model, this means the angle separating the component vectors is 90°. (This research issue is discussed more thoroughly by Macmillan & Creelman, 1991.)

Fidell (1970) accepted a similar logic but with two attributes that one might consider distinct (vision and audition). Instead of the Minkowski metric, he employed the vector model and investigated the detection ability of five observers for a sinusoid embedded in auditory or visual noise. On some trials, the signal was only visual; on others, only auditory, and, in the bimodal case, both signals occurred simultaneously. He used a Two-Interval, Forced-Choice procedure and seemed determined to make sure his subjects were well practiced. They made 20,000 estimates in one condition and 53,000 in another!

The measure of performance was the $d'$ for each of the three conditions: visual, auditory, and bimodal. The vector model predicts the bimodal $d'$ as a function of the two component $d'$s for vision and audition. Fidell compared the additive ($\theta = 0$) and Euclidean ($\theta = 90°$) models, finding the latter to be superior. Figure 16.9a shows the fit, where the model slightly underestimates the bimodal $d'$. This implies that the best-fitting angle in the vector model is somewhat smaller than 90°, because decreasing the angle between the two vectors leads to a larger resultant.

Hughes, Nozawa, and Le (1993) supported Fidell's research in a presentation at the Annual Meeting of the Association for Research in Vision and Opthalmology. In their approach, detection performance is evaluated for auditory and visual signals, alone and in combination, under different conditions of stimulus location and modality uncertainty. In every case, the bimodal detection performance is superior to that of either modality tested alone, and the results are well described by a Euclidean model. Figure 16.9b shows the mean data across conditions and subjects.[1] The bimodal data are remarkably similar to those of Fidell, but with an even better fit of the Euclidean model.

Taken together, the results in Figure 16.9 support the notion that the detection of visual and auditory signals is subadditive, in the sense proposed by Townsend (1992), but the extent of subadditivity may be slightly less than is implied by the Euclidean model. That is, the bimodal $d'$ obtained by both Fidell and by Hughes et al. is less than would be expected by simple addition of the component $d'$s, but more than would be predicted by a Euclidean model. Hughes, Reuter-Lorenz,

---

[1] I am grateful to the authors for providing me with their data.

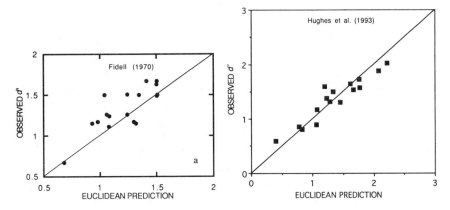

FIG. 16.9.    Detection rates ($d'$) for simultaneous (bimodal) presentation of light–sound pairs as a function of Euclidean combination (Equation 16.12) of detection rates when each attribute is presented alone. (a) After Fidell (1970). (b) After Hughes, Nozawa, and Le (1993).

Nozawa, and Fendrich (1994) reached the same conclusion from experiments on reaction time (detection) to bimodal visual and auditory stimuli. They found that reaction time is faster in the bimodal condition than it is for the component visual or auditory signals, but that this improvement is subadditive. They went on to speculate about the possible neural mechanisms responsible for the results. They pointed out that neurons exist within layers of the superior colliculus that receive convergent visual and acoustic inputs (Jay & Sparks, 1987; Meredith & Stein, 1983, 1986; Peck, 1987; Stein & Meredith, 1993). This neural overlap between the inputs from the two modalities may be responsible for the improvement in bimodal reaction times over the reaction times for isolated auditory or visual signals.

Within the framework of the composition rules outlined earlier, the results on bimodal signal detection suggest that a subpopulation of neurons exists that is uniquely responsive to auditory and visual signals (the additive part of the mix), as well as a subpopulation that responds to both types of input (the interactive part of the mix). The two relative proportions determine the detection performance in the laboratory.

## GLOBAL PSYCHOPHYSICS

The most direct applications of the composition models are to the method of Magnitude Estimation of supraliminal stimuli. In these experiments, psychophysical functions are first determined for each component attribute and these responses are the elements for predicting the judgment of the joint stimuli created by various combinations of component intensities.

One experiment (Feldman & Baird, 1971) combined sounds and lights orthogonally to form a 5 × 5 matrix of joint intensities. In separate experimental phases, subjects estimated the intensities of either the lights alone, the sounds alone, or the light–sound combinations. Unlike the detection analyses just reviewed, estimates of the combined intensities of light and sound were a linear addition of the estimates of the components. These results are reproduced in Figure 16.10. The predicted values for the compound are based on the addition of the responses calculated from the two best-fitting power functions relating response magnitude to stimulus intensity for the lights and sounds presented alone. The necessity of scale factors (slope and y intercept of the equation on the x axis) for achieving a good fit may reflect differences between the use of the number scale in rendering judgments of unidimensional and multidimensional stimuli (cf. Hornung & Enns, 1986).

These results imply that light and sound are separable dimensions, and hence, the additive part of the Averaging Model is emphasized relative to the interactive part. This is not the conclusion reached from the detection data. Why are the two data sets at odds with each other?

One possibility is that the distribution of cells coactivated by light and sound behave differently near absolute threshold than they do at suprathreshold levels. A second possibility is that detection and reaction times in the vicinity of absolute threshold depend on the pattern of stimulation within a relatively small cell ensemble, which is independent of the firing rates of individual cells. Judgments above threshold may depend on the distributions of firing rates across larger cell populations.

Similar independence between the contributions of component dimensions occurs in smell and taste (Murphy & Cain, 1980). Here subjects estimate the intensity of a suprathreshold odor presented alone, a suprathreshold taste pre-

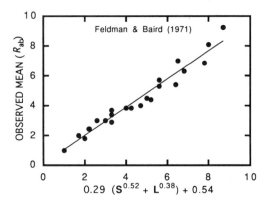

FIG. 16.10. Magnitude estimates of sound–light pairs as a function of linear combination of estimates when each attribute is presented alone. After Feldman and Baird (1971).

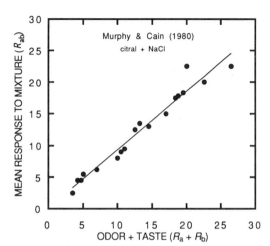

FIG. 16.11. Mean response to mixtures of citral odor and NaCl taste as a function of the addition of their perceived intensities when presented alone. After Murphy and Cain (1980).

sented alone, or both together. When the tendency for making false-positive responses is subtracted from the magnitude estimates, the authors reported almost perfect additivity for the odorant and the tastant. Figure 16.11 illustrates this result. Similar findings are reported in other studies (Gillan, 1983; Hornung & Enns, 1986; Murphy, Cain, & Bartoshuk, 1977).

In the case of taste mixtures, simple additivity does not occur if the two components taste alike. For example, Frijters and Oude Ophuis (1983) found that magnitude estimates of fructose-glucose (both sweet tasting) combinations are predicted by assuming that the exponent of the power function for the combined stimuli is a weighted average of the exponents for the components (for review, see Frijters & De Graaf, 1989).

Evidence for integrality of attributes comes also from the mixing of odors. A person seldom smells only one chemical in the natural environment, just as a person seldom hears only a pure tone or sees only a pure hue. The olfactory sense, in particular, almost always reacts to a mix of airborne chemicals, and therefore, it is of special interest to determine what the relation is between perception of this mixture and of its individual components.

The Vector Addition Model (Equation 16.15) is especially adept at describing such data for the case of odor (reviewed by Cain, 1986), and the findings suggest that the angle between the component vectors exceeds $90°$ (B. Berglund, U. Berglund, & Lindvall, 1976; B. Berglund, U. Berglund, Lindvall, & Svensson, 1973; B. Berglund & Olsson, 1993a, 1993b, 1993c; Cain, 1975; Laing, Panhuber, Willcox, & Pittman, 1984).[2] The angle typically lies within the range of

---

[2]Olsson (1994) reported one of the few exceptions. A Euclidean model best describes his mixture data.

100° to 120° and does not depend systematically on the properties of the chemicals comprising the mixture. The Vector Model also generalizes to mixtures with three or more components (B. Berglund, 1974).

An angle greater than 90° implies that the weight of the interactive portion of the Averaging Model is more than the weight of the additive portion. More integrality is suggested above and beyond that seen in the Euclidean model. In terms of the Dominance Model, such data imply that perception of the strongest component is the same as perception of the overall intensity of the mixture.

## COMPOSITION RULES AND THE VECTOR MODEL

The following calculations help us achieve a clearer understanding of the relation between composition rules and vector models. The programming recipe is this: First, create a 10 × 10 matrix (integers) representing the response to Component A and the response to Component B by substituting pairs of values into the formula for the Vector Model and generating values for response to both stimuli when presented simultaneously. Then vary the angle between the component vectors and generate a set of matrices to simulate a range of empirical results.

Next, manipulate the weights in the Averaging Model to generate simulation results that correspond best to the matrices produced by the vector model. Figure 16.12 compares the two types of models in a by-now-familiar format. As indicated in the figure, each panel represents a different angle in the Vector Model. The weights attached to the separable (additive) and integral (interactive) portions of the Averaging Model are also listed in each panel.

Three conclusions can be drawn from such comparisons. First, the curves converge at the upper end of the scales as the angle between the vectors increases. Second, the Vector Model produces data that could be captured equally well by a Minkowski metric. Third, the Averaging Model offers an excellent characterization of the results produced by the Vector Model—the greater the angle of $\theta$, the greater the interactive contribution. As the angle increases beyond 120°, the Dominance Model provides a better fit. That is to say, olfactory perception is "integral" in respect to the situation in which two chemicals are combined to form a mixture. Although not employing the Vector Model explicitly, Lawless (1977) reached a similar conclusion from studying the perception of single and mixed tastants.

In sum, the mean results for complex mixtures is understood by considering the influence of two factors operating at the level of neural sites: (a) an additive portion in which the contribution of each component is independent of the context, and (b) an interactive portion in which output from a component depends on the strength of the other members of the mixture. Because the importance attached to each of these portions can vary from 0% to 100%, it is misleading to define compounds in exclusionary terms such as "separable" and

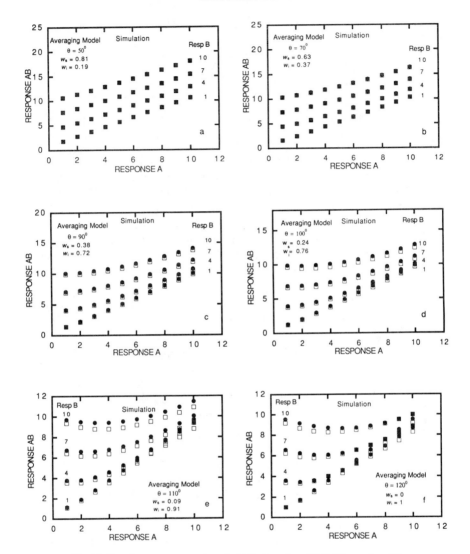

FIG. 16.12.    Response to pairs of attribute values (A & B) as a function of Response A, with Response B a parameter. Data (filled points) generated by evaluating the Vector Model (Equation 16.15) with different angles (θ). Panels a through f show Averaging Model simulations (open points) for six angles (50° to 120°). Best-fitting functions acheived by iterating the weights of the separate and interactive terms in Equation 16.5.

"integral." Most possess features of both (see Ashby & Maddox, 1994; Macmillan & Kingston, 1995).

## RESPONSE VARIABILITY OF MIXTURES

### Qualitative Mixtures

Theorists have proposed a wide assortment of models to deal with the issues of mixing odors and mixing tastants, but it is not easy to declare winners among these models based only on mean responses (B. Berglund & Olsson, 1993c). In attempting to predict the estimation of mixture intensities, vector models rely on the mean responses to components (B. Berglund et al., 1973; Laffort, 1989). Such models are referred to as "perceptual." Other types of models rely on the stimulus concentrations of the component substances, when theorists attempt to predict the response to the compound arrived at by mixing the physical components (Frijters & De Graff, 1989). These models are referred to as "psychophysical."

Although it is difficult to decide between the viability of these two broad types of models on the basis of mean results, it may be possible to draw more definitive conclusions from measures of response variability. For example, if by adding together two chemicals, the result is a third stimulus (compound) that leads to a unique distribution of neural firing, then the mean and standard deviation of that distribution depends on the total intensity of the compound. Therefore, the variance of the responses for the compound is the same as the variance of a hypothetical single stimulus (one of the components) of the same total intensity (if such comparison were technically feasible).

On the other hand, if the addition occurs after each component intensity generates its own neural distribution, the theoretical prediction is quite different. Now we are adding two distributions (some portion of which is assumed to be independent) together when the compound stimulus is presented, and hence, the variance of the compound will be greater than the variances of either of the two components. Assuming the response distributions are normally distributed (or at least symmetric) and independent, it can be proven that (Larsen & Marx, 1981, chap. 7):

$$\sigma_{ab}^2 = \sigma_a^2 + \sigma_b^2.$$

For the Dominance Model, on the other hand, the variance of the judgments to the compound should not exceed that for judgments of the major component. For most situations described in this chapter for smell and taste a clear distinction is possible between "perceptual" and "psychophysical" models by looking at the variability of responses to single components and mixtures. It is also possible to make explicit predictions about response variability for different weights attached to the additive and interactive portions of the complex. Whereas this endeavor might prove mathematically formidable, the predicted variability for any quantitative model, no matter how complex, can always be approximated by computer simulation.

## PROFILE ANALYSIS

Green (1988) and his colleagues expanded the discussion of Weber functions by introducing a new method for obtaining JNDs for a multidimensional complex of tones. The listener detects an increment in amplitude of a single tone embedded in a set of surrounding tones. Using a Two-Alternative Forced-Choice procedure, the task is to select the interval in which the complex stimulus contains the increment. All tones in the standard complex have the same amplitude, and all but one tone in the comparison complex have the same amplitude—one of the components in the comparison includes an additional increment. The overall intensity of the standard and comparison vary from trial to trial, thus making it impossible for the subject to simply concentrate on the single component in discriminating between the two multitone complexes.

Several intriguing findings occur with this procedure. First, when the tones in the complex are closely packed along the frequency dimension, it is difficult for the listener to distinguish between the standard and comparison (Spiegel, Picardi & Green, 1981). As the number of components in this "masker" increases, the threshold for detecting an increment increases. Adding components to a constant range places more masking tones in the vicinity of the standard, so the surrounding tones fall within the critical band of the standard (Scharf & Buus, 1986), and this probably explains why performance is poor.

When the surrounding tones are spread out along the frequency continuum, however, listeners say there is a change in "quality" between the two stimulus ensembles, and this qualitative difference is the basis for their judgment. From such experiments, Green and his colleagues concluded that the listener must be making simultaneous comparisons of tones over the frequency spectrum containing the components; hence, they coined the term *profile analysis*. This situation differs from most psychophysical procedures involving "successive" comparison of tones over time. In profile analysis, the comparison involves tones within each complex. Only after assessing the possibility of a difference in the quality of each complex does the listener make a decision about which interval contains the increment.

A nonintuitive result of this procedure is the effect of the number of components in the ensemble and the spacing between components, determined by the overall frequency range (Green, Kidd, & Picardi, 1983; Green, Mason, & Kidd, 1984). If the center frequency at 1000 Hz is the standard to which an increment is added to form the comparison ensemble, then performance in terms of threshold for detecting the increment improves as the number and range of components increases.

The ability to detect an increment in the standard is enhanced by maximizing the spacing of the tones in the multitone background, at least out to a range of 5000 Hz. This occurs despite the fact that the frequencies at the two boundaries of the range are far removed from the critical band surrounding the standard at 1000 Hz.

At this stage of research on profile analysis it is not clear how one would devise a detailed, quantitative model to handle all the results. Green (1988, 1995) mentioned several candidates, and in one paper (Green, Dai, & Saberi, 1994), it is suggested that different mechanisms underlie the effects depending on the size and location of the spectral band of surrounding frequencies.

## Variability and Composition Rules

In the Sensory Aggregate Model's explanation of the Just-Noticeable-Difference and the Weber function, emphasis is on the variability of firing rates among the ensemble of fibers activated by a stimulus. The greater the variability, the larger the JND and the poorer the discrimination, as indicated by the Weber fraction. Because an increase in the complexity of a stimulus leads to improved discrimination in profile analysis, the Sensory Aggregate Model implies that increased stimulus dimensionality is somehow causing a decrease in the variability of firing rates within the fiber ensemble.

Each auditory fiber has a characteristic frequency to which it is most responsive, but it also responds to other frequencies, though less vigorously. When a profile of diverse frequencies is present, the same fibers are receiving inputs from multiple sources. The variability of the firing rates of all the fibers depends on the composition rule followed by each fiber when it is impacted by more than one frequency. Suppose, for example, that multiple inputs are combined by a winner-take-all rule. When a single frequency is the standard and is then augmented to produce the comparison, the variability is relatively large among the small population of fibers activated by that particular frequency. If many different frequencies are presented, however, it is more likely that each of the fibers in this subpopulation surrounding the target frequency will fire at their maximum rates (given the intensity constraints). This is because at least one of the components will be the characteristic frequency for each fiber. As the number of fibers in the ensemble increases, the variability across the profile will decrease because more and more fibers are firing at this maximum rate. The only fibers not firing at their characteristic rate will be those situated at the ends of the profile, and their relative contribution to the ensemble declines as a function of the number of fibers excited by the multidimensional stimulus. Therefore, an increment in the complex profile is easier to detect because it is perceived as a change against a stable background. Such an explanation only applies when the stimulus frequencies do not fall within the same critical band. The masking effects must correlate with some other neural process.

The key to understanding the results of profile analysis, as well as results in other multidimensional situations, rests with an understanding of the composition rules followed by individual fibers when activated by more than one stimulus quality. Pattern analysis has long played a role in theories of gustation (Schiffman & Erikson, 1971, 1980) and pain (Sherrick & Cholewiak, 1986). Approaches such as these may prove equally valuable in suggesting neural correlates for perception of complex patterns in other sense modalities.

# 17 Sensation and Perception

Psychophysical theory has two primary goals: to provide a sensory platform for inferring processes at the level of neurophysiology and to provide a judgment platform for understanding events at the level of perception. The enterprise is more successful in exploring the downward path to neurophysiology than it is explaining the upward path to perception. The reason for this is that—although it is possible to restrict the options in the laboratory so that only sensory mechanisms prevail—it is more difficult to extrapolate from the relatively impoverished conditions of the laboratory to field situations. The arrow of generalization is asymmetric, straighter toward sensation than toward perception.

## THE VIEW FROM ABOVE: SENSATION

The view of psychophysics motivating its application to neurophysiology holds that the senses can be treated as physical instruments, whose recordings of stimulus events are reliable and valid. The results of such measurement reflect the relative sensitivity of the senses in response to external stimulation. The success of such an outlook, when based on psychophysical measures, rests with the supposition that experimental outcomes are somehow immune to contextual influence. If a different outcome results each time the particulars of an experiment change, then these measures lose their special status for guiding theory construction in the domain of sensory psychology. Theorists must insure that context effects were under control, when they attempt to infer sensory processes from psychophysical outcomes. In point of fact, the laboratory conditions are often so constrained that it is hard for nonstimulus variables to exert themselves anyway.

## Applications of Sensory Psychophysics

Classical psychophysics, the discipline named and popularized by Fechner (1860/1966), represents one of psychology's major contributions to the appreciation of what aspects of human behavior must be explained by physiology. Study after study confirms psychophysical results at the level of sensory physiology. The topic of color vision is a prime example, where experimentation confirms that psychophysical outcomes have identifiable correlates in neurophysiological measures (Armington, 1974; Wandell, 1995). In addition, psychoacoustics isolates phenomena with obvious parallels in the neurophysiology of the auditory receptors and central pathways (Green, 1976; Gulick et al., 1989; Luce, 1993), and significant progress along the same lines is apparent with all the other senses (e.g., Barlow & Mollon, 1989).

Global scaling techniques also furnish insights into neurophysiological underpinnings. This comparatively new tradition furthers our understanding of sensory adaptation, the summation of neural events within sensory channels, and the functioning of the senses at low levels of stimulation (Marks, 1974b; Marks & Algom, 1996; Scharf & Buus, 1986). Although such achievements are less publicized in the research community than those ascribed to the classical methods, they continue to act as behavioral targets for what it is that neurophysiology must explain.

Psychophysical methods are not just relegated to the laboratory, however. They also appear routinely in field and medical settings. Every time individuals have their eyes or ears tested, the behavioral method of choice has historical roots in psychophysics (e.g., Swets & Pickett, 1982). In addition, the scaling methods of global psychophysics are the instruments of choice in many evaluations of environmental health in everyday settings (Baird & B. Berglund, 1989). A specific example is the medical application of the so-called Borg Scale (Borg, 1982), a numerical and verbal scale by which patients express their perceived exertion during physical exercise. For instance, a physician may request subjective ratings from the patient as part of a "stress test" to evaluate the performance of the heart while under physical duress. In hospitals throughout the world, patients make these ratings by using some variation of the Borg Scale.

In the theoretical sphere, the Power Law and its exponent have gained prominence by offering specific suggestions about underlying sensorineural relations. The great variety of physiological measures, however, makes it difficult to establish an indisputable connection between global psychophysics and sensation. Part of the problem is the difficulty in identifying the relevant aspect of neural activity. Is the critical dependent variable the activity of the individual neuron, small squadrons of neurons, or larger populations? Is the critical dependent measure a neural response to the onset of stimulation, the frequency of neural discharge, or the time between pulses arriving at a synapse? The wide scope of possibilities almost guarantees that measures can be found to support the psychophysical Power Law. Still, the question is whether or not such measures are directing us to the relevant causal link between behavioral and neural events.

## The Sensory Aggregate Model

The Sensory Aggregate Model takes a definite stance on such matters. It claims that the concerted action of neural ensembles determines the subjective experience of both stimulus quantity and quality. Subpopulations of neurons respond differently to different types of physical inputs. The fiber activation pattern is stimulus contingent. It is the coordination of local activation that underlies sensory experience, not the activity of fibers that react in lock step to each and every stimulus. Therefore, sensation is the end product of the firing of many specialized units, sharing the task of representing the complexity of environmental events. That is to say, sensory experience is not due to the excitation of identical neural components, whose joint participation is required only to increase redundancy and decrease errors. The enormous range of physical stimulation that must be dealt with by each sense organ demands a system of specialized components, each making its limited, but unique, contribution to the whole.

The Sensory Aggregate Model is a descendant of those theories that stress organization of neurons into integrated patterns, such as the volley principle in hearing (Wever, 1949), and the Gestalt models of pattern perception (Koffka, 1935). The approach also is consistent with more current thinking about how neurons code information (reviewed by Abeles, Bergman, Margalit, & Vaadia, 1993; Engel, Konig, Kreiter, Schillen, & Singer, 1992; Theunissen & Miller, 1995).

If the correlate of psychophysical estimates is the activity of neuronal populations, then the statistical properties of these aggregates must be modeled. At this stage of theory construction, there is less emphasis on the statistical properties of the firing rates of individual neurons, though of course, it will eventually be desirable to include such information in a complete model. This book's approach is one example of how to infer the processes behind psychophysical data. Its main heuristic value may be in pointing out relations among statistical measures that summarize psychophysical estimates. The contention is that the psychophysical laws do not stand alone but, instead, are integral parts of the same unified structure. As such, these laws bear predictable relationships to each other. The goal, in this respect, is the same as that of Norwich (1993), though the roads traveled are very different.

The field's future prospects rest on the ability to expand the richness of dependent measures. It is no longer enough to plot the mean response against the stimulus intensity and determine the form of the psychophysical function. In order to draw conclusions about underlying sensory structures, it is also necessary to describe the relations between the mean and other statistical measures, such as the shape and variability of the response distribution. The pattern emerging from these measures narrows the possible physiological mechanisms that could be responsible for sensory experience. Research of the past half century was devoted to the discovery of psychophysical laws and their specific application for diverse stimulus attributes. The next phase of this agenda should be to determine how these laws interrelate.

## THE VIEW FROM BELOW: PERCEPTION

The conditions of the psychophysics laboratory are rich when compared to those of the physiology laboratory, but stark alongside those of the perception laboratory. The successes of psychophysics in guiding perceptual theory are less visible than in neurophysiology. After a century of research, there still is no theory of perception grounded exclusively in psychophysics. The hope early on was that perceptual experience would prove to consist of a handful of primary elements. Eventually, complex perceptions would be understood from the accumulated knowledge of psychophysics. It is time to admit that this promise has not been fulfilled.

These problems were forecast by the Gestalt movement (Koffka, 1935; Köhler, 1927), and reiterated in the writings of J. J. Gibson (1950, 1966, 1979) and his modern supporters (e.g., Michaels & Carello, 1981; Shaw & Bransford, 1977). The telling point of this critique has remained the same over the years: Perceptual experience cannot be partitioned into a set of elements because the act of partitioning destroys the integrity of the phenomena under study. The attitude permeating this criticism is that whatever is being measured in the psychophysics laboratory, it degenerates in more complex environments and, therefore, cannot underwrite a general theory.

### Perception and Psychophysics

Contrary to the Gestalt view, and its modern counterparts, the reason psychophysics has trouble explaining molar perception has nothing to do with the nature of perceptual experience, or with whether this experience can be meaningfully subdivided. In the context of the Complementarity Theory, such difficulties arise because most attempts place undue weight on sensory explanations and not enough on cognitive ones. If we are to make further progress in weaving the results of psychophysics into those of perception, both sensory and cognitive factors must receive their due. There is a slender research thread that already does this, as in Restle's (1970) approach to perceptual illusions in terms of reference frames, and in some other work on the interrelations between psychophysics, perception, and cognition (Baird, 1982; Baird & Hubbard, 1992; Baird & Wagner, 1982).

There are many points of contact between psychophysics and perception that invite future exploration. Procedural variables—such as instructions, the range of stimulus intensities, and the available response options—all influence the outcome of psychophysical experiments (Poulton, 1989), as documented in the second half of this book. These effects are not limited to the psychophysics laboratory, however, but occur as well in perception studies (Baird, 1970c). A few key examples are noted later.

## Perceptual Contrast

In his critical review of J. J. Gibson's (1950) influential book on perception, E. G. Boring (1952) related an interesting story concerning the role of stimulus contrast in determining perceived size. His example concerned the perceptual experience of an audience at a marionette (puppet) show. While the show is in progress, the puppeteer is hidden by a curtain. At the end of the performance he emerges from behind the curtain to acknowledge the applause of the audience. To everyone's amazement, the person behind the puppets turns out to be a giant! After watching pint-size actors move around a miniature stage, the sudden appearance of a normal-size person comes as a complete shock.

This anecdote has a parallel in conditions Parducci and his colleagues arranged in the psychophysics laboratory for studying the impact of stimulus skewing on category estimates of the visual size of squares (Parducci & Wedell, 1986; chap. 12 of this vol.). If the stimulus series consists of a disproportionate number of small squares, then the appearance of the rarely presented large square comes as a minor surprise to the subject, and it is assigned a category sufficiently large to distinguish it from those assigned to the smaller stimuli. The opposite effect occurs when the majority of squares are large. Now the judgment of a small square tends to contrast with judgments of the larger ones and so the subject assigns it a relatively small category.

## Perceptual Compromise

A common view of the perceptual constancies is that one's experience of stimulus magnitude represents a compromise between the proximal stimulus at the receptor and the distal stimulus in the environment (Brunswik, 1956; Sedgwick, 1986). A familiar example for academics is the perception of individuals walking across campus. Their perceived size does not just depend on the visual angle subtended at the observer's eye, but also on the widely acknowledged fact that most objects remain the same physical size regardless of their distance. The observer arrives at some sort of compromise between two opposing sizes. A receding object is perceived as larger than predicted by the changing visual angle, but smaller than predicted by the object's fixed physical size. Size constancy is incomplete.

The effects of stimulus range on the exponent of the power function may have implications for the perceptual compromise (involving other types of stimulus attributes as well) so often apparent in perception. Imagine two objects of the same size, but one is located twice as far away as the other. The visual angle (linear extent) subtended by the distant object will be half that of the near one. Suppose a stationary observer notes their relative sizes. Now imagine that the farther object moves away, and the observer assesses its relative size in respect to the nearby stationary object. Because the exponent of the Power Law declines with increasing stimulus range (Poulton, 1989), the observer perceives (judges) the receding object as not shrinking in size as rapidly as expected from its visual angle. If the range is not the sole determinant of size, as is usually true experimentally, then this means that the receding object is perceived (judged) to be greater than expected from its visual angle and less than expected from its metric size. The perception of size is a compromise between the object's proximal and distal values.

An alternative explanation of the perception of size-at-a-distance might claim that proximal size is assessed by sensory transducers, but distal size is assessed by contextual constraints on the judgment process. The complementarity inherent in this theoretical position echoes J. J. Gibson's (1950) distinction between the "visual field" and the "visual world."

## Instruction Effects

The extent to which perceptual constancy occurs depends on the experimenter's exact instructions to the subject. Instruction effects in size perception have been thoroughly investigated (reviewed in Baird, 1970c, and Baird & Wagner, 1991), and similar arguments apply to other constancies such as shape, velocity, loudness, and lightness.

Different functional relations obtain between size and distance depending on what the subject is told to do in estimating size. Three different types of instructions are common: *apparent*, *objective*, and *projective*. Apparent instructions generally lead to constancy. Objective ones yield judgments indicating "overconstancy" in the sense that a target of fixed metric size is seen to increase in perceived size with increasing distance. Projective instructions produce estimates indicating "underconstancy" in that a target appears to shrink in size with increasing distance. These instructions are typically given in data-rich environments, containing many cues to aid in the estimation process. Hence, there is ample room for the subject to consider alternative features of the stimulus display in arriving at a judgment.

Two results from these studies are noteworthy. First, whereas size judgments depend systematically on instructions, distance judgments are approximately the same under all instructional sets (Epstein, 1963). Second, the data are roughly linear in the log–log plots, indicating that the power function offers an adequate mathematical description (Baird, 1970c). The implications are that size and distance perception are not coupled in the same way for all instructions. Instructional set has a massive influence on size matches, yet very little on corresponding distance judgments. Something more than sensory processing is involved, and there seems to be no way to decide which of the alternative stimulus–response functions are "true" or preferable, when a theorist endeavors to attribute results to sensory causes.

More recent experiments (Loomis et al., 1992) employ conditions that produce more constancy judgments than in previous investigations. In the name of "ecological validity" one might even claim that such conditions are the "correct" ones because they produce constancy. In other words, the philosophical assumption is made beforehand that constancy is the "normal" perceptual experience, and therefore, any experimental condition that produces constancy must be valid, and any that does not must be invalid. This book does not subscribe to this philosophical view.

There are many findings in psychophysics that depend on instructions, and these are clarified by the Judgment Option Model. A strict sensory model faces more barriers in coming to grips with such data. In the study by Birnbaum and Mellers (1980), the exponent of the power function depends on the sample numbers used in the instructions to signify stimulus magnitude. In the experiment by Baird, Kreindler, and Jones (1971), diverse exponents are obtained for the judgment of line lengths, depending on the values the experimenter attaches to the smallest and largest line. These instruction effects imply that alternative means are available for estimating stimulus magnitude. It is impossible to say which of these alternative instructions leads to a "true" psychophysical scale. In the same way with perception, alternative instructions lead to different perceived magnitudes, and there is no way to tell which of these represents "true" perceptual experience. Gibsonian arguments would have us believe that the instructions leading to the various constancies are in some sense the "correct" ones. Some advocates of Stevens's scaling methods would have us believe that magnitude estimation or one of its variations leads to exponents of the power function that are more "real" than the "virtual" exponents of other methods.

Neither of these viewpoints fosters the kind of scientific atmosphere needed for modeling perceptual or psychophysical judgments. They only admit half the story into evidence, and must explain away large bodies of reliable data. The other half of the story must include cognitive mechanisms whose influence appears in literally hundreds of studies on judgments of stimulus magnitude in psychophysics and perception.

# MAXIMIZING EFFECTS

In the early days of psychophysics, experimenters were content to perform one or maybe two analyses on a data set. The current practice is to do multiple analyses. Such a trend deserves encouragement. Many of the conclusions in this book would have been impossible if experimenters had only performed a single type of analysis. On only rare occasions can a theorist reach a definitive conclusion about the causes behind a phenomenon without examining it under more than one light. The way in which alternative measures interrelate is especially critical in formulating a theoretical model of the underlying sensory and judgment processes. As a rule, the greater the number of perspectives on a data set, the greater the probability of gaining insight into the processes underlying it.

Beyond the foregoing considerations, the complementarity perspective suggests guidelines about the experimental designs most likely to maximize effects.

## Sensory Effects

The Sensory Aggregate Model states that psychophysical laws represent different sides of the same neurophysiological coin. To determine the validity of this claim, it is necessary to test subjects with a variety of methods that yield data in accord with the psychophysical laws discussed in chapters 3, 4, and 5. One central question in this regard is this: Should one employ a within-subjects or a between-subjects design? Both have advantages and disadvantages, but the chances of success improve with a between-subjects design. The problem with using only a few subjects is that individual differences arise with all the psychophysical methods, and there is no guarantee that these differences are the same for all methods. A subject with a predilection for using unusual numbers in magnitude estimation may have either a low or high threshold for responding in a reaction-time study. There is simply no way to tell without doing the experiment. For this reason, the cards are stacked against finding patterns across methods if the subject pool is small. Summary statistics taken over the database from a larger group are more likely to reveal consistent patterns by which one can infer sensory processes.

On the other hand, once a psychophysical relation is established, specific parameter values tied to stimulus conditions are best determined by a within-subject design. This has been the scientific approach throughout the history of psychophysics, and it is one of the most successful in all of psychology.

## Judgment Effects

The situation is slightly different when the aim is to uncover judgment principles that transcend method and attribute. Here, the best experimental strategy is to use a small number of subjects tested with the same procedure. By evaluating performance on a common task it is possible to uncover the relevant judgment strategies. Averaging performance over a large group of participants dims the hope for reaching a satisfactory understanding of these individual strategies. Indiscriminant lumping together of data across subjects can easily lead to pseudoexplanations devised to account for phantom phenomena—present in the average corpus of data but absent from the data of any single individual. And it is the judgment strategy of the individual we are trying to understand. Thus, within-subject designs are preferable in testing the implications of the Judgment Option Model.

## Attribute Effects

The effects of different stimulus qualities on psychophysical judgments are maximized either by the use of small or large subject pools, all utilizing the same method and set of attributes. For large-group studies, the averaging of results has the net effect of washing out idiosyncracies in judgment strategies across subjects. In this way, the differences between attributes are more readily apparent. On the other hand, by using a small number of subjects, it is possible to institute controls for evaluating the impact of idiosyncratic judgment strategies. If money and time are no obstacles, the best research plan is to use a large number of subjects who are each tested with every attribute.

## CHOICE AND COMPLEMENTARITY

This book proposes two complementary ways of viewing psychophysical experiments. The first assumes that psychophysical results are due to sensory processes. According to this view, statistical measures describing responses faithfully mirror the underlying neurophysiology. The alternative concept is that psychophysics involves additional cognitive processing. These processes have no known correlates in sensory physiology, though certainly they have correlates elsewhere in the nervous system.

The critical distinction between the two perspectives concerns the source of response variability. According to the sensory perspective, response variability is due to the different neuronal firing rates that comprise an ensemble of fibers signaling stimulus presence and character. According to the judgment perspective, response variability occurs because subjects are uncertain about which response they should select from the available options.

The question naturally arises as to how one decides which of the two models should be favored under any specified set of conditions. No hard and fast rules exist. The Sensory Aggregate Model is usually appropriate when the dependent measures (e.g., means, variance, skew) are monotonic with changing stimulus intensity. The Judgment Option Model is usually a better choice when monotonicity is violated.

For example, if the standard deviation is plotted as a function of the mean (Ekman function) and the relation is continuously increasing, then the Sensory Aggregate Model probably offers the better interpretation. On the contrary, if the function initially increases but then dips down somewhere along its course, then the Judgment Option Model is more appropriate. The dip would suggest the subject relied on an implicit standard located in the middle of the series and this standard exerted an influence on the judgments of nearby stimuli.

For practical purposes, the model chosen should be the one that yields the clearest picture of the underlying causes. This is how the physical sciences react when deciding whether light is discrete or wavelike. The complementarity doctrine exists because, through trial and error, the theory that light comes in packets best explains certain experimental results, whereas in other experiments the theory that light is a wave is a more appropriate choice (Feynman et al., 1963). There is no definitive way to decide beforehand which of these two conceptions of light will be most helpful in understanding the results of a not-yet-tried experiment. In a similar fashion, the field of psychophysics must also learn to tolerate the uncertainty that comes with acceptance of two complementary and mutually completing viewpoints.

# REFERENCES

Abeles, M., Bergman, H., Margalit, E., & Vaadia, E. (1993). Spatiotemporal firing patterns in the frontal cortex of behaving monkeys. *Journal of Neurophysiology*, *70*, 1629–1638.

Ahlström, R., & Baird, J. C. (1989). Shift in stimulus range and the exponent of the power function for loudness. *Perception and Psychophysics*, *46*, 603–607.

Algom, D. (1992a). Memory psychophysics: An examination of its perceptual and cognitive prospects. In D. Algom (Ed.), *Psychophysical approaches to cognition* (pp. 441–513). Amsterdam: North-Holland & Elsevier.

Algom, D. (1992b). (Ed.). *Psychophysical approaches to cognition*. Amsterdam: North-Holland & Elsevier.

Algom, D., & Cain, W. S. (1991a). Chemosensory representation in perception and memory. In S. J. Bolanowski, Jr. & G. A. Gescheider (Eds.), *Ratio scaling of psychological magnitude*. (pp. 183–198). Hillsdale, NJ: Lawrence Erlbaum Associates.

Algom, D., & Cain, W. S. (1991b). Remembered odors and mental mixtures: tapping reservoirs of olfactory knowledge. *Journal of Experimental Psychology: Human Perception and Performance*, *17*, 1104–1119.

Algom, D., & Marks, L. E. (1989). Memory psychophysics for taste. *Bulletin of the Psychonomic Society*, *27*, 257–259.

Anderson, N. S., & Fitts, P. M. (1958). Amount of information gained during brief exposures of numerals and colors. *Journal of Experimental Psychology*, *56*, 362–369.

Anderson, N. H. (1981). *Foundations of information integration theory*. New York: Academic Press.

Anderson, N. H. (1982). *Methods of information integration theory*. New York: Academic Press.

Anderson, N. H. (1992). Integration psychophysics and cognition. In D. Algom (Ed.), *Psychophysical approaches to cognition* (pp. 13–113). Amsterdam: North-Holland & Elsevier.

Angel, A. (1973). Input–output relations in simple reaction time experiments. *Quarterly Journal of Experimental Psychology*, *25*, 193–200.

Armington, J. C. (1974). *The electroretinogram*. New York: Academic Press.

Ashby, F. G., & Maddox, W. T. (1994). A response time theory of separability and integrality in speeded classification. *Journal of Mathematical Psychology*, *38*, 423–466.

Attneave, F. (1959). *Applications of information theory to psychology*. New York: Holt, Rinehart & Winston.

317

Baddeley, A. D. (1994). The magical number seven: Still magic after all these years? *Psychological Review, 101*, 353–356.

Baird, J. C. (1970a). A cognitive theory of psychophysics: I. Information transmission, partitioning, and Weber's law. *Scandinavian Journal of Psychology, 11*, 35–46.

Baird, J. C. (1970b). A cognitive theory of psychophysics: II. Fechner's law and Stevens' law. *Scandinavian Journal of Psychology, 11*, 89–102.

Baird, J. C. (1970c). *Psychophysical analysis of visual space*. London: Pergamon.

Baird, J. C. (1975a). Psychophysical study of numbers: IV. Generalized preferred state theory. *Psychological Research, 38*, 175–187.

Baird, J. C. (1975b). Psychophysical study of numbers: V. Preferred state theory of matching functions. *Psychological Research, 38*, 189–207.

Baird, J. C. (1979). Studies of the cognitive representation of spatial relations: I. Overview. *Journal of Experimental Psychology: General, 108*, 90–91.

Baird, J. C. (1981). Psychophysical theory: On the avoidance of contradiction. *Behavioral and Brain Sciences, 4*, 190.

Baird, J. C. (1982). The moon illusion: II. A reference theory. *Journal of Experimental Psychology: General, 111*, 304–315.

Baird, J. C. (1986). Numbers and exponents. In B. Berglund, U. Berglund, & R. Teghtsoonian (Eds.), Stockholm: International Society for Psychophysics. *Fechner day 86.* (pp. 101–106).

Baird, J. C. (1989a). The fickle measuring instrument. *Behavioral and Brain Sciences, 12*(2), 269–270.

Baird, J. C. (1989b). Reinterpreting the power law. In G. Canevet, B., Scharf, A. Bonnel, & C. Possamai (Eds.), Cassis, France: International Society for Psychophysics. *Fechner day 89* pp. 42–47.

Baird, J. C. (1990). Modelling sequence effects among many magnitude estimates. In F. Müller (Ed.), *Fechner day 90* (pp. 159–164). International Society for Psychophysics: Wurzburg, Germany.

Baird, J. C. (1995). Judgment windows and perceived magnitude. In R. D. Luce, M. D'Zmura, D. Hoffman, G. J. Iverson, & A. K. Romney (Eds.), *Geometric representations of perceptual phenomena: Papers in honor of Tarow Indow on his 70th birthday.* (pp. 235–251). Hillsdale, NJ: Lawrence Erlbaum Associates.

Baird, J. C., & Berglund, B. (1989). Thesis for environmental psychophysics. *Journal of Environmental Psychology, 9*, 345–356.

Baird, J. C., Berglund, B., Berglund, U., & Lindberg, S. (1991). Stimulus sequence and the exponent of the power function for loudness. *Perceptual and Motor Skills, 73*, 3–17.

Baird, J. C., Berglund, B., & Olsson, M. J. (1996). Magnitude estimation of perceived odor intensity: Empirical and theoretical properties. *Journal of Experimental Psychology: Human Perception and Performance, 22*, 244–255.

Baird, J. C., Degerman, R., Paris, R., & Noma, E. (1972). Student planning of town configuration. *Environment and Behavior, 4*, 159–188.

Baird, J. C., Green, D. M., & Luce, R. D. (1980). Variability and sequential effects in cross modality matching of area and loudness. *Journal of Experimental Psychology: Human Perception and Performance, 6*, 277–289.

Baird, J. C., Harder, K., & Preis, A. (1996). *Annoyance and community noise: Psychophysical model of dose-response relationships.* Manuscript submitted for publication.

Baird, J. C., & Hubbard, T. L. (1992). Psychophysics of visual imagery. In D. Algom (Ed.), *Psychophysical approaches to cognition* (pp. 389–440). Amsterdam: North-Holland & Elsevier.

Baird, J. C., Kreindler, M., & Jones, K. (1971). Generation of multiple ratio scales with a fixed stimulus attribute. *Perception and Psychophysics, 9*, 399–403.

Baird, J. C., Lewis, C., & Romer, D. (1970). Relative frequencies of numerical responses in ratio estimation. *Perception and Psychophysics, 8*, 358–362.

Baird, J. C., & Noma, E. (1975). Psychophysical study of numbers: I. Generation of numerical responses. *Psychological Research, 37*, 281–297.

Baird, J. C., & Noma, E. (1978). *Fundamentals of scaling and psychophysics.* New York: Wiley.

Baird, J. C., & Szilagyi, P. (1977). Perception of psychophysical experiments: II. Model of scale values. *Psychological Research, 39*, 325–343.

Baird, J. C., & Wagner, M. (1982). The moon illusion: I. How high is the sky? *Journal of Experimental Psychology: General, 111*, 296–303.

Baird, J. C., & Wagner, M. (1991). Transformation theory of size judgment. *Journal of Experimental Psychology: Human Perception and Performance, 17*, 852–864.

Baird, J. C., Weissmann, S. M., & McHugo, G. (1977). Perception of psychophysical experiments: I. Scaling of methods. *Psychological Research, 39*, 311–323.

Baldwin, J. M., & Shaw, W. J. (1895). Studies from the Princeton laboratory: I. Memory for square size. *Psychological Review, 2*, 236–239.

Banks, W. P., & Hill, D. K. (1974). The apparent magnitude of number scaled by random production. *Journal of Experimental Psychology, 102*, 353–376.

Barlow, H. B. (1989a). General principles: The senses considered as physical instruments. In H. B. Barlow & J. D. Mollon (Eds.), *The senses* (pp. 1–35). Cambridge, England: Cambridge University Press.

Barlow, H. B. (1989b). Physiology of the retina. In H. B. Barlow & J. D. Mollon (Eds.), *The senses* (pp. 103–113). Cambridge, England: Cambridge University Press.

Barlow, H. B., & Mollon, J. D. (1989). (Eds.). *The senses.* Cambridge, England: Cambridge University Press.

Bartlett, R. J. (1939). Measurement in psychology. *Advancement of Science, 1*, 422–441.

Bartoshuk, L. M. (1986). Taste. In R. C. Atkinson, R. J. Herrnstein, G. Lindzey, & R. D. Luce (Eds.), *Stevens' handbook of experimental psychology: Vol 1. Perception and motivation* (2nd ed., pp. 461–499). New York: Wiley.

Békésy, G. v. (1947). A new audiometer. *Acta Oto-laryngology, 35*, 411–422.

Berglund, B. (1974). Quantitative and qualitative analysis of industrial odors with human observers. *Annals of the New York Academy of Sciences, 237*, 35–51.

Berglund, B., Berglund, U., Ekman, G., & Engen, T. (1971). Individual psychophysical functions for 28 odorants. *Perception and Psychophysics, 9*, 379–384.

Berglund, B., Berglund, U., & Lindvall, T. (1971). On the principle of odor interaction. *Acta Psychologica, 35*, 255–268.

Berglund, B., Berglund, U., & Lindvall, T. (1976). Psychological processing of odor mixtures. *Psychological Review, 83*, 432–441.

Berglund, B., Berglund, U., Lindvall, T., & Svensson, L. T. (1973). A quantitative principle of perceived intensity summation in odor mixtures. *Journal of Experimental Psychology, 100*, 29–38.

Berglund, B., & Olsson, M. J. (1993a). Odor-intensity interaction in binary mixtures. *Journal of Experimental Psychology: Human Perception and Performance, 19*, 302–314.

Berglund, B., & Olsson, M. J. (1993b). Odor-intensity interaction in binary and ternary mixtures. *Perception and Psychophysics, 53*, 475–482.

Berglund, B., & Olsson, M. J. (1993c). Perceptual and psychophysical models for odor intensity interaction. In A. Garriga-Trillo, P. R. Minon, C. Garcia-Gallego, P. Lubin, J. M. Merino, & A. Villarino (Eds.), *Fechner Day '93 (pp. 35–40).* Palma de Mallorca, Spain: International Society for Psychophysics.

Bevan, W., Barker, H., & Pritchard, J. F. (1963). The Newhall scaling method, psychophysical bowing, and adaptation level. *Journal of General Psychology, 69*, 95–111.

Birnbaum, M. H. (1973). The devil rides again: Correlation as an index of fit. *Psychological Bulletin, 79*, 239–242.

Birnbaum, M. H. (1982). Controversies in psychological measurement. In B. Wegener (Ed.), *So-*

*cial attitudes and psychophysical measurement* (pp. 401–485). Hillsdale, NJ: Lawrence Erlbaum Associates.

Birnbaum, M. H., & Elmasian, R. (1977). Loudness "ratios" and "differences" involve the same psychophysical operation. *Perception and Psychophysics, 22,* 383–391.

Birnbaum, M. H., & Mellers, B. A. (1980). *Context effects in category rating and magnitude estimation.* Unpublished manuscript.

Björkman, M. (1958). Some relationships between psychophysical parameters. *Reports from the Psychology Laboratory, University of Stockholm,* No. 65.

Björkman, M. (1960). Variability data and direct quantitative judgment for scaling subjective magnitude. *Reports from the Psychological Laboratory, University of Stockholm,* No. 78.

Björkman, M., Lundberg, I., & Tarnblom, S. (1960). On the relationship between percept and memory: A psychophysical approach. *Scandinavian Journal of Psychology, 1,* 136–144.

Björkman, M., & Strangert, B. (1960). The relationship between ratio estimates and stimulus dispersion. *Reports from the Psychological Laboratory, Stockholm University,* No. 81.

Bohr, N. (1928). The quantum postulate and the recent development of atomic theory. *Nature, 121,* 580–590.

Bohr, N. (1961). *Atomic theory and the description of nature.* Cambridge, England: Cambridge University Press.

Bonnet, C. (1986). *Manuel pratique de psychophysique.* Paris: Armand Colin.

Borg, G. (1982). Psychophysical bases of perceived exertion. *Medicine and Science in Sports and Exercise, 14,* 377–381.

Boring, E. G. (1950). *A history of experimental psychology.* New York: Appleton-Century-Crofts.

Boring, E. G. (1952). The Gibsonian visual field. *Psychological Review, 59,* 246–247.

Brachman, M. L. (1980). *Dynamic response characteristics of single auditory-nerve fibers.* Unpublished doctoral dissertation and special Rep. No. ISR-S-19, Institute for Sensory Research, Syracuse Unversity, Syracuse, New York.

Braida, L. D., & Durlach, N. I. (1972). Intensity perception: II. Resolution in one-interval paradigms. *Journal of the Acoustical Society of America, 51,* 483–502.

Brentano, F. (1874). *Psychologie vom empirischen Standpunkte.* [Psychology from an empirical standpoint]. Leipzig: Duncker & Humbolt.

Brunswik, E. (1956). *Perception and the representative design of psychological experiments* (2nd ed.). Berkeley: University of California Press.

Bujas, Z., Szabo, S., Kovacic, M., & Rohacek, A. (1975). Sensory scales for electrical stimuli in three sense modalities. *Acta Institute of Psychology,* No. 74–78, 17–23.

Bury, K. V. (1975). *Statistical models in applied science.* New York: Wiley.

Butler, D. L., & Overshiner, C. (1983). The role of mental computations in judgments of area and volume. *Perception and Psychophysics, 34,* 593–598.

Cain, W. S. (1975). Odor intensity: Mixtures and masking. *Chemical Senses and Flavor, 1,* 339–352.

Cain, W. S. (1977). Differential sensitivity for smell: "Noise" at the nose. *Science, 195,* 796–798.

Cain, W. S. (1986). Olfaction. In R. C. Atkinson, R. J. Herrnstein, G. Lindzey & R. D. Luce (Eds.), *Stevens' handbook of experimental psychology: Vol. 1. Perception and motivation* (2nd ed., pp. 409–459). New York: Wiley.

Cain, W. S., & Engen, T. (1969). Olfactory adaptation and the scaling of odor intensity. In C. Pfaffmann (Ed.), *Olfaction and taste: Proceedings of the Third International Symposium* (pp. 127–141). New York: Rockefeller University Press.

Cardello, A. V. (1970). *Absolute judgment: Perception or learning?* Unpublished honors thesis, Dartmouth College, Hanover, NH.

Carstens, E., Fraunhoffer, M., & Suberg, S. N. (1983). Inhibition of spinal dorsal horn neuronal responses to noxious skin heating by lateral hypothalamic stimulation in the cat. *Journal of Neurophysiology, 50,* 192–204.

Chocholle, R. (1940). Variations des temps de réaction auditifs en fonction de l'intensité a diverses fréquences [Variation of auditory reaction time as a function of the intensity of different frequencies]. *L'Anné Psychologique, 41*, 65–124.

Cornsweet, T. N. (1962). The staircase method in psychophysics. *American Journal of Psychology, 75*, 485–491.

Cross, D. V. (1973). Sequential dependencies and regression in psychophysical judgments. *Perception and Psychophysics, 14*, 547–552.

Cross, D. V., Tursky, B., & Lodge, M. (1975). The role of regression and range effects in determination of the power function for electric shock. *Perception and Psychophysics, 18*, 9–14.

Cross, D. V. (1974). Some technical notes on psychophysical scaling. In H. Moskowitz, B. Scharf, & J. C. Stevens (Eds.), *Sensation and measurement: Papers in honor of S. S. Stevens* (pp. 23–36). Dordrecht, The Netherlands: Reidel.

Curtis, D. W., Attneave, F., & Harrington, T. L. (1968). A test of a two-stage model for magnitude estimation. *Perception and Psychophysics, 3*, 25–31.

DeCarlo, L. T. (1992). Intertrial interval and sequential dependencies in magnitude scaling. *Journal of Experimental Psychology: Human Perception and Performance, 18*, 1080–1088.

DeCarlo, L. T. (1994). A dynamic theory of proportional judgment: Context and judgment of length, heaviness, and roughness. *Journal of Experimental Psychology: Human Perception and Performance, 20*, 372–381.

DeCarlo, L. T., & Cross, D. V. (1990). Sequential effects in magnitude scaling: Models and theory. *Journal of Experimental Psychology: General, 119*, 375–396.

DeValois, R. L., & DeValois, K. K. (1988). *Spatial vision*. New York: Oxford University Press.

Dimmick, F. L., & Olson, R. M. (1941). The intensive difference limen in audition. *Journal of the Acoustical Society of America, 12*, 517–525.

Durlach, N. I., & Braida, L. D. (1969). Intensity perception: I. Preliminary theory of intensity resolution. *Journal of the Acoustical Society of America, 46*, 372–383.

Ekman, G. (1956a). Discriminal sensitivity on the subjective continuum. *Acta Psychologica, 12*, 233–243.

Ekman, G. (1956b). Subjective power functions and the method of fractionation. *Reports from the Psychological Laboratory, The University of Stockholm*, No. 34.

Ekman, G. (1959). Weber's law and related functions. *Journal of Psychology, 47*, 343–352.

Ekman, G., & Bratfish, O. (1965). Subjective distance and emotional involvement: A psychological mechanism. *Acta Psychologica, 24*, 430–437.

Ekman, G., Eisler, H., & Künnapas, T. (1960a). Brightness of monochromatic light as measured by the method of magnitude production. *Acta Psychologica, 17*, 392–397.

Ekman, G., Eisler, H., & Künnapas, T. (1960b). Brightness scales for monochromatic light. *Scandinavian Journal of Psychology, 1*, 41–48.

Ekman, G., Frankenhaeuser, M., Levander, S., & Mellis, I. (1964). Scales of unpleasantness of electrical stimulation. *Scandinavian Journal of Psychology, 68*, 530–534.

Ekman, G., Fröberg, J., & Frankenhaeuser, M. (1968). Temporal integration of perceptual response to supraliminal electrical stimulation. *Scandinavian Journal of Psychology, 9*, 83–88.

Ekman, G., & Künnapas, T. M. (1957). Subjective dispersion and the Weber fraction. *Reports from the Psychological Laboratory, the University of Stockholm*, No. 41.

Ekman, G., & Sjöberg, L. (1965). Scaling. In P. R. Farnsworth, O. McNemar, & Q. McNemar (Eds.), *Annual review of psychology* (Vol. 16, pp. 451–474).

Eisler, H. (1962). On the problem of category scales in psychophysics. *Scandinavian Journal of Psychology, 3*, 81–87.

Engel, A. K., Konig, P., Kreiter, A. K., Schillen, T. B., & Singer, W. (1992). Temporal coding in the visual cortex: New vistas on integration in the nervous system. *TINS, 155*, 218–226.

Engen, T. (1972). Psychophysics. I. Discrimination and detection. In J. W. Kling & L. A. Riggs (Ed.), *Woodworth and Schlosberg's experimental psychology: Vol. 1. Sensation and perception* (pp. 11–46). New York: Holt, Rinehart & Winston.

Engen, T., & Levy, N. (1955). The influrence of standards on psychophysical judgments. *Perceptual and Motor Skills*, *5*, 193–197.

Engen, T., & Pfaffman, C. (1959). Absolute judgments of odor intensity. *Journal of Experimental Psychology*, *58*, 23–26.

Engen, T., & Pfaffman, C. (1960). Absolute judgments of odor quality. *Journal of Experimental Psychology*, *59*, 214–219.

Engen, T., & Ross, B. M. (1966). Effect of reference number on magnitude estimation. *Perception and Psychophysics*, *1*, 74–76.

Epstein, W. (1963). Attitudes of judgment and the size-distance invariance hypothesis. *Journal of Experimental Psychology*, *66*, 78–83.

Evans, E. F. (1981). The dynamic range problem: Place and time coding at the level of cochlear nerve and nucleus. In J. Syka & L. Aitkin (Eds.), *Neuronal mechanisms of hearing* (pp. 69–85). New York: Plenum.

Evans, E. F. (1989). Functions of the auditory system. In H. B. Barlow & J. D. Mollon (Eds.), *The senses* (pp. 307–332). Cambridge, England: Cambridge University Press.

Falmagne, J. C. (1985). *Elements of psychophysical theory*. New York: Oxford University Press.

Falmagne, J. C. (1986). Psychophysical measurement and theory. In K. R. Boff, L. Kaufman, & J. P. Thomas (Eds.), *Handbook of perception and human performance: Vol. 1. Sensory processes and perception* (pp. 1–66). New York: Wiley.

Fechner, G. T. (1966). *Elements of psychophysics*. (Vol. 1; H. E. Adler, Trans.). New York: Holt, Rinehart & Winston. (Original work published 1860)

Feldman, J., & Baird, J. C. (1971). Magnitude estimation of multidimensional stimuli. *Perception and Psychophysics*, *10*, 418–422.

Feynman, R. P., Leighton, R. B., & Sands, M. (1963). *The Feynman lectures on physics: Mainly mechanics, radiation, and heat*. Reading, MA: Addison-Wesley.

Fidell, S. (1970). Sensory function in multimodal signal detection. *Journal of the Acoustical Society of America*, *47*, 1009–1015.

Fletcher, H., & Munson, W. A. (1933). Loudness, its definition, measurement and calculation. *Journal of the Acoustical Society of America*, *5*, 82–108.

Foley, H. J., Cross, D. V., Foley, M. A., & Reeder, R. (1983). Stimulus range, number of categories, and the "virtual" exponent. *Perception and Psychophysics*, *34*, 505–512.

Fraisse, P. (1948). Les erreurs constantes dans la reproduction de courts intervalles temporels [Constant errors in the reproduction of short time intervals]. *Archives de Psychologie*, *32*, 161–176.

Frank, M. (1973). An analysis of hamster afferent taste nerve response functions. *Journal of General Physiology*, *61*, 588–618.

Frank, M. (1975). Response patterns of rat glossopharyngeal taste neurons. In D. A. Denton & J. P. Coghlan (Eds.), *Olfaction and taste* (Vol. 5, pp. 59–69). New York: Academic Press.

Frijters, J.E.R., & De Graaf, C. (1989). Modeling taste mixture interactions in equiratio mixtures. In D. G. Laing, W. S. Cain, R. L. McBride, & B. W. Ache (Eds.), *Perception of complex smells and tastes* (pp. 245–264). New York: Academic Press.

Frijters, J.E.R., & Oude Ophuis, P.A.M. (1983). The construction and prediction of psychophysical power functions for the sweetness of equiratio sugar mixtures. *Perception*, *12*, 753–767.

Garriga-Trillo, A. (1995). Thurstone's and Stevens' scaling models: Toward a unifying paradigm. In C.-A. Possamaï (Ed.), *Fechner day 95*. (pp. 195–200). Marseille: International Society for Psychophysics.

Garner, W. R. (1962). *Uncertainty and structure as psychological concepts*. New York: Wiley.

Garner, W. R. (1974). *The processing of information and structure*. Potomac, Md: Lawrence Erlbaum Associates.

Geldard, F. A. (1972). *The human senses* (2nd ed.). New York: Wiley.

Gescheider, G. A. (1985). *Psychophysics: Method, theory, and application* (2nd ed.). Hillsdale, NJ: Lawrence Erlbaum Associates.

Gescheider, G. A. (1988). Psychophysical scaling. *Annual Review of Psychology, 39*, 169–200.

Getchell, T. V. (1986). Functional properties of vertebrate olfactory receptor neurons. *Physiological Reviews, 66*, 772–818.

Gibson, J. J. (1950). *The perception of the visual world*. Boston: Houghton Mifflin.

Gibson, J. J. (1966). *The senses considered as perceptual systems*. Boston: Houghton Mifflin.

Gibson, J. J. (1979). *The ecological approach to visual perception*. Boston: Houghton Mifflin.

Gibson, R. H., & Tomko, D. L. (1972). The relation between category and magnitude estimates of tactile intensity. *Perception and Psychophysics, 12*, 135–138.

Gillan, D. G. (1983). Taste-taste, odor-odor, and taste-odor mixtures: Greater suppression within than between modalities. *Perception and Psychophysics, 33*, 183–185.

Graf, V., Baird, J. C., & Glesman, G. (1974). An empirical test of two psychophysical models. *Acta Psychologica, 38*, 59–72.

Gravetter, F., & Lockhead, G. R. (1973). Criterial range as a frame of reference for stimulus judgment. *Psychological Review, 80*, 203–216.

Green, D. M. (1958). Detection of multiple component signals in noise. *Journal of the Acoustical Society of America, 30*, 904–911.

Green, D. M. (1976). *An introduction to hearing*. Hillsdale, NJ: Lawrence Erlbaum Associates.

Green, D. M. (1988). *Profile analysis: Auditory intensity discrimination*. New York: Oxford University Press.

Green, D. M. (1995). Weber's law in auditory intensity discrimination. In C-A Possamaï (Ed.), *Proceedings of the 11th Annual Meeting of the International Society for Psychophysics* (pp. 1–20).Marseille: International Society for Psychophysics.

Green, D. M., Dai, H., & Saberi, K. (1995). Shape discrimination of spectra with various bandwidths. In *Advances in hearing research*. Singapore: World Scientific Publishers.

Green, D. M., Kidd, G. Jr., & Picardi, M. C. (1983). Successive versus simultaneous comparison in auditory intensity discrimination. *Journal of the Acoustical Society of America, 73*, 639–643.

Green, D. M., & Luce, R. D. (1971). Detection of auditory signals presented at random times: III. *Perception and Psychophysics, 9*, 257–268.

Green, D. M., Luce, R. D., & Duncan, J. E. (1977). Variability and sequential effects in magnitude production and estimation of auditory intensity. *Perception and Psychophysics, 22*, 450–456.

Green, D. M., Mason, C. R., & Kidd, G., Jr. (1984). Profile analysis: Critical bands and duration. *Journal of the Acoustical Society of America, 75*, 1163–1167.

Green, D. M. & Swets, J. A. (1974). *Signal detection theory and psychophysics*. Huntington, NY: Krieger. (Original work published 1966)

Guilford, J. P. (1932). A generalized psychophysical law. *Psychological Review, 39*, 73–85.

Gulick, W. L., Gescheider, G. A., & Frisina, R. D. (1989). *Hearing: Physiological acoustics, neural coding, and psychoacoustics*. New York: Oxford University Press.

Gulick, W. L., & Lawson, R. B. (1976). *Human stereopsis: A psychophysical approach*. New York: Oxford University Press.

Hake, H. W., & Garner, W. R. (1951). The effect of presenting various numbers of discrete steps on scale reading accuracy. *Journal of Experimental Psychology, 42*, 358–366.

Hanna, T. E., von Gierke, S. M., & Green, D. M. (1986). Detection and intensity discrimination of a sinusoid. *Journal of the Acoustical Society of America, 80*, 1335–1340.

Harder, K., & Baird, J. C. (1995). *Psychophysical analysis of imagery*. Unpublished manuscript, Dartmouth College, Hanover, NH.

Harper, R., & Stevens, S. S. (1948). A psychological scale of weight and a formula for its derivation. *American Journal of Psychology, 61*, 343–351.

Harris, J. D. (1963). Loudness discrimination. *Journal of Speech Hearing Disorders Monograph Supplement, 11*, 1–63.

Hartline, H. K., & Graham, C. H. (1932). Nerve impulses from single receptors in the eye. *Journal of Cellular and Comparative Physiology, 1*, 277–295.

Haubensak, G. (1992a). The consistency model: A process model for absolute judgments. *Journal of Experimental Psychology: Human Perception and Performance, 18*, 303–309.

Haubensak, G. (1992b). The consistency model: A reply to Parducci. *Journal of Experimental Psychology: Human Perception and Performance, 18*, 314–315.

Hellman, R. P., & Meiselman, C. H. (1990). Loudness relations for individuals and groups in normal and impaired hearing. *Journal of the Acoustical Society of America, 88*, 2596–2606.

Hellman, R. P., & Zwislocki, J. J. (1968). Loudness determination at low sound frequencies. *Journal of the Acoustical Society of America 43*, 60–64.

Helm, C. E., Messick, S., & Tucker, L. R. (1961). Psychological models for relating discrimination and magnitude estimation scales. *Psychological Review, 68*, 167–177.

Helson, H. (1964). *Adaptation-level theory.* New York: Harper & Row.

Hellström, Å. (1977). Time errors are perceptual. An experimental investigation of duration and a quantitative successive-comparison model. *Psychological Research, 39*, 345–388.

Hellström, Å. (1978). Factors producing and factors not producing time errors: An experiment with loudness comparisons. *Perception and Psychophysics, 23*, 433–444.

Hellström, Å. (1979). Time errors and differential sensation weighting. *Journal of Experimental Psychology: Human Perception and Performance, 5*, 460–477.

Hellström, Å. (1985). The time-order error and its relatives: Mirrors of cognitive processes in comparing. *Psychological Bulletin, 97*, 35–61.

Henning, H. (1916). Die Qualitätenreihe des Geschmacks. [Range of taste qualities]. *Zeitschrift für Psychologie, 74*, 203–219.

Holland, M. K., & Lockhead, G. R. (1968). Sequential effects in absolute judgments of loudness. *Perception and Psychophysics, 3*, 409–414.

Hollingworth, H. L. (1910). The central tendency of judgment. *Journal of Philosophy, Psychology, and Scientific Methods, 7*, 461–469.

Hornung, D. E., & Enns, M. P. (1986). The contributions of smell and taste to overall intensity: A model. *Perception and Psychophysics, 39*, 385–391.

Hovland, C. I. (1938). A note on Guilford's generalized psychophysical law. *Psychological Review, 35*, 430–434.

Hubbard, T. L. (1991). *Temporal aspects of memory psychophysics.* Unpublished doctoral dissertation, Dartmouth College, Hanover, NH.

Hughes, H. C., Nozawa, G., & Le, W. (1993). *Bimodal interactions between near-threshold signals: Detection and identification.* Paper presented at the Annual Meeting of the Association for Research in Vision and Opthalmology.

Hughes, H. C., Reuter-Lorenz, P. A., Nozawa, G., & Fendrich, R. (1994). Visual-auditory interactions in sensorimotor processing: Saccades versus manual responses. *Journal of Experimental Psychology: Human Perception and Performance, 20*, 131–153.

Huttenlocher, J., Hedges, L. U., & Duncan, S. (1991). Categories and particulars: Prototype effects in estimating spatial location. *Psychological Review, 98*, 352–376.

Jay, M. F., & Sparks, D. L. (1987). Sensorimotor integration in the primate superior colloculus: II. Coordinates of auditory signals. *Journal of Neurophysiology, 57*, 35–55.

Jesteadt, W., Luce, R. D., & Green, D. M. (1977). Sequential effects in judgments of loudness. *Journal of Experimental Psychology, 3*, 92–104.

Jesteadt, W., Wier, C. C., & Green, D. M. (1977). Intensity discrimination as a function of frequency and sensation level. *Journal of the Acoustical Society of America, 61*, 169–178.

Johnson, N. L. & Kotz, S. (1970). *Continuous univariate distributions–1: Distributions in statistics.* New York: Wiley.

Judd, D. B. (1951). Basic correlates of the visual stimulus. In S. S. Stevens (Ed.), *Handbook of experimental psychology* (pp. 811–867). New York: Wiley.

Kauer, J. S. (1974). Response patterns of amphibian olfactory bulb neurones to odour stimulation. *Journal of Physiology, 243*, 695–715.

Keppel, G., & Underwood, B. J. (1962). Proactive inhibition in short-term retention of single items. *Journal of Verbal Learning and Verbal Behavior, 1*, 153–161.

Kerst, S. M., & Howard, J. H. (1978). Memory psychophysics for visual area and length. *Memory and Cognition, 6*, 327–335.

Kiang, N. Y.-S. (1965). *Discharge patterns of single fibers in the cat's auditory nerve.* (Research Monograph 35). Cambridge, MA: MIT Press.

Kiesow, E. (1926). Über die Vergleichung linearer Strecken und ihre Beziehung zum Weberschen Gesetze [On the comparison of line lengths and its significance for Weber's Law]. *Archive für die gesamte Psychologie, 56*, 421–451.

Kingston, J., & Macmillan, N. A. (1995). Integrality of nasalization and F1 in vowels in isolation and before oral and nasal consonants: A detection-theoretic application of the Garner paradigm. *Journal of the Acoustical Society of America, 97*, 1261–1285.

Koffka, K. (1935). *Principles of gestalt psychology.* New York: Harcourt, Brace.

Kohfeld, D. L., Santee, J. L., & Wallace, N. D. (1981a). Loudness and reaction time: I. *Perception and Psychophysics, 29*, 535–549.

Kohfeld, D. L., Santee, J. L., & Wallace, N. D. (1981b). Loudness and reaction time: II. Identification of detection components at different intensities and frequencies. *Perception and Psychophysics, 29*, 550–562.

Köhler, W. (1923). Zur Analyse des Sukzessivvergleichs und der Zeitfehler [On the analysis of successive comparisons and time-order errors]. *Psychologische Forschung, 4*, 115–175.

Köhler, W. (1927). *The mentality of apes.* New York: Harcourt, Brace.

König, A., & Brodhun, E. (1889). Experimentelle Untersuchungen über die psychophysische Fundamentalformel in Bezug auf den Gesichtsinn [Experimental investigation of the psychophysical relation in respect to vision]. *Akademie der Wissenschaften, Berlin Sitzungsberichte, 2*, 641–644.

Krantz, D. H. (1972). A theory of magnitude estimation and cross-modality matching. *Journal of Mathematical Psychology, 9*, 168–199.

Krueger, L. E. (1991). Toward a unified psychophysical law and beyond. In S. J. Bolanowski, Jr. & G. A. Gescheider (Eds.), *Ratio scaling of psychological magnitude* (pp. 101–111). Hillsdale, NJ: Lawrence Erlbaum Associates.

Künnapas, T. M. (1960). Scales for subjective distance. *Scandinavian Journal of Psychology, 1*, 187–192.

Lacouture, Y. (1994). *Bow, range and sequential effects in absolute identification: A response time analysis.* Unpublished manuscript, Université Laval, Québec.

Lacouture, Y., & Marley, A.A.J. (1991). A connectionist model of choice and reaction time in absolute identification. *Connection Science, 3*, 401–433.

Laffort, P. (1989). Models for describing intensity interactions in odor mixtures: a reappraisal. In D. G. Laing, W. S. Cain, R. L. McBride, & B. W. Ache (Eds.), *Perception of complex smells and tastes* (pp. 205–223). New York: Academic Press.

Laing, D. G., Panhuber, H., Willcox, M. E., & Pittman, E. A. (1984). Quality and intensity of binary odor mixtures. *Physiology and Behavior, 33*, 309–319.

Laming, D. (1984). The relativity of "absolute" judgements. *British Journal of Mathematical and Statistical Psychology, 37*, 152–183.

Laming, D. (1986). *Sensory analysis.* New York: Academic Press.

Laming, D. (1989). Experimental evidence for Fechner's and Stevens's laws. *Behavioral and Brain Sciences, 12*, 277–280.

Laming, D. (1991). Reconciling Fechner and Stevens? *Behavioral and Brain Sciences, 14*, 188–191.

Larsen, R. J., & Marx, M. L. (1981). *An introduction to mathematical statistics and its applications.* Englewood Cliffs, NJ: Prentice-Hall.

Lawless, H. T. (1977). The pleasantness of mixtures in taste and olfaction. *Sensory Processes, 1*, 227–237.

LeGrand, Y. (1957). *Light, colour and vision.* New York: Wiley.

Leuba, J. H. (1892). A new instrument for Weber's law; with indications of a law of sense memory. *American Journal of Psychology, 5*, 370–384.

Link, S. W. (1992). *The wave theory of difference and similarity.* Hillsdale, NJ: Lawrence Erlbaum Associates.

Lockhead, G. R. (1966). Effects of dimensional redundancy on visual discrimination. *Journal of Experimental Psychology, 72*, 95–104.

Lockhead, G. R. (1984). Sequential predictors of choice in psychophysical tasks. In S. Kornblum, & J. Requin (Eds.), *Preparatory states and processes* (p. 27–47). Hillsdale, NJ: Lawrence Erlbaum Associates.

Lockhead, G. R. (1992). Psychophysical scaling: Judgments of attributes or objects? *Behavioral and Brain Sciences, 15*, 543–601.

Lockhead, G. R., & King, M. C. (1983). A memory model of sequential effects in scaling tasks. *Journal of Experimental Psychology: Human Perception and Performance, 9*, 461–473.

Loomis, J. M., Da Silva, J. A., & Fujita, N. (1992). Visual space perception and visually directed action. *Journal of Experimental Psychology: Human Perception and Performance, 18*, 906–921.

Luce, R. D. (1960). The theory of selective information and some of its behavioral applications. In R. D. Luce (Ed.), *Developments in mathematical psychology* (pp. 5–119). Glencoe, Il.: The Free Press.

Luce, R. D. (1977). The choice axiom after twenty years. *Journal of Mathematical Psychology, 15*, 215–233.

Luce, R. D. (1986). *Response times: Their role in inferring elementary mental organization.* New York: Oxford University Press.

Luce, R. D. (1990). "On the possible psychophysical laws" revisited: Remarks on cross-modal matching. *Psychological Review, 97*, 66–77.

Luce, R. D. (1993). *Sound and hearing: A conceptual introduction.* Hillsdale, NJ: Lawrence Erlbaum Associates.

Luce, R. D. (1994). Thurstone and sensory scaling. *Psychological Review, 101*, 271–277.

Luce, R. D., Baird, J. C., Green, D. M., & Smith, A. F. (1980). Two classes of models for magnitude estimation. *Journal of Mathematical Psychology, 22*, 121–148.

Luce, R. D., & Edwards, W. (1958). The derivation of subjective scales from just noticeable differences. *Psychological Review, 65*, 222–237.

Luce, R. D., & Green, D. M. (1972). A neural timing theory for response times and the psychophysics of intensity. *Psychological Review, 79*, 14–57.

Luce, R. D., & Green, D. M. (1974). The response ratio hypothesis for magnitude estimation. *Journal of Mathematical Psychology, 11*, 1–14.

Luce, R. D., Green, D. M., & Weber, D. L. (1976). Attention bands in absolute identification. *Perception and Psychophysics, 20*, 49–54.

Luce, R. D., Krantz, D. H., Suppes, P., & Tversky, A. (1990). *Foundations of measurement: Vol. 3. Representation, axiomatization, and invariance.* New York: Academic Press.

Luce, R. D., & Krumhansl, C. L. (1988). Measurement, scaling, and psychophysics. In R. C. Atkinson, R. J. Herrnstein, G. Lindzey, & R. D. Luce (Eds.), *Stevens' handbook of experimental psychology: Vol. 1. Perception and motivation.* (2nd ed., pp. 3–74). New York: Wiley.

Luce, R. D., & Nosofsky, R. M. (1984). Attention, stimulus range, and identification of loudness. In S. Kornblum, & J. Requin, (Eds.), *Preparatory states and processes* (pp. 3–25). Hillsdale, NJ: Lawrence Erlbaum Associates.

Luce, R. D., Nosofsky, R. M., Green, D. M., & Smith, A. F. (1982). The bow and sequential effects in absolute identification. *Perception and Psychophysics, 32*, 397–408.

Macmillan, N., & Creelman, C. D. (1991). *Detection theory: A user's guide.* New York: Cambridge University Press.

Macmillan, N., & Kingston, J. (1995). Integrality, correspondence, and configurality represent different degrees of perceptual interaction, not different types. In C–A Possamaï (Ed.), *Fechner day 95* (pp. 243–248). Marseille: International Society for Psychophysics.

Mansfield, R.J.W. (1973). Latency functions in human vision. *Vision Research, 13*, 2219–2234.

Marks, L. E. (1968). Stimulus-range, number of categories, and form of the category scale. *American Journal of Psychology, 81*, 467–479.

Marks, L. E. (1974a). On scales of sensation: Prolegomena to any future psychophysics that will come forth as science. *Perception and Psychophysics, 16*, 358–376.

Marks, L. E. (1974b). *Sensory processes: The new psychophysics.* New York: Academic Press.

Marks, L. E. (1988). Magnitude estimation and sensory matching. *Perception and Psychophysics, 43*, 511–525.

Marks, L. E. (1992). "What thin partititions sense from thought divide": Toward a new cognitive psychophysics. In D. Algom (Ed.), *Psychophysical approaches to cognition* (pp. 115–186). Amsterdam: North-Holland & Elsevier.

Marks, L. E. (1993). Contextual processing of multidimensional and unidimensional auditory stimuli. *Journal of Experimental Psychology: Human Perception and Performance, 19*, 227–249.

Marks, L. E., & Algom, D. (1996). Psychophysical scaling. (In M. H. Birnbaum (ed.), *Handbook of perception and cognition: Vol. 3. Measurement, judgment, and decision.* San Diego: Academic Press. (in press)

Marks, L. E., & Warner, E. (1991). The slippery context effect and critical bands. *Journal of Experimental Psychology: Human Perception and Performance, 17*, 986–996.

Marley, A.A.J., & Cook, V. T. (1984). A fixed rehearsal capacity interpretation of limits on absolute identification performance. *British Journal of Mathematical and Statistical Psychology, 30*, 339–390.

Marley, A.A.J., & Cook, V. T. (1986). A limited capacity rehearsal model for psychophysical judgments applied to magnitude estimation. *Journal of Mathematical Psychology, 37*, 136–151.

Mashhour, M., & Hosman, J. (1968). On Stevens' "psychophysical law": A validation study. *Perception and Psychophysics, 3*, 367–375.

McBride, R. L. (1986). Sweetness of binary mixtures of sucrose, fructose, and glucose. *Journal of Experimental Psychology: Human Perception and Performance, 12*, 584–591.

McBride, R. L. (1988). Taste reception of binary sugar mixtures: psychophysical comparison of two models. *Perception and Psychophysics, 44*, 167–171.

McBride, R. L. (1989). Three models for taste mixtures. In D. G. Laing, W. S. Cain, R. L. McBride & B. W. Ache (Eds.), *Perception of complex smells and tastes* (pp. 265–282). Sydney: Academic Press.

McBride, R. L., & Anderson, N. H. (1990). Integration psychophysics. In R. L. McBride & H.J.H. MacFie (Eds.), *Psychological basis of sensory evaluation* (pp. 93–115). London: Elsevier.

McBride, R. L., & Johnson, R. L. (1987). Perception of sugar-acid mixtures in lemon juice drink. *International Journal of Food Science and Technology, 22*, 399–408.

McGill, W. J. (1961). Loudness and reaction time. *Acta Psychologica, 19*, 193–199.

McGill, W. J., & Goldberg, J. P. (1968). A study of the near-miss involving Weber's law and pure-tone intensity discrimination. *Perception and Psychophysics, 4*, 105–109.

Melara, R. D. (1992). The concept of perceptual similarity: From psychophysics to cognitive psychology. In D. Algom (Ed.), *Psychophysical approaches to cognition* (pp. 303–388). Amsterdam: North-Holland & Elsevier.

Mellers, B. A. (1983). Evidence against "absolute" scaling. *Perception and Psychophysics, 33*, 523–526.

Meredith, M. A., & Stein, B. E. (1983). Interactions among converging sensory inputs in the superior colliculus. *Science*, *221*, 389–391.

Meredith, M. A., & Stein, B. E. (1986). Spatial factors determine the activity of multisensory neurons in cat superior colliculus. *Brain Research*, *365*, 350–354.

Michaels, C. F., & Carello, C. (1981). *Direct perception*. Englewood Cliffs, NJ: Prentice-Hall.

Miller, G. A. (1947). Sensitivity to changes in the intensity of white noise and its relation to loudness and masking. *Journal of the Acoustical Society of America*, *19*, 609–619.

Miller, G. A. (1956). The magical number seven, plus or minus two: Some limits on capacity for processing information. *Psychological Review*, *63*, 81–97.

Montgomery, H. (1975). Direct estimation: Effect of methodological factors on scale type. *Scandinavian Journal of Psychology*, *16*, 19–29.

Mori, S. (1988). Two response processes in a guessing task. *Perception and Psychophysics*, 44, 50–58.

Mori, S. (1989). A limited-capacity response process in absolute identification. *Perception and Psychophysics*, 46, 167–173.

Moyer, R. S., Bradley, D. R., Sorenson, M. H., Whiting, J. C., & Mansfield, D. F. (1978). Psychophysical functions of perceived and remembered size. *Science*, *200*, 330–332.

Murdoch, D. (1987). *Niels Bohr's philosophy of physics*. Cambridge, England: Cambridge University Press.

Murphy, C., & Cain, W. S. (1980). Taste and olfaction: Independence vs. interaction. *Physiology & Behavior*, 24, 601–605.

Murphy, C., Cain, W. S., & Bartoshuk, L. M. (1977). Mutual action of taste and olfaction. *Sensory Processes*, *1*, 204–211.

Murray, D. J. (1992). A perspective for viewing the history of psychophysics. *Behavioral and Brain Sciences*, *16*, 115–137.

Myers, A. K. (1982). Psychophysical scaling and scales of physical stimulus measurement. *Psychological Bulletin*, *92*, 203–214.

Naka, K.-I., & Rushton, W. A. (1966). S-potentials from colour units in the retina of fish (Cryinidae). *Journal of Physiology (London)*, *185*, 536–555.

Narens, L., & Mausfeld, R. (1992). On the relationship of the psychological and the physical in psychophysics. *Psychological Review*, *99*, 467–479.

Needham, J. G. (1935). The effect of the time interval upon the time error at different intensive levels. *Journal of Experimental Psychology*, *18*, 539–543.

Noma, E., & Baird, J. C. (1975). Psychophysical study of numbers: II. Theoretical models of number generation. *Psychological Research*, *38*, 81–95.

Nordin, S. (1994). Context effects, reliability, and internal consistency of intermodal joint scaling. *Perception and Psychophysics*, *55*, 180–189.

Norwich, K. H. (1993). *Information, sensation, and perception*. New York: Academic Press.

Nosofsky, R. M. (1983a). Information integration and the identification of stimulus noise in absolute judgment. *Journal of Experimental Psychology: Human perception and Performance*, *9*, 299–309.

Nosofsky, R. M. (1983b). Shifts of attention in the identification of intensity. *Perception and Psychophysics*, *33*, 103–112.

Olsson, M. J. (1994). An interaction model for odor quality and intensity. *Perception and Psychophysics*, *55*, 363–372.

Olsson, M. J., Harder, K., & Baird, J. C. (1993). What Ekman really said. *Behavioral and Brain Sciences*, *16*, 157–158.

Ono, H. (1967). Difference threshold for stimulus length under simultaneous and nonsimultaneous viewing conditions. *Perception and Psychophysics*, *2*, 201–207.

Parducci, A. (1965). Category judgment: A range-frequency model. *Psychological Review*, *72*, 407–418.

Parducci, A. (1982). Category ratings: Still more contextual effects. In B. Wegener (Ed.), *Social attitudes and psychophysical measurement* (pp. 262–282). Hillsdale, NJ: Lawrence Erlbaum Associates.

Parducci, A. (1992). Comment on Haubensak's associative theory of judgment. *Journal of Experimental Psychology: Human Perception and Performance, 18,* 310–313.

Parducci, A., Calfee, R. C., Marshall, L. M., & Davidson, L. P. (1960). Context effects in judgment: Adaptation level as a function of the mean, midpoint, and median of the stimuli. *Journal of Experimental Psychology, 60,* 65–77.

Parducci, A., & Wedell, D. H. (1986). The category effect with rating scales: Number of categories, number of stimuli, and method of presentation. *Journal of Experimental Psychology: Human Perception and Performance, 12,* 496–516.

Peck, C. K. (1987). Visual-auditory interactions in cat superior colliculus: Their role in control of gaze. *Brain Research, 420,* 162–166.

Penner, M. J., Leshowitz, B., Cudahy, E., & Richard, G. (1974). Intensity discrimination for pulsed sinusoids of various frequencies. *Perception and Psychophysics, 15,* 568–570.

Peterson, L. R., & Peterson, M. J. (1959). Sort-term retention of individual verbal items. *Journal of Experimental Psychology, 58,* 193–198.

Pickles, J. O. (1988). *An introduction to the physiology of hearing.* New York: Academic Press.

Piéron, H. (1914). Recherches sur les lois de variation des temps de latence sensorielle en fonction des intensités excitatrices [Research on the laws of variation of sensory reaction time as a function of stimulus intensity]. *L'Année Psychologique, 20,* 17–96.

Piéron, H. (1920). Nouvelles recherches sur l'analyse du temps de latence sensorialle et sur la loi qui relie de temp a l'intensité d'excitation. [New research on the analysis of sensory reaction time and on the law relating time to stimulus intensity]. *L'Année Psychologique, 22,* 58–142.

Piéron, H. (1952). *The sensations: Their functions, processes, and mechanisms.* (M. H. Pirenne & B. C. Abbot, Trans.) New Haven, Ct: Yale University Press.

Pollack, I. (1952). The information of elementary auditory displays. *Journal of the Acoustical Society of America, 24,* 745–749.

Pollack, I., & Ficks, L. (1954). Information of elementary multidimensional auditory displays. *Journal of the Acoustical Society of America, 26,* 155–158.

Potts, B. C. (1991). *The horizontal-vertical illusion: A confluence of configural, contextual, and framing factors.* Unpublished doctoral dissertation, Yale University.

Poulton, E. C. (1967). Population norms of top sensory magnitudes and S. S. Stevens' exponents. *Perception and Psychophysics, 2,* 312–316.

Poulton, E. C. (1989). *Bias in quantifying judgments.* Hillsdale, NJ: Lawrence Erlbaum Associates.

Pugh, E. N., Jr. (1988). Vision: Physics and retinal physiology. In R. C. Atkinson, R. J. Herrnstein, G. Lindzey, & R. D. Luce (Eds.) *Stevens' handbook of experimental psychology: Vol 1. Perception and motivation* (2nd ed., pp. 75–163). New York: Wiley.

Raab, D. H., Osman, E., & Rich, E. (1963). Effects of waveform correlation and signal duration on detection of noise bursts in continuous noise. *Journal of the Acoustical Society of America, 35,* 1942–1946.

Rankin, K. M., & Marks, L. E. (1991). Differential context effects in taste perception. *Chemical Senses, 16,* 617–629.

Ratcliff, R. (1993). Methods for dealing with reaction time outliers. *Psychological Bulletin, 114,* 510–532.

Restle, F. (1961). *The psychology of judgment and choice: A theoretical essay.* New York: Wiley.

Restle, F. (1970). Moon illusion explained on the basis of relative size. *Science. 167,* 1092–1096.

Riesz, R. R. (1928). Differential intensity sensitivity of the ear for pure tones. *Physical Review, 31,* 867–875.

Robinson, E. S., & Robinson, F. R. (1929). A simple series of abilities. *American Journal of Psychology, 41,* 33–53.

Robinson, G. H. (1976). Biasing power law exponents by magnitude estimation instructions. *Perception and Psychophysics*, *19*, 80–84.

Ross, B. M., & Engen, T. (1959). Effects of round number preferences in a guessing task. *Journal of Experimental Psychology*, *58*, 462–468.

Rule, S. J., Curtis, D. W., & Markley, R. P. (1970). Input and output transformations from magnitude estimation. *Journal of Experimental Psychology*, 86, 343–349.

Sachs, M. B., & Abbas, P. J. (1974). Rate versus level functions for auditory-nerve fibers in cats: Tone burst stimuli. *Journal of the Acoustical Society of America*, *56*, 1835–1847.

Schacknow, P. N., & Raab, D. H. (1973). Intensity descimination of tone bursts and the form of the Weber function, *Perception and Psychophysics*, *14*, 449–450.

Scharf, B., & Buus, S. (1986). Audition I: Stimulus, physiology, thresholds. In K. R. Boff, L. Kaufman, & J. P. Thomas (Eds.), *Handbook of perception and human performance: Vol. I. Sensory processes and perception*. New York: Wiley.

Schiffman, S. S., & Erickson, R. P. (1971). A psychophysical model for gustatory quality. *Physiology and Behavior*, *7*, 617–633.

Schiffman, S. S., & Erickson, R. P. (1980). The issue of primary tastes versus a taste continuum. *Neuroscience & Biobehavioral Reviews*, *4*, 109–117.

Schneider, B., & Parker, S. (1990). Does stimulus context affect loudness or only loudness judgments? *Perception and Psychophysics*, *48*, 409–418.

Schneider, B., & Parker, S. (1994). Stimulus context effects and the psychophysical law: Is coexistence possible? In L. M. Ward (Ed.), *Fechner day 94* International Society for Psychophysics, (pp. 71–76). Vancouver.

Schneider, B., Wright, A. A., Edelheit, W., Hock, P., & Humphrey, C. (1972). Equal loudness contours derived from sensory magnitude judgments. *Journal of the Acoustical Society of America*, *51*, 1951–1959.

Sedgwick, H. A. (1986). Space perception. In K. R. Boff, L. Kaufman, & J. P. Thomas (Eds.), *Handbook of perception and human performance* (*Vol. 1*, pp. 21-1–21-57). New York: Wiley.

Senders, V. L. (1958). *Measurement and statistics*. New York: Oxford.

Shaw, R., & Bransford, J. (1977). (Eds.). *James J. Gibon's strategy for perceiving: Ask not what's inside your head, but what your head's inside of*. Hillsdale, NJ: Lawrence Erlbaum Associates.

Shepard, R. N. (1978). On the status of "direct" psychophysical measurement. In C. W. Savage (Ed.), *Minnesota studies in the philosophy of science* (Vol. 9, pp. 441–490). Minneapolis: University of Minnesota Press.

Shepard, R. N. (1991). Integrality versus separability of stimulus dimensions: From an early convergence of evidence to a proposed theoretical basis. In G. R. Lockhead & J. R. Pomerantz (Eds.), *The perception of structure* (pp. 53–71). Washington, DC: American Psychological Association.

Shepherd, G. M. (1983). *Neurobiology*. New York: Oxford University Press.

Shepherd, G. M. (1990). Membrane properties and neurotransmitter actions. In G. M. Shepherd (Ed.), *The synaptic organization of the brain* (3rd ed. pp. 32–66). New York: Oxford University Press.

Sherrick, C. E., & Cholewiak, R. W. (1986). Cutaneous sensitivity. In K. R. Boff, L. Kaufman, & J. P. Thomas (Eds.), *Handbook of perception and human performance* (pp. 12.1–12.58). New York: Wiley.

Shiffrin, R. M., & Nosofsky, R. M. (1994). Seven plus or minus two: A commentary on capacity limitations. *Psychological Review*, *101*, 357–361.

Sicard, G., & Holley, A. (1984). Receptor cell responses to odorants: Similarities and differences among odorants. *Brain Research*, *292*, 284–296.

Siegel, J. A., & Siegel, W. (1972). Absolute judgment and paired-associate learning: Kissing cousins or identical twins? *Psychological Review*, *79*, 300–316.

Siegel, W. (1972). Memory effects in the method of absolute judgment. *Journal of Experimental Psychology*, *94*, 121–131.

Smith, R. L. (1988). Encoding of sound intensity by auditory neurons. In G. M. Edelman, W. E. Gall, & W. M. Cowan (Eds.), *Auditory function: Neurobiological bases of hearing* (pp. 243–274). New York: Wiley.

Spiegel, M. F., Picardi, M. C., & Green, D. M. (1981). Signal and masker uncertainty in intensity discrimination. *Journal of the Acoustical Society of America*, *70*, 1015–1019.

Staddon, J.E.R., King, M., & Lockhead, G. R. (1980). On sequential effects in absolute judgment experiments. *Journal of Experimental Psychology: Human Perception and Performance*, *6*, 290–301.

Stein, B. E., & Meredith, M. A. (1993). *The merging of the senses*. Cambridge, MA: MIT Press.

Sternbach, R. A., & Tursky, B. (1964). On the psychophysical power function in electric shock. *Psychonomic Science*, *1*, 217–218.

Stevens, J. C. (1958). Stimulus spacing and the judgment of loudness. *Journal of Experimental Psychology*, *56*, 246–250.

Stevens, J. C. (1974). Families of converging power functions. In H. R. Moskowitz, B. Scharf, & J. C. Stevens (Eds.), *Sensation and measurement* (pp. 157–165). Dordrecht, The Netherlands: Reidel.

Stevens, J. C., Mack, J. D., & Stevens, S. S. (1960). Growth of sensation on seven continua as measured by force of handgrip. *Journal of Experimental Psychology*, *59*, 60–67.

Stevens, J. C., & Marks, L. E. (1965). Cross-modality matching of brightness and loudness. *Proceedings of the National Academy of Sciences*, *54*, 407–411.

Stevens, J. C., & Stevens, S. S. (1963). Brightness function: Effects of adaptation. *Journal of the Optical Society of America*, *53*, 375–385.

Stevens, J. C., & Tulving, E. (1957). Estimations of loudness by a group of untrained observers. *American Journal of Psychology*, *70*, 600–605.

Stevens, S. S. (1946). On the theory of scales of measurement. *Science*, *103*, 677–680.

Stevens, S. S. (1951). Mathematics, measurement, and psychophysics. In S. S. Stevens (Ed.), *Handbook of experimental psychology* (pp. 1–49). New York: Wiley.

Stevens, S. S. (1953). On the brightness of lights and the loudness of sounds [Abstract]. *Science*, *118*, 576.

Stevens, S. S. (1970). Neural events and the psychophysical law. *Science*, *170*, 1043–1050.

Stevens, S. S. (1971a). Issues in psychophysical measurement. *Psychological Review*, *78*, 426–450.

Stevens, S. S. (1971b). Sensory power functions and neural events. In *Handbook of sensory physiology* (Vol. 1, pp. 226–242). New York: Springer-Verlag.

Stevens, S. S. (1975). *Psychophysics: Introduction to its perceptual, neural and social prospects*. New York: Wiley.

Stevens, S. S., Carton, A. S., & Shickman, G. M. (1958). A scale of apparent intensity of electric shock. *Journal of Experimental Psychology*, *56*, 328–334.

Stevens, S. S., & Galanter, E. H. (1957). Ratio scales and category scales for a dozen perceptual continua. *Journal of Experimental Psychology*, *54*, 377–411.

Stevens, S. S., & Greenbaum, H. B. (1966). Regression effect in psychophysical judgment. *Perception and Psychophysics*, *1*, 439–446.

Strangert, B. (1961). A validation study of the method of ratio estimation. *Reports from the Psychological Laboratory, University of Stockholm*. (No. 95).

Svenson, O., & Åkesson, C. A. (1967). A further note on fractional and multiple estimates in ratio scaling. *Report from the Psychological Laboratory, University of Stockholm* (No. 224).

Swets, J. A., & Birdsall, T. G. (1967). Deferred decision in human signal detection: A preliminary experiment. *Perception and Psychophysics*, *2*, 15–24.

Swets, J. A., & Pickett, R. M. (1982). *Evaluation of diagnostic systems*. New York: Academic Press.

Swets, J. A., Shipley, E. F., McKey, M. J., & Green, D. M. (1959). Multiple observations of signals in noise. *Journal of the Acoustical Society of America, 31*, 514–521.

Tanner, W. P., Jr. (1956). Theory of recognition. *Journal of the Acoustical Society of America, 28*, 882–888.

Teghtsoonian, R. (1971). On the exponents in Stevens' law and the constant in Ekman's law. *Psychological Review, 78*, 71–80.

Teghtsoonian, R. (1973). Range effects in psychophysical scaling and a revision of Stevens' law. *American Journal of Psychology, 86*, 3–27.

Teghtsoonian, R. (1974). On facts and theories in psychophysics: Does Ekman's law exist? In H. R. Moskowitz et al. (Eds.), *Sensation and measurement: Papers in honor of S. S. Stevens* (pp. 167–176). Dordrecht, The Netherlands: Reidel.

Teghtsoonian, R. (1978). Range and regression effects in magnitude scaling. *Perception and Psychophysics, 24*, 305–314.

Teghtsoonian, R., Teghtsoonian, M., & Baird, J. C. (1995). On the nature and meaning of sinuosity in magnitude estimation functions. *Psychological Research, 57*, 63–69.

Thalman, R. (1965). Cross-modality matching in the study of abnormal loudness functions. *Laryngoscope, 75*, 1708–1726.

Theunissen, F., & Miller, J. P. (1995). Temporal encoding in nervous systems: A rigorous definition. *Journal of Computational Neuroscience, 2*, 149–162.

Thurstone, L. L. (1927). A law of comparative judgment. *Psychological Review, 34*, 273–286.

Townsend, J. T. (1992). On the proper scales for reaction time. In H. G. Geissler, S. W. Link, & J. T. Townsend (Eds.), *Cognition, information processing, and psychophysics: Basic issues* (pp. 105–120). Hillsdale, NJ: Lawrence Erlbaum Associates.

Treisman, M. (1984). A theory of criterion setting: An alternative to the attention band and response ratio hypotheses in magnitude estimation and cross-modality matching. *Journal of Experimental Psychology: General, 113*, 443–463.

Tversky, A., & Gati, I. (1982). Similarity, separability, and the triangle inequality. *Psychological Review, 89*, 123–154.

Valter, V. (1970). Deduction and verification of a quantum psychophysical equation. *Reports from the Institute of Applied Psychology*, University of Stockholm. (No. 13).

Viemeister, N. F. (1988). Psychophysical aspects of auditory intensity coding. In G. M. Edelman, W. E. Gall, & W. M. Cowan (Eds.), *Auditory function: Neurobiological bases of hearing* (pp. 213–241). New York: Wiley.

Wagner, M. (1985). The metric of visual space. *Perception and Psychophysics, 38*, 483–495.

Wagner, M., & Baird, J. C. (1981). A quantitative analysis of sequential effects with numeric stimuli. *Perception and Psychophysics, 29*, 359–364.

Wandell, B. (1995). *Foundations of vision*. Sunderland, MA: Sinauer Associates.

Ward, L. M. (1973). Repeated magnitude estimations with a variable standard: Sequential effects and other properties. *Perception and Psychophysics, 13*, 193–200.

Ward, L. M. (1975). Sequential dependencies and response range in cross-modlaity matches of duration to loudness. *Perception and Psychophysics, 18*, 217–223.

Ward, L. M. (1979). Stimulus information and sequential dependencies in magnitude estimation and cross-modality matching. *Journal of Experimental Psychology: Human Perception and Performance, 5*, 444–459.

Ward, L. M. (1987). Remembrance of sounds past: Memory and psychophysical scaling. *Journal of Experimental Psychology: Human Perception and Performance, 13*, 216–227.

Ward, L. M. (1990a). Mixed-method mixed-modality psychophysical scaling. *Perception and Psychophysics, 48*, 571–582.

Ward, L. M. (1990b). Two-slit psychophysics. In F. Müller (Ed.), *Fechner day 90* (pp. 261–266). Würzburg: International Society for Psychophysics.

Ward, L. M., & Davidson, K. P. (1993). Where the action is: Weber fractions as a function of sound pressure at low frequencies. *Journal of the Acoustical Society of America, 94*, 2587–2594.

Ward, L. M., & Lockhead, G. R. (1970). Sequential effects and memory in category judgments. *Journal of Experimental Psychology, 84*, 27–34.

Ward, L. M., & Lockhead, G. R. (1971). Response system processes in absolute judgment. *Perception and Psychophysics, 9*, 73–78.

Warren, H. C., & Shaw, W. J. (1895). Studies from the Princeton laboratory: II. Further experiments on memory for square size. *Psychological Review, 2*, 239–244.

Warren, R. M. (1981). Measurement of sensory intensity. *Behavioral and Brain Sciences, 4*, 175–223.

Wasserman, G. S., Felsten, G., & Easland, G. S. (1979). The psychophysical function: Harmonizing Fechner and Stevens. *Science, 204*, 85–87.

Weber, E. H. (1846). Der Tastsinn und das Gemeinfühl [the sense of touch and general sensation]. In R. Wagner (Ed.), *Handwörterbuch der Physiologie* (Vol. 3, pp. 481–588). Braunschweig: Vieweg.

Weiss, D. J. (1981). The impossible dream of Fechner and Stevens. *Perception, 10*, 431–434.

Weissman, S. M., Hollingsworth, S. R., & Baird, J. C. (1975). Psychophysical study of numbers: III. Methodological applications. *Psychological Research, 38*, 97–115.

Wever, E. G. (1949). *Theory of hearing.* New York: Wiley.

Wever, E. G., & Zener, K. E. (1928). The method of absolute judgment in psychophysics. *Psychological Review, 35*, 466–493.

Wiest, W. M., & Bell, B. (1985). Stevens's exponent for psychophysical scaling of perceived, remembered, and inferred distance. *Psychological Bulletin, 98*, 457–470.

Wilkinson, L., Hill, M. A., & Vang, E. (1992). *Systat for the Macintosh, Version 5.2*, SYSTAT, Inc., Evanston, Illinois.

Wilson, B. C. (1964). *An experimental examination of the spectral luminosity construct.* Unpublished doctoral dissertation, New York University.

Woodworth, R. S., & Schlosberg, H. (1954). *Experimental psychology.* New York: Holt, Rinehart & Winston.

Youngs, W. M. (1974). *The coding of disparity as a function of directional separation and feature similarity.* Unpublished doctoral dissertation, Dartmouth College, Hanover, NH.

Zwicker, E., & Fastl, H. (1990). *Psychoacoustics: Facts and models.* Berlin Heidelberg: Springer-Verlag.

Zwislocki, J. J. (1983). Absolute and other scales: Question of validity. *Perception and Psychophysics, 33*, 593–594.

Zwislocki, J. J., & Goodman, D. A. (1980). Absolute scaling of sensory magnitudes: A validation. *Perception and Psychophysics, 28*, 28–38.

# Author Index

# Subject Index